难结难分

一名中国女律师的真实婚姻案例集

HARD TO TIE HARDER TO UNTIE

CHRONICLES OF REAL MATRIMONIAL CASES BY A CHINESE FEMALE LITIGATOR

iCultures Publications
3769 Peralta Blvd. Suite I
Fremont, CA 94536

Book Title 書名：《难结难分——一名中国女律师的真实婚姻案例集》 Hard to Tie, Harder to Untie — Chronicles of Real Matrimonial Cases by a Chinese Female Litigator
Author 作者 : Rachel J. Ye 叶剑秋
Photography 摄影 : Joseph Xu 徐剑峰
Translater 翻译 : Victoria Chen 陈慧英
Cover Calligraphy by 封面书法题字 : Guoqing Cai 蔡国庆
Planned by 策劃 : Phoenix Huan 郇桓
Designer 設計製作 : Jay Li

ISBN : 979-8-90259-026-2
Trim Size 開本 : 7.20 × 10.20 inches (182.9 × 259.1 mm)
Publisher 出版社 : iCultures Publications
Address 地址 : 3769 Peralta Blvd. Ste I Fremont CA 94536
Website 網站 : icultures.org
Email 郵箱 : info@icultures.org
Publishing Entity 出品 : Eastwest Art Culture & Education Center

Typefaces licensed under the SIL Open Font License (OFL 1.1)

Printed in the United States

特别说明

本书中所有案例均系作者亲自承办的真实案例。
为了保护当事人隐私，所有案例中的人物姓名、时间地点等关键信息以及部分案情均已作改编处理，切勿对号入座。

Author's Note

The cases chronicled in this book are based on actual legal matters personally handled by the author. To safeguard client confidentiality and privacy, names, dates, locations, and other identifying details have been altered. Certain factual circumstances have also been adapted. Any resemblance to actual persons, living or dead, or specific events is entirely coincidental.

作者介绍 ｜ 叶剑秋

高级合伙人律师 ｜ 管理合伙人律师

叶剑秋律师是中国优秀知名的婚姻家事专业律师，她从事律师职业二十多年，长期深耕于婚姻家事法律服务领域，成功办理逾千件疑难典型的婚姻家事案件，包括错综复杂的离婚诉讼、家族财富分割、遗产继承纠纷、子女抚养权争夺和非婚生子女亲子关系认定、跨国婚姻财产处置等类型。她凭借女性律师特有的细腻视角与深厚专业的法律智慧，尤其擅长处理多重婚姻关系、夫妻财产争议、婚姻危机化解、当事人心理疏导和家族矛盾协调等棘手难题。

叶剑秋律师是温州人，她的家乡温州是全中国最著名的侨乡，全世界各地都遍布温州人拼搏奋斗的身影，叶律师为广大的海外华侨处理了大量的涉外家事纠纷，为保护华侨权益不遗余力。叶律师任职的兰迪律师事务所是一家国际化律所，在全球拥有近 70 家分支机构。她在兰迪律所带领婚姻家事律师成立“涉外婚姻家事法律服务中心”，针对中国和世界各国当事人之间建立的跨法域、跨文化的跨国婚姻家庭在结婚离婚、子女抚养、财产分割、遗产继承、财富传承等方面出现的复杂法律问题，提供高度专业化、精细化、人性化的综合解决方案。叶剑秋律师以极度专注的敬业精神和勇敢无畏的正义感，始终致力于高质量的服务好每一位当事人，高品质的办理好每一个案件，成为同行和客户心目中优秀律师的标杆，深受他们的信赖和赞赏。

Rachel J. Ye | Profile

Senior Partner | Managing Partner

Executive Director
Zhejiang-Hainan Regional Management Committee, Landing Law Offices
Managing Partner, Landing Law Offices (Yiwu)

Professional Profile

With over two decades of distinguished legal practice, Rachel J. Ye is a prominent and highly esteemed attorney in China, dedicating her career exclusively to matrimonial and family law. She has successfully navigated over a thousand complex and landmark family law cases, encompassing intricate divorce litigation, division of family wealth, estate succession disputes, child custody battles, paternity determination for non-marital children, and the disposition of cross-border matrimonial assets. Combining profound legal acumen with a highly empathetic and meticulous approach, she is particularly adept at untangling multifaceted matrimonial relationships, resolving marital property disputes, and navigating the thorny challenges of crisis intervention, psychological counseling, and the mediation of deep-rooted family conflicts.

Hailing from Wenzhou—a city renowned as the most prominent hub for the global Chinese diaspora—Rachel has handled a vast array of international family disputes for overseas Chinese, sparing no effort in safeguarding their rights and interests. Landing Law Offices, where she practices, is a leading international law firm with nearly 70 branches worldwide. Under her leadership, the firm established the "Cross-Border Matrimonial and Family Law Service Center." This center provides highly specialized, meticulous, and compassionate comprehensive legal solutions for cross-jurisdictional and cross-cultural families, addressing complex issues ranging from marriage and divorce to child custody, property division, and wealth inheritance. Driven by profound dedication and a fearless sense of justice, Rachel remains unwavering in her commitment to delivering exceptional service and achieving optimal outcomes for every client. She stands as a paragon of excellence in the eyes of her peers and clients, earning their deepest trust and admiration.

主要荣誉

- 中华人民共和国“全国维护妇女儿童权益先进个人”
- 致公党中央参政议政全国先进个人
- 中国浙江省优秀女律师
- 中国浙江省婚姻家事优秀专业律师
- 中国浙江省巾帼建功标兵
- 中国温州市政协履职突出委员
- 中国温州市首届最美律师

出版著作

- 《难结难分——一名中国女律师的真实婚姻案例集》
- 《若结若离——女律师笔下的典型婚姻案例实录》（中国大陆出版）

职务：

兰迪浙江海南区域管委会｜执行主任
上海兰迪（义乌）律师事务所｜主任

工作邮箱：346956339@QQ.COM
联系方式：13088662121

兰迪义乌律所办公地址：
中国浙江义乌市商城大道 288 号伟业大厦 21 层 2102 室

兰迪浙江海南区域综合行政办公地址：
中国浙江温州市温州大道 878 号顺富大厦 A 幢 3 层

Selected Honors & Awards

• National Advanced Individual in Safeguarding the Rights and Interests of Women and Children
• National Advanced Individual in Participation and Deliberation of State Affairs, China Zhi Gong Party
• Outstanding Female Lawyer of Zhejiang Province
• Outstanding Professional Lawyer in Matrimonial and Family Law, Zhejiang Province
• Zhejiang Provincial "Women's Meritorious Service" Pacesetter
• Outstanding Member for Performance of Duties, Wenzhou Municipal Committee of the CPPCC
• Inaugural "Exemplary Lawyer" of Wenzhou Municipality

Publications

• Hard to Tie, Harder to Untie: Chronicles of Real Matrimonial Cases by a Chinese Female Litigator
• To Have and to Let Go: A Female Counsel's Chronicles of Landmark Matrimonial Cases (Published in Mainland China)

Contact Information

• Email: 346956339@qq.com
• Phone: +86 130-8866-2121
• Landing Law Offices (Yiwu): Room 2102, Floor 21, Weiye Building, No. 288 Shangcheng Avenue, Yiwu, Zhejiang, China
• Landing Zhejiang-Hainan Regional Administrative Office: Floor 3, Building A, Shunfu Building, No. 878 Wenzhou Avenue, Wenzhou, Zhejiang, China

前言

自2018年我的作品《若结若离——女律师笔下的典型婚姻案例实录》一书在中国出版以来，不仅得到了国内众多读者的喜爱与共鸣，也受到了海外人士的关注与赞赏。很多读者纷纷向我表达了他们相同的人生经历和婚姻故事，那些深夜里的私信、见面时的倾诉、阅读后的感慨，都让我真切感受到，一名专业婚姻律师帮助当事人维权，既要依仗对法律条文的精准解读和深刻诠释，更需要把人间最柔软、最复杂、也最真实的婚姻情感予以感化和升华。正是来自社会、来自读者、来自我的当事人的长期的认可和鼓励，让我更加坚信：婚姻家事的法理与情理，是共通的人间命题。也让我在婚姻家事律师的专业追求上，始终不敢懈怠，惟精惟一，更加审慎，更加用心。

时光流转，又是数载春秋。这些年里，我专注深耕在婚姻家事法律服务的第一线，亲自经办一宗宗跌宕起伏、疑难复杂的经典婚姻案件。法庭内外，我亲历众多悲欢离合、爱恨情仇的场景，看过相爱相杀的纠缠，也见证过好聚好散的体面；目睹过财富迷雾中的人性挣扎，也陪伴过困境之中的坚守与重生。每一段故事，都藏着一个家庭的命运；每一次抉择，都牵动着当事人未来的人生走向。我始终以专业为刃，以良知为尺，在法理与情理之间为我的当事人争取最大利益，竭力为每一位当事人守住尊严，追寻正义，帮助他们应对人生的风暴，重新出发，向阳而行。

也正是这些沉甸甸的经历与感悟，让我萌生了续写新的案例、再成一书，并在全球市场发行的心愿，这便诞生了《难结难分—— 一名中国女律师的真实婚姻案例集》一书，作为《若结若离》的姊妹篇，与前作一脉相承。

这本书的写作，陆陆续续历时两年。与《若结若离》一书标题取自中国成语"若即若离"的谐音的创意相似，我构思的本书标题《难结难分》，取自中国成语"难解难分"，意即，在婚姻的迷局中，当事人往往陷入既难结合又难分离的抉择困扰中。我还保留了读者熟悉的《若结若离》的体例：以引言提炼案件核心要旨、以办案经历还原案情真相、以案后结语沉淀法律和人性的思考。但与《若结若离》按照不同的婚姻家事主题分章布局所不同的是，这本书里，我采用"傲慢（Pride）、嫉妒（Envy）、暴怒（Wrath）、懒惰（Sloth）、贪婪（Greed）、暴食（Gluttony）、色欲（Lust）"七大主题词，将30个案例分布在七大章节中，通过提炼最容易破坏婚姻家庭的这七宗罪，让读者从具体的案例中引发更多的思索。与此同时，这本书的案例均改编自我近些年亲自办理的真实婚姻案例，包含了跨国婚姻的文化多元与法律冲突、涉外离婚的管辖争议与实体法适用、境内外复杂财产的界定与分割、家族资产与婚姻财产的交织与隔离……它们更贴近当下，也更具现实警示与法律参考价值。它既可以作为国际化婚恋文学作品让读者们品读，也可以作为普法类读物供喜爱法律的朋友们研读，还可以作为中西方婚姻文化的社会学文献供学者们参考阅读。

这本书的编写得到了很多亲友的帮助和支持，书中所选取的插图均来自我深爱的先生 Joseph Xu 创作的摄影作品，他以他独有的风格和温柔的方式一直坚定地支持着我的事业，是我坚实的臂膀和依靠。这本书的封面书法题字，是我最长久的事业伙伴蔡国庆先生亲自而作。长期来，他的国际化视野始终指引着我的发展方向，也激励着我成为更好的自己。同时我还要特别鸣谢这本书的翻译陈慧英 Victoria 女士——一位杰出的美国华裔女企业家、女画家和女诗人，她以她超凡的文学才华和语言艺术，以她对婚姻的深度理解和生命悟性，以她坚韧的品格和豁达的素养，为本书的完美呈现提供了出色的帮助。

长期持续的律师执业，经手案件无数，我愈发深刻地体会到：婚姻不单是一场两个人相遇相知相惜的同行，更是一场需要理性与智慧共同经营的修行；法律更不是用来伤害彼此的武器，而是守护边界、厘清责任、重建秩序的底线。好的婚姻，让人彼此成就；坏的婚姻，让人学会成长。而我作为一名婚姻家事专业律师，最大的价值，不仅在于赢得一场场法庭上的诉讼，更要让离散者体面落幕，让迷茫者看清方向，让受伤者重获力量，让"难结难分"终能好聚好散。

愿翻开这本书的你，既能在真实案例中看见法律的逻辑，也能在人间故事里照见自己的内心。愿每一份深情不被辜负，每一次抉择皆有归途。愿爱有尊严，行有底气，心有光芒。

是为序

——叶剑秋

Preface

Since the publication of my book To Have and to Let Go: A Female Counsel's Chronicles of Landmark Matrimonial Cases in China in 2018, it has not only won the affection and resonance of numerous domestic readers but also attracted the attention and admiration of overseas audiences. Many readers have shared with me their similar life experiences and marital stories. Those late-night private messages, heartfelt outpourings in person, and emotional reflections after reading have made me truly realize that as a professional matrimonial lawyer, when helping clients protect their rights and interests, I must rely not only on the accurate interpretation and profound understanding of legal provisions but also on guiding and elevating the softest, most complex, and most authentic marital emotions. It is the enduring recognition and encouragement from society, readers, and my clients that have strengthened my conviction: the interplay of legal principles and human emotions in matrimonial affairs is a universal human proposition. They have also kept me diligent, focused, prudent, and dedicated in my professional pursuit as a family lawyer, inspiring me to never slacken my efforts.

Time flows on, and several years have passed. Over these years, I have remained deeply engaged on the frontline of matrimonial legal services, personally handling a series of turbulent, difficult, and complex landmark marriage cases. Inside and outside the courtroom, I have witnessed countless joys and sorrows, partings and reunions, loves and hatreds. I have seen the agonizing entanglements of mutually destructive lovers, and also witnessed the dignified grace of amicable separations. I have observed human struggles amid the fog of wealth, and accompanied clients through their perseverance and rebirth in adversity. Every story holds the fate of a family; every choice shapes the future trajectory of the client's life. I have always wielded my professional expertise as a blade and my conscience as a compass, striving for the best interests of my clients between legal principles and human compassion, doing my utmost to safeguard their dignity, pursue justice, and help them weather life's storms to start anew and step into the light.

These profound experiences and insights have inspired my wish to compile new cases into another book for global release, thus giving birth to Hard to Tie, Harder to Untie: Chronicles of Real Matrimonial Cases by a Chinese Female Litigator. As a sister volume to To Have and to Let Go, it carries on the spirit of the previous work.

The writing of this book took two years on and off. Similar to the title of To

Have and to Let Go, which adopts a homophonic twist of the Chinese idiom "ruò jí ruò lí" (seemingly close yet distant), the title of this book, Hard to Tie, Harder to Untie, is adapted from the Chinese idiom "nán jiě nán fēn" (inextricably intertwined), meaning that in the maze of marriage, parties are often trapped in the dilemma of finding it hard to bond, yet equally hard to part. I have also retained the structure familiar to readers of To Have and to Let Go: an introduction distilling the core of each case, a narrative of my handling to reconstruct the truth, and a post-case conclusion reflecting on legal and human insights. However, unlike To Have and to Let Go, which was structurally organized by distinct matrimonial and family themes, this book distributes its 30 cases across seven chapters anchored by the themes of Pride, Envy, Wrath, Sloth, Greed, Gluttony, and Lust. By distilling these seven deadly sins that most easily corrode marital and family bonds, I hope to inspire deeper reflection among readers through these concrete accounts. Meanwhile, all the cases within this book are adapted from real matrimonial disputes I have personally handled in recent years. They encompass the cultural pluralism and legal conflicts inherent in cross-border marriages, jurisdictional disputes and the application of substantive law in international divorces, the identification and division of complex domestic and overseas assets, and the intricate intertwining and segregation of family wealth and marital property. These accounts resonate more deeply with the contemporary landscape, offering profound cautionary insights and practical legal reference value. Ultimately, this book can be savored by general readers as an international literary narrative on marriage and romance, studied by legal enthusiasts as an accessible guide to the law, and consulted by scholars as a sociological document exploring Eastern and Western matrimonial cultures.

The compilation of this book has received help and support from many relatives and friends. All illustrations selected are photographic works created by my beloved husband, Joseph Xu. With his unique style and gentle manner, he has firmly supported my career and remains my solid pillar and reliance. The calligraphic inscription on the cover of this book was personally penned by my longest-standing professional partner, Mr. Cai Guoqing. Over the years, his global vision has consistently guided my professional trajectory, inspiring me to continually become a better version of myself. I would also like to express my special gratitude to Ms. Victoria Huiying Chen, the translator of this book—an outstanding Chinese-American entrepreneur, painter, and poet. With her extraordinary literary talent, linguistic artistry, profound understanding of marriage and life, as well as her fortitude and open-mindedness, she has provided exceptional support for the perfect presentation of this book.

After years of sustained legal practice and countless cases handled, I have come to understand more deeply: marriage is not merely a journey of two people meeting, knowing, and cherishing each other, but a rigorous cultivation that requires joint management with reason and wisdom. The law is not a weapon to hurt each other, but the ultimate baseline to guard boundaries, clarify responsibilities, and restore order. A good marriage helps people achieve mutual success; a broken one teaches people to grow. As a professional matrimonial lawyer, my greatest value lies not only in winning lawsuits in court, but also in helping those who part ways end with dignity, guiding the confused to find their direction, empowering the injured to regain strength, and ensuring that even the most "hard to tie, harder to untie" can ultimately part on terms of grace.

May you, upon opening this book, see the logic of the law in real cases and reflect upon your inner self through human stories. May every sincere affection be cherished, and every choice find its way home. May love be dignified, your actions grounded in strength, and your heart full of light.

These words are offered as my preface.

— Rachel J. Ye

目录

第一章 | 傲慢 Pride 1

当澳洲"事实婚姻"的枷锁，遇上中国法律的清醒 3
When the Shackles of Australian "De Facto Relationship"
Met the Clarity of Chinese Law

尘埃里的背叛与法庭上的坚守 —— 一场追还婚外赠与款的全程较量 10
Betrayal in the Dust and Perseverance in Court:
A Full Battle to Recover Illicit Gifts to a Third Party

温商跨国婚变：亿级资产里的尊严与突围 19
A Cross-Border Marriage Breakdown of a Wenzhou Merchant:
Dignity and Breakthrough Amid Hundreds of Millions in Assets

跨境婚约下的财富守护，一份婚前协议的双向安全感 29
Cross-Border Marriages & Wealth Safeguards:
The Dual Protection of a Prenuptial Agreement

中澳婚姻里的无声牺牲，全职妈妈争得离婚经济补偿 41
A Full-Time Mother Wins Economic Compensation in Divorce

第二章 | 嫉妒 Envy 53

跨国婚约的倒塌与温商二代的债务迷局 55
The Collapse of a Transnational Marriage
and the Debt Quagmire of a Second-Generation Wenzhou Businessman

秦氏家族传承启示录：
家族信托，何以成为富人守业传家的终极答案 63
Revelations from the Qin Family Legacy: Why Family Trusts Are the
Ultimate Solution for Wealthy Families to Preserve Their Legacy

Table of Contents

倾尽家财赠子女，为何晚年悔断肠——三起亲子财富赠与的法律警醒 71
Giving All to Children, Regretting in Twilight Years:
Legal Lessons from Three Parental Gifting Disputes

异国相恋情深意浓，分手怎可索回赠款 82
A Devoted Cross-Border Romance:
Can Gifts Be Reclaimed After a Breakup?

第三章 | 暴怒 Wrath 93

爱到极致是疯狂 95
Love at Its Extreme Is Madness

情杀利刃下的家破人亡，刑事附带民事的正义追讨 103
A Family Destroyed in a Crime of Passion:
Seeking Justice via Civil Claims in Criminal Proceedings

涉外离婚之诉，挣脱家暴与谎言的跨国婚姻囚笼 113
A Cross-Border Divorce: Breaking Free from the Cage of Transnational Marriage Built on Domestic Violence and Deception

糟糠之妻焉能弃 121
A Wife Who Shared Hard Times Should Never Be Forsaken

第四章 | 懒惰 Sloth 131

罗马抉择，抢在窗口期的“快进”离婚 133
A Choice in Rome: Fast-Track Divorce Within a Critical Window

消失的遗产管理人 142
The Vanishing Estate Administrator

英伦遥望：十年空守，一纸传票唤醒良知，跨境调解终获解脱 150
Across the Oceans: A Decade of Waiting, a Summons to Conscience, and Freedom Through Cross-Border Mediation

孕途风波里，法理与温情共护新生 160
Safeguarding New Life with Law and Warmth Amid Pregnancy Disputes

第五章 | 贪婪 Greed 171

法庭微光：以未成年人之名，修复一段濒临破碎的婚姻 173
A Glimmer of Light in Court:
In the Name of a Minor, Mending a Marriage on the Brink

跨国婚姻父女分离，"首诉不离"下的贪婪之欲 182
Separation of Father and Daughter in a Cross-Border Marriage:
Greed Under the "No Divorce in First Action" Rule

狮城余波：新加坡离婚后，我为当事人追回宁波学区房 193
Aftermath in the Lion City: Recovering Ningbo School-District Property for My Client After a Singapore Divorce

一纸离婚约定，十四年的侵占，与一场迟来的归还 200
A Divorce Agreement,
14 Years of Illegal Occupation, and a Long-Overdue Return

致命的婚姻——哀悼一位沉入海底的美丽新娘 208
A Deadly Union — Mourning the Beautiful Bride
Who Sank to the Ocean Depths

Table of Contents

第六章 | 暴食 Gluttony 221

恋爱炼狱——伪装的“高富帅”的重重骗局 223
Love's Inferno:
The Elaborate Scams of a Fake "Rich, Tall and Handsome" Player

塞纳河畔的亲情谜题：一场中法跨国非婚生子抚养权的拉锯战 230
Family Puzzle on the Banks of the Seine: A Sino-French Transnational Custody Battle Over a Child Born Out of Wedlock

一纸遗嘱锁终身：当继承权困住婚姻自由权 238
A Will Bound for Life: When Inheritance Traps the Freedom of Marriage

隐瞒配偶“被网络诈骗”，离婚因“挥霍”而少分财产 245
Concealing that the Spouse Was "Online Scam", and the Divorce Divided Less Property Due to "Squander"

第七章 | 色欲 Lust 257

分手后的“阴影期”，终有“人身安全保护令”的守护 259
The Post-Breakup "Shadow":
Finally Guarded by a Personal Safety Protection Order

新婚疑云，揭开亲子谜团的惊天秘密 266
Newlywed Doubts: Uncovering the Shocking Truth Behind Parentage

性瘾执念下的婚姻废墟，绝望主妇的涅槃重生 277
The Ruins of Marriage Under Sex Addiction:
The Nirvana and Rebirth of a Desperate Housewife

一场婚外虐恋引发的亲子鉴定之诉 287
Extramarital Love Woes Leading to a Paternity Suit

CHAPTER 1 | PRIDE

第一章 | 傲慢

引文

"一个人若是傲慢自大，便会在自己筑起的高墙内，
看不见世界，也看不见他人。"

——【古希腊】苏格拉底

傲慢是人性深处最不易察觉的劣性，它往往以自我为中心，在最亲密的关系里筑起无形的壁垒。在婚姻的围城中，它常常表现为居高临下的俯视、不肯妥协的执拗、拒绝共情的偏执，或是由财富、地位、认知所滋生的虚妄优越感。许多家庭的崩塌并非始于激烈的争吵与背叛，而是始于一方对另一方长期的漠视，对平等关系的背离，对边界感的肆意践踏。

在我多年深耕婚姻家事法律的执业历程中，亲眼见证太多纷争由傲慢而起：家事协商中的寸步不让，法庭对峙中的互不相容，抚养权争夺里的自说自话，家族事务处理中的独断专行。傲慢让沟通彻底失效，让和解变得遥不可及，让本该温情脉脉的亲密关系，一步步走向冰冷的对峙与割裂。

法律能够厘清权责、判定是非，却难以修复被傲慢长久灼伤的心；能够重建秩序，却无法强制一个人放下执念。真正的亲密关系从不是征服与支配，而是平视与尊重；真正的强大从不是永不低头，而是懂得在爱与亲情面前，放下虚妄的骄傲，拥抱理解与柔软。这是婚姻的修行，亦是人性的觉醒。

Epigraph

"If a man is proud and arrogant, he will live within walls of his own making, blind to the world and to others."

— Socrates, Ancient Greece

Pride is one of the most insidious vices deep in human nature. It centers on the self and erects invisible barriers even in the closest relationships. Within the confines of marriage, it often manifests as condescension, stubborn refusal to compromise, paranoia without empathy, or false superiority bred by wealth, status, or perceived intellectual advantage. Many families do not collapse from fierce quarrels or betrayal, but from long-term disregard for one another, abandonment of equality, and reckless violation of personal boundaries.

In my years of practice in family and marital law, I have witnessed countless disputes rooted in pride: unyielding rigidity in family negotiations, bitter antagonism in court, self-serving arguments in custody battles, and arbitrary dominance in family affairs. Pride shatters communication, makes reconciliation unattainable, and turns once tender intimacy into cold confrontation and division.

The law can clarify rights and responsibilities, judge right and wrong, yet cannot easily mend hearts scarred by pride. It can restore order, but cannot force anyone to let go of obsession. True intimacy is not about conquest and control, but about mutual respect and equal regard. True strength is not in never yielding, but knowing to lay down false pride in the face of love and family, embracing understanding and tenderness. This is the cultivation of marriage, and the awakening of humanity.

当澳洲 "事实婚姻" 的枷锁，遇上中国法律的清醒

引言

国境线不仅划分了地域，某种程度上，也割裂了法律对亲密关系的定义。在澳洲，五年同居或许能被贴上"事实婚姻"的标签；但在中国，未登记的结合，却只是一段可随时终止的非法同居关系。我的当事人许呜呜，困在墨尔本的公寓里，被男友以"离婚程序"相要挟，进退维谷。我以跨境法律的精准研判为剑，斩断了这层莫须有的身份捆绑，让她带着尊严，从这场跨国情感的泥沼中全身而退。

许呜呜第一次向我描述墨尔本的冬天时，语气里还带着未散尽的寒意。她 34 岁，是一名才华横溢的室内设计师，常年穿梭于工作室和咖啡馆，对生活琐事向来随性。五年前，为了寻找创作灵感，她远赴澳洲发展。在一场华人社区的创作分享会上，她遇见了 36 岁的建筑工程师江哲。

彼时的江哲，刚从国内移民澳洲不久，身上带着中式传统的温文尔雅，又融入了些许西式的绅士风度。两人相识交往后，江哲会在许呜呜熬夜绘制图纸时煮上一碗热汤，会细心记住她对色彩搭配的喜好，会在她创作瓶颈焦虑时，安静地陪在身边。这份在异国他乡稀缺的暖意，让许呜呜迅速沦陷，两人很快确定了恋爱关系。

随后，两人在墨尔本东区租下一套带落地窗的公寓，开始了同居生活。许呜呜的生活节奏随性而浪漫，常常为了一幅设计稿，花上数天时间沉浸在色彩与线条的世界里，甚至会为了寻找独特的创作素材，飞往不同的城市；江哲却是典型的工科男，生活严谨刻板，作息规律到分秒不差，甚至有些锱铢必较。起初，这种差异是互补：江哲帮许呜呜处理生活琐事，许呜呜用画笔装点两人的生活；可日子一长，裂痕便悄然蔓延。

消费观的冲突，成了两人争吵的导火索。许呜呜为了一个设计灵感，会斥巨资购买限量版的家具；江哲却为了超市里几澳元的差价，驱车半小时去折扣店采购食材。许呜呜会随手给江哲添置质感出众的衬衫与配饰，江哲却反复念叨"太浪费""没必要"。那些日积月累的争执，像细密的针，渐渐扎破了两人感情的泡沫。

真正让许呜呜心死的，是那个飘着细雨的午后。她提前结束外地的采风行程，想给江哲一个生日惊喜，却在公寓的卧室里，撞见了他与公司女同事的亲密瞬间。空气中弥漫的香水味与凌乱的床铺，像一把重锤，狠狠砸在许呜呜的心上。那场歇斯底里的争吵，耗尽了许呜呜五年来所有的隐忍与期待。她麻木地收拾行李，决绝地提出分手，却被江哲冰冷的话语钉在原地："我们在澳洲同居五年，对外以伴侣相称，经济上相互扶持，已经构成了事实婚姻。你想走，可

以，按离婚程序来，分割共同财产，承担这段时间的生活开支。"

许鸣鸣懵了。她从未与江哲在任何国家办理结婚登记，怎么就成了"夫妻"？江哲拿出澳洲家庭法的条文，一条条念给她听，甚至拿出两人的共同账户流水、公寓租赁合同，以分割她的作品版权、冻结联名账户相要挟。孤立无援的许鸣鸣，看着陌生的城市、遥不可及的故乡，最终订了回国的机票，敲响了我的办公室大门。

"叶律师，我只是想分手，不想被他绑一辈子，我不想在异国他乡被他拿捏。"许鸣鸣的声音带着颤抖，眼底满是惶恐。我看着她眼底的疲惫与无助，表示非常理解，同时明确告诉她："在中国法律框架下，你们从未建立婚姻关系。澳洲虽有'事实婚姻'的规定，但作为中国的公民，你仍有权选择自由分手。"

接受委托后，我尽快为许鸣鸣搭建起跨境法律防御体系，每一步都细致严谨。

第一步，我指导她全面梳理证据链，关注到每一个细节：收集五年间的租房合同，上面始终只有江哲一人的签名，且租赁登记信息也仅为他个人；整理银行流水，双方账户长期独立，仅有零星的日常开支往来，无大额共同财产混同；导出社交平台动态与聊天记录，所有的合影与文字，从未以"夫妻"自居，仅标注"伴侣""朋友"；收集创作版权证明，明确许鸣鸣的室内设计作品均为个人原创，与江哲无任何关联。这些证据，层层递进，完全能证明两人在经济与社会认知上，始终保持着独立的边界。

第二步，我依据中澳法律差异，为许鸣鸣起草了一份专业的《法律意见书》。在这份文书里，我清晰阐明：中国法律自 1994 年《婚姻登记管理条例》实施后，便不再承认事实婚姻；根据中国《民法典》和司法解释的规定，未办理结婚登记的同居关系，不受婚姻法保护；而澳洲的事实婚姻认定，虽需满足同居时长、亲密程度、财务依赖等多重条件，但江哲所主张的"事实婚姻"，缺乏共同子女、大额共同财产混同、对外以夫妻名义公示等核心要件，亦无实质支撑。

第三步，我通过跨境律师协作渠道，将这份《法律意见书》与正式律师函送达江哲。函中明确告知：若继续以"事实婚姻"为名进行要挟、限制许鸣鸣出入境的人身自由或转移财产，许鸣鸣将保留追究其侵权责任、提起相应诉讼的权利。

一周后，许鸣鸣收到了江哲的回复。他不再提"离婚"二字，只是简单地回复了一句："好聚好散，互不打扰。"这场看似复杂的跨境同居纠纷，在法律的清晰界定下，迎刃而解。许鸣鸣没有分割任何财产，也没有承担任何额外责任，她带着自己的作品与行李，彻底摆脱了那段窒息的关系，回到了熟悉的生活轨道。

案后结语

许鸣鸣的经历，揭示了跨境同居的最大风险——法律认知的错位。当我们跨越国境去追寻爱情时，往往容易忽略：不同的法律体系，对"爱"与"责任"的定义有着天壤之别。

作为家事律师，我的价值，不仅在于熟悉本国法律，更在于拥有跨境法律的视野。我为许鸣鸣所做的，是用法律的理性，驱散她情感上的迷雾，用细致的证据梳理与专业的函件，帮她厘清关系性质、摆脱法律要挟，告诉她：你有选择结束的自由，也有不被错误法律认知绑架的权利。

爱情或许没有国界，但法律有。守住法律的底线，便是守住了自己在亲密关系中的尊严与自由。

When the Shackles of Australian "De Facto Relationship" Met the Clarity of Chinese Law

Introduction

Borders not only divide territories but also, to some extent, separate legal definitions of intimate relationships. In Australia, five years of cohabitation may be labeled a De Facto Relationship. But in China, an unregistered union is merely an illegal cohabitation that can be terminated at any time. My client Xu Mingming was trapped in an apartment in Melbourne, blackmailed by her boyfriend with so-called "divorce proceedings," caught between a rock and a hard place. Using precise cross-border legal analysis as a sword, I cut through this false identity bond and helped her extricate herself from the quagmire of this cross-border relationship with dignity.

When Xu Mingming first described the winter in Melbourne to me, her voice still carried a lingering chill. At 34, she was a talented interior designer, moving between studios and cafés, easygoing about daily trivialities. Five years ago, seeking creative inspiration, she went to Australia to develop her career. At a creative sharing session in the Chinese community, she met Jiang Zhe, a 36-year-old structural engineer.

Jiang Zhe had recently immigrated to Australia from mainland China. He carried the gentle elegance of traditional Chinese culture, blended with a touch of Western gentlemanliness. After they met and started dating, he would make a bowl of hot soup for Xu Mingming when she stayed up late drawing plans, remember her color preferences carefully, and stay quietly by her side when she felt anxious about creative blocks. This rare warmth in a foreign land made Xu Mingming fall quickly, and the two soon entered a romantic relationship.

They then rented an apartment with floor-to-ceiling windows in Melbourne's eastern suburbs and began living together. Xu Mingming lived a casual, romantic rhythm: she would immerse herself in color and lines for days for a single design, even flying to different cities for unique creative materials. Jiang Zhe, however, had the temperament of a typical engineer: strict, rigid, with a precise schedule down to the minute, and even somewhat penny-pinching. At first, these differences complemented each other. Jiang Zhe handled daily chores for her; Xu Mingming decorated their life with her art. But as time went on, cracks quietly spread.

Conflicts over consumption became the trigger for quarrels. Xu Mingming would spend heavily on limited-edition furniture for a design spark; Jiang Zhe would drive half an hour to a discount store for groceries just to save a few Australian dollars. Xu Mingming would buy high-quality shirts and accessories for Jiang Zhe on a whim, only to be told repeatedly it was "too wasteful" and "unnecessary." These accumulated disputes, like fine needles, gradually pricked the bubble of their relationship.

What truly broke Xu Mingming's heart was a drizzling afternoon. She ended her field trip early to surprise Jiang Zhe for his birthday, only to catch him being intimate with a female colleague in their bedroom. The smell of perfume and the messy bed struck her like a heavy hammer. That hysterical quarrel drained all her patience and expectations from five years together. Numb, she packed her luggage and resolutely asked to break up—only to be frozen by Jiang Zhe's cold words: "We've lived together in Australia for five years, presented ourselves as partners, and supported each other financially. We already constitute a De Facto Relationship. If you want to leave, fine—go through divorce procedures, divide joint property, and share living expenses from this period."

Xu Mingming was stunned. She had never registered a marriage with Jiang Zhe in any country. How could they be "husband and wife"? Jiang Zhe took out provisions of Australian family law and read them to her one by one. He even showed their joint account statements and the apartment lease, threatening to divide her copyrights and freeze their joint account. Helpless and isolated, in an unfamiliar city far from home, Xu Mingming finally booked a flight back to China and knocked on the door of my office.

"Lawyer Rachel J. Ye, I just want to break up. I don't want to be tied down for my whole life. I don't want to be controlled by him in a foreign country." Her voice trembled, her eyes filled with fear. I looked at her exhaustion and helplessness, expressed my deep understanding, and told her firmly: "Under Chinese law, you never established a marital relationship. Although Australia recognizes De Facto Relationship, as a Chinese citizen, you still have the right to break up freely."

After accepting the mandate, I quickly built a cross-border legal defense system for her, step by step with extreme care. First, I guided her to fully organize the evidence chain, paying attention to every detail:

The rental contract for five years was signed only by Jiang Zhe, and the lease registration information was solely under his name.

Bank records showed separate accounts, no major mixed property, with only sporadic daily expense transactions.

Exported social media posts and chat records—all photos and texts never referred to each other as "husband and wife," only as "partner" or "friend."

Copyright certificates for her creations—confirming that all of Xu Mingming's interior design works were independently created by her alone, with no connection to Jiang Zhe. These pieces of evidence, layer by layer, fully proved that the two maintained independent boundaries both financially and socially.

Second step: Based on the legal differences between China and Australia, I drafted a professional Legal Opinion for Xu Mingming. In this document, I clearly stated: Chinese law has not recognized De Facto Relationship since the implementation of the Marriage Registration Administration Regulations in 1994. Under the Civil Code of the People's Republic of China and judicial interpretations, unregistered cohabitation relationships are not protected by marriage law. Although Australian law recognizes De Facto Relationships, which require cohabitation duration, emotional intimacy, financial interdependence and other conditions, Jiang Zhe's claimed "De Facto Relationship" lacked essential elements: no joint children, no substantial commingling of large joint property, no holding out as spouses to the public, and therefore had no factual support.

Third step: Through cross-border legal cooperation channels, I delivered the Legal Opinion and an official lawyer's letter to Jiang Zhe. The letter clearly warned: If he continued to blackmail her in the name of a "De Facto Relationship," restricted her personal freedom including exit and entry, or transferred property, Xu Mingming would reserve the right to pursue his tort liability and file corresponding lawsuits.

One week later, Xu Mingming received Jiang Zhe's reply. He no longer mentioned the word "divorce." He only wrote briefly: "Let's part amicably and not disturb each other." This seemingly complicated cross-border cohabitation dispute was easily resolved under clear legal definition. Xu Mingming was not required to divide any property or assume any additional liability. She left with her works and luggage, completely freed from that suffocating relationship, and returned to her familiar life.

Post-Case Conclusion

Xu Mingming's experience reveals the greatest risk in cross-border cohabitation: misalignment of legal understanding. When we cross national borders to pursue love, we often overlook that different legal systems define "love" and "responsibility" in vastly different ways. As a family lawyer, my value lies not only in being familiar with domestic law, but also in having a cross-border legal vision. What I did for Xu Mingming was to use legal rationality to clear the fog of emotion, and, through meticulous evidence organization and professional correspondence, help her clarify the nature of the relationship, and break free from legal blackmail. I told her: You have the freedom to choose to end it, and you have the right not to be held hostage by false legal perceptions.

Love may know no borders, but the law does. Holding fast to the bottom line of the law means protecting your dignity and freedom in intimate relationships.

尘埃里的背叛与法庭上的坚守 —— 一场追还婚外赠与款的全程较量

引言

有些真相，总是在最痛的时刻才被揭开。我的当事人袁梅女士，在悉心照料患癌丈夫直至离世后，才在遗物中发现了丈夫长达近十年的婚外情，以及数十万元夫妻共同财产被擅自赠与第三者的残酷事实。悲痛与愤怒之下，她委托我提起诉讼，而庭审之路远比想象艰难：被告当庭证据突袭、临时申请证人作证、层层抗辩狡辩，试图将侵占的财产合理化。我沉着应对，以扎实证据为盾，以严密逻辑为矛，逐一攻破对方防线，最终帮助袁梅女士一审胜诉、二审维持原判，让违背公序良俗的行为，付出了应有的代价。

我第一次见到袁梅女士，是在她丈夫丰先生去世后的第三个星期。

她坐在会客椅上，面色苍白，眼底是未散尽的哀伤与疲惫，捏着一叠刚打印出来的银行流水、转账记录和订单截图，纸张边缘被指尖攥得发皱。那不是普通的财务凭证，而是压垮她的最后一根稻草——是她倾尽所有照顾的丈夫，在婚内瞒着她，与另一个女人近十年的情感纠缠与金钱往来。

袁梅与丰先生结婚数十年，夫妻二人原本在一个大型的商贸市场经营外贸生意，日子安稳平淡，育有一子，孩子勤奋上进，也已长大成人。在外人眼中，这是一个安稳和睦的家庭，可只有袁女士知道，近几年的日子有多艰难。

丰先生确诊癌症后，袁女士放下了手中的生意，全身心照料丈夫的起居与治疗。北京、上海各地奔波求医，排队、挂号、陪床、熬药，她从无怨言；为了凑齐高昂的治疗费，家中四处借款，经济捉襟见肘，她咬牙支撑，从没有让丈夫受过一点委屈。她以为，自己的不离不弃，能换来夫妻一场的真心相待，却不知道，在她省吃俭用、四处筹钱救命的时候，丈夫正在偷偷将夫妻共同财产，一笔笔转给婚外的第三者夏某。

直到料理完后事，袁梅整理丈夫的手机、银行卡与支付记录时，那些被刻意隐藏的秘密，才毫无保留地摊开在她眼前。从 2016 年到 2025 年，近十年时间里，丰先生通过银行、微信、支付宝，持续不断地向夏某转账，金额从几百、几千到数万不等，还频繁为夏某点外卖、订酒店、购买机票，甚至在他去广州老家参加同学会期间，都拒绝妻子陪同，却悄悄安排夏某随行。流水里那些带有特殊含义的转账数字、私密的酒店订单、寄往夏某家中的隐私用品，像一把把尖刀，扎进袁梅的心里。

她这才明白，丈夫那些”工作忙””要静养””不方便视频”的借口，全都是谎言；她省吃俭用省下的钱、四处借来的治疗费，有一部分，竟被丈夫用来维系婚外情，花在了另一个女人身上。

更让她心寒的是，2025 年 3 月，儿子过 18 岁生日的时候，作为父亲的丰先生却说自己出差在外赶不回来，没能陪伴儿子，事实却是订了酒店与夏某厮混。甚至在生命最后的时光里，他对家庭、对妻子、对孩子极尽亏欠，对第三者却慷慨大方。

袁梅无数次彻夜难眠，眼泪流干，心口像被掏空一样疼。她试图联系夏某，想痛斥她的卑劣无耻，想要回丈夫生前打给她的钱，这些钱本就属于夫妻共同财产，可对方电话不接、信息不回。对方的冷漠与回避，让她彻底清醒：这段被背叛的婚姻，这笔被侵占的财产，必须通过法律，讨回公道。

带着绝望与坚定，袁梅女士找到了我，委托我代理这起婚外赠与纠纷案。接受委托后，我和团队律师没有急于立案，而是沉下心，细致严谨地梳理全部证据。近十年的流水，几千条交易记录，我们一笔笔核对、分类、统计，剔除夏某转回的小额款项，精准核算出丰先生赠与付出的总金额，其中包含转账、机票、餐饮、住宿等全部支出。同时，我们固定了不雅照片、私密订单、亲密转账备注等关键证据，形成完整的证据链，清晰证明丰先生与夏某存在不正当男女关系。

一切准备就绪，我们正式向法院提起诉讼，请求确认赠与行为无效，并判令夏某返还全部款项。庭审伊始，夏某的律师便抛出她的抗辩理由：

第一，声称夏某对丰先生已婚的事实并不知情，误以为丰先生和原告袁梅早已离婚，主观无过错；

第二，主张大额转账不是赠与，其中有 18 万元是合伙投资款，不是赠与款。另有 10 万元是丰先生支付的还款，不是赠与款；

第三，辩称机票、住宿、外卖是合伙进货、陪同就医、日常开销，与婚外情无关；

第四，试图以”十年平均每年花费不多”，淡化行为的违法性。

更棘手的是，对方当庭进行证据突袭，提交了所谓的借款记录、店铺租赁协议、租金凭证，且临时申请证人出庭作证，试图证明存在合伙关系。按照民事诉讼规则，此类关键证据本应在举证期限内提交，当庭突袭既不合法，也违背诉讼诚信原则。面对突发状况，袁梅女士又着急又生气。

我始终保持冷静，没有被对方打乱节奏。法庭之上，最考验律师的，不是慷慨激昂的言辞，而是临危不乱的定力和对证据、法条的精准把控。

首先，针对证据突袭，我当庭向法庭提出意见，明确指出被告逾期举证、当庭抛证，程序严重违法，不应被采纳，同时对这种不诚信的诉讼行为予以严肃谴责。

随后，我对被告提交的全部"新证据"，逐一质证驳斥：

针对 10 万元还款的主张，我指出，被告提供的转账记录系信用卡刷卡，结合丰先生的账户流水与双方无任何借贷合意的事实，该操作更符合信用卡套现特征，根本不存在真实借贷关系，丰先生的转款就是纯粹的赠与；

针对 18 万元合伙投资款的抗辩，我质证，被告提交的租赁协议仅有其个人签字，无丰先生署名，无合伙合同、无出资约定、无分红记录、无共担风险的任何凭证，所谓合伙，完全是事后拼凑的虚假说辞；

针对证人证言，我一针见血点明，证人与夏某系朋友关系，证言存在明显倾向性，且证人仅听闻口头提议，从未见过合伙协议、账目、收益，根本无法证明存在真实合法的合伙关系。

对于被告核心的"不知情已婚"抗辩，我用铁证予以回击：双方近十年的隐秘往来、不敢公开的合照、刻意隐瞒的相处模式，足以证明夏某对丰先生有配偶的事实心知肚明，这种辩解违背常理，不足为信。

而对于机票、住宿、外卖等支出，我清晰向法庭陈述：丰先生同学会拒绝妻子陪同，却与夏某同行；孩子生日人生重大时刻，他却与夏某入住酒店；所有消费均基于不正当男女关系产生，绝非正常往来或人道主义帮助。

整个庭审过程，我没有情绪化表达，而是以判决书式的严谨，逐条对应证据、法条与事实，把对方每一个抗辩点，都从逻辑、证据、常理上彻底推翻。我向法庭强调：丰先生在婚姻存续期间，擅自处分大额夫妻共同财产赠与第三者，既非日常生活需要，也未取得原告袁梅女士的同意，严重侵害夫妻共同财产权，更违背公序良俗，该赠与行为自始无效，被告夏某理应全额返还。

法庭认真听取了双方意见，对证据逐一审核，最终采纳了我方全部核心观点，对被告的证据、证人证言均不予采信。一审法院作出判决：确认已故的丰先生生前对夏某的赠与行为无效；夏某应返还原告袁梅全部诉请的款项及相应利息。

一审胜诉后，被告夏某不服判决，提起上诉。二审中，我们坚持一审的证据与逻辑，沉着应对对方的上诉理由，最终二审法院经审理，作出终审裁定：驳回上诉，维持原判。拿到二审判决书那天，袁梅终于卸下了压在心头的巨石。她没有欢呼，只是轻声说了一句："总算，对得起自己这么多年的付出了。"

案后结语

这是一起典型的婚外赠与纠纷，它藏着最真实的人性与婚姻之痛。袁梅的遭遇，是无数被背叛配偶的缩影——倾尽真心照料家庭，却在最脆弱的时候，遭遇最彻底的背叛；明明是受害者，却要鼓起巨大的勇气，才能走进法庭，维护自己的合法权益。

作为律师，我们能做的，不仅仅是替当事人抚平情感的创伤，更要用最专业、最细致、最沉稳的工作，为她守住法律的底线。从近十年流水的逐笔核对，到庭审中应对证据突袭、质证虚假抗辩，再到一二审全程坚守立场，我们始终以事实为依据，以法律为准绳，不夸大、不退缩、不妥协。

法律不会纵容违背公序良俗的行为，也不会辜负坚守正义的人。夫妻共同财产不是个人私产，婚外赠与终究无效，所有试图以感情为名侵占他人财产的行为，终将在法庭上无处遁形。

对袁梅女士而言，这场官司赢回的不仅是几十万钱款，更是尊严、公平，以及走出伤痛、重新开始生活的勇气。而对我们而言，这场案件再次提醒我们：家事法律服务的核心，是用专业守护弱者，用正义修复不公，让每一份被辜负的真心，都能得到法律最坚实的托举。

Betrayal in the Dust and Perseverance in Court: A Full Battle to Recover Illicit Gifts to a Third Party

Introduction

Some truths only come to light at the most painful moment. My client Ms. Yuan Mei, after faithfully caring for her cancer-stricken husband until his passing, discovered in his belongings the cruel reality: he had carried on an extramarital affair for nearly a decade, and improperly gifted hundreds of thousands of yuan in marital joint property to a third party. Overwhelmed by grief and anger, she entrusted me to file a lawsuit. The trial proved far more difficult than expected: the defendant ambushed the court with last-minute evidence, hastily applied for witnesses to testify, and raised layers of defenses and sophistry in an attempt to justify the misappropriated property. I remained calm and composed, using solid evidence as my shield and rigorous logic as my sword, dismantling the defendant's defenses one by one. In the end, I helped Ms. Yuan Mei win the case at first instance, and the judgment was upheld on appeal. Conduct violating public order and good morals was made to pay its due price.

I first met Ms. Yuan Mei three weeks after her husband Mr. Feng passed away. She sat in the reception chair, pale-faced, her eyes still clouded with sorrow and exhaustion, clutching a stack of freshly printed bank statements, transfer records and order screenshots, their edges crumpled from being tightly squeezed. These were not ordinary financial documents—they were the final straw that broke her. They revealed nearly a decade of emotional and financial dealings between the husband she had devoted everything to caring for, and another woman, all hidden from her during the marriage.

Yuan Mei and Mr. Feng had been married for decades. They originally ran a foreign trade business in a large commercial market, living a steady and ordinary life, and raised a son who was diligent and ambitious, now fully grown. To outsiders, theirs seemed a stable and harmonious family. Yet only Ms. Yuan knew how difficult life had been in recent years.

After Mr. Feng was diagnosed with cancer, Ms. Yuan put aside her business and devoted herself entirely to his daily care and treatment. She traveled to seek medical treatment in Beijing, Shanghai and other cities—queuing, registering, accompanying him in the hospital, preparing medicine—never a word of complaint. To cover the high medical costs, the family borrowed heavily and struggled financially, yet she endured silently, never letting her husband suffer. She believed her unwavering devotion would be rewarded with genuine affection. What she did not know was that while she lived frugally and raised money to save his life, her husband was secretly transferring their joint property, bit by bit, to his extramarital lover, Ms. Xia.

It was only when she finished handling the funeral affairs and sorted through her husband's phone, bank cards and payment records that the deliberately hidden secrets were fully exposed before her eyes. From 2016 to 2025, over nearly a decade, Mr. Feng continuously transferred money to Xia via bank, WeChat and Alipay, ranging from a few hundred to tens of thousands of yuan. He frequently ordered takeaways, booked hotels and bought flight tickets for her. Even when he went to his hometown Guangzhou to attend a class reunion, he refused his wife's company but secretly arranged for Xia to accompany him. The transfer amounts with special symbolic meanings, private hotel orders, and personal items sent to Xia's home pierced Yuan Mei's heart like knives.

She then realized all his excuses—"busy with work," "need to rest," "inconvenient for video calls"—were all lies. Part of the money she had saved through frugality and borrowed for medical treatment was being used by her husband to sustain an extramarital affair, spent on another woman.

What broke her heart even more was that in March 2025, when their son celebrated his 18th birthday, Mr. Feng, as a father, claimed he was on a business trip and could not make it back to accompany his son, but the truth was he booked a hotel to meet Xia. In his final days, he failed his family, his wife and his child miserably, yet remained extraordinarily generous to the third party.

Yuan Mei lay awake countless nights, her tears dried up, her heart feeling hollow and torn. She tried to contact Xia, wanting to bitterly denounce her despicability and shamelessness, and ask back the money her husband had sent her during his lifetime, which rightfully belonged to the marital joint property. But the calls went unanswered, messages ignored. The coldness and avoidance finally woke her up: this betrayed marriage, this misappropriated property—she must seek justice through law.

In despair yet with firm resolve, Ms. Yuan Mei came to me and entrusted me to represent her in this dispute over extramarital gifts. After accepting the mandate, my team and I did not rush to file the case. Instead, we settled down and sorted through all evidence with meticulous and rigorous attention. We reviewed, classified and counted thousands of transaction records spanning nearly a decade, deducted small amounts returned by Xia, and accurately calculated the total value of the unconditional gifts made by Mr. Feng, including transfers, air tickets, catering, accommodation and other expenses. Meanwhile, we preserved key evidence such as inappropriate photos, private orders and intimate transfer remarks, forming a complete chain of evidence that clearly proved the improper sexual relationship between Mr. Feng and Xia.

With full preparation, we formally filed a lawsuit with the court, requesting to declare the gift invalid and order Xia to return all the money. At the start of the trial, Xia's attorney raised a full set of defenses: 1. Claiming lack of knowledge that Mr. Feng was married, mistakenly believing he was divorced, thus having no subjective fault; 2. Arguing that large transfers were not gifts—claiming 180,000 yuan was for partnership investment and another 100,000 yuan was repayment of a debt; 3. Asserting that air tickets, accommodation and takeaways were for partnership purchasing, medical accompaniment and daily expenses, unrelated to the extramarital affair; 4. Attempting to downplay the illegality by claiming "the annual spending over ten years was not large."

To make matters worse, the defendant ambushed the court with last-minute evidence, submitting so-called loan records, shop rental agreements and rent receipts, and hastily applied for witnesses to testify, trying to prove the existence of a partnership. Under civil procedure rules, such crucial evidence should have been submitted within the time limit. An ambush in court was not only illegal but also violated the principle of good faith in litigation. Faced with this sudden turn, Ms. Yuan Mei was both anxious and angry.

Yet I stayed calm and did not let the other side disrupt my pace. In court, what truly tests a lawyer is not impassioned rhetoric, but composure under pressure and precise command of evidence and law.

First, regarding the evidence ambush, I submitted an objection in court, clearly pointing out that the defendant's late submission and ambush were seriously procedurally illegal and should not be admitted, while strongly condemning this bad-faith litigation conduct.

Then I dismantled and refuted all the defendant's "new evidence" one by one: As to the claim that 100,000 yuan was debt repayment, I pointed out that the defendant's record was a credit card transaction; combined with Mr. Feng's account flow and the absence of any loan agreement between the two parties, the transaction was more consistent with credit card cashing, meaning there was no real loan relationship—Mr. Feng's transfer was a pure gift. As to the claim that 180,000 yuan was partnership investment, I noted in court that the rental agreement bore only the defendant's signature, not Mr. Feng's, and there was no partnership contract, no capital contribution agreement, no profit distribution record, and no proof of shared risk; the so-called partnership was nothing but an after-the-fact fabrication. As to witness testimony, I pointed out sharply that the witnesses were friends of Xia, their testimony obviously biased, and they had only heard verbal proposals and never seen any partnership agreement, accounts or profits, making them unable to prove a genuine and legal partnership.

Against the defendant's core defense of "unaware of marriage," I countered with irrefutable proof: nearly a decade of secret dealings, undisclosed photos, and a deliberately concealed relationship sufficiently proved that Xia knew perfectly well Mr. Feng had a spouse. Such a claim defied common sense and was not credible.

Regarding expenses such as air tickets, accommodation and takeaways, I clearly stated to the court: Mr. Feng refused his wife's company to attend a class reunion but went with Xia; at the crucial moment of his son's 18th birthday, he checked into a hotel with Xia. All expenses arose from an improper sexual relationship, far from normal interactions or humanitarian assistance.

Throughout the trial, I avoided emotional expressions. Instead, with the rigor of a judgment, we matched evidence, law and facts point by point, completely overthrowing every defense from logical, evidential and reasonable perspectives. I emphasized to the court: During the marriage, Mr. Feng improperly disposed of a large amount of marital joint property as gifts to a third party. This was neither for daily life needs nor consented to by the plaintiff Ms. Yuan Mei. It seriously infringed the right to marital joint property and violated public order and good morals. The gift was invalid ab initio, and the defendant Xia ought to return the full amount.

The court carefully heard both sides, examined all evidence, and ultimately accepted all our core arguments, rejecting the defendant's evidence and witness testimony. The court of first instance ruled: The gifts made by the late Mr. Feng to Xia during his lifetime were declared invalid; Xia shall return to the plaintiff Yuan Mei all claimed funds and corresponding interest.

After winning at first instance, the defendant Xia refused to accept the judgment and filed an appeal. In the second instance, we adhered to the evidence and logic of the first instance, calmly responding to the appeal grounds. Eventually, the court of second instance heard the case and issued a final ruling: dismissing the appeal and upholding the original judgment. On the day she received the second-instance judgment, Yuan Mei finally lifted the boulder from her heart. She did not cheer, but whispered softly: "Finally, I have lived up to all these years of devotion."

Post-Case Conclusion

This is a typical dispute over extramarital gifts, hiding the most real pain of human nature and marriage. Yuan Mei's experience reflects countless betrayed spouses—those who give their all to care for the family, only to suffer the ultimate betrayal at their most vulnerable moment. Though the innocent victim, they must summon immense courage to step into court and defend their legitimate rights.

As lawyers, what we can do is not only ease our clients' emotional wounds, but also uphold the bottom line of justice for them through the most professional, meticulous and steady work. From verifying each entry in nearly a decade of statements, to countering evidence ambushes and dismantling false defenses in court, to standing firm throughout both trials, we have always taken facts as the basis and law as the criterion—without exaggeration, retreat or compromise.

The law never tolerates conduct violating public order and good morals, nor does it fail those who uphold justice. Marital joint property is not personal private property; extramarital gifts are ultimately invalid. All attempts to encroach on others' property in the name of love will eventually be exposed in court.

For Ms. Yuan Mei, this lawsuit won back not just hundreds of thousands of yuan, but also dignity, fairness, and the courage to move past pain and restart her life. For us, this case reminds us once again: the core of family legal services is to protect the vulnerable with professionalism, redress injustice with justice, and let every true heart that has been let down be firmly supported by the law.

温商跨国婚变：亿级资产里的尊严与突围

引言

一场横跨中美两国的婚姻，一对白手起家的温商华侨，一段纠缠三十年的再婚情缘，最终崩塌在亿级资产的漩涡之中。婚外情、转移隐匿财产、跨境房产、股权代持、巨额债权、复杂债务、前婚子女与共同子女的产权交织……这起案件几乎囊括了婚姻家事领域所有最疑难、最尖锐的争议焦点。作为代理律师，我陪伴当事人走过近两年的漫长诉讼，在层层迷雾与利益困局里，以专业破局，以谈判制胜，不仅帮他守住了半生财富，更夺回了尊严与安宁。这是一场婚姻的落幕，更是一场财产与人性的终极较量。

在我二十年的婚姻家事执业生涯里，经手的大案、难案不计其数，但程锦云诉杨望贞这起涉外离婚案，依旧是最特殊、最典型、最复杂的一桩。它集合了婚姻案件里几乎所有的争议元素：再婚家庭、跨境资产、婚前祖宅、婚后房产加名、子女赠与、婚外情过错、隐瞒转移财产、巨额共同债权、股权代持、家族信托基金、商业人身保险、银行抵押贷款……涉案资产规模过亿，境内境外盘根错节，关系错综复杂，稍有不慎，便会让当事人的半生心血付诸东流。

我的当事人程锦云，是典型的一代温商。年轻时出国闯荡，在美国加州打拼多年，与妻子杨望贞同为华侨，共同经历过白手起家的艰辛，也共同拥有过风光体面的生活。两人均是再婚，婚前各有与前婚配偶生育的子女，婚后又共同生育了一双儿女。三十年婚姻，从中国到美国，从中餐馆到跨境生意，风雨同舟，在外人眼中是安稳圆满的家庭。可只有程锦云自己知道，这段婚姻早已千疮百孔。

矛盾的爆发，始于财产的失控。

杨望贞性格强势，长期独揽家中财政大权，从房产处置到资金流转，经常不与程锦云商量就擅自做主。多年来，她将夫妻共同财产或出借给他人，或抵押房产用于投资，或私自将房产登记至自己前婚的女儿名下，或暗中进行股权代持、隐匿出售货品的收益，甚至在婚姻存续期间，与他人发生不正当男女关系。

最让程锦云无法接受的，是他倾尽半生守护的温州祖宅。这是他婚前的个人财产，是家族根基，却在婚后被杨望贞的姐姐杨望芬一家人长期占有使用，也未承担过一分钱租金。与此同时，一笔高达近 3000 万元的巨额债权，也成了悬在他头顶的巨石。这笔钱由杨望贞瞒着他私自出借给一家融资平台公司，借条上的出借人却只写了杨望贞一个人的名字。程锦云多次要求杨望贞向债务人催讨该笔借款，杨望贞却回避不与配合。程锦云曾拿着这张借条试图起诉该融资公司，却被法院认定其不具有原告主体资格，而被拒之门外。讨债无门，程锦云的这笔资金又面临长期悬空。

而另一边，近千万元的夫妻共同债务像阴影般笼罩而来，房产被反复抵押，资金被莫名挪用，账户被不断掏空，银行频频催债而来。而他却像一个局外人，守着一个看似光鲜的家，却对自己的财产完全失去掌控。

两人也早已分房居住长达十年，沟通彻底中断，夫妻感情早已消磨殆尽，再无和好可能。2023 年，在忍无可忍、退无可退的情况下，程锦云找到我，决心提起离婚诉讼，请求解除婚姻关系、分割夫妻共同财产、确认巨额共同债权，并彻底隔离自身不应承担的债务风险。

我接受委托后，第一件事便是梳理这团缠绕了三十年的乱麻。本案涉案财产错综复杂：价值约 4500 万元的境内外多处房产，包含婚前祖宅、婚后共同购房、登记在各自子女名下的混合产权房；高达 3000 万元的夫妻共同债权悬而未决；在香港设立的 800 万元的家族信托基金和人身保险利益；以及高达 900 万元的银行贷款债务争议。再加上中美两国跨境资产、前婚子女与共同子女产权交织、婚内多次财产协议效力争议、婚外情过错、转移财产行为……这早已不是一桩简单的离婚案，而是一场系统性的家族财富保卫战。

系统性的梳理了全案后和听取了当事人程锦云的主要诉求之后，我们确立了本案的三大核心攻坚目标：

第一、夺回温州祖宅控制权，守住委托人最在意的家族根基；

第二、锁定 3000 万元巨额债权，打通维权路径，确保财产不落空；

第三、一揽子解决全部争议，将房产、子女共有份额、股权、债权、债务在一案中处理完毕，杜绝案中案、累讼缠身。

为实现这一目标，在长达两年的诉讼历程中，我们近乎将诉讼手段和策略用到极致。我们第一时间申请财产保全，冻结对方账户与房产，遏制财产继续转移；全面申请调查令，穿透资金流水、股权代持、房产抵押、出借记录；及时申请房产评估，在市场下行周期掌握定价主动权；根据庭审进展和变化，我们及时变更、增加诉讼请求，牢牢把控诉讼节奏。

庭审中，我通过连续、精准、层层递进的当庭询问，一步步突破对方防线，成功固定 3000 万元借贷事实，让这笔险些灭失的债权，成为我方最关键的制胜证据。同时，我们将 AI 与可视化图表引入庭审，把三十年财产演变、资金流向、产权结构、债务链条全部绘制成清晰思维导图，让法官对复杂案情一目了然。我们逐条梳理婚内财产协议的效力边界，精准区分婚前财产、婚后共同财产、子女赠与份额、个人债务与夫妻共同债务，将混乱的事实，梳理成逻辑严密的证据链。

而真正决定案件走向的，是谈判。

我们手握两大关键筹码：一是杨望贞在婚姻存续期间存在婚外不正当关系的过错证据；二是其长期隐瞒、转移、擅自处分夫妻共同财产的事实已被充分固定。

在多次庭前会议、三次正式庭审的高压之下，我们同步释放调解信号，以理服人，以法制衡，既守住底线，又留有余地，最终促使对方放下对抗，坐到谈判桌前。

这场谈判，不仅是财产的分割，更是尊严的博弈。

我们坚持：祖宅必须归还程锦云；巨额债权必须司法确认；所有财产一揽子分割；债务风险彻底隔离。

历经近两年的拉锯战和诉辩博弈，2025 年 11 月，本案终于迎来圆满结果。在法院主持下，双方达成调解，我的当事人程锦云的全部核心诉求均得以实现：

一、成功夺回祖宅，当事人最在意的家族根基失而复得；
二、境内房产一次性全部分割完毕，财产利益最大化；
三、3000 万元巨额债权以民事调解书正式确认，成为合法有效的债权凭据；
四、家族信托、股权、保险等资产全部清晰分割，无遗留争议；
五、成功隔离 900 万元债务风险，委托人无需承担不合理负债；
六、所有涉及子女、案外人的产权争议一案了结，彻底杜绝后续累讼；
七、美国境内资产依托中国调解书办理公证，跨境分割顺利落地。

拿到调解书那天，这位在商场上叱咤半生的温商，终于松了一口气。这段早已破碎的婚姻，终于让他赢回了财产、控制权和人格尊严，以及下半生的安宁。同时也让双方平息了缠绕的纠葛，化解了深刻的积怨，回归到生活的正轨。

案后结语

这起涉外再婚离婚案，是我执业二十年非常具有代表性的经典案例。它集合了婚姻家事领域几乎全部疑难争议点，跨境、巨额、复杂、多主体、多财产类型、多法律关系，每一步都如履薄冰，每一个决定都影响深远。

案件的圆满解决，再次印证了婚姻家事法律服务的真正价值：它不止是解除一段关系，更是财富的保全、风险的隔离、权利的救济、尊严的守护。

在再婚家庭、跨境资产、高净值人群的家事纠纷中，财产边界极易模糊，权利极易受损。婚前财产与婚后财产混同、共同财产被擅自处分、登记在子女名下房产引发争议、巨额债权悬空、债务莫名上身……都是高净值家庭最常见的风险陷阱。

法律的意义，在于厘清边界；律师的价值，在于保护利益；调解的智慧，在于案结事了。本案最终以调解收官，没有两败俱伤，没有无休止的上诉与申诉，没有案外生案。当事人体面离婚，财产安全落地，债权得到保障，债务得以隔离，子女利益亦得到妥善安排。这正是家事审判最理想的状态——辨是非、分财产、护弱者、了事端、保安宁。

婚姻可散，家财可分，但尊严不可丢，底线不可破。在爱与利益的尽头，法律永远是最坚实的依靠。

A Cross-Border Marriage Breakdown of a Wenzhou Merchant: Dignity and Breakthrough Amid Hundreds of Millions in Assets

Introduction

A marriage spanning China and the United States, a Chinese overseas couple from Wenzhou who built their fortune from scratch, a 30-year bond of remarriage finally collapsing in the vortex of hundreds of millions in assets. Extramarital affairs, concealed asset transfers, cross-border real estate, nominee shareholding, huge creditor's rights, complicated debts, intertwined property rights between children from previous marriages and joint children... This case covers almost all the most difficult and contentious issues in family and marital law. As the attorney in charge, I accompanied my client through nearly two years of prolonged litigation. Amid layers of confusion and interest dilemmas, we broke the deadlock with professionalism and won through negotiation. We not only helped him preserve the wealth accumulated over half a lifetime but also helped him regain his dignity and peace. This was the end of a marriage and a final showdown between property and human nature.

In my twenty-year legal career focusing on marital and family affairs, I have handled countless major and complex cases. Yet the cross-border divorce case of Cheng Jinyun v. Yang Wangzhen remains one of the most unique, typical, and intricate matters. It contains nearly every controversial element in divorce litigation: remarried family, cross-border assets, pre-marital ancestral property, post-marital title addition, gifts to children, fault of extramarital affairs, concealed asset transfer, substantial joint creditor's rights, nominee shareholding, family trust funds, commercial personal insurance, bank mortgage loans, and more. The assets involved exceeded 100 million yuan, intricately intertwined both domestically and overseas, with highly complex relationships. One careless move could have cost my client half a lifetime of hard work.

My client, Cheng Jinyun, is a classic first-generation Wenzhou merchant. He ventured abroad at a young age and built a career in California, USA. He and his wife Yang Wangzhen, both overseas Chinese, shared the hardships of starting from nothing and later enjoyed a prosperous life. Both were remarried, each with children from previous unions, and they had two children together after marriage. Over 30 years of marriage, they moved from China to the United States, from running a Chinese restaurant to cross-border business, standing together through thick and thin. To outsiders, they appeared to have a stable and complete family. But only Cheng Jinyun knew that the marriage had long been riddled with holes.

The conflict erupted when he lost control over his property.

Yang Wangzhen had a strong personality and long held sole financial control over the household. She never consulted Cheng Jinyun on anything, from real estate transactions to fund transfers. Over the years, she unilaterally made decisions to lend out joint property, mortgage real estate for investments, privately register properties under the name of her daughter from a previous marriage, secretly engage in nominee shareholding, conceal proceeds from goods sales, and even engage in improper sexual relations with others during the marriage.

What Cheng Jinyun found most unacceptable was his Wenzhou ancestral home, which he had guarded for half his life. It was his pre-marital personal property, the foundation of his family, yet it had been occupied for years by Yang Wangzhen's sister Yang Wangfen and her family without paying any rent. Meanwhile, a huge creditor's claim of nearly 30 million yuan hung over him like a boulder. Yang Wangzhen had secretly lent this sum to a financing platform without his knowledge, with only her name listed as the lender on the loan agreement. Cheng Jinyun repeatedly demanded that she pursue repayment, but she refused to cooperate. When he attempted to sue the financing company using the loan document, the court ruled he lacked standing as a plaintiff and dismissed the case. With no way to recover the debt, the funds remained indefinitely stranded.

On the other side, joint debts of nearly 10 million yuan loomed like a shadow. Properties were repeatedly mortgaged, funds misappropriated without explanation, accounts continuously drained, and banks pressed constantly for repayment. Yet he was like an outsider, living in an outwardly prosperous home but having completely lost control over his own assets.

The couple had lived separately for a full decade, with all communication severed. The marital bond had long been exhausted, with no possibility of reconciliation. In 2023, having endured all he could and with no room left to retreat, Cheng Jinyun came to me, determined to file for divorce. He sought dissolution of the marriage, division of joint property, confirmation of the substantial joint creditor's rights, and complete isolation from improper debt risks.

After accepting the mandate, my first task was to untangle this 30-year-old knot. The property involved in this case was intricate and complex: various domestic and overseas properties worth approximately 45 million yuan, including pre-marital ancestral homes, jointly purchased post-marital properties, and mixed-title properties registered under their children; an unsettled joint creditor's right of 30 million yuan; an 8-million-yuan family trust fund and personal insurance benefits established in Hong Kong; and a disputed 9-million-yuan bank loan debt. Coupled with cross-border assets between China and the U.S., intertwined property rights involving children from previous and current marriages, disputes over the validity of multiple marital property agreements, fault of extramarital affairs, and asset transfers... this was far from a simple divorce case. It was a systematic defense of family wealth.

After systematically reviewing the entire case and listening to the main demands of my client Cheng Jinyun, we established three core strategic objectives:

1. Regain control of the Wenzhou ancestral home and safeguard the family foundation most precious to my client;

2. Secure the 30-million-yuan creditor's claim, clear a path for rights protection, and ensure the assets were not lost;

3. Resolve all disputes in a single package, including real estate, co-owned shares by children, equity, creditor's rights, and debts, to prevent collateral cases and prolonged litigation.

To achieve these goals, over the two-year litigation process, we employed litigation tactics and strategies to their fullest extent. We immediately applied for property preservation to freeze the opposing party's accounts and real estate, halting further asset transfers; we obtained comprehensive investigation orders to trace capital flows, nominee shareholding, real estate mortgages, and lending records; we timely applied for real estate appraisal to seize pricing initiative amid a market downturn; and we continuously amended and added claims in line with trial progress, firmly controlling the litigation rhythm.

During the trial, through continuous, precise, and layered cross-examination, we gradually broke through the opposing party's defenses and successfully established the facts of the 30-million-yuan loan, turning this nearly lost claim into our key decisive evidence. We also introduced AI and visual charts into the courtroom, mapping out the 30-year evolution of property, capital flows, ownership structures, and debt chains into clear mind maps, allowing the judge to grasp the complex case at a glance. We analyzed the validity boundaries of marital property agreements clause by clause, accurately distinguishing pre-marital property, post-marital joint property, gifted shares to children, personal debts, and joint marital debts, organizing chaotic facts into a tightly logical evidence chain.

Yet what truly determined the case's outcome was negotiation.

We held two critical bargaining chips: first, evidence of Yang Wangzhen's fault in having an extramarital affair during the marriage; second, well-established facts that she had long concealed, transferred, and arbitrarily disposed of marital joint property. Under the high pressure of multiple pre-trial conferences and three formal hearings, we consistently signaled a willingness to mediate, persuading with reason and balancing with legal leverage, holding firm to our bottom lines while leaving room for compromise. We finally persuaded the opposing party to set aside confrontation and come to the negotiating table.

This negotiation was not only about dividing property but also a battle for dignity. We insisted: the ancestral home must be returned to Cheng Jinyun; the huge creditor's rights must be judicially confirmed; all property must be divided in a comprehensive package; and debt risks must be completely isolated.

After nearly two years of stalemate and litigation wrangling, a satisfactory result was finally reached in November 2025. With the court's assistance, the parties reached a settlement, and all of my client Cheng Jinyun's core demands were fulfilled:

1. The ancestral home was successfully recovered, restoring the family foundation he cherished most;

2. Domestic real estate was fully divided in one go, maximizing property interests;

3. The 30-million-yuan creditor's claim was formally confirmed by a civil mediation statement, becoming legally valid;

4. Family trusts, equity, insurance, and other assets were clearly divided with no remaining disputes;

5. The 9-million-yuan debt risk was successfully isolated, with the client

free from unreasonable liabilities;

6. All property disputes involving children and third parties were resolved in one case, eliminating future prolonged litigation;

7. U.S. overseas assets were notarized based on the domestic mediation statement, enabling smooth cross-border division.

On the day he received the mediation document, this Wenzhou merchant who had dominated the business world for half a lifetime finally breathed a sigh of relief. Through the resolution of this long-broken marriage, he had regained his property, control, personal dignity, and peace for the rest of his life. The tangled disputes between both sides were settled, deep-seated resentment resolved, and life returned to order.

Post-Case Conclusion

This cross-border remarriage divorce case is a highly representative classic matter from my twenty-year practice. It encompasses nearly all complex disputes in marital and family law: cross-border elements, huge value, complexity, multiple parties, diverse asset types, and multiple legal relationships. Every step was taken with extreme caution, and every decision carried profound consequences.

The successful resolution once again confirms the true value of family legal services: it is not merely about dissolving a relationship, but about preserving wealth, isolating risks, remedying rights, and safeguarding dignity.

In family disputes involving remarried families, cross-border assets, and high-net-worth individuals, property boundaries are easily blurred and rights easily violated. Commingling of pre- and post-marital assets, arbitrary disposal of joint property, disputes over real estate registered under children's names, stranded huge creditor's rights, and unexpected liabilities are among the most common risk traps for wealthy families.

The law clarifies boundaries; the attorney protects interests; the wisdom of mediation brings matters to a complete close. This case ultimately ended in settlement, with no mutual destruction, no endless appeals, and no collateral disputes. The parties divorced with dignity, property was safely settled, creditor's rights protected, debts isolated, and children's interests properly arranged. This represents the ideal state of family justice: distinguishing right from wrong, dividing property, protecting the vulnerable, resolving disputes, and safeguarding peace.

Marriage can end, family wealth can be divided, but dignity must not be lost and bottom lines must not be broken. At the end of love and interest, the law remains the most solid support.

跨境婚约下的财富守护，一份婚前协议的双向安全感

引言

当爱情跨越山海，当财富遇上高净值家庭的传承思维，婚姻便不再只是情感的联结，更藏着财产与人性的双重考量。在婚恋自由的当下，婚前协议已不是"不信任"的代名词，而是高净值人群守护家族资产、规避婚姻风险的理性选择。本案当事人袁洛珈，是一位资深的金融从业者，在杭州和上海都有她经营的公司。面对浙港跨境婚恋，她没有被爱情冲昏头脑，而是选择用法律工具为婚姻筑牢防线。作为她的代理律师，我全程参与这份涉港婚前协议的拟定，破解两地法律差异的实务难题，既守住女方家族传承的财富底线，也兼顾男方的情感与权益，让这份协议成为婚姻的稳定器，而非感情的隔阂。这起案例，也为众多跨境婚恋的高净值家庭，提供了可借鉴的财富保护范本。

初识袁洛珈，是在我律所的会客室，她身着简约职业装，谈吐从容干练，举止透露着的顶尖金融公司精英金领的气质。年仅三十出头的她，已年收入数百万。她的原生家庭在浙江深耕实业，家底殷实，作为家中独女，她不仅继承了父辈的商业头脑，更有着超乎常人的法律风险意识。

此次找到我，袁洛珈是为了自己的终身大事。她与男友肖驰相恋多年，已步入谈婚论嫁的阶段。肖驰是香港居民，因工作业务常年往返浙沪港澳多地，两人感情稳定，对未来的婚姻生活满怀期许。而让袁洛珈下定决心拟定婚前协议，既源于男友的主动提议，也来自闺蜜宋珠珠的惨痛前车之鉴。

肖驰在谈及婚事时，曾主动向袁洛珈提出："你家的家族资产是父母一辈子的心血，属于你个人所有，婚后我们一起打拼、共同投资的收益，才属于我们夫妻双方，我们可以签一份婚前协议，我身边很多香港朋友结婚前都会做这样的安排，既能分清财产，也能避免日后纠纷。"男友的坦诚，让袁洛珈心生认可，而闺蜜宋珠珠的经历，更让她坚定了签署婚前协议的想法。

宋珠珠同样家世优渥，父母为其置办了巨额婚前资产，婚后她嫁给了一位香港富家子弟，因为信任爱情，她没有做任何财产隔离，婚后将自己的婚前财产与夫妻共同财产混同打理，一同购置房产、做多项目的投资运营等。可婚姻终究没能抵过人性的考验，婚后不久男方出轨，执意提出离婚，离婚分割财产时，宋珠珠的大量婚前资产因混同与婚后财产而难以区分边界，被男方分走大半，损失惨重，原本属于自己的家族财富，最终因一场失败的婚姻大幅缩水。

"叶律师，我和肖驰是相互信任的。不过我们都很理性，都不希望让人性去经受试探和考验。而且婚姻也有太多未知，尤其是我们一个在内地、一个在香港，涉及两地财产，我必须守住父母留给我的家族财富，婚前协议不是为了防备谁，而是用法律约束人性，给彼此一个清晰的边界，让婚姻更纯粹。"袁洛珈的

诉求很明确，希望通过一份严谨的婚前协议，将家族传承的巨额财富，与婚后共同收益彻底隔离，同时兼顾两地法律规定，确保协议合法有效。

接手案件后，我们团队立刻梳理核心案情，很快发现这起案件的最大难点：双方分属内地与香港两个法域，法律规定差异极大，单一法域的常规婚前协议，显然无法适配跨境婚姻的风险，一旦后续产生纠纷，协议效力将面临巨大挑战。

首先是两地法律底层逻辑的核心差异。在内地，婚前协议的效力有着明确的成文法支撑。《民法典》第一千零六十五条清晰规定，男女双方可以约定婚姻关系存续期间所得财产以及婚前财产归各自所有、共同所有或部分各自所有、部分共同所有。内地法院秉持"意思自治优先"原则，只要协议是双方真实意思表示、内容不违反法律强制性规定与公序良俗，一般会直接认可其效力，审查重点集中在内容合法性，如是否限制离婚自由、是否剥夺一方基本生存权等。

而香港作为普通法地区，法律逻辑截然不同：

1. 无夫妻共同财产法定制：香港依《已婚者地位条例》实行严格分别财产制，婚后财产原则上各自独立，但离婚时法院依据《婚姻法律程序与财产条例》第 7 条，拥有极大自由裁量权，会综合考量双方收入、财产、婚姻时长、家庭贡献等"所有情况"，而非机械按协议判决。

2. 婚前协议非绝对有效：香港无专门婚前协议成文法，协议仅被视为重要考量因素，而非绝对约束力的合同。香港司法判例支持审判原则：仅当协议满足"自愿签署、充分披露、独立法律意见、内容公平"四要件时，法院才会赋予"决定性权重"，否则可直接调整或推翻。

3. 审查重心不同：内地重"内容公平"，香港重程序合规——法院更关注签署时是否有胁迫、是否隐瞒资产、是否各自聘请律师，程序瑕疵往往直接导致协议失效。这种底层差异，意味着同一份协议在内地有效，在香港可能因为程序和实体上的瑕疵而被否定，这也是本案必须攻克的核心难题。

针对袁洛珈的资产结构与跨境婚姻的特殊性，我们首先明确核心原则：协议必须在婚前完成签署，既要筑牢女方家族财富的隔离防线，也要平衡男方权益，让双方都能带着诚意步入婚姻。基于此，我们先在内地协议文本中，搭建了完整的财产隔离架构。

第一，完整梳理界定女方的婚前个人财产范围，这是守护袁洛珈家族资产的核心。我们在协议中明确约定，登记在袁洛珈名下的婚前房产、存款，以及父母单独转入其指定专属账户的资金，无论婚后是否产生孳息、投资收益，均属于袁洛珈个人财产；同时，父母赠与的家族企业股权、股权分红及后续增值收益，无论婚姻存续多久，都严格界定为女方个人财产，与婚姻无关，彻底阻断婚后财产混同的风险。

第二，规范和构建夫妻共同财产的"安全港"，兼顾肖驰的权益与安全感。协议约定，婚后双方共同投资的项目、共同经营所得收益，即便以单方名义投资但双方共同参与的，其收益均纳入夫妻共同财产，归双方共同所有，明确婚后共创价值的归属，让肖驰清晰知晓，婚后共同努力的成果，双方均可共享，消除他对"财产分得太清"的顾虑。

第三，增加兜底隔离条款，明确财产边界。除上述约定的共同财产外，双方各自名下的其他资产，包括肖驰在香港的房产、存款等个人资产，婚后仍归各自所有，互不干涉，实现财产边界的清晰划分。

在此研判基础上，我们针对香港司法标准，梳理出五大合规要素，并按照五大要素制定了一套兼顾两地法律的完整婚前协议方案。

第一要素：时间底线——阻断"胁迫与不当影响"。

香港法院高度关注签署自愿性，婚礼前夕仓促签署极易被认定为"最后一刻施压"，曾有婚期前 21 天签署的协议被判定无效。我们要求协议至少在婚期前 45 天完成签署，远超香港判例认可的安全期限，确保肖驰有充足时间审阅、咨询律师，排除"被迫签署"可能，这是香港程序审查的首要门槛。

第二要素：全面财务透明——香港效力基石

香港法院将完整财务披露视为协议效力的前提，任何隐瞒不仅会推翻协议，还可能构成藐视法庭。我们要求双方均予以披露：袁洛珈提交内地房产、股权、银行流水；肖驰提交香港房产、公司股份、资产凭证，所有材料附入协议附件，满足香港"无隐瞒"的刚性要求。

第三要素：独立法律意见——两地最核心差异

这是内地当事人最易忽视的环节：香港严禁双方共用律师，必须各自聘请独立律师，且不得由一方代付律师费，否则法院直接质疑"是否理解放弃权利的后果"。本案中，袁洛珈委托我们内地律师梳理财产、共同制定法律方案，并同步委托她的香港律师参与协议的签订见证和全程合规审核，建立双团队律师；肖驰则自行聘请独立香港律师，双方律师分别出具意见，这是香港认可协议的必备程序。

第四要素：实质公平底线——两地平衡关键

内地要求协议内容公平，香港则更关注不导致一方陷入经济困境。依据香港《婚姻法律程序与财产条例》第 7 条，若协议使一方离婚后无法维持基本生活，法院有权干预。我们在协议中加入弹性平衡条款：若婚姻满十年以上，一方经济发生危机以致难以从家庭的共同财产中保障其正常生活的，则可向另一方请求支付经济补偿金，另一方在合理的资产范围内给予不超过其年收入 30% 的补偿金。这样既守住家族财富底线，又能为未来可能出现的不确定情形给予一定的弹性调整空间，更好的实现两地公平标准的衔接。

第五要素：签署规范——证据留存闭环

香港不强制公证，但要求签署可追溯。我们安排双方在各自律师见证下亲自签署、全程录像，所有披露文件、律师意见书装订成册，形成完整证据链——这既是香港程序审查的要求，也契合内地"证据充分"的司法习惯，并由香港律师进行本土化改造，嵌入独立法律意见确认书、财务披露清单，满足香港判例要求，杜绝后续效力争议。

因着双方当事人的坦诚和理性，以及双方律师的专业和负责，方案很快顺畅推进和实施。在婚期前 45 天的安全窗口期，袁洛珈和肖驰在双方律师的见证下完成签署。婚礼后，袁洛珈向我寄来一幅美丽幸福的婚照，我由衷地为他们感到喜悦和祝福。

一年后，当我得知袁洛珈与肖驰婚姻安稳美满，且生育了一个健康的男孩，内心充满了欣慰。后来，我还陆续为他们办理将婚内共同财产陆续赠与儿子，设立家族信托的法律事务的处理，见证了这对新人一路走来的相爱相守和人间值得。爱情回归纯粹，婚姻少了内耗，这份两地合规审查的协议，成为了他们最坚实的法律屏障。

案后结语

这起浙港跨境婚前协议案例，打破了"婚前协议伤感情"的刻板认知，也为跨境婚恋、高净值家庭的财富保护提供了清晰的实务思路。婚姻的本质是爱与陪伴，但理性的法律防护，并不是对感情的否定，而是对彼此、对家族财富的负责。

袁洛珈和肖驰的清醒与理性，值得所有身处婚恋中的人借鉴。尤其是高净值人群、跨境婚姻群体，面对两地法律差异、财产结构复杂的现状，提前做好财产隔离，不是防备，而是未雨绸缪。一份严谨的婚前协议，既能守住家族传承的心血，避免因婚姻破裂导致资产流失，也能明确双方权益边界，减少婚后财产纠纷，让爱情回归纯粹，让婚姻更有安全感。

内地与香港法律体系的核心差异，在于内地重意思自治与内容公平，香港重程序合规与裁量平衡。跨境婚前协议的关键，是同时满足两地审查标准：内地合法、香港合规——独立法律意见、全面财务披露、充足签署时间、公平弹性条款，这些看似繁琐的细节，实则是协议在两地生效的核心前提。

真正好的婚姻，既有相爱的真心，也有应对风险的理性。婚前协议的意义：其目的远非离婚分财产这么单一和不近人情，而是为了更好地守护婚姻，立下财产界限，立下坦诚态度，更立下对彼此长远未来的尊重。这，便是跨境婚恋中，法律与爱情最好的共存方式。

Cross-Border Marriages & Wealth Safeguards: The Dual Protection of a Prenuptial Agreement

Introduction

When love crosses borders, and wealth intersects with the inheritance mindset of high-net-worth families, marriage becomes more than just an emotional bond — it also involves dual considerations of property and human nature. In an era of free love and marriage, prenuptial agreements are no longer synonymous with "distrust." Instead, they are a rational choice for high-net-worth individuals to safeguard family assets and avoid marital risks. Yuan Luojia, the client in this case, is a senior financial professional with businesses in both Hangzhou and Shanghai. Faced with a cross-border relationship between Zhejiang and Hong Kong, she did not let love cloud her judgment. Instead, she chose to use legal tools to build a solid defense for her marriage. As her attorney, I participated in the entire drafting process of this Hong Kong-related prenuptial agreement, solving practical challenges arising from legal differences between the two jurisdictions. The agreement not only protected the wife's family wealth inheritance but also respected the husband's emotions and rights, making it a stabilizer for marriage rather than a barrier to affection. This case also provides a replicable wealth protection model for many high-net-worth families in cross-border relationships.

I first met Yuan Luojia in the reception room of my law firm. Dressed in a simple professional outfit, she spoke calmly and competently, with the air of an elite professional from a top financial institution. In her early thirties, she already earned an annual income of several million yuan. Her family of origin had deep roots in industrial business in Zhejiang, with substantial family wealth. As the only child, she not only inherited her parents' business acumen but also possessed extraordinary legal risk awareness.

She came to me regarding her lifelong marriage. She had been in a relationship with her boyfriend Xiao Chi for many years, and they were preparing for marriage. Xiao Chi is a Hong Kong resident who travels frequently between Zhejiang, Shanghai, Hong Kong, and Macao for work. Their relationship was stable, and both were full of expectations for their married life. Yuan Luojia's decision to sign a prenuptial agreement stemmed from both her boyfriend's proactive suggestion and the painful lesson learned by her best friend, Song Zhuzhu.

When discussing marriage, Xiao Chi voluntarily proposed to Yuan Luojia: "Your family assets are the lifelong effort of your parents and belong to you personally. After marriage, the income from our joint endeavors and investments will belong to both of us as a couple. We can sign a prenuptial agreement. Many of my Hong Kong friends make such arrangements before marriage — it clarifies property ownership and avoids future disputes." Her boyfriend's honesty earned her approval, and her best friend's experience further strengthened her resolve to sign a prenuptial agreement.

Song Zhuzhu also came from a wealthy background, with substantial pre-marital assets provided by her parents. She married a Hong Kong heir and, out of trust in love, did not arrange any asset segregation. After marriage, she commingled her pre-marital assets with marital joint property, purchasing real estate and investing in various projects together. However, the marriage failed the test of human nature. Shortly after the wedding, the husband had an affair and insisted on divorce. During the property division, a large portion of Song Zhuzhu's pre-marital assets was difficult to distinguish due to commingling with post-marital property and was mostly awarded to her husband, resulting in heavy losses. Family wealth that rightfully belonged to her was severely diminished due to a failed marriage.

"Lawyer Rachel J. Ye, Xiao Chi and I trust each other. But we are both rational and do not want to put human nature to the test. Besides, marriage holds many unknowns — especially since one of us is from the Mainland and the other from Hong Kong, involving cross-border assets. I must protect the family wealth left to me by my parents. A prenuptial agreement is not about guarding against anyone. It is about using the law to regulate human nature, setting clear boundaries for both parties, and making marriage more pure." Yuan Luojia's request was clear: to completely segregate the substantial inherited family wealth from post-marital joint income through a rigorous prenuptial agreement, while complying with the laws of both jurisdictions to ensure the agreement's legal validity.

Upon taking on the case, our team immediately sorted out the core facts and soon identified the greatest difficulty: the parties are domiciled in two jurisdictions, the Chinese mainland and Hong Kong, with vastly different legal provisions. A conventional prenuptial agreement governed by a single jurisdiction is completely inadequate to address the risks inherent in a cross-border marriage. Should a dispute arise in the future, the validity of such an agreement would face enormous challenges.

The fundamental divergence lies in the underlying legal logic of the two jurisdictions. On the Chinese mainland, the validity of prenuptial agreements is firmly supported by statutory law. Article 1065 of the Civil Code clearly stipulates that a man and a woman may agree that property acquired during the marriage and their respective premarital property shall be owned separately, jointly, or partly separately and partly jointly. Mainland courts adhere to the principle of party autonomy. So long as the agreement represents the true intent of both parties and its contents do not violate mandatory provisions of law or public order and good morals, the court will generally uphold its validity, focusing its review on the legality of the terms (such as whether they restrict freedom of divorce or deprive one party of the right to basic subsistence).

As a common law jurisdiction, Hong Kong follows a distinctly different legal logic:

1. No statutory regime of community property: Pursuant to the Married Persons Status Ordinance, Hong Kong adopts a strict separate property regime, under which post-marital property is in principle owned separately. However, in divorce proceedings, the court exercises wide discretionary power under Section 7 of the Matrimonial Proceedings and Property Ordinance. It will take into account all the circumstances, including the parties' income, assets, duration of marriage, and family contributions, rather than mechanically enforcing the terms of the agreement.

2. A prenuptial agreement is not absolutely effective: Hong Kong has no specific statute governing prenuptial agreements. Such agreements are regarded only as important considerations, not as absolutely binding contracts. Hong Kong judicial precedents uphold the principle that the court will grant a prenuptial agreement determinative weight only if it fulfills four requirements: voluntary execution, full financial disclosure, independent legal advice, and substantive fairness. Otherwise, the court may directly revise or set aside the agreement.

3. Different focus of judicial review: The Chinese mainland emphasizes substantive fairness, while Hong Kong emphasizes procedural compliance. Hong Kong courts focus closely on whether there was duress, concealment of assets, or joint legal representation at the time of signing. Procedural defects often result in the agreement being held invalid.

These fundamental differences mean that an agreement valid in the mainland may be rejected in Hong Kong due to procedural or substantive flaws. This was the core challenge to overcome in this case.

Given Yuan Luojia's asset structure and the special nature of this cross-border marriage, we first established a core principle: the agreement must be signed before marriage, establishing a robust firewall for the wife's family wealth while balancing the husband's interests, so that both parties could enter the marriage in good faith. On this basis, we first built a complete asset isolation framework in the mainland version of the agreement.

First, clearly define the wife's full scope of pre-marital personal property. This is the core of protecting Yuan Luojia's family assets. The agreement stipulated that pre-marital real estate and bank deposits registered under Yuan Luojia's name, as well as funds separately transferred by her parents into her designated exclusive account, shall remain her personal property regardless of whether they generate interest or investment returns after marriage. Furthermore, equity in the family business gifted by her parents, dividend distributions, and subsequent appreciation shall be strictly defined as her personal property, unrelated to the marriage, no matter how long the marriage lasts. This completely eliminates the risk of commingling of assets after marriage.

Second, establish a "safe harbor" for marital joint property. The agreement provides that projects jointly invested in and income from joint operations after marriage, even if invested in one party's name but jointly participated in by both spouses, shall be classified as marital joint property and owned equally by both parties. This clarifies the ownership of value created together after marriage, reassuring Xiao Chi that the fruits of their joint efforts would be shared, and easing his concern about overly rigid asset division.

Third, add catch-all isolation clauses to clarify property boundaries. Except for the agreed joint property, all other assets under each party's name – including Xiao Chi's real estate and deposits in Hong Kong – remain their separate personal property after marriage, with no mutual interference.

Based on this analysis, we identified five compliance elements aligned with Hong Kong judicial standards and drafted a comprehensive cross-border prenuptial agreement compatible with both jurisdictions.

Element One: Time Requirement – Eliminating Duress and Undue Influence

Hong Kong courts attach great importance to voluntary signing. A hastily signed agreement on the eve of the wedding is easily deemed "last-minute pressure." There have been cases where an agreement signed only 21 days before the wedding was ruled invalid. We required the agreement to be signed at least 45 days before the wedding, well beyond the safe period recognized in Hong Kong precedents. This ensured Xiao Chi had sufficient time to review the document and seek legal advice, eliminating any possibility of being "forced to sign" — the primary threshold for procedural review in Hong Kong.

Element Two: Full Financial Transparency — Foundation of Validity in Hong Kong

Hong Kong courts treat complete financial disclosure as a prerequisite for a valid agreement. Any concealment may not only invalidate the agreement but also constitute contempt of court. We required full disclosure from both parties: Yuan Luojia provided mainland real estate, equity holdings, and bank statements; Xiao Chi provided Hong Kong property, company shares, and asset certificates. All materials were attached as annexes to satisfy Hong Kong's strict "no concealment" requirement.

Element Three: Independent Legal Advice — Core Difference Between the Two Jurisdictions

This is the point most easily overlooked by mainland parties: Hong Kong strictly prohibits shared legal representation. Each party must retain separate, independent lawyers, and legal fees must not be paid by one party on behalf of the other. Otherwise, the court will directly question whether they understand the consequences of waiving their rights. In this case, Yuan Luojia entrusted our mainland lawyers to organize the assets and jointly formulate the legal plan, while simultaneously entrusting her Hong Kong lawyer to participate in witnessing the signing of the agreement and conducting a full compliance review, establishing a dual-lawyer team. Xiao Chi hired an independent Hong Kong lawyer himself, and the lawyers of both parties issued separate opinions. This is an essential procedure for the agreement to be recognized in Hong Kong.

Element Four: Substantive Fairness Baseline — The Key to Balancing Both Jurisdictions

The mainland requires the content of the agreement to be fair, while Hong Kong focuses more on ensuring that it does not lead to one party falling into financial hardship. Under Section 7 of the Matrimonial Proceedings and Property Ordinance in Hong Kong, if an agreement renders a party unable to maintain basic living standards after divorce, the court has the power to intervene. We included a flexible balance clause in the agreement: if the marriage lasts for more than ten years and one party experiences a financial crisis that makes it difficult to secure a normal living from the family's joint property, they may request economic compensation from the other party, and the other party shall provide compensation not exceeding 30% of their annual income within a reasonable range of assets. This not only secures the baseline of family wealth but also provides a certain degree of flexible adjustment space for uncertain situations that may arise in the future, better connecting the fairness standards of both jurisdictions.

Element Five: Signing Protocol — A Closed Loop for Evidence Preservation

Notarization is not mandatory in Hong Kong, but traceable execution is required. We arranged for both parties to sign in person under the witness of their respective lawyers, with the entire process video-recorded. All disclosure documents and legal opinions were bound into a complete file, forming a full chain of evidence. This complies with Hong Kong's procedural review requirements and aligns with the Mainland judicial practice of "sufficient evidence." Furthermore, Hong Kong counsel localized the agreement, incorporating an independent legal opinion confirmation letter and a financial disclosure checklist to meet Hong Kong case law requirements and eliminate future disputes over validity.

Thanks to the openness and rationality of both parties, as well as the professionalism and dedication of their legal teams, the plan was smoothly advanced and implemented. During the safe 45-day window before the wedding, Yuan Luojia and Xiao Chi signed the agreement under the witness of their respective lawyers. After the wedding, Yuan Luojia sent me a beautiful and joyful wedding photo. I was truly delighted for them and offered my sincere blessings.

A year later, I was greatly relieved to learn that Yuan Luojia and Xiao Chi enjoyed a stable and happy marriage and had welcomed a healthy baby boy. Later, I also assisted them with successive legal matters: gifting their marital joint property to their son and establishing a family trust. I witnessed this couple's enduring love and commitment, proof that a loving relationship is truly worthwhile. Love returned to its purest form, and marriage was free of internal strife. This cross-jurisdictional agreement, fully compliant with the laws of both regions, became their most solid legal safeguard.

Post-Case Conclusion

This cross-border prenuptial agreement case between Zhejiang and Hong Kong challenges the stereotype that "prenuptial agreements harm romantic relationships." It also provides clear practical guidance for wealth protection in cross-border marriages and high-net-worth families. Marriage is essentially about love and companionship, yet rational legal protection does not negate affection — it represents responsibility toward each other and toward family wealth.

The clarity and rationality shown by Yuan Luojia and Xiao Chi offer valuable lessons for everyone in a relationship. Especially for high-net-worth individuals and those in cross-border marriages, who face differing legal systems and complex asset structures, proactive asset segregation is not suspicion but foresight. A well-drafted prenuptial agreement preserves the fruits of family legacy, prevents asset erosion due to marital breakdown, clarifies the boundaries of rights between spouses, reduces post-marital property disputes, allows love to remain pure, and brings greater security to marriage.

The core difference between the legal systems of the Mainland and Hong Kong lies in this: the Mainland emphasizes party autonomy and substantive fairness, while Hong Kong emphasizes procedural compliance and discretionary balance. The key to a valid cross-border prenuptial agreement is satisfying the review standards of both jurisdictions — legally valid in the Mainland and compliant in Hong Kong. Independent legal advice, full financial disclosure, sufficient time for execution, and fair and flexible clauses — these seemingly tedious details form the essential prerequisites for the agreement to take effect in both regions.

A truly good marriage combines sincere love with rational risk preparedness. The purpose of a prenuptial agreement goes far beyond the narrow and cold idea of dividing assets upon divorce. It is designed to better protect the marriage, set clear property boundaries, uphold honesty between partners, and affirm respect for each other's long-term future. This is the finest way for law and love to coexist in cross-border relationships.

中澳婚姻里的无声牺牲，全职妈妈争得离婚经济补偿

引言

婚姻里最易被忽视的，往往是一方默默扛起家庭重担的无声付出。尤其是跨境婚姻中，放弃职业、远赴异国、独自育儿持家的全职妈妈，她们的牺牲藏在日夜的操劳里，藏在放弃自我成长的妥协中，一旦婚姻破碎，这些付出往往成了无人提及的过往。作为婚姻家事律师，我代理过无数离婚纠纷，接触过太多在婚姻里牺牲了自我的家庭主妇。而这起中澳跨境离婚案，始终让我印象深刻。我以女方陆倩倩代理人的身份，陪她走过家暴后的绝望、跨境诉讼的艰难，用法律为她九年的家庭付出讨回公道，也让法律真正看见全职妈妈的价值，让每一份隐忍与坚守，都能得到应有的慰藉。

陆倩倩初次来找我的时候，我正在律所开会，她等候在洽谈室，身形消瘦，眼底藏着化不开的疲惫与委屈。见到我，她将手里捏着的澳大利亚医院的诊断报告和法院出具的禁止接触令递到我面前，指尖微微发抖，说话都带着哽咽。那时的她，刚从澳大利亚回国，身心都还笼罩在家暴的阴影里，婚生子邹文皓才刚满五岁，九年的婚姻，最终以一场暴力、一场跨境离婚诉讼，彻底走向破碎。

陆倩倩经朋友介绍，了解到我专业办理婚姻家事案件，于是找到我。她的诉求很明晰，只希望我能帮她顺利解除这段痛苦的婚姻，拿到儿子邹文皓的抚养权，更重要的是，为自己九年全职妈妈的付出，争取应有的离婚经济补偿。

她向我讲述了她的故事。2015 年 3 月，陆倩倩与邹阳俊在上海登记结婚，那时的两人，也曾有过安稳幸福的时光。2019 年儿子邹文皓出生后，为了更好地照顾孩子、打理家庭，也为了全力支持丈夫邹阳俊的事业，陆倩倩毅然辞去了前景不错的工作，做起了全职太太。后来，夫妻俩一同申请并取得了澳大利亚永久居住资格，举家移居海外，本以为生活会越来越好，可这段跨境婚姻，却渐渐露出了狰狞的面目。

邹阳俊因工作时常在中澳两地奔波，家里大小事、照顾幼子的重担，全都压在了陆倩倩一个人身上。她每天围着孩子、家务打转，放弃了自己的社交、职业梦想，甚至没有属于自己的时间，从职场女性彻底变成了围着家庭打转的全职妈妈，整整五年，没有一分钱收入，所有的生活开销都仰仗丈夫，可她从未有过怨言，只想着守好家庭、照顾好儿子。但她没想到的是，丈夫的心悄然发生了改变，他在婚外已经有了一位长期相好的女伴。

陆倩倩的付出，终究没能换来珍惜。2024 年 1 月，在澳大利亚的家中，邹阳俊酒后因一点家庭琐事，突然对陆倩倩大打出手，拳头狠狠落在她身上，导致她右侧两根肋骨轻微移位骨折。事发后，澳大利亚当地医院出具了详细的伤情诊断

报告，心理机构的测评也显示，陆倩倩因这次家暴，出现了严重的抑郁情绪和创伤后应激障碍，整夜失眠、情绪崩溃，甚至不敢靠近邹阳俊。当地法院也依法向邹阳俊签发了家庭暴力禁止接触令，勒令他不得靠近陆倩倩母子，两人自此正式分居，这段九年的婚姻，彻底走到了尽头。

可让她没想到的是，邹阳俊在分居期间，向中国法院提起离婚诉讼，要求离婚、争夺儿子抚养权，还颠倒黑白，称陆倩倩阻挠他探望孩子，完全不提自己家暴、出轨的事实。

接到法院传票时，陆倩倩彻底崩溃了，她哭着对我说：″叶律师，我为这个家放弃了一切，伺候他、照顾孩子，操持所有家务，到头来他打我、背叛我，还要抢孩子、说我坏话，我九年的付出，难道就一文不值吗？″我告诉她，你要勇敢地拿起法律的武器，我会帮助你为自己和孩子的权利全力争取。随即，我正式接受陆倩倩的委托，成为她的诉讼代理人，全面梳理案情，制定代理方案，开启了这场艰难的跨境离婚维权之路。

接手案件后，我首先梳理出案件的核心难点：

一是跨境证据的固定。将澳洲的诊断报告、禁止接触令、出轨相关证据转化为国内法院认可的有效证据；

二是离婚经济补偿的举证，陆倩倩是全职太太，没有直接收入证明，需要举证她多年的家庭付出、放弃职业的损失，这也是本案的核心代理重点；

三是孩子抚养权的争取，这点更为关键，既要证明陆倩倩作为母亲，在抚养权争取上具有各方面条件优于男方邹阳俊的优势，又要考虑到她的全职太太的现实的经济情况，从力争抚养费给付更有保障性的角度来陈述观点和举证。

尤其是在抚养权的争取上，我制定了″过去的抚养贡献 + 当下的抚养能力 + 未来的抚养规划″三个时间维度上的充分举证，为确保陆倩倩争取孩子的抚养权做好充分的应对和准备。

庭审中，邹阳俊的代理人依旧矢口否认家暴、出轨，辩称是家庭纠纷，还坚持要求抚养权，对陆倩倩提出的离婚经济补偿，更是嗤之以鼻，认为全职家务不算付出，不该补偿。我当庭逐一驳斥对方观点，提交所有固化后的证据，清晰阐述代理意见，也将相关法律规定融入其中：

首先，邹阳俊存在家暴、婚内出轨行为，是婚姻破裂的完全过错方，澳洲的司法法律文书与医疗报告均已证实，其行为不仅违背夫妻忠诚义务，更对陆倩倩造成严重身心伤害，法院应认定其过错。

其次，婚生子邹文皓应由陆倩倩抚养，孩子自幼由母亲独自照料，与母亲感情深厚，邹阳俊有家暴恶习，不利于孩子身心健康成长，且陆倩倩虽为全职太太，但有能力抚养孩子，邹阳俊应依法支付抚养费。三个时间维度的抚养权证据，也充分印证了陆倩倩抚养孩子最有利于未成年人利益。

最后，也是本案的核心，陆倩倩有权主张离婚经济补偿。根据我国《民法典》第一千零八十八条明确规定，夫妻一方因抚育子女、照料老年人、协助另一方工作等负担较多义务的，离婚时有权向另一方请求补偿，另一方应当给予补偿。不管夫妻是共同财产制还是分别财产制，只要一方负担了更多家庭义务，离婚时都可以主张这项补偿，这是法律对家务劳动价值的明确认可，和夫妻共同财产分割是相互独立、不可替代的权利，并非简单的财产分割。

同时，结合最新的婚姻家庭编司法解释，法院在确定补偿数额时，会综合考量负担家庭义务投入的时间、精力，对双方职业发展的影响，以及给付方的负担能力、当地生活水平等因素，这也为陆倩倩的诉求提供了充分的法律依据。我向法庭详细陈述，陆倩倩婚后九年，彻底放弃职业发展，独自承担起抚育幼子、操持家务的全部责任，尤其是在澳洲生活期间，邹阳俊常年在外，家里大小事均是陆倩倩打理，陆倩倩的付出远超普通婚姻中的一方，理应获得相应的经济补偿。

我逐一还原案件真相，用扎实的证据戳破邹阳俊的谎言，清晰阐释法律规定与案件事实的关联，让法官全面了解陆倩倩九年的无声付出与遭遇的不公。法院经审理后，采纳了我的代理意见，依法认定邹阳俊存在家庭暴力与婚内不忠行为，系婚姻过错方。

法院综合考量双方九年的婚姻存续时长、陆倩倩全身心投入家庭的付出程度、其放弃职业发展的机会损失，以及邹阳俊的经济收入与实际支付能力，最终作出判决：准予双方离婚；婚生子邹文皓由陆倩倩直接抚养，邹阳俊按月支付抚养费；邹阳俊向陆倩倩支付离婚经济补偿款，款项从其个人财产中支取，同时对子女探望权作出合理安排，既保障了陆倩倩母子的权益，也认可了她多年的家庭付出。

拿到判决书的那一刻，陆倩倩如释重负，终于舒展眉头，连声道谢。这场跨境离婚诉讼，终于画上了圆满的句号，邹阳俊没有提起上诉，判决顺利生效，陆倩倩不仅摆脱了痛苦的婚姻，拿到了儿子的抚养权，更重要的是，她九年的全职付出，得到了法律的认可与补偿，那些无人看见的日夜操劳，终于有了应有的价值。

案后结语

办结这起案件，我内心久久不能平静。在太多婚姻里，全职妈妈、家庭主妇的付出，总被视作"理所当然"，家务、育儿、照料家庭，这些无形的劳动，没有薪资、没有表彰，却撑起了整个家庭的运转，尤其是跨境婚姻中的女性，远离故土、放弃自我，在异国他乡的锅碗瓢盆、吃喝拉撒里，她们的牺牲更值得被尊重、被保障。

我国的离婚经济补偿制度，其立法本质意义就是为了填补家务劳动的价值空白，弥补付出较多一方的机会损失，守护婚姻里的公平正义。它是对一份付出的认可，对一段牺牲的慰藉，让婚姻里的双向奔赴有了底线，让默默付出的人不再被辜负。

陆倩倩的胜诉，不仅是法律的胜利，更是对所有家庭付出者的肯定。婚姻不是单方的消耗，而是双向的扶持，无论男女，为家庭做出的牺牲都不该被漠视。而我，也会始终站在法律的立场，为每一位遭遇不公的当事人发声，让法律的温度，抚平婚姻破碎的伤痛，让每一份无声的付出，都能被看见、被善待、被尊重。

A Full-Time Mother Wins Economic Compensation in Divorce

Introduction

What is most easily overlooked in marriage is often the silent devotion of one spouse who shoulders the burden of the family without complaint. This is especially true in cross-border marriages, where full-time mothers may give up their careers, move abroad, and raise children while managing the household alone. Their sacrifices are hidden in the exhaustion of daily life and in the compromises that require them to set aside their own growth and aspirations. When the marriage breaks down, those years of devotion are often reduced to an unspoken past. As a family law attorney, I have handled countless divorce disputes and represented many homemakers who sacrificed themselves for their families. Yet this particular China–Australia cross-border divorce case has remained especially vivid in my mind. Acting for the wife, Lu Qianqian, I stood beside her through the despair that followed domestic violence and the difficulties of cross-border litigation. Through the law, I sought justice for her nine years of contribution to the family and helped ensure that the law truly recognized the value of a full-time mother, so that every act of silent endurance and steadfast devotion could receive the acknowledgment it deserved.

When Lu Qianqian first came to see me, I was in a meeting at the firm. She waited in the consultation room, thin and exhausted, with grief and fatigue lingering in her eyes. When I met her, she handed me medical reports issued by an Australian hospital and a restraining order issued by the court. Her fingers trembled slightly, and her voice was choked with emotion. She had only just returned from Australia and was still living under the shadow of domestic violence. Her son, Zou Wenhao, had only just turned five. After nine years of marriage, her relationship had completely collapsed in the wake of violence and a cross-border divorce lawsuit.

Referred by a friend who knew I specialized in family law, she came to me with a clear goal: to end her painful marriage, gain custody of her son Zou Wenhao, and, most importantly, obtain fair divorce economic compensation for her nine years of devotion as a full-time mother.

She told me her story. In March 2015, Lu Qianqian and Zou Yangjun registered their marriage in Shanghai. For a time, they enjoyed a stable and happy life together. After their son Zou Wenhao was born in 2019, Lu Qianqian resolutely resigned from a promising job to become a full-time housewife, so she could better care for the child, manage the home, and fully support her husband's career. Later, the couple applied for and obtained Australian permanent residency and moved overseas. They hoped life would only get better, but their cross-border marriage gradually turned ugly.

Zou Yangjun traveled frequently between China and Australia for work, leaving all household affairs and the burden of caring for their young son entirely to Lu Qianqian. Her days revolved around the child and housework. She gave up her social life, career dreams, and even personal time, transforming completely from a career woman to a full-time mother. For five years, she had no income of her own and relied entirely on her husband for living expenses. Yet she never complained, hoping only to keep the family together and care for her son. But what she did not expect was that her husband's heart had quietly changed; he already had a long-term female companion outside their marriage. Her devotion ultimately failed to win his cherishing.

In January 2024, at their home in Australia, Zou Yangjun, under the influence of alcohol, suddenly launched a violent assault on Lu Qianqian over a trivial family dispute. He repeatedly punched her, causing slight displacement and fractures of two ribs on her right side. Following the incident, a local Australian hospital issued a detailed medical diagnosis report. Psychological assessments also confirmed that Lu Qianqian had developed severe depression and post-traumatic stress disorder (PTSD) as a result of the domestic violence. She suffered from insomnia throughout the night, frequent emotional breakdowns, and was even afraid to go anywhere near Zou Yangjun. The local court subsequently granted a domestic violence restraining order against Zou Yangjun, prohibiting him from contacting or approaching Lu Qianqian and their child. The couple formally separated, and their nine-year marriage came to an irrevocable end.

To her shock, during their separation, Zou Yangjun filed for divorce in a Chinese court, demanding a divorce, seeking custody of their son, and even distorting the truth by claiming that Lu Qianqian had obstructed his visitation rights — all while completely concealing his history of domestic violence and infidelity.

When Lu Qianqian received the court summons, she completely broke down. Through tears, she said to me: "Lawyer Rachel J. Ye, I gave up everything for this family. I waited on him, raised our child, and did all the housework. In the end, he hit me, betrayed me, wants to take our son, and slanders me. Are my nine years of devotion really worth nothing?" I told her: "You must bravely take up the weapon of the law. I will help you fight for your rights and your child's rights with all my strength." I then formally accepted Lu Qianqian's retainer as her litigation representative, thoroughly analyzed the case, developed a legal strategy, and embarked on this difficult cross-border divorce case to defend her rights.

After taking on the case, I first identified the core challenges: First, preservation and authentication of cross-border evidence. Medical diagnosis reports, restraining orders, and infidelity evidence from Australia had to be converted into valid evidence admissible in Chinese courts. Second, proof for divorce economic compensation. As a full-time housewife with no direct income records, Lu Qianqian needed evidence showing her years of family contributions and the opportunity cost of abandoning her career — the central focus of our representation. Third, fighting for child custody, the most critical issue. I needed to prove that Lu Qianqian, as the mother, was far more suitable for custody than Zou Yangjun, while also addressing her financial situation as a full-time homemaker and arguing for secure and adequate child support.

I first guided Lu Qianqian to collect and organize a complete set of evidence: local medical injury diagnoses and psychological evaluation reports from Australia, as well as Australian court restraining orders, directly proving Zou Yangjun's domestic violence; records of their separation between China and Australia, childcare receipts, and witness statements from relatives and friends, confirming that Lu Qianqian had long raised the child alone and managed all household duties; pre-marriage employment certificates and resignation records, proving she gave up her career for the family; and relevant evidence of Zou Yangjun's extramarital affairs, establishing him as the sole at-fault party in the marriage.

Especially regarding child custody, I built a comprehensive evidence framework across three time dimensions: past caregiving contributions, present caregiving capacity, and future parenting plan, fully preparing Lu Qianqian to secure custody.

During the trial, Zou Yangjun's counsel categorically denied domestic violence and infidelity, framing the matter as mere family conflict. They insisted on custody, and scoffed at Lu Qianqian's claim for divorce economic compensation, arguing that full-time housework did not count as meaningful contribution and deserved no compensation. I refuted each of their arguments in court, submitted all formalized evidence, clearly presented our legal positions, and integrated the relevant legal provisions:

First, Zou Yangjun's acts of domestic violence and marital infidelity made him the complete at-fault party responsible for the breakdown of the marriage. Australian judicial documents and medical reports confirmed this. His behavior not only violated the spousal duty of fidelity but also caused severe physical and psychological harm to Lu Qianqian. The court should affirm his fault.

Second, their son Zou Wenhao should be placed in Lu Qianqian's custody. The child had been raised solely by his mother since infancy and shared a deep bond with her. Zou Yangjun's history of domestic violence was harmful to the child's physical and mental health. Although Lu Qianqian was a full-time homemaker, she was fully capable of raising the child, and Zou Yangjun was legally obligated to pay child support. The three-dimensional evidence of custody fully confirmed that placing the child with Lu Qianqian would best serve the minor's best interests.

Finally, and central to this case: Lu Qianqian was entitled to claim divorce economic compensation. Under Article 1088 of the Civil Code of the People's Republic of China, where one spouse undertakes more obligations in raising children, caring for the elderly, assisting the other spouse in work, or other household matters, that spouse has the right to claim compensation from the other party upon divorce, and the other party shall provide such compensation. This right applies regardless of whether the marital property regime is community property or separate property. It constitutes a legal recognition of the value of domestic labor, and is an independent, non-substitutable right separate from ordinary property division.

Furthermore, under the latest judicial interpretations of the Marriage and Family Part, courts determining the amount of compensation will comprehensively consider the time and energy devoted to family duties, the impact on both parties' career development, the payer's financial capacity, and the local standard of living. This provided solid legal support for Lu Qianqian's claim. I argued in detail to the court that, over nine years of marriage, Lu Qianqian had completely abandoned her career and single-handedly taken responsibility for raising their young son and managing all household affairs. Especially during their cross-border life, Zou Yangjun was frequently away and never fulfilled his family duties. Her contributions far exceeded those of the average spouse, and she deserved corresponding economic compensation.

I reconstructed the full truth of the case, refuted Zou Yangjun's lies with solid evidence, and clearly explained the connection between the law and the facts, enabling the court to fully understand Lu Qianqian's silent devotion and unfair treatment over nine years. After trial, the court accepted my submissions and legally confirmed that Zou Yangjun had committed domestic violence and marital infidelity, making him the at-fault party.

Taking into account the nine-year duration of the marriage, the extent of Lu Qianqian's full-time devotion to the family, the opportunity cost of abandoning her career, and Zou Yangjun's income and payment ability, the court rendered its judgment: the divorce was granted; their son Zou Wenhao was placed in the direct custody of Lu Qianqian, with Zou Yangjun to pay monthly child support; Zou Yangjun was ordered to pay divorce economic compensation to Lu Qianqian from his personal property; and reasonable visitation arrangements were also made. The judgment protected the rights of Lu Qianqian and her son while legally acknowledging her years of family service.

Upon receiving the judgment, Lu Qianqian was greatly relieved, her face finally relaxed, and she thanked me repeatedly. This cross-border divorce case came to a satisfactory conclusion. Zou Yangjun did not appeal, and the judgment took effect. Lu Qianqian not only escaped an unhappy marriage and gained custody of her son but, more importantly, her nine years of full-time family labor were recognized and compensated by law. Those unseen days and nights of hard work finally received their due value.

Post-Case Conclusion

After concluding this case, my thoughts lingered long. In far too many marriages, the contributions of full-time mothers and housewives are taken for granted. The invisible labor of housework, childcare, and family care goes unpaid and unrecognized yet sustains the entire household. For women in cross-border marriages, especially, who leave their homeland and abandon their personal growth to manage daily life abroad, their sacrifice deserves particular respect and protection.

The essential purpose of China's divorce economic compensation system is to recognize the value of domestic labor, compensate the opportunity losses of the contributing spouse, and uphold fairness and justice in marriage. It affirms dedication, consoles sacrifice, sets a bottom line for mutual commitment, and ensures that silent givers are not let down.

Lu Qianqian's victory is not only a legal triumph but also a recognition of all who devote themselves to family life. Marriage is not one-sided exhaustion but mutual support. Sacrifices for the family, regardless of gender, should never be ignored. I will continue to stand on the side of the law, speaking up for every wronged client. May the warmth of law heal the pain of broken marriages, and may every silent contribution be seen, valued, and respected.

Photograph by Joseph Xu

CHAPTER 2 | ENVY

第二章 | 嫉妒

引文

"嫉妒是一个游荡的鬼魂，它看似伤害别人，其实一直在折磨自己。"

——【英】莎士比亚

嫉妒是一把沉默而锋利的刀刃，它从不声张，却能在悄无声息中割裂亲情、磨损爱情、摧毁最坚固的信任。在婚姻里，它化作无端的猜忌、过度的控制、偏执的窥探与情绪勒索；在家族之中，它演变为无休止的攀比、心理的失衡、心底的怨怼与挥之不去的不公感。

兄弟姐妹因父母的厚薄之分而生出隔阂，夫妻因无谓的比较与怀疑而渐行渐远，亲人因一时的得失计较而彼此疏离、反目。许多看似激烈的财产争夺、抚养权对抗、遗产继承纠纷，剥开层层表象，底层皆是长期压抑的嫉妒与不甘。在无数调解与诉讼现场，我常常慨叹：最无解的难题，不止是复杂的法律问题，而是人心深处的执念；最昂贵的代价，不是财富得失，而是被负面情绪彻底消耗的人生。

嫉妒让人困在原地，只看见缺憾，看不见拥有；只计较输赢，看不见珍惜。唯有放下无谓的比较，心怀坦荡与包容，方能在亲密关系中获得真正的自由，在漫长人生里寻得内心的安宁与平和。

Epigraph

"Envy is a wandering ghost. It seems to hurt others, yet it torments no one more than itself."

— William Shakespeare, England

Envy is a silent yet sharp blade. It makes no sound, yet quietly severs family bonds, erodes love and destroys the strongest trust. In marriage, it turns into groundless suspicion, excessive control, paranoid prying and emotional blackmail; within families, it evolves into endless comparison, psychological imbalance, hidden resentment and lingering feelings of injustice.

Siblings grow alienated from unequal parental affection; couples drift apart over meaningless comparison and doubt; relatives become distant and hostile over temporary gains and losses. Behind many fierce property battles, custody fights and inheritance disputes, stripped of superficial layers, lie long-suppressed envy and resentment. At countless mediations and trials, I often sigh: the most unsolvable problems are not complex legal issues, but obsessions deep in the heart; the most costly price is not wealth, but a life completely consumed by negative emotions.

Envy traps people in place, making them see only what they lack, not what they have; only winning and losing, not what to cherish. Only by letting go of meaningless comparison, with openness and tolerance, can one attain true freedom in intimate relationships and find inner peace and calm in a long life.

跨国婚约的倒塌与温商二代的债务迷局

引言

温州商人的足迹遍布全球，他们的二代，带着海归的视野与温州人的基因，在世界各国开拓事业。然而，在婚姻的选择上，这群看似开放的"创二代"，骨子里却依旧秉持着最传统的"本土化"执念。我的当事人霍浩，一位拥有荷兰国籍的温商海归，遵从父母意愿回乡择偶，与温州本土的女强人刘蕊缔结了跨国婚姻。本以为是门当户对的良缘，却因各自为政的家族事业、牵一发而动全身的债务担保，最终演变成一场无法圆满的婚姻浩劫。从情投意合到对簿公堂，从海外高管到负债缠身，这段跨越国界的婚姻，终究在现实的重压下，变得支离破碎。

霍浩的故事，是许多海外温商二代的真实写照。

他出生在典型的海外创一代家庭，父母早年远赴欧洲，在意大利、荷兰、比利时等国辗转打拼。凭借温州人特有的精明与韧劲，霍家在海外商界积累了丰厚家业，在当地温商圈中拥有稳固的地位。霍浩小学毕业后便随父母移居海外，接受了完整的国际教育，后又赴英国伦敦攻读硕士学位。2005 年，25 岁的他拿到硕士学历，回到家族在荷兰的酒店担任高管，负责亚洲区营销。

彼时的霍浩，身边不乏优秀女性的追求，但他内心深处，却对故乡温州有着一种特殊的眷恋。父母虽半辈子旅居海外，却对儿子的婚事秉持着"肥水不流外人田"的传统观念，极力希望他找一位温州本土的妻子。霍浩是个孝子，他也认为温州女人特有的温婉与聪慧，远比异国女性更懂家庭与生活。于是，在 2005 年的春天，这个多年未归的青年，第一次带着明确的择偶的心愿回到了温州。

那一个多月，霍浩的生活被相亲填满。姑婶婆姨竞相牵线，他见了不下二十位年轻女子，平均两天见一位。在这茫茫人海中，他遇见了刘蕊。刘蕊与霍浩相似，也是海归出身，曾留学西班牙，家境优渥，父母是温州当地知名服饰公司的创始人。她长相靓丽，性格干练，接手家族产业后经营得有声有色。两人因相似的留学背景和共同话题，一见如故。经过半年多的异地恋与相处，双方父母满意，情投意合。2005 年 11 月，两人按照温州风俗举行了订婚仪式；同年 12 月，霍浩带着刘蕊前往荷兰，并在当地办理了结婚登记。

婚姻初期，生活充满了美好的憧憬。刘蕊想将家族服饰品牌开拓到海外，希望丈夫能伸出援手。霍浩心疼妻子，也看好市场潜力，便放下了自己在荷兰蒸蒸日上的酒店生意，回到国内，全力支持刘蕊的事业扩张。他们还迎来了可爱的儿子锐锐，一家三口的日子看似安稳美满。

然而，现实的裂痕往往藏在美好的表象之下。刘蕊是个事业心极强的女人，她一心想将产业做大，对海外市场充满野心。由于前期投入巨大，她希望霍浩利用其酒店产业做担保，向银行申请巨额贷款。霍浩出于信任和爱意，同意了这一请求。但刘蕊对海外市场的风险预估不足，屡屡试水失败，巨额投资款打了水漂。霍浩心急如焚，多次劝阻她歇手，回到自己的酒店板块发展，但性格倔强的刘蕊并不甘心。

夫妻二人开始为了各自的事业争执不休。霍浩想稳守荷兰家业，刘蕊却执意继续冒险。这种理念的冲突，让两人的感情在一次次争吵中逐渐冷却。结婚五年后，霍浩返回荷兰打理酒店，刘蕊则远赴法国继续开拓市场。两地的距离、各自的忙碌，让原本就淡薄的感情彻底渐行渐远。直到 2011 年 3 月，霍浩在荷兰接到了温州法院的传票，才如梦初醒。

原来，刘蕊父母经营的公司因无力偿还银行贷款被起诉，而霍浩与刘蕊是共同的担保人。霍浩这才想起，此前曾数次应刘蕊的要求，为其娘家公司的贷款签字担保。他立刻联系刘蕊，却发现对方早已无力偿债。屋漏偏逢连夜雨。当时正值温州民间借贷金融危机爆发，民营企业资金链全线断裂，刘蕊娘家的产业一夜之间资产缩水、负债数亿。霍浩不得不匆匆回国，处理这堆烂摊子。几番调解与诉讼下来，不仅夫妻共同房产被拍卖执行，就连霍浩在荷兰酒店的股权也受到了严重牵连，惊动了远在海外的父母。

两家人终于坐到了谈判桌前。霍父看着被搞得一团糟的局面，言语间难免流露出对儿子的失望与责备。刘蕊却认为公公是在借机打压她，自尊心极强的她出言反击。言语冲突瞬间升级，双方家长的争吵彻底撕破了霍浩与刘蕊之间仅存的最后一丝情分。2011 年底，这段维持了六年的婚姻，走到了尽头。

两人在民政局协商离婚，却因结婚登记在荷兰，且霍浩已拥有荷兰国籍，无法通过民政部门办理协议离婚，只能通过法院诉讼程序。最终，双方各自委托律师，经法院调解达成协议，出具了民事调解书。此时的他们，已没有任何共同财产，只剩下沉重的连带债务，和一个年幼的儿子。儿子由霍浩带回荷兰抚养，刘蕊放弃了抚养权。她表示，自己还要东山再起，不能让家族产业在她手中衰败，她要为事业再拼一次。

时间来到 2015 年正月，距离离婚已过去三年多。我突然接到了刘蕊的电话。她因之前的借贷诉讼被纳入了失信被执行人名单，被限制出境，无法去荷兰看望儿子。思子心切的她，希望我能从中调解，劝说霍浩将孩子的抚养权变更给她。霍浩接到我的转达时，态度异常坚决。他表示自己已经组建了新的家庭，孩子在新环境中适应得很好，快乐无忧，他不希望刘蕊再去打扰孩子原本平静的生活。

刘蕊得知后心急如焚，委托我继续做霍浩的工作。我向霍浩详细转达了刘蕊作为母亲的思念与苦衷，并从孩子成长的角度，耐心劝说他创造条件，让孩子与母亲相见。起初，霍浩严词拒绝。但经过我多番的调解与沟通，他最终松口，同意了刘蕊的探望孩子的请求。一场纠缠了数年的抚养权争议，在法律与情理的平衡下，得以妥善解决。

案后结语

这起案件，是一起典型的涉外婚姻解体纠纷，更是一场因家族利益冲突引发的婚姻悲剧。

它深刻揭示了"海归创二代"在择偶与婚姻中的深层矛盾：外表看似接受了西方开放观念，内心却始终被温州传统家庭观念束缚。霍浩回乡择偶，看似是自由选择，实则是父母意志与传统观念的产物。这种"本土化"的婚姻开端，在面对截然不同的事业追求和现实风险时，显得格外脆弱。

案件的核心转折点，在于债务担保。霍浩出于对妻子的爱与信任，为其娘家产业提供了巨额担保，却最终因温州金融危机的爆发，将整个家庭拖入债务深渊，也彻底摧毁了婚姻的基础。这提醒我们：在婚姻关系中，尤其是涉及家族企业的夫妻，财产边界与风险隔离至关重要。个人担保不是儿戏，它可能成为婚姻的保护伞，也可能成为压垮婚姻的最后一根稻草。

于霍浩与刘蕊而言，这段婚姻已成过往，债务与伤痛或许难以完全抹去。但法律的介入，让他们在分开时尽可能地厘清了界限，为孩子的未来保留了一丝温情与体面。而作为律师，我们能做的，就是在每一段复杂的关系中，用专业为当事人厘清是非，用规则为破碎的关系画上一个相对公平的句号。

The Collapse of a Transnational Marriage and the Debt Quagmire of a Second-Generation Wenzhou Businessman

Introduction

Wenzhou merchants have left their footprints all over the world. Their second-generation heirs, equipped with an international perspective and the innate spirit of Wenzhou people, have forged careers in various countries. Yet when it comes to marriage, this seemingly open-minded group of "second-generation entrepreneurs" still clings deep down to the most traditional obsession with "localization". My client, Huo Hao, a Dutch national and returnee from a Wenzhou business family, followed his parents' wishes to return home to find a spouse, and married Liu Rui, a powerful local businesswoman from Wenzhou, in a transnational union. What was expected to be a well-matched marriage eventually turned into a devastating marital disaster, torn apart by divided family businesses and debt guarantees that affected the whole family. From mutual affection to courtroom confrontation, from an overseas executive to a man burdened with heavy liabilities, this cross-border marriage finally shattered completely under the weight of reality.

Huo Hao's story is a true reflection of many second-generation Wenzhou businessmen living overseas. He was born into a typical family of first-generation overseas entrepreneurs; his parents traveled to Europe in their early years and built their careers across Italy, the Netherlands, Belgium, and other countries. With the typical shrewdness and perseverance of Wenzhou people, the Huo family accumulated substantial wealth overseas and secured a stable position in the local Wenzhou business community. After finishing primary school, Huo Hao moved abroad with his parents and received a complete international education, later pursuing a master's degree in London, the UK. In 2005, at the age of 25, he obtained his master's degree and returned to work as an executive at his family's hotel in the Netherlands, responsible for Asian marketing.

At that time, Huo Hao had many outstanding women pursuing him, but deep down, he held a special affection for his hometown, Wenzhou. Although his parents had lived overseas for half their lives, they held the traditional view that "wealth should not flow to outsiders" regarding their son's marriage, and strongly hoped he would marry a local Wenzhou woman. A filial son, Huo Hao also believed that the unique gentleness and intelligence of Wenzhou women made them far more understanding of family and life than foreign women. So in the spring of 2005, this young man who had been away for years returned to Wenzhou for the first time with a clear purpose of finding a spouse.

For more than a month, Huo Hao's life was filled with blind dates. Aunts and relatives competed to arrange introductions, and he met no fewer than twenty young women, averaging one date every two days. Amid this crowd, he met Liu Rui. Like Huo Hao, Liu Rui was also a returnee who had studied in Spain, from a wealthy family whose parents founded a well-known local apparel company in Wenzhou. She was beautiful, capable, and ran the family business successfully after taking it over. The two hit it off immediately due to their similar overseas study backgrounds and shared topics. After more than half a year of long-distance dating and getting along, both sets of parents were satisfied, and the couple was deeply in love. In November 2005, they held an engagement ceremony according to Wenzhou customs; that December, Huo Hao took Liu Rui to the Netherlands, where they registered their marriage locally.

In the early days of marriage, life was full of beautiful hopes. Liu Rui wanted to expand her family's apparel brand overseas and hoped her husband would lend a hand. Loving his wife and optimistic about the market potential, Huo Hao put aside his thriving hotel career in the Netherlands and returned to China to fully support Liu Rui's business expansion. They also welcomed their lovely son, Ruirui, and the family of three seemed to live a stable and happy life.

However, cracks in reality often hide beneath a beautiful surface. Liu Rui was an extremely ambitious woman, determined to expand her business and full of ambition for overseas markets. Due to massive upfront investment, she hoped Huo Hao would use his hotel business as collateral to apply for large bank loans. Out of trust and love, Huo Hao agreed. But Liu Rui underestimated the risks of overseas markets, failed repeatedly in her attempts, and lost huge sums of investment capital. Huo Hao was extremely anxious and repeatedly advised her to stop and return to develop his hotel business, but the stubborn Liu Rui refused to give up.

The couple began to argue constantly over their respective careers. Huo Hao wanted to steadily maintain the family business in the Netherlands, while Liu Rui insisted on continuing to take risks. This conflict of ideas gradually cooled their relationship amid quarrels. Five years after marriage, Huo Hao returned to the Netherlands to manage the hotel, and Liu Rui traveled to France to continue expanding the market. The long-distance separation and their respective busyness drove the already weakening relationship even further apart. It was not until March 2011, when Huo Hao received a court summons from Wenzhou in the Netherlands, that he finally woke up to the truth.

It turned out that the company run by Liu Rui's parents had been sued for failing to repay bank loans, and both Huo Hao and Liu Rui were joint guarantors. Only then did Huo Hao recall that he had signed guarantees for loans taken by his wife's family company several times at Liu Rui's request. He immediately contacted Liu Rui, only to find that she was already unable to repay the debts. Troubles never come singly. At that time, the private lending financial crisis erupted in Wenzhou, and the capital chains of private enterprises collapsed across the board. Liu Rui's family business suffered a sharp drop in assets overnight and was saddled with hundreds of millions in liabilities. Huo Hao had to rush back to China to clean up the mess. After several mediations and lawsuits, not only was the couple's joint property auctioned off for enforcement, but even Huo Hao's equity in the Dutch hotel was seriously implicated, shocking his parents overseas.

The two families finally sat down at the negotiation table. Looking at the utter mess, Mr. Huo, Huo Hao's father, could not help expressing disappointment and blame toward his son. However, Liu Rui saw this as her father-in-law taking the opportunity to suppress her. With her strong self-esteem, she spoke back in retaliation. The verbal conflict quickly escalated, and the quarrel between the parents completely destroyed the last shred of affection remaining between Huo Hao and Liu Rui. By the end of 2011, this six-year marriage had come to an end.

The two attempted to negotiate a divorce at the civil affairs bureau, only to find it unavailable. Since their marriage was registered in the Netherlands and Huo Hao had already obtained Dutch citizenship, they could not process a consensual divorce through the civil affairs authority and had to resort to court litigation. Eventually, each party retained legal counsel, reached an agreement through court mediation, and obtained a civil mediation statement. By then, they had no community property left, only heavy joint and several debts, and a young son. The boy was taken back to the Netherlands by Huo Hao for custody, and Liu Rui renounced her custody rights. She stated that she had to rebuild her career and could not let the family business decline under her watch; she wanted to fight for her career once more.

Time moved to the first lunar month of 2015, more than three years after the divorce. I suddenly received a call from Liu Rui. She had been listed as a dishonest judgment debtor due to previous loan lawsuits and was restricted from leaving the country, making her unable to visit her son in the Netherlands. Overwhelmed by longing for her child, she asked me to mediate and persuade Huo Hao to transfer custody of the child to her. When I relayed her request to Huo Hao, his attitude was extremely firm. He said he had built a new family, the child was adapting well to the new environment and living happily and carefree, and he did not want Liu Rui to disturb the boy's peaceful life.

Upon hearing this, Liu Rui was extremely anxious and entrusted me to continue persuading Huo Hao. I conveyed to him in detail a mother's longing and hardship, and patiently urged him to make arrangements for the child to meet his mother, from the perspective of the child's best interests. At first, Huo Hao refused firmly. But after repeated mediation and communication on my part, he finally relented and agreed to Liu Rui's visitation request. A custody dispute that had dragged on for years was properly resolved through a balance of law and human decency.

Post-Case Conclusion

This case is a typical dispute involving the dissolution of a cross-border marriage, and also a marital tragedy triggered by conflicts of family interests. It profoundly reveals the deep-seated contradictions of "second-generation returnee entrepreneurs" in mate selection and marriage: on the surface, they seem to have embraced open Western values, yet deep down they remain bound by traditional Wenzhou family concepts. Huo Hao's choice of a spouse back in his hometown, seemingly a free decision, was in fact a product of his parents' will and traditional values. Such a "localized" beginning to marriage proved especially fragile when confronted with vastly different career pursuits and real-life risks.

The core turning point of the case lay in the debt guarantee. Out of love and trust for his wife, Huo Hao provided a huge guarantee for her family's business, yet the outbreak of the Wenzhou financial crisis eventually dragged the entire family into a deep pit of debt and completely destroyed the foundation of their marriage. This reminds us that in marital relationships, especially for couples involved in family businesses, clear asset boundaries and risk isolation are crucial. Personal guarantees are not trivial matters; they can serve as a protective umbrella for marriage, yet may also become the final straw that crushes it.

For Huo Hao and Liu Rui, this marriage is now in the past, and the debt and pain may never be fully erased. However, legal intervention has allowed them to clarify boundaries as much as possible upon separation, preserving a measure of warmth and dignity for their child's future. As lawyers, what we can do is to use professional expertise to help clients distinguish right from wrong in every complicated relationship, and draw a relatively fair conclusion to broken relationships through legal rules.

秦氏家族传承启示录：家族信托，何以成为富人守业传家的终极答案

引言

在我二十年深耕婚姻家事与财富传承的执业生涯中，见过诸多豪门兴衰起落：一代创业者白手起家、积攒亿万家财，却因传承失当，短短数年便资产散尽、亲情反目。秦氏集团的传承困局，正是无数高净值家庭的真实缩影——子女不堪托付、亲情暗藏风险、家业无人接班、财富随时面临崩塌。而秦氏夫妇最终摒弃传统继承，选择以家族信托重构家业版图，不仅守住了半生打拼的财富根基，更护住了家族安宁与亲情底色。这起案例，道破了一个真相：真正的富人传承，并不是简单的分家产，而是用制度，守护人性与未来。

秦功鑫夫妇的名字，在商圈里是成功创业的代名词。

两人白手起家，一手创立秦氏集团，历经半生风雨，终创下令人艳羡的商业版图与家族财富。夫妻二人膝下两儿一女，在外人看来，本应是子承父业、家业永续的圆满剧本，可现实却充满无奈与隐忧。

长子秦山性格孤僻、性情冥顽，与父母关系常年紧绷隔阂，对家族生意毫无兴趣亦无能力，根本无法扛起接班重任。唯有长媳贤良淑德、沉稳通透，不仅处事得体，更具备出色的商业经营与管理头脑，多年来与公婆相处和睦、深得信任，已是家族里最靠谱、最能托付的人。长子夫妻二人育有一对双胞胎孙子，是秦家最珍贵的未来希望。

次子秦河则性情放纵、嗜赌成性，早已离异，独自抚养一个女儿，身边往来人员复杂，常年被各类人情与欲望裹挟，别说管理资产，连自身都管不住。

最小的女儿秦瑶早已远嫁，女婿是外籍人士，已生育有三个孩子，一家五口长期定居境外，对国内产业、资产状况全然不熟，既无法近身尽孝，更无力接管家业。

三个子女，各有各的短板与困境，无一人能稳妥承接这份庞大家业。秦功鑫夫妇看在眼里，忧在心上，日夜难安。他们比谁都清楚：巨额财富，遇上不堪托付的后人，福泽也会变成灾难。直接分钱，只会助长挥霍、嗜赌、被人算计；直接交权，只会让半生基业迅速败落；传统继承，更会引发子女猜忌、内斗不休，最终家财散尽、亲情破碎。

无数个日夜斟酌，反复权衡家族成员品性、能力、未来风险之后，秦氏夫妇做出了一个在亲友间引发巨大争议的决定：放弃传统继承模式，设立家族专项基金，将资产管理权交予长媳，所有家族成员按规则定向受益。消息一出，质疑声四起。有人认为父母偏心，有人指责不合传统，有人觉得资产交予儿媳风险难测，甚至有人挑拨离间，试图搅乱这份安排。

在一片争议声中，秦氏夫妇找到了我。希望专业律师给予他们更完善的论证

与解答。他们想要的，不是简单的财产分配，而是让财富真正守护家人，而非毁掉家人；让家业长久安稳，而非昙花一现；让亲情纯粹温暖，而非被利益撕裂。听完他们的顾虑与规划，我肯定了他们的智慧和选择，并讲述我的意见。你们的选择，不是特例，而是高净值家庭传承的最优解。你们心中的家族基金，其内核逻辑，正是法律层面最成熟、最安全、最长效的财富传承工具——家族信托。

在我处理过的大量财富传承案件里，无数惨痛教训反复印证：富人守护财富的第一核心，不应是财富的增值，而是守住本金、隔绝风险、约束人性、长效可控。而家族信托，正是实现这一切的最佳载体。

其一，它能从根源上杜绝"后代败家、财富流失"。

传统继承一旦完成，财产便完全归于继承人，挥霍、赌博、被骗、盲目投资，都能在短时间内掏空家产。而家族信托实现了管理权与受益权分离，资产被锁定为独立信托财产，后代只能按约定领取生活、教育、医疗等费用，却无法随意处置本金，从制度上阻断了财富被挥霍、侵吞、损耗的可能。

其二，它拥有强大的资产隔离与法律保护功能。

信托财产独立于委托人、管理人、受益人之外，不受个人债务、婚姻变动、经营风险的牵连。即便子女日后出现婚变、负债、纠纷，核心家族资产依然安全无虞，这是普通赠与、遗嘱完全无法比拟的风险防火墙。

其三，它能让委托人的意愿跨越代际、精准落地。

家族信托可以量身定制：孙辈教育金如何发放、子女生活费标准、创业支持条件、养老医疗保障、甚至行为激励与约束……所有对家族的期许、责任、关爱，都能以法律规则固定下来，长久执行，真正破解"富不过三代"的宿命。

其四，它能彻底化解家族内斗，守护亲情和睦。

遗产争夺，是亲情最大的杀手。而家族信托规则清晰、分配透明、执行刚性，没有模糊空间，没有猜忌纷争，让亲属关系回归情感本身，从源头杜绝因财产引发的家庭破裂。

其五，由靠谱之人管理，兼顾制度刚性与人情温度。

秦氏夫妇将管理权交予长媳，是历经人性考验后的明智选择。她品行端正、能力出众、与家族利益高度绑定，既懂规则，又懂亲情，既能守住资产安全，又能照顾家族成员实际所需。在规范的信托结构下，管理人权限受法律与监督机制双重约束，安全与稳妥兼得。

秦氏夫妇的安排，看似另类，实则极具远见。他们没有把财富当成"给予"，而是当成"守护"；没有把传承当成"交付"，而是当成"规划"；没有依赖人情，而是依赖制度。

在我的专业建议下，他们进一步完善了传承架构：不仅为两位儿子设定稳定生活受益，为境外女儿一家做好境外资产衔接，更将所有孙辈的教育、成长、生活保障全部纳入信托体系，让每一个家族成员都被妥善安放，让秦家的财富与温暖，真正实现代际延续。

从争议四起，到格局落定；从忧心忡忡，到安心笃定。秦氏夫妇更加相信：真正的传家之宝，不是金钱，不是房产，不是股权，而是一套能抵御人性弱点、抵御外部风险、守护家族安宁的科学传承制度。

案后结语

秦氏家族的传承选择，为所有高净值家庭敲响了警钟，也提供了示范。财富越大，责任越重；家业越厚，约束越要刚性。我们这一代婚姻家事与财富传承律师，真正的价值，是在处理离婚、继承、纠纷之时，在悲剧发生之前，为家族筑起安全屏障；在亲情破裂之前，用规则理顺利益；在财富消散之前，用制度锁定长久。

家族信托的意义，远不止资产保全。

它是对后代的保护，让财富不成为腐蚀人心的毒药；

它是对家业的守护，让创业者的心血不被轻易败落；

它是对亲情的维系，让利益不再成为撕裂家庭的利刃；

它是对责任的兑现，让一代人的奋斗，真正福泽子孙、绵延世代。

秦功鑫夫妇的智慧，在于他们看清了财富的本质：金钱最好的归宿，不是放任挥霍，不是无序传承，而是在法律框架之下，用制度和亲情共同守护整个家族安稳和长久。这，才是富人传家的最高境界，也是家族信托最动人的价值所在。

Revelations from the Qin Family Legacy: Why Family Trusts Are the Ultimate Solution for Wealthy Families to Preserve Their Legacy

Introduction

Over my two-decade career specializing in family law, marital disputes, and wealth succession, I have witnessed the rise and fall of numerous prominent families: founders built fortunes from scratch, amassing hundreds of millions in assets, only to see their wealth squandered and family bonds torn apart within a few years due to poor succession planning. The succession dilemma of the Qin Group is a true microcosm of countless high-net-worth families: unfit heirs, hidden familial risks, no capable successor for the family business, and wealth constantly on the brink of collapse. In the end, Mr. and Mrs. Qin abandoned traditional inheritance and restructured their family estate through a family trust. This not only safeguarded the wealth they had built over a lifetime but also preserved family harmony and affection. This case reveals a profound truth: true wealth succession for the affluent is never about simply dividing assets, but about protecting human nature and the future through institutional frameworks.

Mr. and Mrs. Qin Gongxin are synonymous with entrepreneurial success in business circles. Starting from nothing, they founded the Qin Group and, through decades of trials and hardships, finally built an enviable business empire and family fortune. They have two sons and one daughter. To outsiders, it seemed destined to be a perfect story of sons inheriting the family business and lasting prosperity, yet reality was fraught with helplessness and hidden worries.

The eldest son, Qin Shan, is withdrawn and stubborn, with a long history of tense estrangement from his parents. He has no interest or ability in the family business and is utterly incapable of taking over the reins. In contrast, the eldest daughter-in-law is virtuous, calm, and insightful. Not only does she conduct herself with grace, but she also possesses exceptional business acumen and management skills. Having maintained a harmonious relationship with her parents-in-law for years and earned their deep trust, she has become the most reliable and trustworthy member of the family. The eldest couple has twin grandsons, the most precious hope for the Qin family's future.

The second son, Qin He, is indulgent and compulsive in gambling. Divorced long ago, he raises his daughter alone, associates with dubious people, and is constantly entangled in worldly obligations and desires. He cannot even manage himself, let alone family assets.

The youngest daughter, Qin Yao, married abroad long ago to a foreign husband, with whom she has three children. The family of five has settled overseas permanently, with no familiarity with domestic businesses or asset conditions. They can neither provide close care for their parents nor take over the family enterprise.

Each of the three children has their own shortcomings and dilemmas, and none can steadily inherit the vast family estate. Qin Gongxin and his wife watched with heavy hearts, losing sleep over the matter. They knew better than anyone that immense wealth, when placed in unworthy hands, could turn from a blessing into a disaster. Direct distribution of money would only fuel extravagance, gambling, and exploitation by others; direct transfer of power would quickly ruin a lifetime's achievements; traditional inheritance would spark suspicion and infighting among children, ultimately dissipating wealth and shattering family bonds.

After countless nights of deliberation, repeatedly weighing the character, abilities, and future risks of every family member, the Qin couple made a decision that sparked intense controversy among relatives and friends: abandoning traditional inheritance, establishing a dedicated family fund, entrusting asset management to the eldest daughter-in-law, and designating benefits for all family members in accordance with established rules. The announcement drew waves of doubt. Some accused the parents of favoritism, others deemed it inconsistent with tradition, some argued that entrusting assets to a daughter-in-law carried unforeseeable risks, and some even sowed discord to disrupt the arrangement.

Amid the controversy, the Qin couple turned to me, hoping for professional legal advice to refine and validate their plan. What they sought was not mere asset distribution, but to have wealth truly protect rather than destroy their family; to ensure lasting stability of the family business rather than a fleeting existence; and to keep family bonds pure and warm rather than torn apart by interests. After listening to their concerns and plans, I affirmed their wisdom and choice, and shared my professional opinion: "Your decision is not an exception, but the optimal solution for wealth succession in high-net-worth families. The family fund you have in mind is, in its core logic, the most mature, secure, and long-lasting wealth succession tool under the law — a family trust."

In the numerous wealth succession cases I have handled, countless painful lessons have repeatedly proven one thing: the top priority for wealthy families in protecting wealth should not be wealth appreciation, but preserving principal, isolating risks, restraining human weaknesses, and ensuring long-term control. And a family trust is the best vehicle to achieve all of this.

First, it fundamentally prevents descendants from squandering family wealth and causing asset erosion. Once traditional inheritance is completed, property belongs entirely to the heirs, who may squander, gamble, fall victim to fraud, or make reckless investments – all of which can deplete the family fortune in a short time. A family trust realizes the separation of management rights and beneficial rights, with assets locked as independent trust property. Descendants may only receive funds for living, education, medical care, and other expenses as agreed, but cannot freely dispose of the principal. This institutionally blocks the possibility of wealth being squandered, embezzled, or depleted.

Second, it provides strong asset isolation and legal protection. Trust assets are independent of the settlor, trustee, and beneficiaries, and are not affected by personal debts, marital changes, or business risks. Even if children face divorce, debt, or disputes in the future, the core family assets remain safe and secure. This is a risk firewall that ordinary gifts and wills simply cannot match.

Third, it enables the settlor's wishes to cross generations and be precisely implemented. Family trusts are highly customizable: how education funds for grandchildren are disbursed, living expense standards for children, conditions for entrepreneurial support, elderly care and medical security, and even behavioral incentives and restrictions... All expectations, responsibilities, and care for the family can be fixed in legal provisions and enforced for a long time, truly breaking the curse that "wealth does not last three generations."

Fourth, it completely resolves internal family conflicts and preserves harmony. Estate disputes are the greatest killer of family bonds. A family trust features clear rules, transparent distribution, and rigid enforcement, leaving no room for ambiguity or suspicion. It allows family relationships to return to emotional connection itself, and prevents family breakdown caused by property disputes at the source.

Fifth, management by a reliable person balances institutional rigidity with human warmth. Mr. and Mrs. Qin's decision to entrust management to their eldest daughter-in-law was a wise choice tested by human nature. She is upright in character, capable, and highly aligned with the family's interests. She understands both rules and family affection, and can protect asset security while attending to the practical needs of family members. Under a standardized trust structure, the trustee's powers are bound by both law and supervision mechanisms, ensuring both safety and prudence.

The arrangement made by Mr. and Mrs. Qin, though unconventional at first glance, is in fact highly forward-looking. They did not treat wealth as a "gift," but as a "protection"; they did not view succession as a "transfer," but as "planning"; they did not rely on personal feelings, but on institutions.

With my professional advice, they further refined their succession structure: they not only set up stable living benefits for their two sons and arranged cross-border asset connections for their daughter's family overseas, but also included education, growth, and living support for all grandchildren in the trust system, allowing every family member to be properly provided for, and allowing the Qin family's wealth and warmth to truly realize intergenerational continuation.

From widespread controversy to a settled plan; from deep anxiety to complete peace of mind. Mr. and Mrs. Qin became even more convinced: the true heirloom is not money, real estate, or equity, but a scientific succession system that can defend against human weaknesses, resist external risks, and safeguard family peace.

Post-Case Conclusion

The succession choice of the Qin family serves as a warning and a guide for all high-net-worth families. The greater the wealth, the heavier the responsibility; the larger the family estate, the stricter the constraints must be. The true value of our generation of lawyers specializing in marriage, family, and wealth succession is to build a safety barrier for families before tragedies occur, sort out interests through rules before family bonds break, and lock in lasting prosperity through institutions before wealth vanishes.

The significance of family trusts goes far beyond asset preservation. It protects future generations, so that wealth does not become a poison that corrupts the heart. It safeguards the family business, so that the founder's lifelong efforts are not easily ruined. It sustains family affection, so that interests do not become a blade that tears families apart. It fulfills responsibility, so that one generation's struggles truly bless descendants and extend for generations.

The wisdom of Mr. and Mrs. Qin Gongxin lies in their understanding of the true nature of wealth: the best destiny for money is not unrestrained squandering or disorderly succession, but to protect the entire family steadily and permanently within a legal framework — with institutions and family affection. This is the highest realm of wealth succession for the affluent, and the most touching value of family trusts.

倾尽家财赠子女，为何晚年悔断肠——三起亲子财富赠与的法律警醒

引言

父母之爱子，则为之计深远。可现实中，不少父母倾尽半生心血，将房产、股权、巨额财富悉数赠与子女，本以为是血脉传承、亲情托付，到头来却落得财产失控、亲情疏离，满心委屈与悔恨却求助无门。作为婚姻家事与财富传承律师，我在一年内接连接待了三位境遇相似的当事人：离婚后将股权赠与女儿的父亲，婚内把全部家产转给儿子的母亲，再婚前置办资产赠与爱子的母亲，他们都在对子女付出全部后陷入困境，急切想要追回赠与的财产。

这三起案件，起因不同、困境各异，却踩中了同一个财富传承的误区。我依据法律，为他们逐一剖析困境根源、给出专业意见，既点明赠与无法随意撤销的法律现实，也指导亲子传承与婚姻家庭中的相处智慧，更希望以此警醒世人：爱子女无需倾尽所有，财富传承更要守住底线，别让深情的付出，变成晚年的伤痛。

做财富传承法律服务多年，我始终觉得，亲子之间的财富纠纷，比普通离婚家事案更让人心酸。短短半年内，我先后接待了赵先生、费女士、纪女士三位当事人，他们的故事各有不同，却又那么相似，更有着一模一样的执念与后悔，都抱着"追回赠与子女财产"的诉求而来，最终都在法律的理性分析中，认清现实、重新寻找亲情与财富的平衡。

一、赵先生：离婚赠股护女，父女反目追悔莫及

第一位找到我的是赵先生，年逾五旬，神色憔悴，一提起女儿赵颖莹，眼眶就泛红，满是无奈与懊悔。

赵先生与前妻冯女士离婚时，夫妻二人名下最核心的资产，就是赵先生持有的一家科技公司的全部股权。为了弥补离婚对女儿的亏欠，也想给女儿一份终身保障，夫妻俩在离婚协议中明确约定，将该股权全部赠与女儿赵颖莹，离婚后很快办理了工商变更登记，股权全部过户到女儿名下，赵先生彻底失去了公司的股东身份与控制权。

起初父女关系还算和睦，可没过两年，赵先生再婚重组家庭，女儿对继母十分抵触，父女矛盾日渐激化，从最初的争吵冷战，到后来彻底断了往来。赵先生想过问公司经营，女儿直接拒绝；他想拿回部分股权保障晚年生活，女儿更是一口回绝。

看着自己一手打拼的公司，自己再也无权插手，曾经贴心的女儿如今形同陌路，赵先生夜夜难眠，满心都是后悔。他找到我，语气急切又带着一丝侥幸："叶

律师，这股权是我一辈子的心血，当初是离婚时一时冲动送给她的，现在我跟她关系这么差，我能不能反悔，把股权要回来？”

我看着赵先生焦灼的模样，先安抚他的情绪，再向他剖析法律现实：赵先生与前妻在离婚协议中约定的股权赠与，是双方真实意思表示，且已完成工商变更，财产权利完全转移给女儿，依据《民法典》第658条规定，赠与人在财产权利转移后，不再享有任意撤销权。而父女关系不和、女儿不让父亲干预公司经营，远未达到《民法典》第663条规定的"严重侵害赠与人权益、不履行扶养义务"等法定撤销情形，更何况这是夫妻共同财产的共同赠与，前妻作为共有人，也不会同意单方撤销，贸然起诉不仅无法追回股权，还会彻底斩断仅剩的父女情分。

赵先生听完，沉默良久，长叹一口气，他明白，自己一时冲动的赠与，早已没有回头路，如今能做的，只有试着修复父女关系，而非执着于法律诉讼。

二、费女士：家产全部赠与儿子，再婚之后却亲情尽疏

第二位当事人费女士，是一位气质温婉却满心委屈的女士，她的困境，比赵先生更让人心酸。

费女士是典型的女强人，与前夫婚内共同创业，她是家里的主要经济支柱，打拼多年积累下巨额财富，有房有存款，还有多处投资资产。两人育有一个儿子，早已成年，费女士对儿子百般疼爱，视若珍宝，总觉得儿子是自己最亲的人，早晚财产都是他的，不如早早交付。

但费女士与前夫感情不合，基于不愿意离婚将财产分给前夫的想法，费女士在与前夫协议离婚前，便将家里大部分核心资产，陆续转移到儿子名下，房产过户、存款转账，无一遗漏。离婚后，费女士遇见了郑先生，两人情投意合，选择再婚，本想安安稳稳度过晚年，可没想到，儿子与继父郑先生水火不容，处处抵触，甚至连带着对费女士也心生不满。

自从费女士再婚，儿子便很少回家，逢年过节也不登门，电话不接、消息不回，费女士想跟儿子沟通，却屡屡被拒之门外。她看着空荡荡的家，再想想自己倾尽所有转给儿子的家产，如今自己无房无大额存款，晚年生活全靠再婚丈夫支撑，儿子却如此疏远，一点也指望不上，她满心都是委屈与不甘。

"叶律师，我这辈子挣的钱，全给了他，我现在老了，他不管我，还要跟我断绝来往来气我，我想把给他的房子、存款都要回来，难道不行吗？"费女士说着，忍不住落泪，语气里满是绝望。

我耐心为费女士分析：她赠与儿子的资产，多为婚内共同财产，且已完成过户、交付，赠与行为合法有效，儿子仅是不沟通、不亲近，并未达到法定撤销赠与的条件，法律无法强行追回。而且费女士当初是自愿赠与，并非附条件传

承，如今以亲子疏远为由主张撤销，于法无据。我劝慰她，与其纠结财产，不如放下执念，先经营好自己的再婚家庭，等彼此情绪平复，再慢慢与儿子修复亲情，毕竟血缘难断，亲情远比财产更珍贵。

三、纪女士：再婚护子赠产，儿子败家无力回天

第三位当事人纪女士，是再婚重组家庭的母亲，她的遭遇，更具警示意义。

纪女士与前夫离婚后，独自带着儿子生活，对儿子极度溺爱，生怕儿子在重组家庭中受委屈。再婚前，她为了做好资产隔离，避免再婚财产纠纷，也想给儿子一份稳稳的保障，将自己一手创业打拼的公司股权、全部个人资产，悉数赠与儿子，还让儿子接手公司经营，自己彻底交出所有控制权。

可她万万没想到，儿子接手公司后，好赌好酒、玩物丧志，根本无心经营，对纪女士的劝说全然不听，甚至直接禁止她干预公司事务。短短时间内，公司业务大幅萎缩，业绩一落千丈，资产不断缩水，纪女士看在眼里，急在心里，却因为股权早已全部过户，自己没有任何股东权利，根本无法阻止儿子的荒唐行为。

看着自己半生心血创办的公司，即将毁在儿子手里，纪女士又急又悔，找到我时，语气满是愤恨与无奈："叶律师，我真是瞎了眼，早早把财产都给他，现在他败我家产，我管不了，我要撤销赠与，把公司和钱都要回来！"

针对纪女士的情况，我向她分析解答：纪女士的赠与行为已完成，财产权利完全转移，儿子虽不善经营、挥霍资产，但并未实施严重侵害纪女士权益的行为，也未拒绝履行扶养义务，不符合法定撤销赠与的情形。且公司股权已登记在儿子名下，其拥有独立的经营决策权，纪女士无权强行干预，起诉撤销并没有胜诉可能，当下最该做的，是放下对抗情绪，与儿子坦诚沟通，尝试引导儿子回归正途，或是及时止损，避免公司资产进一步流失。

四、三案共性解析：赠与易撤销难，传承需有智慧

梳理这三起案件，三位当事人的诉求都是"追回已赠与给子女的财产"，但法律层面的结论高度一致：赠与完成即生效，无正当理由不得撤销，诉讼绝非良策。

其一，财产权利转移后，任意撤销权消灭。根据《民法典》第 658 条，无论是股权、房产还是存款，只要完成过户、登记、交付，赠与人就不能随意反悔，这是法律维护交易稳定与合同效力的基本原则。

其二，法定撤销门槛极高，普通亲子矛盾不构成理由。《民法典》第 663 条明确的撤销情形，仅包括严重侵害赠与人、不履行扶养义务、不履行赠与约定

义务三种，单纯的关系不和、子女不善经营，远未达到法定标准，无法通过诉讼撤销。

其三，夫妻共同财产赠与，单方无权撤销。赵先生、费女士赠与的均是夫妻共同财产，单方主张撤销，必然遭到前配偶反对，赠与行为早已履行完毕，根本无法推翻。

其四，诉讼只会激化亲情矛盾。亲子之间的财富纠纷，一旦对簿公堂，仅存的亲情也会彻底破裂，即便胜诉，也会落得人财两空、亲情尽失的结局，远不如理性沟通、修复关系更有意义。

而这三位当事人的困境，根源都在于财富传承的认知误区：把一次性赠与等同于传承，过早交出全部财产控制权，既没培养子女的财富管理能力，也没给自己留下晚年保障的底线，最终陷入"付出一切却一无所有"的被动境地。

同时，三起案件也各有个性痛点：赵先生的矛盾源于再婚家庭的关系隔阂，费女士的遗憾在于再婚之后亲子疏离，纪女士的悔恨则是子女败家、资产失控。针对不同痛点，我也给出了差异化建议：赵先生重点修复父女与再婚家庭的双重关系，费女士先经营好自身晚年生活再缓和亲子矛盾，纪女士则直面子女问题，及时沟通止损，为后续财富传承预留空间。

案后结语

这三起亲子财富赠与反悔案，道尽了为人父母的深情与无奈。父母爱子女，本是天性，倾尽所有给予财富，初衷都是为了子女安稳、亲情绵长，可往往因为不懂法律、不懂传承智慧，让深情变成了枷锁，让付出变成了悔恨。

很多父母都陷入一个误区：认为财富传承就是把资产过户给子女，一劳永逸。殊不知，真正的财富传承，不可能是简单的财产转移，而是理念、能力、责任的系统传递。子女尚未具备匹配财富的认知与担当，过早交出全部控制权，只会让子女坐享其成、不懂感恩，甚至挥霍败家，父母也会失去晚年的尊严与底气。

法律的规则清晰而理性：赠与一旦完成，便难以回头。法定撤销权的设立，是为了保护赠与人的合法权益，而非纵容随意反悔，亲子亲情、财产权属，都需要在法律框架内理性对待。为人父母，不必为了子女牺牲全部，更不能过早放弃财产控制权，财富是晚年独立的保障，是尊严的底线，留有余地的爱，才是对自己、对子女、对亲情最负责的态度。

愿每一位父母都能明白：爱子女，要适度；传财富，要守拙。先保全自身安稳，再传递亲情温暖，别让倾尽家财的付出，换来晚年的孤独与悔恨；也别让血脉亲情，困在财产的纠葛里，最终两败俱伤。理性传承，守住底线，亲情与财富，方能长久相伴。

Giving All to Children, Regretting in Twilight Years: Legal Lessons from Three Parental Gifting Disputes

Introduction

A parent's love for a child plans far and deep. Yet in reality, many parents devote half a lifetime's effort to gifting real estate, equity, and substantial wealth to their children. What they expect to be a legacy of blood ties and trust often ends in lost control over assets, estrangement from their children, and bitter regret with nowhere to turn. As a lawyer specializing in marriage, family, and wealth succession, I advised three clients in similar situations within one year: a father who gifted company shares to his daughter after divorce, a mother who transferred all family assets to her son during marriage, and a mother who settled property on her beloved son before remarrying. All found themselves in trouble after giving everything, urgently seeking to reclaim the gifted property.

These cases arose from different circumstances and led to different hardships, yet all fell into the same trap in wealth succession. Using legal principles as my guide, I analyzed the root of their difficulties and provided professional opinions. I clarified the legal reality that gifts cannot be revoked at will, while also offering wisdom for parent-child relationships and family dynamics. My deeper hope is to warn everyone: loving your children does not mean giving everything, and wealth succession requires firm boundaries. Do not let affectionate giving become lifelong pain in old age.

Having practiced wealth succession law for many years, I have always found parent-child financial disputes more heartbreaking than ordinary divorce cases. Within half a year, I met with Mr. Zhao, Ms. Fei, and Ms. Ji. Their stories differed, yet were strikingly similar, marked by identical obsession and regret. All came seeking to "recover property gifted to their children," yet through rational legal analysis, they eventually came to accept reality and seek a new balance between family affection and wealth.

I. Mr. Zhao: Gave Shares to Protect Daughter in Divorce, Only to Regret Bitterly After Falling Out

The first client to approach me was Mr. Zhao, nearly fifty, haggard and worn. At the mention of his daughter Zhao Yingying, his eyes reddened with helplessness and remorse.

At the time of his divorce from his ex-wife Ms. Feng, the core asset in their joint name was all equity in a technology company held by Mr. Zhao. To compensate his daughter for the divorce and secure her lifelong future, the couple clearly agreed in their divorce settlement to gift all shares to their daughter Zhao Yingying. Shortly after the divorce, they completed industrial and commercial registration changes, transferring full equity to her. Mr. Zhao completely lost his shareholder status and control of the company.

At first, the father-daughter relationship remained harmonious. But within two years, Mr. Zhao remarried and formed a new family. His daughter strongly opposed his new wife, and conflicts between father and daughter intensified. What began as quarrels and cold wars turned into total estrangement. When Mr. Zhao tried to oversee the company's operations, his daughter refused outright; when he asked to regain part of the equity to support his old age, she rejected him flatly.

Watching the company he built from scratch slip beyond his control, and his once loving daughter become a stranger, Mr. Zhao lost sleep nightly, consumed by regret. He came to me, urgent yet holding onto a glimmer of hope: "Lawyer Rachel J. Ye, these shares are my life's work. I gave them to her impulsively during the divorce. Now our relationship is terrible. Can I go back on my word and take the shares back?"

Seeing his distress, I first calmed his emotions before explaining the legal reality: The equity gift agreed in the divorce settlement by Mr. Zhao and his ex-wife reflected their true intent, and having completed the commercial registration changes, the property rights were fully transferred to the daughter. Under Article 658 of the Civil Code, a donor loses the right of arbitrary revocation once property rights are transferred. Furthermore, poor father-daughter relations and the daughter's refusal to let him manage the company fall far short of the statutory grounds for revocation under Article 663 of the Civil Code, such as "serious infringement of the donor's rights or failure to provide support." Moreover, the gift was made from joint marital property; as a co-owner, his ex-wife would not consent to a unilateral revocation. A reckless lawsuit would not only fail to recover the shares but also permanently destroy the last remaining bond between father and daughter.

Mr. Zhao fell silent for a long time and sighed deeply. He realized his impulsive gift could not be undone. All he could do now was try to repair their relationship, not pursue legal action.

II. Ms. Fei: Gave All Assets to Her Son, Only to Be Alienated After Remarriage

The second client, Ms. Fei, was a gentle yet deeply wronged lady. Her plight was even more heartbreaking than Mr. Zhao's.

Ms. Fei was a typical strong woman. She had built a successful business together with her ex-husband and was the main breadwinner of the family. After years of hard work, she had accumulated substantial wealth: real estate, savings, and multiple investment assets. They had one son, already an adult. Ms. Fei doted on him, seeing him as a treasure and her closest relative. She believed her property would belong to him eventually anyway, so she might as well transfer it early.

However, her relationship with her ex-husband had broken down. Based on the thought of being unwilling to split her assets with her ex-husband in a divorce, Ms. Fei transferred most of the family's core assets to her son before their divorce by agreement — including real estate title transfers and bank transfers, leaving nothing out. After the divorce, Ms. Fei met Mr. Zheng. They fell in love and chose to remarry, hoping to spend her old age peacefully. But to her surprise, her son and his stepfather Mr. Zheng were completely incompatible and clashed constantly, and the son even grew resentful toward Ms. Fei herself.

Since Ms. Fei's remarriage, her son rarely came home, did not visit during festivals, did not answer calls, and left messages unreplied. Whenever Ms. Fei tried to communicate with him, she was repeatedly shut out. Looking at her empty home, and thinking of the family fortune she had given entirely to her son—now finding herself with no house or large savings, relying entirely on her remarried husband for support in her old age, while her son was so distant and unsupportive—she was filled with grievance and unwillingness.

"Lawyer Rachel J. Ye, I gave him everything I earned in my life. Now I'm old, and he ignores me. He even wants to cut off ties to anger me. Can't I get back the houses and savings I gave him?" Ms. Fei said, unable to hold back her tears, her tone full of despair.

I patiently analyzed it for Ms. Fei: Most of the assets she gifted her son were marital community property, and the title transfers and deliveries had been completed. The gift was legally valid. Her son's mere lack of communication and closeness did not meet the statutory conditions for revoking a gift, and the law could not force the assets to be returned. Moreover, Ms. Fei had gifted them voluntarily, not as a conditional succession. Claiming revocation now on the grounds of parent-child estrangement lacked legal basis. I comforted her that instead of obsessing over the property, it would be better to let go of her fixation, focus on managing her new marriage well first, and wait until both sides' emotions calmed down before slowly repairing the relationship with her son. After all, blood ties are hard to sever, and family affection is far more precious than property.

III. Ms. Ji: Gifted Assets to Protect Her Son in Remarriage, Only for Him to Ruin the Family Fortune

The third client, Ms. Ji, was a mother in a reconstituted remarried family. Her experience carries an even stronger warning significance.

After divorcing her ex-husband, Ms. Ji raised her son alone and doted on him extremely, fearing he would suffer in a reconstituted family. Before remarrying, in order to properly isolate assets, avoid future property disputes in the remarriage, and provide a steady guarantee for her son, she gifted all her company equity built from scratch and her personal assets entirely to her son. She even let her son take over the company's management, completely handing over all control herself.

But she never imagined that after taking over the company, her son became addicted to gambling and drinking, lost his ambition, and had no intention of running the business. He completely ignored Ms. Ji's advice and even directly forbade her from intervening in company affairs. Within a short time, the company's business shrank drastically, performance plummeted, and assets dwindled continuously. Ms. Ji watched anxiously, yet because the equity had long been fully transferred and she held no shareholder rights, she was completely unable to stop her son's absurd behavior.

Watching the company she built with half her lifetime's effort about to be ruined in her son's hands, Ms. Ji was both anxious and regretful. When she came to me, her tone was full of resentment and helplessness: "Lawyer Rachel J. Ye, I was really blind to give him all the property so early. Now he is ruining my family fortune and I can't control him. I want to revoke the gift and get the company and the money back!"

Regarding Ms. Ji's situation, I analyzed and explained to her: Ms. Ji's gift had been completed, and the property rights had been fully transferred. Although her son was poor at managing the business and squandered assets, he had not committed acts that seriously infringed upon Ms. Ji's rights and interests, nor had he refused to fulfill his obligation of support, which did not meet the statutory circumstances for revoking a gift. Furthermore, the company equity was already registered in her son's name, granting him independent operational decision-making power. Ms. Ji had no right to forcibly intervene, and a lawsuit for revocation had no chance of success. The most appropriate thing to do right now was to let go of confrontational emotions, communicate honestly with her son, and try to guide him back to the right path, or to cut losses promptly to prevent further depletion of the company's assets.

IV. Analysis of the Commonality of the Three Cases: Gifting is Easy but Difficult to Revoke; Succession Requires Wisdom

Sorting out these three cases, the demand of all three clients was to "recover the property already gifted to their children", but the conclusion at the legal level was highly consistent: a gift takes effect upon completion, cannot be revoked without justifiable reasons, and litigation is by no means a good strategy.

First, after the transfer of property rights, the right of arbitrary revocation is extinguished. According to Article 658 of the Civil Code, whether it is equity, real estate or deposits, as long as the transfer, registration, and delivery are completed, the donor cannot repent at will. This is a basic principle of the law to maintain transaction stability and contract effectiveness.

Second, the threshold for statutory revocation is extremely high, and ordinary parent-child conflicts do not constitute a reason. The circumstances for revocation specified in Article 663 of the Civil Code only include three types: seriously infringing upon the donor, failing to fulfill the obligation of support, and failing to fulfill the obligations agreed upon in the gift. Simple relationship discord or a child's poor management falls far short of statutory standards and cannot be revoked through litigation.

Third, a unilateral revocation of gifts made from joint marital property is not permitted. Both Mr. Zhao and Ms. Fei gifted assets that belonged to their marital joint property. A unilateral claim to revoke it would inevitably be opposed by the former spouse, and since the gift had long been fully executed, it could not be overturned at all.

Fourth, litigation will only intensify family conflicts. Once financial disputes between parent and child go to court, the remaining family affection will be completely shattered. Even if one wins the case, it will end up with both wealth and family affection lost. It is far less meaningful than rational communication and repairing the relationship.

The predicament of these three clients was rooted in a cognitive misunderstanding about wealth succession: equating a one-time gift with succession, and handing over all property control too early. They neither cultivated their children's ability to manage wealth nor left themselves a basic safety net for old age, ultimately landing in a passive situation of "giving everything yet having nothing."

At the same time, the three cases each had their individual pain points: Mr. Zhao's conflict originated from the relationship barriers in a remarried family; Ms. Fei's regret lay in the parent-child alienation after her remarriage; and Ms. Ji's remorse was due to her child's squandering and loss of asset control. Aimed at these different pain points, I also provided differentiated advice: Mr. Zhao should focus on repairing the dual relationships with his daughter and his remarried family; Ms. Fei should first manage her own later life well before easing the parent-child conflict; and Ms. Ji should face her child's problems directly, communicate in time to stop losses, and reserve space for subsequent wealth succession.

Post-Case Conclusion

These three cases of parents attempting to go back on wealth gifts to their children fully express the deep love and helplessness of parenthood. It is natural for parents to love their children, and giving all their wealth is originally intended to ensure their children's stability and everlasting family affection. However, often due to a lack of legal knowledge and succession wisdom, deep affection turns into a shackle, and dedication turns into regret.

Many parents fall into a misunderstanding: they believe that wealth succession is simply transferring assets to their children once and for all. Little do they know that true wealth succession can never be a simple transfer of property, but a systematic transmission of concepts, capabilities, and responsibilities. When children do not yet possess the cognition and responsibility to match the wealth, handing over full control too early will only make them sit back and enjoy the fruits, fail to understand gratitude, and even squander the family fortune, while parents will also lose their dignity and confidence in their later years.

The rules of the law are clear and rational: once a gift is completed, it is difficult to turn back. The establishment of the statutory right of revocation is to protect the legitimate rights and interests of the donor, not to condone arbitrary repentance. Both parent-child affection and property ownership need to be treated rationally within the legal framework. As parents, there is no need to sacrifice everything for their children, nor should they give up control of property too early. Wealth is the guarantee of independence and the bottom line of dignity in later years. A love that leaves room is the most responsible attitude towards oneself, one's children, and family affection.

May every parent understand this: love your children in moderation; transfer wealth with prudence. First preserve your own stability, and then pass on the warmth of family affection. Do not let the dedication of giving all your family wealth be exchanged for loneliness and regret in your later years; nor let blood ties be trapped in property disputes, eventually ending up with both sides hurt. With rational succession and keeping the bottom line, family affection and wealth can accompany each other for a long time.

异国相恋情深意浓，分手怎可索回赠款

引言

恋爱时的转账是情分，分手时的追讨是裂痕。男女交往期间的红包、转账、礼品馈赠，本是爱意流淌的痕迹，可一旦情缘散尽，昔日温情便极易沦为法庭上的针锋相对。这笔钱究竟是无条件赠与、附条件赠与，还是民间借贷？边界模糊之间，藏着情感与法理的拉扯。我代理的这起跨国恋爱财产纠纷案，便将热恋时的付出、异国分居的煎熬、消费观念的碰撞、婚史带来的隐秘负重，尽数铺展在法律面前，最终为女方守住了应有的尊严与财产。

2016 年的日本，成了谷先生与南女士缘分开始的地方。

彼时两人同在日本东京打拼，孤独的异乡生活里，一句乡音、一次照面，都轻易拉近了彼此的距离。相似的异乡漂泊感，让两人迅速靠近，感情日渐浓烈。两人很快建立恋爱关系。在日本期间，谷先生在一家日料店工作。谷先生此前已有一段婚姻，并独自抚养着与前妻所生的儿子小谷，身上背负着父亲的责任与异国生活的不俗开销。南女士独立坚韧，却也渴望一份安稳的依靠。两人交往了一段时间，南女士回到国内经营着自己的事业，谷先生则常年往返中日两国之间。

2018 年 1 月，两人在中国正式订婚，谷先生精心挑选了一枚钻石戒指赠予南女士，以表心意。南女士亦满心欢喜地回赠了爱马仕皮带扣头、高端定制西装等昂贵礼品，还包了大额款项的红包赠送给谷先生。她不愿计较物质得失，只觉得真心相待，便能换来长久相守。同年 9 月，两人按照民间风俗，在国内酒店举办了热闹的婚礼，宴请亲友，昭告彼此的身份。虽然未办理法律意义上的结婚登记，但此后两人始终以夫妻名义共同生活，在南女士看来，这场婚礼，便是她认定一生的承诺。

婚礼后的温馨时光并未持续太久，现实的矛盾便随着异国分居悄然滋生。为了陪伴在日本读书的儿子小谷，谷先生在婚礼一年后便返回日本定居，从此两人开始了漫长的中日跨国分居生活。南女士割舍不下国内苦心经营的事业，也放不下身边的亲友，只能一次次放下手中工作，漂洋过海奔赴日本，只为维系这段来之不易的感情。飞机往返的疲惫、时差颠倒的煎熬、独自等待的孤寂，成了她感情里的常态，可她从未抱怨，只觉得真心付出，总能跨越距离的阻碍。

但相处越久，两人骨子里的差异却逐渐凸显。谷先生因有过婚史，独自承担着儿子在日本的学费、生活费、住房开销，经济本就背负着重担，消费观念愈发谨慎克制，甚至对日常开支斤斤计较；而南女士生性大方，恋爱中向来愿意双向付出，平日里衣食住行、人情往来，从不吝啬，她始终认为，情侣之间相互馈赠、共同承担开销，是爱意最直接的表达。

观念的分歧、异国的距离、婚史带来的隐形压力，渐渐让这段感情蒙上阴影。谷先生开始要求南女士放下国内的一切，远赴日本陪他定居，并不能顾及到南女士多年打拼的事业，也无视她在异国无亲无故的不安。他将工作之余的精力几乎都放在前妻的儿子身上，给南女士的承诺迟迟无法兑现，安全感一点点崩塌。南女士则坦言，她不是不愿奔赴，而是不敢奔赴一场她看不到稳定的未来，感受不到被坚定选择的底气，更无法抛下自己的人生，奔向一场毫无保障的生活。

长期的意见不合、跨国分居的疏离、需求与安全感的错位，最终让感情彻底走向破裂。

2022 年，谷先生率先提出分手，随之而来的，不是好聚好散，而是一纸诉状。他将恋爱期间所有的转账、红包、订婚戒指尽数清算，主张逾百万元款项均为附结婚条件的赠与，要求南女士返还款项等共计 130 余万元。

昔日在日本街头的并肩同行、婚礼上的温情誓言、跨国奔赴的满心欢喜，转眼变成了法庭上的追讨与算计。情感与经济的双重打击，让南女士陷入崩溃，她满心委屈却无力辩驳，最终找到了我，希望能理清这段感情里的是非，守住自己的合法权益。

接受委托后，我一点点还原了这段感情的全貌：南女士在这段关系里，从来不是一味索取的一方。她回赠高价礼品、赠送大额红包，独自承担共同生活中的诸多开销，漂洋过海奔赴异国维系感情，付出的情感与物质，从未少于男方；她通过微信、支付宝转账给谷先生的钱一时难以计数，这些都是她实实在在的付出。

庭审中，我逐一提供证据，驳回对方的主张，将法理与情理尽数呈现。我提出，双方早已举办民俗婚礼，以夫妻名义共同生活，谷先生的转账、红包均为恋爱期间增进感情的无条件赠与，未附任何登记结婚的条件，且财产权利已实际转移，无权要求返还；两人最终未办理结婚登记，系谷先生长期定居日本、无法回国，两人情感淡漠最终分离所致，未能结婚的原因在于现实所迫，而非被告南女士的责任。对于钻石戒指与订婚红包，南女士已回赠高价礼品，以及诸多的款项消费付出形成对价，结合双方共同生活的事实，彩礼亦无需全额返还。

我的辩论逻辑清晰、证据充分，将这段跨国恋情里的付出、拉扯、委屈与真相，完整呈现在法庭之上。最终，法院充分采纳了我的代理意见，依法作出公正判决：谷先生主张的恋爱期间红包、转账，均为增进感情的无条件赠与，且南女士也进行了回赠和持续消费投入，故南女士无需返还；钻石戒指归属南女士所有，基于公平原则，南女士向谷先生酌情返还 5 万元彩礼款。

这场突如其来的追讨之战，最终以南女士免于承担百余万元款项落下帷幕，昔日的情感伤痛，终有法律为她托底。

案后结语

情侣之间的金钱往来，不应只是冰冷的数字，而是藏着彼时的心意与付出。法律不会偏袒任何一方，更不会将热恋时的自愿赠与，强行认定为需要返还的借款或附条件赠与。恋爱期间为表达爱意、维系感情、共同生活支出的款项，属于无偿赠与，财产权利转移后，赠与人无权随意撤销。

这起案件也让我们看清，爱情里的双向奔赴，不该在分手时沦为算计。情浓时的馈赠是真心，情散时的体面是底线。而法律的意义，便是在情感消散之后，守住公平与正义，让真心付出的人，不被辜负，不被损害。对我而言，我守护的不仅是当事人的财产，更是她在这段感情里，毫无保留的真心与尊严。

A Devoted Cross-Border Romance: Can Gifts Be Reclaimed After a Breakup?

Introduction

Transfers during love are tokens of affection; claims after a breakup are scars of separation. Red envelopes, money transfers and gifts between lovers are naturally traces of love. Yet once affection fades, past tenderness can easily turn into confrontation in court. Are such payments unconditional gifts, conditional gifts, or private loans? Behind the blurred legal boundaries lies a conflict between emotion and justice. This cross-border relationship property dispute I represented lays bare the devotion in passionate love, the agony of living apart across borders, the clash of consumption attitudes, and the hidden burdens of marital history. In the end, I helped the client defend her due dignity and property.

Their fate began in Japan in 2016.

Back then, both were building their lives in Tokyo. Amid the loneliness of living abroad, a familiar accent or a casual encounter quickly drew them close. Sharing the same feeling of drifting in a foreign land, they grew attached rapidly and their love deepened. They soon entered a romantic relationship. During their time in Japan, Mr. Gu worked at a Japanese restaurant. He had previously been married and raised his son Xiaogu from his ex-wife alone, shouldering the responsibilities of fatherhood and considerable living expenses abroad. After dating for some time, Ms. Nan returned to China alone to run her own business: independent and resilient, yet also longing for stable support. Meanwhile, Mr. Gu traveled frequently between China and Japan.

In January 2018, the couple got officially engaged. Mr. Gu presented Ms. Nan with a carefully chosen diamond ring as a token of his love. In return, Ms. Nan happily gave him expensive gifts including a Hermès belt buckle and high-end custom suits, along with several large red envelopes. She cared little about material gains and losses, believing that sincere devotion would bring lifelong companionship. In September of the same year, they held a lively traditional wedding banquet at a hotel in China, inviting relatives and friends to announce their union. Although they never completed legal marriage registration, they thereafter lived together as husband and wife. To Ms. Nan, this wedding represented a lifelong commitment.

The warm days after the wedding did not last long. Real-life conflicts quietly emerged along with their cross-border separation. To accompany his son Xiaogu, who was studying in Japan, Mr. Gu returned to settle in Japan one year after the wedding. Since then, the couple began a long period of long-distance separation between China and Japan. Unable to give up her hard-built career in China or her relatives and friends, Ms. Nan had to put aside her work repeatedly and travel across the ocean to Japan, just to preserve this hard-won relationship. Exhaustion from frequent flights, torment of jet lag, and loneliness of waiting alone became her constant companions. Yet she never complained, believing that sincere devotion could eventually overcome the distance.

However, as they spent more time together, deep-rooted differences gradually surfaced. Having been married before and shouldering his son's tuition, living costs and housing expenses in Japan alone, Mr. Gu was under heavy financial pressure and grew increasingly cautious and even calculating about daily spending. In contrast, Ms. Nan was generous by nature, always willing to give equally in the relationship. She never hesitated to cover expenses for food, clothing, housing, transportation and social interactions. She firmly believed that mutual giving and shared expenses between lovers were the most direct expression of love. Diverging values, the physical distance between countries, and the invisible pressure brought by previous marriages gradually cast a shadow over this relationship. Mr. Gu began demanding that Ms. Nan abandon everything in her home country and move to Japan to settle down with him, disregarding the career she had built over many years and ignoring her anxiety of living in a foreign land without family or friends. He devoted nearly all his spare time to his son from his ex-wife, repeatedly failing to fulfill his promises to Ms. Nan, and her sense of security crumbled little by little. For her part, Ms. Nan admitted that it was not that she was unwilling to make the move, but that she dared not commit to a future with no stability, no assurance of being firmly chosen, and no possibility of abandoning her own life for an insecure existence.

Long-standing disagreements, the estrangement of cross-border separation, and a mismatch between emotional needs and security finally led the relationship to a complete breakdown.

In 2022, Mr. Gu took the initiative to end the relationship. What followed was not an amicable separation, but a formal lawsuit. He itemized every transfer, red envelope, engagement ring, and renovation expense during their relationship, claiming that more than one million yuan in total was conditional gifts based on marriage, and that over 500,000 yuan in renovation costs was a loan. He demanded that Ms. Nan return more than 1.3 million yuan in total, including betrothal gifts, red envelopes, and the alleged loan.

The days of walking side by side on the streets of Japan, the tender vows at their wedding ceremony, and the joy of traveling across borders for each other quickly turned into claims and calculations in court. The double blow of emotional and financial loss pushed Ms. Nan to the brink of collapse. Filled with grievances yet powerless to defend herself, she eventually turned to me, hoping to clarify the rights and wrongs of this relationship and protect her legitimate rights and interests.

After accepting the mandate, I gradually reconstructed the full picture of their relationship: Ms. Nan was never the one who only took and never gave. She reciprocated with expensive gifts, sent large red envelopes, bore many of the couple's living expenses alone, and traveled overseas across the ocean to maintain their relationship. Her emotional and material devotion was no less than that of the man. The transfers and red envelopes via WeChat and Alipay were merely daily expenses to strengthen their bond as lovers, and the renovation costs were for the home they shared, with no loan agreement ever made.

During the trial, I organized the evidence piece by piece, refuted the opposing claims layer by layer, and presented both legal principles and human considerations. I argued that the two had already held a traditional wedding ceremony and lived together as husband and wife. Mr. Gu's transfers and red envelopes were unconditional gifts to nurture affection during their relationship, not subject to any condition of civil marriage registration. Since property rights had been effectively transferred, he had no right to demand their return. The reason the couple never formally registered their marriage was that Mr. Gu had settled in Japan long-term and refused to return to China to complete the procedure, making him primarily liable rather than the defendant Ms. Nan.

Regarding the renovation expenses of more than 500,000 yuan, our position is that there were no loan receipts, IOUs, or other debt evidence, nor was there any intent to form a loan relationship. The property involved was Ms. Nan's premarital personal asset, and Mr. Gu, as a cohabitant, bearing the renovation cost constituted reasonable expenses for the couple's shared life. The so-called "repayment statements" were merely in jest and did not represent a genuine legal intention.

As for the diamond ring and engagement red envelope, Ms. Nan had already given high-value gifts in return as consideration. Moreover, Mr. Gu was the party who called off the engagement. Combined with the fact that the two had lived together, there was no requirement for full restitution of the betrothal gifts.

With clear logic and sufficient evidence, I fully presented the devotion, disputes, grievances, and truth of this cross-border romance in court. In the end, the court fully adopted our agency opinions and rendered a fair judgment in accordance with the law: the red envelopes and transfers claimed by Mr. Gu during their relationship were unconditional gifts to foster affection, and Ms. Nan had also given gifts in return and made continuous consumption contributions; therefore, Ms. Nan was not required to return them. The renovation expenses did not constitute a loan, so Ms. Nan had no obligation to repay them. The diamond ring belonged to Ms. Nan, and based on the principle of fairness, Ms. Nan would appropriately return 50,000 yuan of betrothal gifts to Mr. Gu.

This unexpected claim dispute finally concluded with Ms. Nan being exempted from bearing more than one million yuan in payments. The emotional pain of the past was finally supported by the law.

Post-Case Conclusion

Monetary transactions between lovers should not be just cold numbers, but embody the affection and devotion of that time. The law does not favor either party, nor does it arbitrarily characterize voluntary gifts given during passionate love as loans or conditional gifts subject to restitution.

A romantic relationship is not a specific status prescribed by law. The establishment of a private lending relationship must be centered on the intent to borrow. Mere transfer records without supporting evidence such as loan receipts or chat logs cannot validate a lending relationship. Funds spent during a relationship to express affection, maintain the bond, or cover shared living expenses are gratuitous gifts. Once property rights are transferred, the donor has no right to revoke them at will.

This case also makes it clear that mutual devotion in love should not degenerate into calculation after a breakup. Gifts given when love is strong come from sincerity, and dignity when love fades is the bottom line. The role of the law is to uphold fairness and justice after emotions fade, ensuring that those who give wholeheartedly are not betrayed or harmed. For me, I safeguard not only my client's property but also her unreserved sincerity and dignity in this relationship.

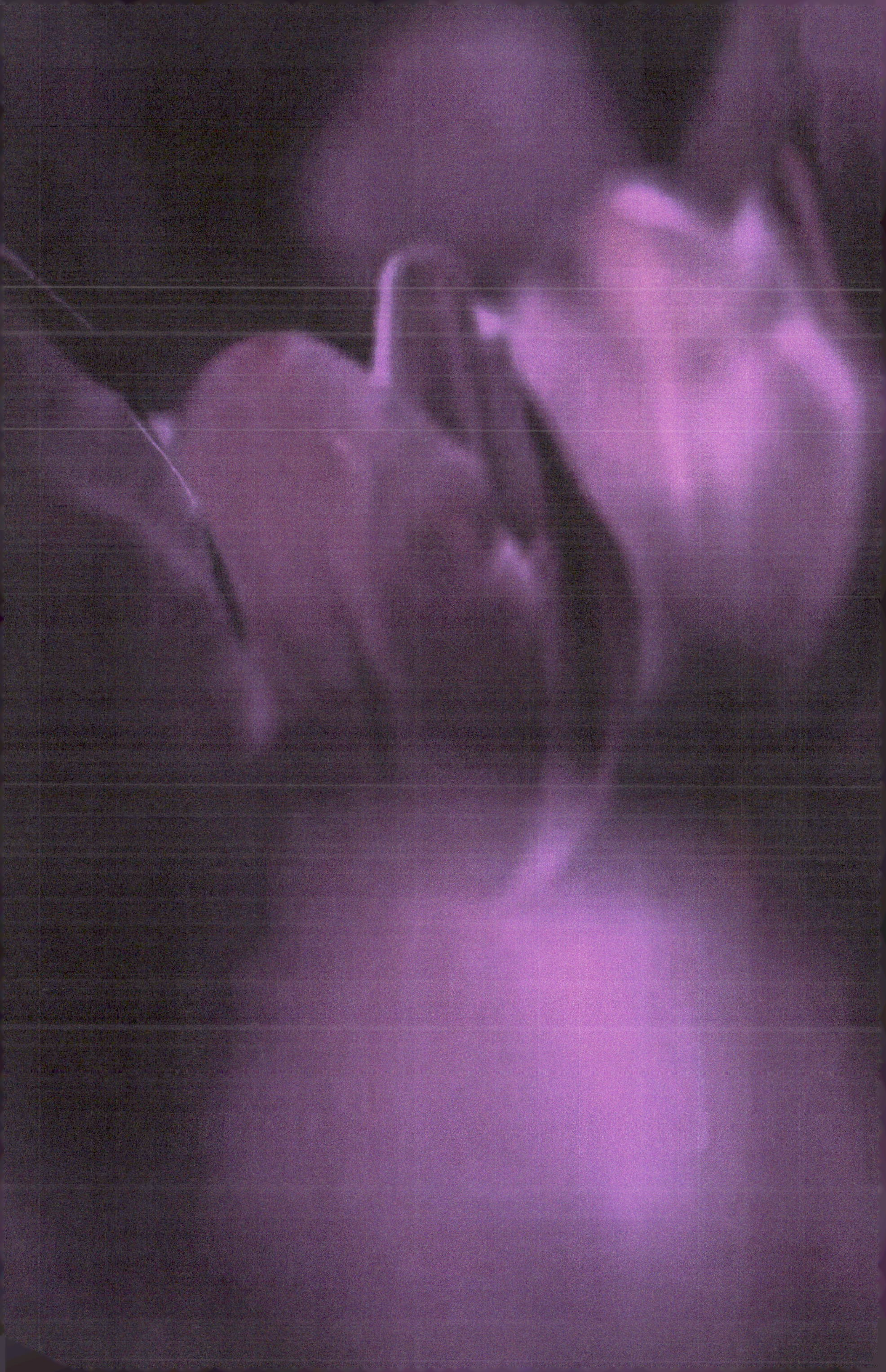

PHOTOGRAPH BY JOSEPH XU

CHAPTER 3 | WRATH

第三章 | 暴怒

引文

"愤怒就像火焰，燃烧的首先是自己；控制情绪，远比战胜他人更接近强大。"

——【古罗马】塞内卡

暴怒是情绪的决堤，是亲密关系里最直接、最残酷的暴力。它或者是言语上的利刃攻击，或者是肢体上的伤害控制，或者是极端的报复行为，甚至是不顾一切的自我与他人毁灭。在婚姻家事法律领域，暴怒常常以最令人心痛的方式呈现：家庭暴力中的控制与伤害、离婚冲突中的诋毁与威胁、抚养权争夺里的极端行为、家族争产中的仇恨宣泄。

我在无数真实案件中深刻见证：一时的情绪失控，足以摧毁数十年相濡以沫的情感；一句脱口而出的狠话，足以割裂血脉相连的至亲；一次失去理智的举动，足以让一个完整的家庭坠入长久的深渊。暴怒带来的短暂掌控感，背后是无尽的伤害、恐惧与无法挽回的破碎。

法律为人身安全筑起坚实屏障，为受害者赋予正当权利，为施暴者划定不可逾越的边界，却难以抹去那些刻在生命里的创伤与阴影。真正的力量，并非是发泄愤怒，而是驾驭情绪；真正的成熟，也不是绝不退让，而是懂得在爱与亲情面前保持克制与慈悲。婚姻与家庭的终极意义，是守护、包容与救赎。

Epigraph

"Anger is like flame; it burns the wielder first. To master one's emotions is far closer to strength than to conquer others."

— Seneca, Ancient Rome

Wrath is an emotional outburst, the most direct and cruel form of violence in intimate relationships. It may be cutting verbal attacks, physical harm and control, extreme acts of revenge, or even reckless self-destruction and harm to others. In the field of family and marriage law, wrath often presents itself in heartbreaking ways: control and abuse in domestic violence, slander and threats in divorce conflicts, extreme behavior in custody battles, and the venting of hatred in family property disputes.

I have deeply witnessed in countless real cases: a moment of emotional outburst can destroy decades of shared devotion; a single harsh remark can sever blood ties; one irrational act can plunge a whole family into lasting despair. The brief sense of control brought by wrath hides endless harm, fear and irreversible brokenness.

The law builds a solid barrier for personal safety, grants legitimate rights to victims and draws uncrossable lines for abusers, yet it cannot erase the trauma and shadows etched into lives. True power is not venting anger, but controlling emotions; true maturity is not never yielding, but knowing to remain restrained and compassionate in the face of love and family. The ultimate meaning of marriage and family is protection, tolerance and redemption.

爱到极致是疯狂

引言

你曾是佛前的莲
转瞬间
弥散消亡
爱已浑然不见
极致 如月的背面
疯狂滴落
无尽的折磨
哀怨绵绵

“肖法官，一切都是我的错，是我亲手葬送了这个婚姻，是我一次次将婚姻逼进死胡同，逼走了我的丈夫，请再给我一次挽救婚姻的机会！”当小青在法庭调解时，痛哭流涕地说出这番话时，她的丈夫小方在一旁面色凝峻，他默默地走出法庭，对我说：“叶律师，我已经再三给过她机会，现在说什么也没用了，这个婚，我离定了。”

这是我执业二十多年来经办的惟一一例男方遭受家暴的特殊离婚案。小方与小青曾经是一对天造地设，人人钦羡的璧人。小方纯良温善、宽厚沉稳，在一次朋友聚会上对美丽聪颖的小青一见钟情，暗恋了半年后终于向小青表白。双方交往后，小方的诚实善良和专一痴情感动了小青，小青答应了小方的求婚，双方幸福地走进婚姻殿堂。婚后，小青享受着小方对她毫无保留的迁就、包容和隐忍，然而性格任性暴躁的小青，并不能尊重和照顾丈夫的感受，小方长期承受着难以名状的苦闷、压抑、困惑和迷茫，最终演变至矛盾的爆发。

在小青一次次无理取闹、反复纠缠下，甚至对丈夫踢打谩骂下，小方最终忍无可忍，选择起诉离婚，小青难以置信一向珍视她比自己的生命还要重要的丈夫竟然会向法院提出离婚，她无法接受，也根本不能承受。于是发生了后来的这件事，据小方的陈述：“我在外地经营某品牌皮鞋专卖店，那天，小青突然出现在我的专卖店门口，让我一下子惊奇地差点认不出来，但她还是不改一贯粗暴蛮横无理的脾气，喊道‘没想到我会从家里来这里吧，把你们的帐本拿出来，不然就有你们好看的’，说着就拿起茶几上的果盆往地上摔去，弄了一地干果，又拿起茶几上的茶壶向地上猛摔，茶壶碎了一地，这一情形把我和正在上班的员工都吓得不知所措。我缓过神来，想将她拉住，劝她冷静下来，而她甩手打了我两个耳光，把我当场打愣了，员工们都惊呆了，那时我非常尴尬难堪，但是我知道她的性格，她经常不计后果，要把事情闹大，丢我的脸。我让她离开，她却在我的专卖店到处翻找账本，我拉她，她从桌上拿起剪刀就刺过来，一下子把我的衣服划破了，员工看此情景，赶紧打电话报警。她就冲过去要打员工。我使劲夺过她手里的剪刀，但是我真的怕她了，我让员工不要报警，并把她抱住往外拖，但是她又喊又叫又踢又打，在我肩上狠咬，脸上乱抓。她真的疯了，我当时非常恐慌惊吓，在推搡中，她把桌子踢翻了，抽屉里的账本掉了出来，她一下子就拣到了账本，我冲过去把账本夺来，跑进里面办公室锁门。她在外大闹，拿灭火器把店里砸地乱七八糟。最后我忍无可忍报警。警察来了，她才罢休。我无数次地容忍她，但是她一次次逼人太甚。这个婚姻我已经受够了，我坚决要求离婚，否则我也要被她逼死。"

2010 年 5 月 11 日，上午九时，法院不公开开庭审理小方诉小青离婚纠纷案。庭前，被告小青告知法院其因赴越南出差，无法出庭，故委托代理人到庭参与庭审。至上午十一时许，该案第一次庭审结束。说来很难让人相信，小方签完笔录，先行离开，十多分钟后，小方突然打我手机，称他刚从法院大门走出来，突然他的老婆小青出现在马路对面直冲过来扑到他身上发疯的扭打、撕咬、脚踹，小方只顾躲避并没有还手。小青见法警要过来，遂一面辱骂一面跳上一旁等候的车子，但还不甘心，从车窗里探出上身，继续狂骂。

小方打我手机，我隐约有不祥之感，等我赶出来时，刚巧看见那辆车子绝尘而去。这时发觉小方的衬衫已被对方扯破，胸口也被抓出血。整个过程中，小方始终未曾还手。这一事发经过，有法院门口的视频监控录像和前来的法警可以证实。我们立刻向经办法官报告此情况，很显然，小青在法院门口公然对小方实施暴力的行为，进一步证明了小方遭受家暴的事实。同时，这一行为也严重干扰了正常的诉讼程序，侵害了小方的合法权益，应当依法给予处理。

法庭随即传唤了小青。面对法官严厉的质问和小方对婚姻完全绝望的态度，小青终于留下了悔恨的泪水。她说，过去一切的错都在她，小方并没有任何过错，是小方对她太好了，时时事事容忍她，迁就她，纵容了她的任性和霸道，使得她忽视了丈夫的尊严。到最后，双方无法正常沟通和交流。在长期的分居生活中，她一面享受小方的经济供给，一面顾自在外玩乐甚至吸毒被拘，即便如此，小方也没有骂过他一句，因而她绝没有想到小方竟然会主动起诉离婚。她从心理上无法接受小方的起诉，她恨小方，因而坚决不同意离婚，并且谎称出国拒绝出庭应诉。

这个案件并不复杂，然而在随后的第二次开庭中，我仍然详细陈述我的代理意见：

1、双方的婚姻现状表明离婚势在必行。原告的性格太过懦弱，一味回避问题，优柔寡断，使得矛盾一再堆积。被告个性强硬，专横娇纵，从不顾及原告的感受，阻却了双方的正常沟通，使得婚姻屡屡陷入危机。双方在婚姻的经营上均有误区。在长达五六年的分居生活中，双方极少联络，互不干涉，婚姻关系已经名存实亡。原告尝试过多种方法跟被告沟通离婚一事，均被被告唾骂如狗血喷头，无奈在半年之前提起离婚诉讼，但被法院判决驳回。然而，这半年来双方关系并无丝毫改善，证明确无和好可能。

2、在对待离婚问题的处理上，被告几次无正当理由拒不到庭应诉，不提交合法答辩，反而以辱骂殴打原告，跟踪监视原告，强夺原告账簿，威胁恐吓原告家人等极端做法对抗原告的合法起诉，被告此行暴露了她对婚姻家庭一贯以来的不理性、不负责和不珍惜。被告虽称不同意离婚，但这是她的心理失衡使然，并非挽回婚姻的真实意愿。婚姻到了破裂的程度，对于双方来说都是无可估量的伤害，但被告应当面对现实，而不是积怨成仇，害人害己。

3、相对被告的强横无理，原告对待婚姻，包括离婚的态度是谦让的、认真的、理智的。原告对于价值逾千万元的夫妻共有财产，主动表态愿意给予被告尽量多的优先照顾，且要求由原告独自负担儿子至独立生活，这是原告作为一名丈夫和父亲，在离婚之时，面对有过错的妻子，所作出的难能可贵的决定。因为原告认为，无论女方在婚姻中有多少的过错，对于离婚而言，女方所遭受的损害总是比男方要多。毕竟夫妻一场，为了尽可能降低离婚对女方可能造成的心理或生活上的损失，原告已经是做了最大的让步。

庭审结束后，法院主持调解，小方愿意主动放弃夫妻共有财产，只要小青肯离婚，并表示不予追究小青之前所有恶意违法侵害行为。最终，在尊重当事人意愿的基础上，法庭形成了调解协议，小青在协议书上默默签下了自己的名字。尽管小青得到了绝大部分财产，但是她失去了最心爱的丈夫，曾经深爱她、包容她、呵护她的生命中的伴侣，这又是多大的再也无法弥补的损失。

案后结语

1、婚姻需要双方共同呵护，共同督促，共同经营。无论是妻子还是丈夫，一方一味的毫无原则的迁就忍让包容另一方，其实是溺爱娇惯纵容了另一方，而隐忍的一方，内心长期积压着不满和愤懑，无法得以宣泄，使得婚姻越来越偏离互爱互谅的轨道，导致互尊互重的天平失衡，从而最终走向破裂。

2、《反家暴法》第五条规定，反家庭暴力工作应当尊重受害人真实意愿，保护当事人隐私。尽管小方在这个案件中是家暴的受害者，但是他选择了放弃权利，让渡利益，以获取和平解决离婚纠纷，这是他内心的真实意愿，同时也是他对曾经夫妻一场的小青的作出的善意对待。法律对当事人的意愿予以了尊重。

Love at Its Extreme Is Madness

Introduction

You were once a lotus before the Buddha.
In an instant, you scattered and vanished.
Love is completely gone.
The extreme, like the dark side of the moon,
drips down in madness,
endless torment,
lingering sorrow.

"Judge Xiao, everything is my fault. I destroyed this marriage with my own hands. I pushed our marriage into a dead end again and again, and drove my husband away. Please give me one more chance to save our marriage!" When Xiao Qing tearfully said these words during the court mediation, her husband Xiao Fang sat beside her with a stern face. He silently walked out of the courtroom and said to me: "Lawyer Rachel J. Ye, I have given her chances over and over again. Nothing she says matters now. I am determined to divorce her."

This was the only special divorce case I handled in more than 20 years of practice in which the husband was the victim of domestic violence. Xiao Fang and Xiao Qing were once a perfect, enviable couple. Xiao Fang was kind, gentle, generous and calm. He fell in love at first sight with the beautiful and intelligent Xiao Qing at a friend's gathering. After half a year of secret love, he finally confessed his feelings to her. As they dated, Xiao Fang's honesty, kindness and devotion touched Xiao Qing. She accepted his proposal, and they happily entered marriage. After marriage, Xiao Qing enjoyed Xiao Fang's unreserved accommodation, tolerance and patience. However, Xiao Qing, who was willful and hot-tempered, failed to respect or care for her husband's feelings. Xiao Fang endured unspeakable depression, pressure, confusion and loss for a long time, until the conflict finally erupted.

After Xiao Qing repeatedly acted unreasonably, pestered him, and even kicked, beat and insulted her husband, Xiao Fang could bear it no longer and filed for divorce. Xiao Qing could not believe that the man who had cherished her more than his own life would actually sue for divorce. She could not accept it, nor bear it. Then the incident happened. According to Xiao Fang: "I ran a brand-name shoe store in another city. That day, Xiao Qing suddenly appeared at the door of my store. I was so surprised I almost didn't recognize her. But she was still as rude and unreasonable as ever. She shouted: 'Didn't expect I'd come here from home, did you? Bring out your account books, or you'll be sorry.' With that, she grabbed the fruit bowl from the coffee table and smashed it on the floor, spilling dried fruit everywhere. She then grabbed the teapot and slammed it down, shattering it into pieces. My staff and I were terrified and stunned. I came to my senses and tried to hold her back, telling her to calm down. But she slapped me twice across the face, leaving me dumbfounded on the spot. All the staff were shocked. I was extremely embarrassed, but I know her character: she often acts recklessly, making a scene to shame me. I told her to leave, but she rummaged everywhere in the store looking for account books. When I pulled her away, she picked up a pair of scissors from the table and stabbed at me, slashing my clothes. Seeing this, the staff quickly called the police. She rushed at them to hit the staff. I struggled to take the scissors from her hand. I was truly afraid of her. I told the staff not to call the police, held her and dragged her outside. But she screamed, kicked, bit my shoulder hard and scratched my face wildly. She was truly crazy. I was terrified. During the scuffle, she kicked over a table, and the account books fell out of the drawer. She grabbed them at once. I rushed to take the books from her, ran into the inner office and locked the door. She made a huge scene outside, smashing the store into a mess with a fire extinguisher. In the end, I could take no more and called the police. Only when the police arrived did she stop. I have tolerated her countless times, but she has gone too far again and again. I have had enough of this marriage. I insist on divorce, or she will drive me to death."

At 9 a.m. on May 11, 2010, the court held a closed hearing on Xiao Fang. Xiao Qing divorce case. Before the trial, the defendant Xiao Qing informed the court that she was on a business trip to Vietnam and could not appear in person, so she entrusted an agent to attend. The first hearing ended at around 11 a.m. Incredibly, right after Xiao Fang signed the transcript and left first, he suddenly called me more than ten minutes later. He said he had just walked out of the court gate, when his wife Xiao Qing appeared across the road, rushed straight at him, and attacked him madly – hitting, biting and kicking. Xiao Fang only dodged and did not fight back at all. When Xiao Qing saw the judicial police coming, she cursed and jumped into a waiting car. Not satisfied, she leaned out of the window and continued to scream insults.

When Xiao Fang called my mobile phone, I had a bad feeling. When I rushed out, the car was already speeding away. Xiao Fang's shirt was torn open, and his chest was scratched and bleeding. Throughout the whole incident, Xiao Fang never retaliated. The whole process was recorded by the surveillance camera at the court gate and witnessed by the judicial police. We immediately reported this to the judge. Clearly, Xiao Qing's violent attack on Xiao Fang at the court gate further proved that Xiao Fang was a victim of domestic violence. This act also seriously disrupted the normal litigation process and infringed upon Xiao Fang's legitimate rights and interests, and should be dealt with according to law.

The court immediately summoned Xiao Qing. Faced with the judge's stern questioning and Xiao Fang's complete despair toward the marriage, Xiao Qing finally shed tears of regret. She said all the mistakes in the past were hers; Xiao Fang was completely innocent. Xiao Fang had been too good to her, tolerating and indulging her in everything, which spoiled her willfulness and arrogance, making her ignore her husband's dignity. In the end, they could no longer communicate normally. During their long separation, she enjoyed Xiao Fang's financial support while going out and having fun, even being detained for drug use. Even so, Xiao Fang never scolded her a single word. She never imagined Xiao Fang would take the initiative to sue for divorce. She could not accept it psychologically, hated Xiao Fang, thus firmly refused to divorce, and lied about going abroad to avoid appearing in court.

The case was not complicated, but in the subsequent second hearing, I still presented my detailed agent's opinion:

1. The current state of the marriage makes divorce inevitable. The plaintiff was too weak, avoiding problems and being indecisive, causing conflicts to pile up repeatedly. The defendant was strong, domineering and spoiled, never considering the plaintiff's feelings, blocking normal communication and repeatedly pushing the marriage into crisis. Both parties had misunderstandings in managing the marriage. After five or six years of separation, they rarely contacted each other and lived independent lives. The marriage existed in name only. The plaintiff tried many ways to talk about divorce, only to be violently insulted by the defendant. He had no choice but to file for divorce half a year ago, but the court dismissed the claim. However, there had been no improvement in their relationship in the past six months, proving reconciliation was

impossible.

2. In handling the divorce, the defendant refused to appear in court without justifiable reasons several times, did not file a legitimate reply, and instead fought the legitimate lawsuit through extreme means: insulting and beating the plaintiff, stalking and monitoring him, seizing his account books, threatening and intimidating his family. Her actions exposed her consistent irrationality, irresponsibility and disregard for the marriage and family. Although the defendant claimed she opposed divorce, this stemmed from psychological imbalance, not a genuine will to save the marriage. The breakdown of the marriage caused immeasurable harm to both sides, but the defendant should face reality instead of turning resentment into hatred, harming others and herself.

3. Compared with the defendant's arrogance and unreasonableness, the plaintiff's attitude toward the marriage and divorce was modest, earnest and rational. Regarding the joint marital property worth more than 10 million yuan, the plaintiff voluntarily offered to give the defendant as much priority as possible. He also asked to bear the sole responsibility of raising their son until independence. This was a noble decision made by the plaintiff as a husband and father, facing his at-fault wife during divorce. He believed that no matter how many mistakes the wife made in the marriage, she would suffer more harm than the man in a divorce. After all, they had been husband and wife. To minimize the psychological and life losses divorce might bring to the defendant, the plaintiff had made the greatest concessions.

After the trial, the court presided over mediation. Xiao Fang was willing to voluntarily give up all joint marital property as long as Xiao Qing agreed to divorce, and stated he would not pursue all her previous malicious and illegal violations. Finally, based on respecting the parties' wishes, the court issued a mediation agreement. Xiao Qing silently signed her name on the document. Although Xiao Qing obtained most of the property, she lost the husband she loved most — the partner who had deeply loved, tolerated and cherished her. What an irreparable loss.

Post-Case Conclusion

1. Marriage requires mutual care, supervision and management by both partners. Whether wife or husband, if one party unconditionally accommodates, tolerates and indulges the other without principle, it is in fact overindulgence and spoiling. The tolerant party suppresses dissatisfaction and resentment for a long time with no outlet, causing the marriage to deviate further from the path of mutual love and understanding, unbalancing the scale of mutual respect, and eventually leading to breakdown.

2. Article 5 of the Anti-Domestic Violence Law stipulates that anti-domestic violence work shall respect the true wishes of victims and protect the privacy of the parties. Although Xiao Fang was the victim of domestic violence in this case, he chose to waive his rights and yield interests for a peaceful resolution of the divorce dispute. This was his true will, and also his kindness to Xiao Qing, whom he had once been married to. The law respected the parties' wishes.

情杀利刃下的家破人亡，刑事附带民事的正义追讨

引言

情感的执念一旦沦为疯狂的占有，便会化作刺向他人的利刃，将原本平静的生活彻底撕碎。这是一起因婚外情引发的故意杀人惨案，一段错付的感情，最终酿成了无法挽回的悲剧。我代理了被害人董鸿菲的女儿董嘉臻与外公董柯强的刑事附带民事诉讼案件，亲眼见证了一个单亲母亲被情人残忍杀害，见证了花季少女目睹惨案后的精神创伤，也见证了七旬老人白发人送黑发人的锥心之痛。这场情杀案，不仅是对生命的践踏，更是对人性底线的突破。在法庭上，我们不仅要为逝者讨回公道，更要为破碎的家庭争取应有的赔偿，用法律的正义，慰藉逝者的亡魂，抚平生者的创伤。

我接手这起案件时，眼前的一幕让我久久无法平静。七十多岁的董柯强老人佝偻着身子，布满皱纹的脸上写满了绝望与悲痛，他的身旁，是十六岁的外孙女董嘉臻，女孩眼神空洞，浑身颤抖，面对母亲惨死的事实，早已被恐惧与创伤吞噬。这对祖孙，是本案仅有的两名刑事附带民事诉讼原告人，而夺走他们一切的，是被害人董鸿菲曾经的情人——傅志发。

董鸿菲是一位独立的服装生意人，独自抚养女儿董嘉臻十余年。母亲早逝的她，从小与父亲董柯强相依为命，婚后的感情经历也颇为坎坷。年轻时认识同乡刘某，交往不久就意外怀孕，她曾提出与孩子的父亲刘某结婚，却被对方无情拒绝，刘某从此消失得无影无踪，甚至疑似出境，再也没有音讯。

孤独无助的董鸿菲，舍不得放弃腹中的胎儿，在父亲的支撑下，度过了难捱的漫长的孕期，终于顺利生下一个美丽的女婴，取名董嘉臻。女儿很像她，非常健康可爱，从此母女二人和外公董柯强，构成了这个小小的家。董鸿菲凭借自己的努力，将服装生意经营得有声有色，给女儿提供了安稳的生活，也悉心照料着年迈的父亲，日子虽平淡，却充满温情。

2022 年 9 月，董鸿菲为青田老家的房屋装修，经人介绍认识了从事室内装修工作的傅志发。彼时的傅志发早已组建家庭，却被董鸿菲的经济能力所吸引，主动接近并哄骗她，两人很快发展成情人关系。单纯的董鸿菲，在情感上却容易迷失方向，她对傅志发付出了真心，却换来对方无休止的索取。傅志发频繁向她索要钱财，董鸿菲念及一时的情分，一次次满足他的要求。可当董鸿菲看清傅志发的贪婪与偏执，不堪其扰，下定决心提出分手时，噩梦就此开始。

傅志发不愿接受分手的结局，开始变本加厉地纠缠、威胁。他多次用极端言语恐吓董鸿菲，“那一天把你杀了”的狠话成了家常便饭；他上门堵截，抢夺她的金戒指，用肢体与言语的威胁逼迫她维持关系；同时，依旧不断向她索要金钱。在被多次拒绝后，傅志发的怨恨彻底爆发，萌生了杀人的歹念。

2025 年 1 月 8 日，这个本该平凡的日子，成了董家永远的噩梦。傅志发以寻找钥匙为借口，哄骗孤身一人在家的董鸿菲打开门，恶魔就这样进来了。面对他再次提出的复合要求，董鸿菲严词拒绝，这成了压垮傅志发的最后一根稻草。他恼恨之下，残忍地用枕头蒙住董鸿菲的面部，亲手剥夺了这个女人的生命。

惨剧发生后，董嘉臻恰好放学回家。她发现母亲的房门紧闭，多次呼喊无人应答，心中隐隐不安。但她以为母亲可能还没回家，于是自己在家中简单用餐。之后，她依旧联系不上母亲，这时已有些心急如焚，当她再次去敲母亲的卧室门时，竟听到了房间里异常的动静。恐惧瞬间席卷了这个十六岁的女孩，她颤抖着拨通了亲戚阿婆的电话。阿婆让她待在原地，随即赶过来。与此同时，当地警方接到了凶手傅志发的报警电话。傅在电话中称，他将一个女人杀害在房间里，又割脉自杀，却因求生的念头而放弃自杀，于是拨打了报警电话自首。警方迅速赶到现场，破门而入，将还在屋内的傅志发当场抓获。

董嘉臻亲眼目睹了母亲惨死的现场，但凶手杀死母亲后就躲在家中的那一幕场景，成了她一生无法磨灭的阴影。这场突如其来的惨案，让她患上了严重的创伤后应激障碍，每晚惊醒五六次，无法正常入睡；她开始抵触与外界接触，社交功能严重退化；学习能力也急剧下降，原本处于升学关键阶段的她，学习成绩也一落千丈，学业上遭受了巨大损失。心理医生将董嘉臻的诊断书摆在面前，每一个字都像针一样扎在祖孙二人的心上。

董柯强老人，在古稀之年遭遇了人生最惨痛的打击，白发人送黑发人的剧痛，让他陷入了严重的哀伤障碍，晚年的生活失去了唯一的依靠，凄凉与绝望成了他余生的底色。一个原本安稳幸福的家庭，因为一段错误的感情，彻底支离破碎。

接受委托后，我代理董家祖孙提起了刑事附带民事诉讼，一方面要求法院依法严惩凶手傅志发，从重处罚；另一方面，要求傅志发赔偿死亡赔偿金、被扶养人生活费、精神损害抚慰金、丧葬费等，用以弥补这个家庭遭受的经济与精神双重创伤。董家祖孙的诉求无比坚定，他们不求凶手苟活，只希望法院能判处其死刑立即执行，为惨死的董鸿菲讨回最基本的公道。

庭审过程中，公诉机关出示了完整的证据链，傅志发的犯罪事实清晰、证据确实充分。他因情感纠纷与钱财索取未果，恶意报复杀人，作案手段残忍，犯罪动机卑劣，且毫无悔罪表现，情节极其恶劣。面对我方提交的董嘉臻的精神疾病诊断报告、董柯强的哀伤障碍证明，以及各项经济损失的证据，傅志发的辩护律师试图以自首、悔罪等情节为其减刑，却无法掩盖其残忍杀害他人、摧毁一个家庭的罪行。

最终，法院作出判决：被告人傅志发犯故意杀人罪，判处死刑，缓期两年执行，剥夺政治权利终身。这个结果，未能满足董家祖孙判处死刑立即执行的诉求，却也给了他们一丝慰藉。在附带民事赔偿部分，法院结合案件事实与法律规定，对董家祖孙提出的赔偿请求进行了核定，尽管最终的赔偿金额与他们诉求期望金额存在巨大差距，但这是法律对逝者与伤者的最后一点弥补。

案件落幕，可董家祖孙的伤痛却永难愈合。董嘉臻需要长期接受心理干预治疗，才能慢慢走出阴影；董柯强老人在失去女儿后，只能靠着外孙女相依为命，昔日的欢声笑语，再也无法回到这个破碎的家。而傅志发，这个因贪婪与偏执酿成悲剧的凶手，将在监狱中度过余生，他用自己的双手，毁掉了两个无辜之人的人生，也让自己的人生彻底坠入深渊。

案后结语

这起因情杀引发的故意杀人案，是人性扭曲与情感失控的极端体现，它以最惨烈的方式告诉我们，错误的感情、偏执的占有欲，最终只会酿成无法挽回的悲剧。作为代理律师，我在为逝者维权、为生者争取权益的过程中，深刻感受到了生命的脆弱，也看清了人性在欲望与执念面前的不堪一击。

从情感与人性的角度分析，本案的悲剧，源于傅志发扭曲的占有欲与贪婪的本性。他明知自己有家庭，却刻意接近经济独立的董鸿菲，将感情当作索取钱财的工具；当对方提出分手，触及他的利益时，便从纠缠、威胁升级为残忍的暴力杀人。他的偏执与自私，是摧毁这个家庭的直接原因。而董鸿菲的悲剧，则源于她单纯的性格与匮乏的人生阅历，在一段错误的婚外情中，毫无防备地付出真心，最终被自己信任的人夺走了生命。董嘉臻与董柯强，是这场悲剧最无辜的受害者，一个花季少女失去了母亲，一个古稀老人失去了女儿，他们承受的精神创伤，是任何物质赔偿都无法弥补的。

傅志发的行为，是对生命最赤裸裸的践踏，其犯罪动机卑劣、手段残忍，理应受到法律的严惩。法院判处其死刑缓期两年执行，是结合了其自首情节后的法定判决，尽管未能满足原告人死刑立即执行的诉求，但法律的判决依然彰显了对故意杀人罪的严厉打击。

本案也揭示了深刻的婚姻与情感思考：婚外情是婚姻的毒药，更是滋生悲剧的温床。它违背了婚姻的忠诚原则，也容易让身处其中的人失去理智，沦为欲望的奴隶。董鸿菲在婚外情中付出的真心，最终换来了杀身之祸，这是对所有人的警示：在感情中，保持清醒的头脑，坚守底线，学会及时止损，是保护自己的唯一方式。同时，对于心智尚未成熟的青少年、情感单纯的成年人而言，树立正确的婚恋观，提高自我保护意识，尤为重要。

在司法实践层面，本案也凸显了刑事附带民事诉讼的意义。它将刑事追责与民事赔偿相结合，既实现了对犯罪行为的惩罚，又为被害人家属提供了经济补偿的途径，是法律兼顾惩罚与救济的重要制度

对比西方普通法系国家，在刑事案件的审判中，两大法系均对故意杀人罪保

持着严厉的打击态度，核心原则一致，均以剥夺他人生命的严重程度作为量刑的核心依据。差异主要体现在附带民事赔偿的计算标准、程序细节上，但在惩治恶性犯罪、维护被害人权益的核心目标上，并无本质区别。

人性的贪婪与偏执，是这场悲剧的根源。傅志发用极端的方式，毁掉了他人的人生，也毁掉了自己的未来。而董家祖孙的遭遇，让我们明白，生命无比珍贵，感情需要理性对待。法律可以惩治犯罪、弥补损失，却无法挽回逝去的生命，也无法轻易抚平心灵的创伤。唯有守住内心的底线，远离错误的感情，珍惜身边的人，才能避免这样的悲剧再次上演。这，也是这起情杀惨案留给我们最深刻的思考。

A Family Destroyed in a Crime of Passion: Seeking Justice via Civil Claims in Criminal Proceedings

Introduction

Once emotional obsession turns into frenzied possession, it becomes a blade that tears through otherwise peaceful lives. This is an intentional homicide case triggered by an extramarital affair—a misplaced affection that led to an irreversible tragedy. I represented Dong Jiazhen, the daughter of the victim Dong Hongfei, and Dong Keqiang, her grandfather, in their criminal incidental civil lawsuit. I witnessed firsthand the brutal murder of a single mother by her lover, the psychological trauma of a teenage girl who witnessed the tragedy, and the heart-wrenching pain of a septuagenarian father burying his own child. This crime of passion not only violated the sanctity of life but also crossed the bottom line of humanity. In court, we sought not only justice for the deceased but also due compensation for the shattered family. Through legal justice, we aimed to comfort the departed and heal the wounds of the living.

When I took on this case, the scene before me left me deeply disturbed. The elderly Dong Keqiang, in his seventies, was hunched over, his wrinkled face etched with despair and grief. Beside him stood his 16-year-old granddaughter Dong Jiazhen, her eyes empty, her body trembling, consumed by fear and trauma after her mother's brutal death. This grandfather and granddaughter were the only two plaintiffs in the criminal incidental civil action. The man who had taken everything from them was Fu Zhifa, the former lover of the victim Dong Hongfei.

Dong Hongfei was an independent clothing merchant who had raised her daughter Dong Jiazhen single-handedly for more than a decade. Having lost her mother at an early age, she had grown up relying on her father Dong Keqiang. Her romantic life after marriage had also been fraught with hardship. In her youth, she met Liu, a fellow townsman, and became pregnant unexpectedly after a short relationship. She proposed marriage to Liu, the father of her child, only to be cruelly rejected. Liu vanished without a trace, apparently leaving the country, and was never heard from again.

Lonely and helpless, Dong Hongfei could not bear to give up the unborn baby. Supported by her father, she endured a long and difficult pregnancy and eventually gave birth to a beautiful baby girl named Dong Jiazhen. The daughter took after her, healthy and lovely. From then on, the mother, daughter, and grandfather formed a small but close family. Through her own hard work, Dong Hongfei built a successful clothing business, providing a stable life for her daughter and carefully caring for her elderly father. Life was simple, yet warm.

In September 2022, Dong Hongfei was renovating her family house in Qingtian and was introduced to Fu Zhifa, an interior decorator. Although Fu Zhifa was already married, he was drawn to Dong Hongfei's financial means. He actively pursued and deceived her, and the two soon became lovers. Naive and emotionally vulnerable, Dong Hongfei gave her wholehearted affection to Fu Zhifa, only to be met with endless demands for money. He repeatedly asked her for funds, and out of affection, she gave in time and again. But when Dong Hongfei finally saw Fu Zhifa's greed and paranoia, grew tired of his harassment, and resolutely decided to break up, her nightmare began.

Refusing to accept the breakup, Fu Zhifa intensified his harassment and threats. He repeatedly intimidated her with extreme language, often saying things like "I'll kill you one day." He confronted her at her home, snatched her gold ring, and used physical and verbal threats to force her to continue the relationship, all while still demanding money. After being rejected multiple times, Fu Zhifa's resentment erupted completely, and he formed the intent to kill.

January 8, 2025, an otherwise ordinary day, became an everlasting nightmare for the Dong family. Under the pretext of looking for his keys, Fu Zhifa lured Dong Hongfei, who was home alone, to open the door. Just like that, the devil entered. When Dong Hongfei firmly rejected his renewed request to reconcile, it became the final straw that broke Fu Zhifa. Overwhelmed by resentment and rage, he cruelly pressed a pillow over her face and took the woman's life with his own hands.

At the time of the tragedy, Dong Jiazhen happened to come home from school. She found her mother's bedroom door tightly closed, and after calling out several times with no response, her anxiety grew stronger. But she thought her mother might not have come home yet, so she had a simple meal at home. Afterwards, she still could not reach her mother, and by then, she was burning with anxiety. When she knocked on the bedroom door again, she heard strange noises coming from inside. Fear instantly engulfed the 16-year-old girl. Trembling, she called an elderly relative. The relative told her to stay put and rushed over immediately. Meanwhile, the local police received an emergency call from the murderer, Fu Zhifa. He claimed on the phone that he had murdered a woman in the room, and then attempted suicide by slitting his wrists, but gave up suicide out of an urge to survive, thus calling the police to surrender. The police arrived quickly, broke down the door, and arrested Fu Zhifa on the spot inside the room.

Witnessing the gruesome scene of her mother's tragic death, with the murderer still in the house, left an indelible shadow on Dong Jiazhen for the rest of her life. The sudden tragedy left her suffering from severe post-traumatic stress disorder. She woke up five or six times every night, unable to sleep normally. She began to withdraw from the outside world, with severely impaired social functioning. Her academic ability also declined sharply. Originally at a critical stage of transitioning to higher education, her academic performance plummeted, causing her to suffer a huge loss academically. The psychiatrist's diagnosis lay before them, each word piercing the hearts of the grandfather and granddaughter like needles.

Elder Dong Keqiang, in his seventies, suffered the most painful blow of his life. The agony of losing a child in his old age plunged him into severe grief disorder. Having lost his only support in his later years, desolation and despair became the tone of the rest of his life. A once peaceful and happy family was completely torn apart because of a toxic relationship.

After accepting the mandate, I represented the elderly man and his granddaughter in filing a criminal lawsuit with attached civil claims. On the one hand, we demanded that the court severely punish the murderer Fu Zhifa in accordance with the law and impose a heavy sentence. On the other hand, we demanded that Fu Zhifa pay compensation for death compensation, living expenses for dependents, mental distress damages, funeral expenses, and other items, to compensate for the family's dual economic and psychological trauma. The family's demand was firm: they did not want the murderer to live, and only hoped the court would sentence him to death with immediate execution to secure basic justice for the slain Dong Hongfei.

During the trial, the public prosecution presented a complete chain of evidence. Fu Zhifa's criminal facts were clear and the evidence was solid and sufficient. He committed intentional murder out of retaliation after emotional disputes and failed attempts to extort money. His crime was cruel in method, vile in motive, and showed no sign of remorse, making the circumstances particularly egregious. Faced with the psychiatric diagnosis report of Dong Jiazhen, the grief disorder certification of Dong Keqiang, and evidence of various economic losses submitted by our side, Fu Zhifa's defense attorney attempted to seek a reduced sentence on the grounds of voluntary surrender and remorse, but could not conceal his crime of brutally killing another person and destroying an entire family.

In the end, the court rendered its judgment: the defendant Fu Zhifa was found guilty of intentional homicide and sentenced to death with a two-year reprieve, with deprivation of political rights for life. Although this outcome did not fulfill the family's wish for immediate execution, it still brought them a measure of comfort. Regarding the attached civil compensation, the court examined and verified the claims based on the facts of the case and legal provisions. Although the final compensation amount fell far short of their expected claim amount, it represented the law's final form of redress for the deceased and the survivors.

The case has come to an end, but the pain of Dong Keqiang and his granddaughter will never fully heal. Dong Jiazhen will need long-term psychological intervention to gradually recover from the trauma. Having lost his daughter, the elderly Dong Keqiang can only rely on his granddaughter for company. The laughter and joy of the past will never return to this broken home. As for Fu Zhifa, the perpetrator who brought about this tragedy out of greed and paranoia, he will spend the rest of his life behind bars. With his own hands, he ruined the lives of two innocent people and cast his own life into the abyss.

Post-Case Conclusion

This intentional homicide case, born of a fatal love affair, represents an extreme manifestation of distorted human nature and emotional loss of control. In its most tragic form, it teaches us that misplaced affection and obsessive possessiveness can only lead to irreversible tragedy. As the attorney representing the family, I deeply felt the fragility of life while seeking justice for the deceased and protecting the rights of the survivors, and witnessed how easily human nature collapses in the face of desire and obsession.

From an emotional and human perspective, the tragedy originated from Fu Zhifa's twisted possessiveness and inherent greed. Though he already had a family, he deliberately approached the financially independent Dong Hongfei, using their relationship as a tool to extort money. When she broke up with him and threatened his interests, he escalated from harassment and threats to brutal murder. His paranoia and selfishness directly destroyed the family. Dong Hongfei's tragedy stemmed from her naivety and lack of life experience. She wholeheartedly gave her trust in a wrongful extramarital affair and was ultimately killed by someone she believed in. Dong Jiazhen and Dong Keqiang were the most innocent victims: a teenage girl lost her mother, and an elderly man in his seventies lost his daughter. The psychological trauma they endured cannot be compensated by any material means.

Fu Zhifa's behavior was a blatant violation of human life. With despicable motives and cruel means, he deserved severe legal punishment. The court's sentence of death with a two-year reprieve was a statutory judgment that took into account his voluntary surrender. Although it did not satisfy the plaintiffs' demand for immediate execution, the verdict still demonstrated the severe crackdown on the crime of intentional homicide.

This case also provokes profound reflections on marriage and relationships. Extramarital affairs are always poison to marriage and a breeding ground for tragedy. They violate the principle of marital loyalty and easily drive people to lose their sense and become slaves to desire. Dong Hongfei's sincere devotion to an extramarital affair cost her life, serving as a warning to everyone: in relationships, staying clear-headed, upholding moral boundaries, and knowing when to stop in time are the only ways to protect oneself. Meanwhile, for emotionally naive adults and immature young people, establishing a healthy view of love and marriage and raising self-protection awareness is especially important.

In judicial practice, this case highlights the significance of criminal incidental civil litigation. By combining criminal accountability with civil compensation, it not only punishes criminal conduct but also provides financial relief for the victim's family, representing an important legal mechanism that balances punishment and remedy.

Compared with common law jurisdictions in the West, both legal systems maintain severe attitudes toward intentional homicide, sharing the same core principle: sentencing is based primarily on the gravity of unlawfully depriving a person of life. Differences lie mainly in the calculation standards and procedural details of incidental civil compensation, but there is no essential divergence in the core goals of punishing violent crimes and protecting victims' rights.

Greed and paranoia were the root causes of this tragedy. Fu Zhifa used extreme means to ruin the lives of others as well as his own future. The suffering of the Dong family reminds us that life is precious and relationships must be treated rationally. The law can punish crimes and remedy losses, but it cannot bring back the dead or easily heal emotional wounds. Only by upholding our inner moral bottom line, staying away from harmful relationships, and cherishing those around us can we prevent such tragedies from recurring. This is the deepest lesson left by this horrific crime of passion.

涉外离婚之诉，挣脱家暴与谎言的跨国婚姻囚笼

引言

跨国婚姻的浪漫外衣之下，常常藏着文化冲突、性格撕裂、信息隐瞒，甚至是暴力与危险。当一段在海外缔结的婚姻沦为囚笼，当外籍丈夫失联拒离、远隔重洋，被困的一方该如何自救？我的当事人贺女士，一位美貌高知却涉世未深的自由插画师，38岁时在催婚压力下踏入跨国婚姻，却遭遇丈夫家暴、躁郁症隐瞒的残酷真相，仓皇逃回国内后被名存实亡的婚姻捆绑四年。作为婚姻家事律师，我依据中国法律，全程国内诉讼、涉外公告送达、缺席判决离婚，让她不必再踏回危险之地，彻底挣脱了那段黑暗的跨国婚姻。

贺女士是众人眼中的“优质女性”，一位高学历背景，审美出众，作品细腻的自由插画师。她容貌清丽、气质温婉，无论外在条件还是内在素养，都堪称出众。可这份优秀，却在婚恋路上成了“枷锁”。

她对伴侣的要求始终偏高，总盼着一份契合灵魂的感情，而不愿将就，不知不觉便错过了世俗眼中的“最佳婚配期”。转眼到了 38 岁，看着身边同龄人早已成家立业，父母的催婚从温和提醒变成日日叮嘱，亲友的关切也渐渐变成无形的压力。常年沉浸在创作与理想世界里的她，心思纯粹、社会经验不足，因大龄未婚的焦虑陷入了心智上的不成熟，在自己的人生选择上，渐渐失去了理性判断的能力。

就在这时，麦克出现在了她的网络世界里。麦克是美国当地一家知名餐厅的主厨，谈吐风趣，擅长用文字描绘生活的浪漫，对远在大洋彼岸的贺女士体贴备至。他说自己欣赏东方女性的温婉，向往安稳的家庭生活，那些恰到好处的情话，恰好击中了贺女士渴望被爱、渴望给父母一个交代的软肋。

彼时的她，被催婚的焦虑裹挟，又被跨国恋情的新鲜感吸引，全然忽略了隔着屏幕的信息不对称——麦克刻意隐瞒了自己患有躁郁症的病史，以及情绪极端、自控力极差的本性。这些让婚姻埋下隐患的真相，都被他用浪漫的人设完美掩盖。

在麦克的一再邀约和“终身相伴”的承诺下，贺女士怀着对婚姻的满心憧憬，不顾内心隐约的不安，独自远赴美国。两人很快在美国办理了结婚登记，正式结为夫妻。贺女士以为自己终于找到了归宿，却不知，这场仓促的跨国婚姻，从一开始就披着欺骗和隐瞒的外衣。

共同生活后，东西方文化的巨大差异、生活习惯的剧烈冲突、三观的根本不合，让矛盾一触即发。而真正将贺女士推入恐惧深渊的，是麦克卸下伪装后的真面目。躁郁症带来的情绪剧烈波动，让他时而亢奋暴躁，时而低落阴郁，开始频繁对贺女士实施家庭暴力。推搡、辱骂、恐吓，甚至肢体上的暴力，在那个异国

的小屋里不断上演。作为心思细腻的自由插画师，她曾试图理解、包容麦克的情绪，却换来更变本加厉的伤害。

语言不通、举目无亲，贺女士整日活在惶恐与不安中。在一次严重的家暴后，她拼尽全力挣脱束缚，向邻居求助。邻居当即报警，美国警方出警处置，对麦克出具了训诫书，并依法作出了相应处罚。那段时间，贺女士满心绝望，只想逃离。可在麦克痛哭流涕的忏悔、赌咒发誓的保证下，心软的她，又被"多年等待才遇到的婚姻"这一执念牵绊，选择了暂时原谅，天真地以为对方会真心悔改。

她不知道，躁郁症引发的情绪失控与暴力倾向，根本不会轻易改变。短暂的平静之后，是更深的控制与伤害。这段婚姻早已变成不见天日的囚笼，让这位纯粹优秀的自由插画师濒临崩溃。再也无法忍受的贺女士，不顾一切收拾行李，在一个深夜仓皇逃回国内。这一走，便是四年。

回国后，贺女士终于从焦虑与执念中清醒，决心结束这段充满伤害、欺骗与暴力的婚姻。她多次通过邮件、社交软件联系麦克，明确提出离婚，可对方始终冷漠无视、拒不回应，仿佛那段婚姻只是他困住她的工具。四年分居，四年挣扎。贺女士在国内重新拾起画笔，专注创作，也试图自愈，却始终被一段在美国缔结的婚姻法律束缚。她不敢再踏回美国——那里有她不愿回想的创伤，更有随时可能再次施暴的麦克，语言不通的陌生环境，只会让她再次陷入孤立无援的境地。

"我不去美国，我能不能在国内离婚？"坐在我办公室里的贺女士，褪去了往日的温婉，眼底只剩被拖延四年的疲惫与忐忑。

听完她的遭遇，我既心疼于她的经历，也坚定地告诉她：完全可以。即便在美国登记结婚，你是中国公民，就有权在国内起诉离婚。根据我国民事诉讼法及司法解释规定，中国公民一方居住在国内，不论婚姻缔结地在何处，国内一方住所地法院均有管辖权。对方失联、不配合、远在海外，都不是无法突破的障碍。

接受委托后，我着手为贺女士启动全程在国内法院受理的跨国离婚程序，步步为营，形成系统的法律环节：

第一，确定管辖法院，向贺女士经常居住地人民法院递交立案材料，依法提起离婚诉讼；

第二，规范办理境外证据手续，将美国的结婚登记证书、警方家暴训诫记录等材料完成公证、认证及中文翻译，满足国内法院涉外案件的证据要求；

第三，全面梳理关键事实，整理双方分居四年的证据、贺女士多次提出离婚的沟通记录、麦克家暴及隐瞒躁郁症病史的相关佐证，充分证明夫妻感情彻底破裂，无任何和好可能；

第四，依法启动涉外送达程序，在无法直接联系麦克、邮寄送达无果情况下，向法院申请涉外公告送达，按照法定程序完成起诉状及开庭文书送达；

第五，严密准备庭审方案，向法庭清晰陈述：贺女士因大龄催婚焦虑仓促缔结跨国婚姻，婚后发现男方存在家暴、隐瞒重大精神病史等严重过错，双方分居长达四年，婚姻关系早已名存实亡，符合法定离婚条件，请求法院依法缺席判决。

庭审当天，麦克经合法公告传唤，无正当理由拒不到庭，亦未提交任何答辩意见。我当庭完整呈现事实与法律依据，重点阐述男方的严重过错，以及贺女士因婚恋心智不成熟陷入困境、如今坚决寻求解脱的诉求，让法庭清晰看到这段婚姻的本质。

法院经审理，完全采纳我方全部代理意见，最终依法作出缺席判决：准予贺女士与麦克离婚。当判决生效的消息传来，贺女士红了眼眶。她没有再踏回美国一步，没有面对施暴者，没有承受任何额外的风险，便在自己的祖国，重获了自由与安宁。

案后结语

跨国婚姻并不是解决大龄婚恋焦虑的"捷径"，优秀的自身条件，更需要理性的婚恋判断来匹配。贺女士的经历，是许多大龄高知、心思单纯的女性婚恋困境的缩影——被催婚裹挟，因渴望归宿而降低了风险防范意识，最终陷入始料未及的伤害。

但法律永远是中国公民最坚实的依靠——只要你是中国公民，在国内有经常居住地，即便在国外结婚、外籍配偶失联拒离，中国法院依然可以管辖、可以送达、可以缺席判离。

作为专业婚姻家事律师，我处理过大量涉外离婚案件，深知当事人在异国伤害、跨境困境中的无助与恐惧。我的工作，就是用专业程序降低风险，用法律规则破除障碍，让当事人不必重返危险之地，就能安全、体面、稳妥地结束痛苦婚姻。

爱情不分国界，但婚姻需要理性。愿每一位优秀的女性，都能挣脱世俗的焦虑，守住理性的底线，在婚恋路上，不必将就，更不必因仓促而陷入深渊。而当不幸降临，法律始终跨越山海，守护着每一个寻求解脱的灵魂。

A Cross-Border Divorce: Breaking Free from the Cage of Transnational Marriage Built on Domestic Violence and Deception

Introduction

Beneath the romantic veil of cross-border marriage often lie cultural clashes, personality breakdowns, hidden information, and even violence and danger. When a marriage formed overseas becomes a prison, when the foreign husband disappears and refuses to divorce across vast oceans, how can the trapped party save herself? My client Ms. He, a beautiful, highly-educated yet innocent freelance illustrator, entered a transnational marriage at 38 under pressure to marry. She soon faced the cruel truth: domestic violence and a concealed bipolar disorder from her husband. After fleeing back to China in panic, she remained tied to this hollow marriage for four years. As a family lawyer, I used Chinese law as her shield. The entire case was processed within China, through public service of process and default judgment. She never had to step back into danger, yet completely broke free from that dark transnational marriage.

Ms. He was seen by everyone as an "elite woman": highly educated, a freelance illustrator with exquisite taste and delicate works, elegant and gentle. She was outstanding in both external conditions and internal qualities. Yet this excellence became a "shackle" in her love life. She had high standards for a partner and refused to compromise, always hoping for a soul-matching relationship. Before she knew it, she had passed society's "best marriage age." By 38, watching her peers settle down, her parents' gentle reminders turned into daily pressure, and relatives' concern became invisible stress. Immersed in creation and idealism, she was pure and inexperienced. Anxious about being unmarried at a later age, she gradually lost rational judgment.

Just then, Mike appeared in her online world. Mike was a head chef at a well-known local restaurant in the United States. He spoke wittily, described romantic life with words, and showered Ms. He with thoughtful attention across the ocean. He said he admired the gentleness of Eastern women and longed for a stable family life. Those well-timed sweet words hit her soft spot: she craved to be loved and to give her parents peace of mind. Caught in anxiety and attracted by the novelty of a cross-border romance, she completely ignored the information gap behind the screen. Mike deliberately hid his medical history of bipolar disorder, as well as his extreme emotions and poor self-control. These truths, enough to lay hidden dangers for any marriage, were perfectly covered by his romantic image.

Urged by Mike's repeated invitations and promises of "lifelong companionship," Ms. He, filled with longing for marriage, ignored her faint unease and traveled alone to the US. They soon registered their marriage there and formally became husband and wife. She thought she had finally found a home. Little did she know, this hasty transnational marriage was cloaked in deception and concealment from the very beginning.

After living together, huge cultural differences, conflicting lifestyles, and fundamentally incompatible values set off constant conflicts. What truly pushed Ms. He into the abyss of fear was Mike's true face once he dropped his disguise. Extreme mood swings caused by bipolar disorder made him sometimes agitated and violent, sometimes depressed and gloomy. He began to frequently commit domestic violence against her. Shoving, verbal abuse, threats, and even physical violence were constantly staged in that small foreign apartment. As a sensitive freelance illustrator, she tried to understand and tolerate his emotions, only to receive escalating harm.

Unable to speak the language and with no relatives nearby, Ms. He lived in constant terror and unease all day. After one severe domestic violence incident, she struggled free with all her strength and begged her neighbor for help. The neighbor called the police immediately. US officers responded, issued a reprimand to Mike, and imposed corresponding legal penalties. During that time, Ms. He was full of despair and only wanted to escape. Yet moved by Mike's tearful confessions and sworn guarantees, she, being soft-hearted, was held back by the obsession of "a marriage encountered after years of waiting" and chose to temporarily forgive him, naively believing he would truly repent.

She did not know that emotional outbursts and violent tendencies caused by bipolar disorder would not easily change at all. The brief calm was followed by deeper control and harm. This marriage had long become a dark cage, pushing this pure and excellent freelance illustrator to the brink of collapse. Unable to endure any longer, Ms. He packed her bags desperately and fled back to China in panic late one night. That departure lasted four years.

After returning to China, Ms. He finally woke up from her anxiety and obsession and resolved to end this marriage filled with harm, deception, and violence. She contacted Mike multiple times via email and social media, clearly requesting a divorce, but he remained indifferent and unresponsive, as if the marriage had only been a tool to trap her. Four years of separation, four years of struggle. Ms. He picked up her paintbrush again, focused on creation, and tried to heal, yet she remained legally bound by a marriage registered in the United States. She dared not step back into the US — it held traumatic memories she refused to revisit, and Mike, who might commit violence again at any time. The unfamiliar, language-barriered environment would only leave her isolated and helpless once more.

"Can I get a divorce right here in China without going back to the US?" Sitting in my office, her former gentleness gone, Ms. He's eyes showed only exhaustion and unease after being delayed for four years.

After hearing her story, I felt deep sympathy for her experience and told her firmly: Absolutely you can. Even if you registered your marriage in the United States, as a Chinese citizen, you have the right to sue for divorce in China. Under China's Civil Procedure Law and judicial interpretations, where one Chinese citizen resides in China, the people's court of the domestic party's domicile has jurisdiction regardless of where the marriage was solemnized. The other party's disappearance, refusal to cooperate, and residence overseas are not insurmountable barriers.

After accepting the mandate, I immediately launched a cross-border divorce process handled entirely by domestic courts for Ms. He, proceeding step by step to form a systematic legal chain:

First, confirm the competent court and file the divorce lawsuit at the people's court of her habitual residence in accordance with the law.

Second, standardize the formalities for overseas evidence: notarization, authentication, and Chinese translation of the US marriage certificate and police domestic violence reprimand records, to meet the evidentiary requirements of domestic courts for foreign-related cases.

Third, fully organize key facts: evidence of four years of separation, communication records of Ms. He repeatedly proposing divorce, and supporting evidence of Mike's domestic violence and concealment of his bipolar disorder history, fully demonstrating the irretrievable breakdown of the marriage with no possibility of reconciliation.

Fourth, initiate foreign-related service procedures according to law. Since direct contact and mail service failed, I applied to the court for foreign-related public notice service, completing the service of the complaint and hearing documents in accordance with legal procedures.

Fifth, strictly prepare a trial strategy, clearly stating to the court: Ms. He hastily entered a transnational marriage due to anxiety over late-marriage pressure; post-marriage, she discovered the husband had serious faults including domestic violence and concealing a major mental illness history; the parties had separated for as long as four years; the marital relationship was already dead in name and fact, satisfying the statutory conditions for divorce. We requested the court to grant a default judgment according to law.

On the trial date, Mike, having been legally summoned by public notice, failed to appear without just cause and submitted no defense opinions. I presented all facts and legal bases in full in court, emphasizing the husband's serious faults and Ms. He's sincere request for freedom after being trapped due to immature romantic judgment, allowing the court to clearly see the essence of this marriage.

After hearing the case, the court fully accepted all our agent's opinions and ultimately rendered a default judgment according to law: The divorce between Ms. He and Mike is granted. When the news of the judgment taking effect came, Ms. He's eyes turned red. Without stepping back into the US, without facing her abuser, and without bearing any additional risks, she regained her freedom and peace in her own motherland.

Post-Case Conclusion

Transnational marriage is never a "shortcut" to relieve anxiety about late marriage. Outstanding personal qualities require rational romantic judgment to match. Ms. He's story reflects the plight of many highly educated, pure-hearted women: pressured into marriage, lowering their risk prevention awareness because of a longing for a home, and finally falling into unexpected harm.

But the law is always the most solid support for Chinese citizens. As long as you are a Chinese citizen with a habitual residence in China, even if you married abroad and your foreign spouse disappears and refuses to divorce, Chinese courts can still exercise jurisdiction, serve process, and grant divorce by default.

As a professional family lawyer, I have handled numerous foreign-related divorce cases. I deeply understand the helplessness and fear of clients suffering harm in foreign countries and trapped in cross-border dilemmas. My job is to reduce risks through professional procedures, remove barriers through legal rules, and allow clients to end a painful marriage safely, decently, and securely — without having to return to a dangerous place.

Love knows no borders, but marriage requires rationality. May every outstanding woman break free from secular anxiety, uphold the bottom line of rationality, and never settle or rush into an abyss on the road of love and marriage. And when misfortune comes, the law always crosses mountains and seas to protect every soul seeking liberation.

糟糠之妻焉能弃

引言

十五年后，我还清楚地记得那个案件的点点滴滴，那是我执业最初经办的第一个离婚案件，也是第一个令我因目睹当事人的遭遇而悲恸落泪的案件。十五年后，我在人民路上偶遇年逾80高龄的秀姐，她拎着一个篮子，缓步走来，篮子里面露出青菜和茄子。我看见她，分外惊喜，我说："秀姐，是我。"她认出我："哎呀，叶律师，怎么是你，你还好吗？你没变啊，这些年我经常想起你啊，快到我家坐坐。"我说："你现在还自己出来买菜吗？"她说："是啊，孙子上大学回来住在我这里，我要照顾孙子。"然后我说："老耀还好吗？"她默然片刻道："去年就走了。临终前，我守着他。叶律师，他说他对不起我，他这一辈子最对不起的人就是我。"

原告秀姐 50 年代中期在某市政协委员会工作。1956 年 6 月秀姐因工作关系与当时在该市某兵团服役的被告老耀相识，双方经自由恋爱于同年 12 月在老耀的部队举行了简朴的婚礼并领取结婚证书。婚后，双方相敬如宾，夫妻感情真挚笃实。次年，老耀调任外省部队任职，秀姐作为随军家属亦跟随老耀来到该市过着颠沛波折的行军生活。双方于同年 8 月 27 日生育长女红，期间秀姐将自己的母亲接至身边一起生活。1959 年又生育长子军，1962 年 5 月 27 日生育次子强。1972 年老耀转业回家乡，分配在市某国有工厂工作，一家六口遂结束部队生活迁至该地稳定下来，秀姐就职于当地某银行工作。尽管当时生活比较清苦，但秀姐和老耀却能相濡以沫，和睦共处。

然而，和美的婚姻生活在 90 年代初出现了转折。1990 年，老耀退休之后下海经商，专营钢材买卖。在生意来往中结识了一位叫阿萍的女人，双方交往日益密切，最后发展至暗中保持不正当关系。半年后，此事终于被秀姐发觉，由此两人发生争吵。老耀见秀姐激愤难抑，便顾自携带阿萍去往外地游玩。一个月后，老耀来信称钱已花光，请求家人支援，长子遂赴外地将其带回。之后，通过单位领导、居委会干部、子女等人做工作，老耀有所悔悟，表示不再重犯，并由那名女子写下保证书。秀姐念在几十年的夫妻情分上亦原谅了老耀。

第二年开春，老耀不慎将右腿严重摔伤，卧床治疗了三年，康复后又在家休养了二年多。期间，秀姐任劳任怨、体贴入微的服侍老耀。伤愈后，老耀供职新单位。1999 年 7 月间，老耀在负责市区某地段拆迁工作中与一名拆迁户——一位 40 多岁的离异女子阿玲认识。不久两人频繁往来，关系暧昧。期间，老耀帮助阿玲装修新房，搬家迁居。同年年底，老耀重蹈覆辙，屡屡在外留宿，且对秀姐的态度明显转变，漠然不理。秀姐为此非常伤心，与之理论，却反遭谩骂，夫妻感情严重受挫。

2003 年 3 月的一天晚上，秀姐和老耀又因老耀外遇一事发生争执。争吵间，老耀竟对 60 多岁的秀姐大打出手，秀姐被打得双眼肿胀。次日，老耀全然不顾，离家而去。老耀这一走就是两个月。事后，经双方子女、老耀的单位出面调解，老耀才于同年 5 月 7 日搬回家。但此后，老耀却继续与阿玲私下往来，并屡次向秀姐提出离婚。秀姐不允，老耀则说："你已经老了，我对你早已没有感情了，你不要再勉强我！"令秀姐万分痛心。

2005 年 6 月，秀姐不甘心几十年的夫妻就这样破裂，再次恳求老耀回心转意，但丈夫断然拒绝，且言语更加荒谬、态度更加恶劣，甚至秀姐卧病在床亦不闻不问，双方已然貌合神离。7 月，老耀为能自由"活动"、不受干涉，遂书写了一张所谓的"分居调解书"强迫秀姐签字信守。秀姐此时对他已经心灰意冷，于是提出离婚，老耀表示同意，并拿出身份证让秀姐去办手续。

秀姐辗转找到我来承办这件案子。基于双方当事人就离婚意志达成一致，因此案情本来并不复杂，然而在离婚诉讼过程中，老耀却公然将阿玲带回家里，这激起了秀姐长期压抑的愤怒，秀姐喝令老耀马上带阿玲离开，老耀却当着阿玲的面将秀姐暴打一顿。厮打中，秀姐从楼梯上摔了下来，当场昏迷。当我接到医院的电话赶到病房时，老耀已不知所踪，秀姐独自躺在病床上，身体衰弱，神情痛苦。

"叶律师，我已经对他彻底绝望了！"六十多岁的秀姐，经历了人生无数沧桑，本应安享晚年，此时却被风雨同舟数十年的丈夫打得鼻青脸肿，卧床不起。她凄惨的遭遇令我愤慨，我告诉秀姐，老耀的行为已经构成家庭暴力、故意伤害，并具有婚外出轨事实，具有离婚过错责任，她完全有权利提出赔偿请求，为自己争取应有的尊严。秀姐坚定地点了点头。

此后，在法庭上，我们提出："原、被告的婚姻虽则历经了四十多年的风风雨雨，彼此在共同生活中建立了比较深厚的夫妻感情，但在婚姻生活的后期，由于被告喜新厌旧、绝情抛弃，致使原告忍无可忍，双方矛盾日益尖锐。最终，被告为能堂而皇之地维持婚外姘居，竟向原告全数摊牌，并以种种恶语对之进行刺激，使得原告心力交瘁，夫妻感情遭致破裂。原告幼年丧父、母亲改嫁，由一位阿姨辛苦带大，饱受生活的磨难。婚后随被告来温后，一直把被告当作唯一的依靠，生活上给予全心的关爱，希望能相扶到终老。然而被告晚节不保，抛却糟糠之妻，对原告实施家庭暴力，致使原告身心受到极大的伤害。因此，请求法庭判令准予离婚，并要求被告给予原告精神损害赔偿。"

心力交瘁的秀姐，原本只想把婚离掉，没有其他多余的想法，然而在离婚诉讼期间遭遇老耀的暴力伤害，让她几十年来所受的委屈和痛苦一并迸发，她把老耀以往所有的保证书、承诺书、调解书等统统呈上法庭，她要让法庭彻底看清老耀在这个婚姻中所作的一切，并提出老耀构成婚姻法规定之"有配偶者与他人同居"行为。老耀百般争辩，特别针对"有配偶者与他人同居"，认为自己只是偶尔在其他女人处留宿，并不构成婚姻法意义上的婚外同居行为。对此，我当庭提出观点认为，《中华人民共和国婚姻法》第三条规定，禁止有配偶者与他人同居。这一规定进一步明确了婚姻法中的一夫一妻制及夫妻相互忠诚的义务。什么是有配偶者与他人同居呢？依据最高人民法院关于《婚姻法司法解释（一）》第二条规定，有配偶者与他人同居是指有配偶者与婚外异性，不以夫妻名义，持续、稳定地共同居住。需要特别指出的是，这里的共同居住并不等同于共同居所，这是两个不同的概念，共同居住强调的是共同居住或生活在一起，而共同居所则表示双方有共同的住所。根据司法判例，法院认定的"持续、稳定"通常为共同生活的时间达到三个月以上。但同居时间的长短并不能作为唯一衡量的标准，应将双方同居前存有的不正当关系的稳定程度、双方的主观追求，以及与那些偶然的、无固定场所的通奸、姘居关系进行比较等诸多因素综合起来考虑。本案老耀在婚姻存续期间先后与数名有名有姓的女子共同生活，最长的一次在该女子家中居住长达半年之久，且有该女子书写的保证书为据。因此，老耀已经构成婚外同居行为，以及家庭暴力行为。根据《婚姻法》第四十六条规定，有下列情形之一，导致离婚的，无过错方有权请求损害赔偿：……（二）有配偶者与他人同居的；（三）实施家庭暴力的……"法庭采信了我们的证据和观点，最终，通过调解工作，老耀同意给予秀姐精神损害赔偿。

案子结束了，然而年近七十古稀的秀姐和老耀的故事还在各自的轨道上发展。我没有料到，老耀怀着对秀姐今生难言的愧疚离世，没能获得糟糠之妻的原谅，成为他永远无法弥补的遗憾。

案后结语

"执子之手，与子偕老"，青春夫妻老来相伴的温馨画面并不都是那么和谐的存在，有相濡以沫、恩爱白头的夫妻，也有很多夫或妻在岁月磨折中渐渐厌恶了对方，甚至不惜伤害对方，折磨对方，离开对方。步入老年的老人企求朝夕厮守的老伴能给予精神依托和生活照料，这是其他亲属所不能替代的。当一方因生理变化或发生某些意外而产生烦恼和苦闷时，另一方的心理"搀扶"和生活护理，都会使对方从精神上得到慰藉。然而，如果婚姻真正变成一厢情愿，学会适时放手仍不失明智之举。毕竟，过好自己的生活，比陷入形同地狱的婚姻里苟延残喘，无论如何都是更有生命的意义和价值的。

A Wife Who Shared Hard Times Should Never Be Forsaken

Introduction

Fifteen years later, I still clearly remember every detail of that case. It was the first divorce case I handled at the very beginning of my legal career, and also the first time I wept bitterly after witnessing what my client had suffered. Fifteen years later, I ran into Sister Xiu, who was already over eighty, on Renmin Road. She was walking slowly with a basket, with green vegetables and eggplants sticking out of it. I was overjoyed to see her and said, "Sister Xiu, it's me." She recognized me at once: "Oh, Lawyer Rachel J. Ye! Fancy seeing you! How have you been? You haven't changed a bit. I've often thought of you all these years. Come to my place for a visit." I asked, "Do you still go grocery shopping by yourself?" She said, "Yes. My grandson is home from college and staying with me, so I have to take care of him." Then I asked, "How is Lao Yao?" She fell silent for a moment and said: "He passed away last year. I stayed by his side until his last breath. Lawyer Rachel J. Ye, he said he was sorry to me. The person he had wronged most in his entire life was me."

The plaintiff, Sister Xiu, worked for a Chinese People's Political Consultative Conference (CPPCC) committee in a city in the mid-1950s. In June 1956, she met the defendant, Lao Yao, who was serving in a corps in the same city due to work. They fell in love freely and held a simple wedding at Lao Yao's military unit in December of the same year, registering their marriage legally. After marriage, they treated each other with respect, and their relationship was sincere and deep. The following year, Lao Yao was transferred to a military unit in another province, and Sister Xiu, as a military dependent, followed him, living a nomadic, unstable military life. On August 27 of the same year, they had their eldest daughter, Hong. During this time, Sister Xiu brought her own mother to live with them. They had their eldest son, Jun, in 1959, and their second son, Qiang, on May 27, 1962. In 1972, Lao Yao was transferred to civilian work in his hometown and assigned to a state-owned factory. The family of six finally ended their military life and settled down stably. Sister Xiu worked at a local bank. Although life was hard at that time, Sister Xiu and Lao Yao supported each other through thick and thin and lived in harmony.

However, their happy marriage took a turn in the early 1990s. After retiring in 1990, Lao Yao went into business, specializing in steel trading. In his business dealings, he met a woman named A Ping. They grew closer and eventually developed an improper secret relationship. Half a year later, Sister Xiu discovered the affair, and quarrels broke out between them. Unable to calm Sister Xiu's anger, Lao Yao left with A Ping to travel elsewhere. A month later, Lao Yao sent a letter saying he had run out of money and asked his family for help. Their eldest son went to bring him back. Later, through mediation by leaders of his work unit, neighborhood committee cadres, and their children, Lao Yao showed some remorse and promised not to repeat the mistake. The woman also wrote a guarantee letter. Out of decades of marital affection, Sister Xiu forgave him.

The next spring, Lao Yao seriously injured his right leg in an accident and was bedridden for three years, recovering at home for more than two years after that. During this period, Sister Xiu served him patiently and attentively without complaint. After his recovery, Lao Yao worked in a new unit. In July 1999, while in charge of demolition work in a downtown area, he met A Ling, a divorced woman in her forties whose house was being demolished. Soon they began frequenting each other and had an ambiguous relationship. Lao Yao helped A Ling renovate her new house and move. At the end of the same year, Lao Yao fell back into old habits: he often stayed out overnight, and his attitude toward Sister Xiu turned cold and indifferent. Sister Xiu was heartbroken and confronted him, only to be met with insults. Their relationship was severely damaged.

One night in March 2003, they quarreled again over Lao Yao's affair. During the argument, Lao Yao actually beat Sister Xiu, who was in her sixties, leaving her eyes swollen. The next day, Lao Yao left home without any regard for her. He was gone for two months. Later, through mediation by their children and Lao Yao's work unit, he returned home on May 7 of the same year. But afterward, he continued seeing A Ling in secret and repeatedly asked Sister Xiu for a divorce. When she refused, Lao Yao said: "You're old now. I haven't had any feelings for you for a long time. Stop forcing me!" This broke Sister Xiu's heart.

In June 2005, unwilling to see their decades-long marriage fall apart, Sister Xiu begged Lao Yao to change his mind again. But her husband refused firmly, speaking more absurdly and behaving more harshly. He even ignored her when she was ill in bed. They were only married in name. In July, to "live freely" without interference, Lao Yao wrote a so-called "separation mediation agreement" and forced Sister Xiu to sign it. By then, Sister Xiu had completely lost hope in him, so she filed for divorce. Lao Yao agreed and gave her his ID card to go through the procedures.

Sister Xiu came to me to handle the case. Since both parties agreed to the divorce, the case should not have been complicated. However, during the divorce proceedings, Lao Yao openly brought A Ling home. This ignited Sister Xiu's long-suppressed anger. She ordered Lao Yao to take A Ling away immediately, but Lao Yao beat her violently in front of A Ling. During the struggle, Sister Xiu fell down the stairs and fell unconscious on the spot. When I received a call from the hospital and rushed to the ward, Lao Yao had disappeared. Sister Xiu lay alone in bed, weak and in great pain.

"Lawyer Rachel J. Ye, I have completely despaired of him!" Sister Xiu, in her sixties, had gone through countless hardships in life and deserved to enjoy her later years. Instead, she was beaten black and blue by the husband who had shared weal and woe with her for decades and was confined to bed. Her miserable experience filled me with indignation. I told Sister Xiu that Lao Yao's acts constituted domestic violence and intentional injury, and he was the at-fault party in the divorce due to his extramarital affairs. She had every right to claim compensation and defend her dignity. Sister Xiu nodded firmly.

Thereafter, we argued in court: "Although the marriage between the plaintiff and the defendant has gone through more than 40 years of ups and downs, and they had built a deep marital relationship, in the later stage of the marriage, the defendant abandoned the plaintiff for a new love, leaving the plaintiff with no alternative but to endure. The conflicts between them became increasingly acute. Eventually, to openly maintain an extramarital cohabitation, the defendant laid all his cards on the table, provoked the plaintiff with vicious words, and broke her heart, leading to the breakdown of the marriage. The plaintiff lost her father at a young age, her mother remarried, and she was raised by an aunt through great hardships. After moving to Wenzhou with the defendant after marriage, she regarded him as her only support, loved him wholeheartedly, and hoped to grow old together with him. However, the defendant failed to keep his moral integrity in old age, abandoned his wife who had shared his bitter days, and committed domestic violence against the plaintiff, causing severe physical and mental harm to her. Therefore, we request the court to grant a divorce and order the defendant to pay compensation for mental distress to the plaintiff."

Exhausted, Sister Xiu originally only wanted a divorce with no other demands. But the violent assault by Lao Yao during the proceedings released all the grievances and pain she had endured for decades. She submitted all of Lao Yao's previous guarantee letters, promises, and mediation agreements to the court, laying bare everything he had done in the marriage, and raised that Lao Yao's conduct constituted "cohabitation with another person while being married" as defined by the Marriage Law. Lao Yao argued vehemently, especially regarding "cohabitation with another person while being married," claiming that he only occasionally stayed overnight at other women's places and did not constitute extramarital cohabitation under the Marriage Law. In response to this, I countered in court: Article 3 of the Marriage Law of the People's Republic of China prohibits cohabitation with another person while being married. This provision further clarifies the monogamous system and the duty of mutual loyalty between spouses. What is cohabitation with another person while being married? According to Article 2 of the Judicial Interpretation of the Marriage Law (I) by the Supreme People's Court, cohabitation with another person while being married refers to a married person cohabiting continuously and stably with a person of the opposite sex who is not his or her spouse, not in the name of husband and wife. Notably, "cohabitation" is not equivalent to "shared residence." They are two different concepts; cohabitation emphasizes living together, while shared residence means having a common home. According to judicial precedents, "continuous and stable" usually means living together for more than three months. However, duration is not the only criterion; the court should comprehensively consider factors such as the stability of the improper relationship before cohabitation, the subjective intentions of both parties, and the comparison with casual adultery or cohabitation without a fixed place. In this case, during the marriage, Lao Yao lived with several named women one after another, staying at one woman's home for as long as half a year, supported by her written guarantee. Therefore, Lao Yao has constituted extramarital cohabitation and domestic violence. Pursuant to Article 46 of the Marriage Law, a no-fault party has the right to claim compensation for damages if the divorce results from one of the following circumstances: ... (2) cohabitation with another person while being married; (3) domestic violence..." The court accepted our evidence and arguments. Eventually, through mediation, Lao Yao agreed to pay Sister Xiu compensation for mental distress.

The case was closed, but the stories of Sister Xiu and Lao Yao, both nearly seventy, continued on their separate paths. I never expected that Lao Yao would die with unspeakable guilt toward Sister Xiu in this life, never obtaining forgiveness from the wife who had shared his poverty and hardships—becoming a regret he could never make up for.

Post-Case Conclusion

"Take my hand, and we shall grow old together." The warm picture of young lovers growing old side by side does not always exist harmoniously. Some couples support each other and stay loving until old age, while many gradually grow tired of each other over the years, even harming, torturing, and leaving one another. Elderly people stepping into their twilight years long for the spiritual support and daily care that only a lifelong spouse can provide—something no other relative can replace. When one side suffers from physical changes or unexpected troubles, the other's emotional support and care bring spiritual comfort. However, if a marriage truly becomes one-sided, letting go at the right time is still a wise choice. After all, living one's own life well is far more meaningful and valuable than lingering in a hellish marriage.

Photograph by Joseph Xu

CHAPTER 4 | SLOTH

第四章 | 懒惰

引文

"世上最可怕的不是距离，而是忽视；不是岁月，而是冷漠。"

—— 林清玄

懒惰是婚姻里最沉默、最致命的杀手，它来自行为上的懈怠，更来自情感上的冷漠、经营上的缺位、沟通上的荒芜、责任上的逃避。在很多婚姻里，虽没有激烈的争吵、背叛或贫穷，但日复一日的漠视：不愿倾听，不愿改变，不愿修复，不愿成长，直至让伴侣心冷心寒、绝望离去。

夫妻在沉默中渐行渐远，亲情在忽略中慢慢变淡，问题在拖延中层层堆积，直到一切变得无可挽回。在抚养权纠纷、夫妻关系破裂、家族事务混乱的大量案件背后，我总能清晰看见"精神懒惰"的影子：懒得沟通，懒得负责，懒得解决，懒得执行。人们总以为关系会永远稳固，却忘了婚姻不是一劳永逸的归宿，而是日复一日的用心修行；亲情不是天生不变的联结，而是需要长期浇灌的花朵。

法律确实能正式结束一段关系，却无法替代发自内心的经营与陪伴；可以公平裁定结果，却无法弥补长久缺席的关怀与温暖。唯有以热忱对抗冷漠，以坚守对抗懈怠，以责任对抗逃避，爱才有归处，家才有温度，人生才有真正的圆满。

Epigraph

"The most terrifying thing in the world is not distance, but neglect; not years, but indifference."

— Lin Qingxuan

Sloth is the quietest and deadliest killer in marriage. It stems from physical idleness, and even more from emotional coldness, lack of nurturing, barren communication and avoidance of responsibility. In many marriages, there are no fierce quarrels, betrayal or poverty, only day-to-day neglect: unwillingness to listen, to change, to repair, to grow, until a partner's heart turns cold and leaves in despair.

Couples drift apart in silence; family affection fades through neglect; problems pile up in delay until everything becomes irreparable. Behind numerous cases of custody disputes, marital breakdown and disordered family affairs, I can always clearly see the shadow of "spiritual sloth": too lazy to communicate, to take responsibility, to solve problems, to follow through. People often assume relationships will last forever, forgetting that marriage is never a once-and-for-all destination, but a daily practice requiring care; family bonds are not innate and unchanging, but flowers that need long-term nurturing.

The law can formally end a relationship, yet cannot replace genuine devotion and companionship; it can rule fairly, yet cannot make up for long-absent care and warmth. Only by opposing coldness with enthusiasm, idleness with perseverance, and avoidance with responsibility can love find a home, family retain warmth, and life achieve true fulfillment.

罗马抉择，抢在窗口期的“快进”离婚

引言

跨境婚姻的终局，有时不是情感的拉锯，而是现实利益的竞速。当意大利的“法定分居期”撞上国内创业的“黄金窗口期”，我的当事人陈景明站在了两难的十字路口：一边是筹备数年的商业布局，一边是异国法律设定的离婚诉讼半年等待期。这一次，我没有沿用常规的程序抗辩，而是以国际私法的法律适用规则为核心，将中国法律的效率优势嵌入意大利的裁判体系，用28天的极速办结，为他的事业蓝图扫清了婚姻的法律羁绊。

我的当事人陈景明，40 岁，身上带有温州商人特有的敏锐与果决。他从意大利匆匆赶回国内，出现在我律所的会客室里，手里拿着一个厚厚的牛皮纸文件袋。里面装着的，不仅是他离婚案件的资料，更重要的，是一整套国内高端服装供应链的投资方案、合作框架协议，还有长三角跨境电商园区的入驻批复。

他拿出材料，向我叙述了他的婚姻历程和当下碰到的棘手难题。十二年前，他跟随亲友移民意大利。在罗马的十二年里，他把一家中式服装批发店，做成了服务当地高端买手店的供应商，手里攒下的，是实打实的行业资源与资本。2016 年的罗马时装周，他为了找本土设计师合作，结识了 38 岁的索菲亚。

索菲亚是土生土长的罗马人，供职于当地一家老牌设计师工作室，她的设计里有地中海的热烈，也有对东方元素的好奇。两人的相识，始于这场时装周里一次面料展的洽谈，陈景明欣赏她的设计张力，索菲亚佩服他的商业头脑。那段时间，陈景明的公寓里，总能看到一半是面料样本，一半是红酒杯的画面。他们在台伯河畔的餐厅定情，在市政厅的大理石走廊里登记，所有人都以为，这是一场商业与艺术的完美结合。

可婚姻的底色，终究藏在日常的褶皱里。陈景明的生活，是“订单、物流、现金流”的闭环，他习惯凌晨复盘账目，周末跑面料工厂；索菲亚的生活，是“灵感、展览、下午茶”的节奏，她可以为了一个设计细节泡在美术馆一整天，也会为了朋友的生日派对，临时取消和陈景明的约定。

两人最明显的分歧，出现在财务观念上。陈景明想把两人的收入合并，扩大仓库规模；索菲亚却坚持“财产独立”，甚至不愿在陈景明的生意里挂名。有一次，陈景明拿下了一个重要的欧洲品牌代理，想让索菲亚帮忙设计联名款，索菲亚却直接拒绝：“我的设计是我的，你的生意是你的，我们不该混为一谈。”

这句话，成了两人婚姻的分水岭。从那以后，他们依旧住在同一栋公寓里，却分了房间，分了账单，甚至连冰箱里的食材都分得清清楚楚。没有争吵，没有冷战，只有一种近乎冷漠的“相敬如宾”。这种状态持续了五年，直到 2023 年春天，陈景明收到了国内的招商邀请函。

那是一个足以改变他事业轨迹的机会——长三角跨境电商园区推出专项扶持，针对海外服装供应链企业，给出了税收减免、仓储补贴、渠道对接的三重利好。陈景明敏锐地意识到，这是他“班师回国”的最佳时机。他用三个月时间，敲定了合作工厂，谈妥了电商平台的入驻，甚至连团队核心成员都已就位。

一切准备就绪，但面对与索菲亚的婚姻，陈景明突然冷静了下来。他坦言，他和索菲亚的婚姻已经名存实亡，只是两人一直没有主动提出去办理离婚。而他一旦在婚姻存续期间回国启动项目，即便投资款全部来自他的个人财产，但项目运营产生的收益，也极有可能被认定为夫妻共同财产。索菲亚虽对他的生意不感兴趣，但意大利法律对“婚内收益”的界定极为宽泛，如果未来产生纠纷，他数年的筹备，很可能要被分割走一半。

陈景明找到索菲亚，坦诚地提出了离婚诉求。出乎意料，索菲亚并没有提出异议，她早已习惯了独立的生活，同意与陈景明离婚，双方也没有共同房产和共同债务，各自的生意与收入归各自所有。就在陈景明以为“好聚好散”触手可及时，索菲亚的律师却抛出了意大利法律的“硬规定”：根据《意大利民法典》第151条，即便双方自愿离婚，也必须先行分居，且分居时长不得少于6个月。分居期间，双方需保持独立居住、独立生活的状态，期满后，法院才会受理离婚申请。

分居六个月后才能离婚，意味着还得等六个月之后，他才能启动投资项目，从而与婚内财产相隔离。但这对陈景明而言，意味着错过招商扶持的截止日期，意味着合作工厂的解约，意味着整个项目的搁置。“叶律师，窗口期就像花期，错过了，再等就是下一个轮回。”陈景明的手指划过投资协议上的“生效日期”，语气里是前所未有的急迫。这就是他此行最主要的难题。

我没有急于给出方案，而是先让团队梳理了两个核心问题：第一，意大利法院是否允许当事人选择适用外国法律？第二，中国法律对自愿离婚的程序要求，能否成为突破分居期的关键？

围绕核心和焦点，我们找到了破局的关键——《意大利国际私法法典》第30条的规定：“离婚与别居案件，可适用夫妻双方的本国法；若夫妻国籍不同，可适用共同住所地法，也可由法院根据当事人申请，适用其中一方的本国法。”

这一条，就是打开僵局的钥匙。作为中国公民，陈景明的“本国法”是《中华人民共和国民法典》。而根据中国法律，夫妻双方自愿离婚的，签订书面离婚协议后，即可向婚姻登记机关申请离婚登记，不存在任何“法定分居期”的前置要求。我们的核心策略，就是向意大利法院申请，本案适用中国法律进行裁判。

接下来的工作，是一场精准的“法律翻译”与“程序对接”。我没有采用常规的律师函沟通，而是选择了更具说服力的法律意见书 + 证据组合的方式：

首先，我们帮助陈景明起草了一份《法律适用申请意见书》。不同于以往的文书，这份意见书没有过多赘述情感破裂的事实，而是聚焦于“法律适用的合理性”与“当事人的利益保护”。我在其中明确指出：本案双方对离婚及财产分割无任何争议，适用中国法律，符合双方自愿离婚的意愿，契合“效率与公平”的国际裁判原则。

其次，为了确保程序无缝衔接，我联系了罗马的合作律师马可。马可深耕家事法律多年，由他担任陈景明罗马离婚案的代理律师，负责与承办法官进行书面沟通，提前阐释中国法律的核心规则，避免法官因不熟悉中国法律而产生疑虑。

庭审的那天，采用了视频连线的方式。陈景明在国内我律所的视频会议室，马可在罗马法院的法庭里。法官的提问很直接：“为何不适用意大利法律？”陈景明和马可按照我们既定的方案清晰地回应：“法官阁下，本案的核心争议并非‘是否离婚’，而是‘以何种程序离婚’。双方已就离婚及财产分割达成完全一致，意大利的分居期制度，在此案中已无适用的必要。适用中国法律，既能快速解决当事人的婚姻问题，也能避免其因程序拖延而遭受不必要的商业损失，这与意大利法律追求的‘实质正义’完全一致。”

索菲亚的律师也提交了她的书面声明，表示同意陈景明和马可律师讲述的事实和意见。马可也提交了陈景明准备的商业证据。法官沉默了片刻，翻阅着手中的材料，最终敲下了法槌：“准予申请人的请求，本案适用中华人民共和国法律审理。”

接下来的流程，如同按下了“快进键”。根据中国法律的精神，意大利法院对双方的离婚合意进行了确认，对财产分割清单进行了审核。28 天后，陈景明收到了由罗马法院出具的离婚判决书。判决书的核心条款，与我们起草的离婚协议完全一致：准予离婚，双方财产各自所有，互不干预。

拿到判决书的当天，陈景明就带着团队进驻了长三角的跨境电商园区。他的服装供应链项目，如期启动。那年年底，他的品牌在国内电商平台创下了千万级的销售额。他给我寄来了一份产品手册，扉页上写着：“感谢叶律师，为我的事业，守住了最重要的窗口期。”

案后结语

陈景明的案件，是跨境家事法律实务中，"法律适用策略"的典型范本。它打破了一个常见的误区：涉外离婚，并非只能被动适用婚姻缔结地的法律。

在这个案件中，我们没有将重点放在"情感破裂"的事实陈述上，而是转向了"法律适用的价值判断"——当异国法律的程序规则，与当事人的现实利益产生冲突时，专业律师的职责，是在国际私法的框架内，为当事人寻找最契合其需求的法律规则。虽然作为中国律师，我们并不能直接担任陈景明在罗马离婚案的代理人，但我们依然为他的案件提供了不可替代的价值。

对陈景明而言，这场离婚的意义，不仅是结束一段名存实亡的婚姻，更为他的事业蓝图，划定了清晰的法律边界。而对我而言，这个案件也再次印证：家事法律的服务，并不是单一的"离婚维权"，而是结合当事人的人生规划、事业发展，提供全方位的法律解决方案。法律的生命力，在于解决问题。当跨境婚姻遇上人生机遇，专业的法律策略，就是那把能同时打开"离婚之门"与"事业之门"的钥匙。

A Choice in Rome: Fast-Track Divorce Within a Critical Window

Introduction

The end of a cross-border marriage is sometimes not a battle of emotions, but a race for practical interests. When Italy's statutory separation period collided with a golden window for domestic entrepreneurship in China, my client Chen Jingming stood at a crossroads: on one side, a business layout years in the making; on the other, a six-month waiting period for divorce under foreign law. This time, instead of using ordinary procedural defenses, I focused on the conflict of laws rules in private international law, integrating the efficiency advantage of Chinese law into the Italian judicial system. With a swift conclusion in just 28 days, I cleared the legal marital barrier for his career blueprint.

The end of a cross-border marriage is sometimes not a battle of emotions, but a race for practical interests. When Italy's statutory separation period collided with a golden window for domestic entrepreneurship in China, my client Chen Jingming stood at a crossroads: on one side, a business layout years in the making; on the other, a six-month waiting period for divorce under foreign law. This time, instead of using ordinary procedural defenses, I focused on the conflict of laws rules in private international law, integrating the efficiency advantage of Chinese law into the Italian judicial system. With a swift conclusion in just 28 days, I cleared the legal marital barrier for his career blueprint.

My client Chen Jingming, 40, carries the typical sharpness and decisiveness of a Wenzhou merchant. He rushed back from Italy to my firm, holding a thick kraft paper file bag. Inside were not only his divorce materials but, more importantly, a full set of investment plans for a high-end apparel supply chain, framework cooperation agreements, and approval for entry into the Yangtze River Delta Cross-Border E-Commerce Park.

He laid out the documents and told me his marital story and the urgent dilemma he now faced. Twelve years ago, he emigrated to Italy with relatives. During those twelve years in Rome, he grew a small Chinese clothing wholesale shop into a supplier for local high-end boutiques, building solid industry connections and capital. At Rome Fashion Week in 2016, he met Sofia, 38, while seeking local designers to collaborate with.

Sofia was a native Roman, working at a long-established design studio.

Her designs blended Mediterranean passion with curiosity about Eastern elements. They met during a fabric exhibition at the fashion week. Chen admired her creative energy; Sofia respected his business acumen. During that period, his apartment was always half-filled with fabric samples and half with wine glasses. They pledged their love at a restaurant by the Tiber River and registered their marriage in the marble corridors of the city hall. Everyone thought it was a perfect union of business and art.

Yet the true nature of a marriage lies in the details of daily life. Chen Jingming's world revolved around orders, logistics, and cash flow. He was used to reviewing accounts in the early hours and visiting fabric factories on weekends. Sofia's rhythm was inspiration, exhibitions, and afternoon tea. She could spend an entire day in an art gallery over a single design detail, or cancel plans with Chen at the last minute for a friend's birthday party.

Their most obvious divide was financial. Chen wanted to combine their incomes to expand their warehouse. Sofia insisted on separate property and refused even to be associated with his business. Once, Chen secured a major European brand agency and asked Sofia to design a co-branded line. She flatly refused: "My designs are mine, your business is yours. They should not be mixed."

That remark became the turning point of their marriage. After that, they still lived in the same apartment but in separate rooms, with separate bills, even separate food in the fridge. No quarrels, no cold wars — only an almost indifferent "polite distance." This state lasted five years, until spring 2023, when Chen received an investment invitation from China.

It was an opportunity to change his career: the Yangtze River Delta Cross-Border E-Commerce Park offered tailored support for overseas apparel supply chain enterprises, including tax breaks, storage subsidies, and channel connections. Chen immediately recognized this as his best chance to return to China. Within three months, he finalized partner factories, secured e-commerce platform access, and assembled his core team.

Everything was ready — except for his marriage to Sofia. Chen suddenly calmed down. He admitted their marriage was already dead in name, though neither had filed for divorce. If he launched his project in China while still married, even if funded entirely by his pre-marital assets, the income generated would likely be deemed community property under many legal systems. Sofia might not care about his business, but Italian law defines marital income very broadly. If a future dispute arose, he could lose half of everything he had spent years building.

Chen approached Sofia and honestly proposed divorce. Surprisingly, she did not object. She had long grown used to independent life and agreed to divorce. They owned no joint real estate, had no joint debts, and each would keep their own business and income. Just when Chen thought an amicable divorce was within reach, Sofia's lawyer laid down Italy's strict rule: under Article 151 of the Italian Civil Code, even with mutual consent, the couple must first undergo legal separation for no less than 6 months. During the separation period, both parties must maintain independent residences and independent lives. Only after this period could the court accept a divorce application.

A six-month separation before divorce would mean he had to wait another six months to launch his investment project and separate it from marital property. For Chen Jingming, however, this meant missing the deadline for investment incentives, terminating contracts with cooperative factories, and putting the entire project on hold. "Lawyer Rachel J. Ye, a window of opportunity is like a flowering season. Miss it, and you must wait for the next cycle." Chen's finger traced the "effective date" on the investment agreement, his voice filled with unprecedented urgency. This was the core difficulty that brought him to me.

I did not rush to offer a solution. Instead, I instructed my team to clarify two key issues: First, does an Italian court allow parties to choose the application of foreign law? Second, can the procedural requirements for mutual consent divorce under Chinese law serve as the key to bypassing the separation period?

Focusing on these core questions, we found the breakthrough: Article 30 of the Italian Private International Law Code stipulates that: "Divorce and separation may be governed by the national law of both spouses. If the spouses have different nationalities, the law of their common domicile may apply, or the court may, upon application by the parties, apply the national law of either spouse."

This provision was the key to breaking the deadlock. As a Chinese citizen, Chen Jingming's national law is the Civil Code of the People's Republic of China. Under Chinese law, spouses who mutually agree to a divorce may apply to the marriage registration authority after signing a written divorce agreement, with no prerequisite statutory separation period. Our core strategy was to apply to the Italian court to adjudicate the case under Chinese law.

What followed required precise legal translation and procedural coordination. Instead of a standard lawyer's letter, we adopted a more persuasive combination of a legal opinion and supporting evidence:

First, we helped Chen Jingming draft a Legal Application Opinion. Unlike ordinary documents, it did not dwell excessively on the breakdown of relations, but focused on the reasonableness of the choice of law and the protection of the parties' legitimate interests. I clearly stated that since the parties had no dispute regarding divorce or property division, applying Chinese law honored their mutual consent and aligned with the international judicial principles of efficiency and fairness.

Second, to ensure seamless procedure, I contacted Marco, my cooperating lawyer in Rome. With years of experience in family law, he represented Chen in the divorce proceedings in Rome, communicating with the presiding judge in writing and explaining core rules of Chinese law in advance to prevent the judge from having doubts due to unfamiliarity with Chinese law.

The hearing was conducted via video link: Chen in the video conference room of my law firm in China, and Marco in the courtroom in Rome. The judge asked directly: "Why not apply Italian law?" Following our prearranged strategy, Chen and Marco replied clearly: "Your Honor, the core dispute is not whether to divorce, but by which procedure. The parties have reached full agreement on divorce and property division. The Italian separation period serves no practical purpose in this case. Applying Chinese law will resolve the marriage quickly and avoid unnecessary commercial losses caused by procedural delay. This is fully consistent with the substantive justice pursued by Italian law."

Sofia's lawyer also submitted her written statement, expressing agreement with the facts and opinions presented by Chen Jingming and Lawyer Marco. Marco also submitted the commercial evidence prepared by Chen Jingming. After a moment of silence, the judge reviewed the materials and struck the gavel: "The application is granted. This case shall be heard in accordance with the law of the People's Republic of China."

The proceedings then accelerated dramatically. Following the spirit of Chinese law, the Italian court confirmed the parties' divorce agreement and reviewed the property division list. Twenty-eight days later, Chen Jingming received the divorce judgment issued by the Rome court. Its core terms were identical to the divorce agreement we drafted: divorce granted; each party retains their own property; no further claims between them.

On the very day he received the judgment, Chen moved into the Yangtze River Delta Cross-Border E-Commerce Park with his team. His apparel supply chain project was launched as scheduled. By the end of that year, his brand achieved sales of over ten million yuan on domestic e-commerce platforms. He sent me a product brochure with an inscription on the cover: "Thank you, Lawyer Rachel J. Ye, for protecting the most important window of opportunity for my career."

Post-Case Conclusion

Chen Jingming's case serves as a classic model of application-of-law strategy in cross-border family law practice. It dispels a widespread misconception: in a foreign-related divorce, one is not forced to passively apply the law of the place where the marriage was solemnized.

In this case, we did not focus on proving the breakdown of the relationship, but instead shifted our approach to value judgment in the application of law. When procedural rules of a foreign law conflict with a client's practical interests, it is the professional lawyer's responsibility to find the most suitable legal rules for the client within the framework of private international law. Although as Chinese lawyers we could not directly act as Chen Jingming's representatives in his divorce proceedings in Rome, we still provided irreplaceable value for his case.

For Chen Jingming, this divorce meant more than ending a marriage in name only — it also drew clear legal boundaries for his career blueprint. For me, this case once again confirmed that family legal services are not simply about "protecting rights in divorce", but about providing comprehensive legal solutions integrated with the client's life planning and career development.

The vitality of law lies in solving problems. When a cross-border marriage intersects with life opportunities, a professional legal strategy is the key that opens both the door to divorce and the door to a promising career.

消失的遗产管理人

引言

一份亲笔写下的遗嘱，本应是逝者留给生者最后的安宁与交代。可当遗嘱被指定的执行人牢牢握在手中，却成了一道打不开的门。一方是倾尽所有、在爱人重病期间不离不弃的再婚妻子，一方是认定"继母图谋家产"的前妻之子，还有一位手握遗嘱原件、却始终不肯露面的"消失的遗产管理人"。遗嘱是否有效？遗产该如何分割？本可平静落幕的继承，却因一个关键人物的沉默与逃避，陷入漫长的僵局。我接手这起案件时，当事人几乎已经走到败诉边缘，而我要做的，是在缺乏遗嘱原件的绝境里，为她守住本该属于她的一切。

第一次见到苏晚晴时，她眼底的疲惫与无助，让我至今难忘。她坐在我办公室的沙发上，声音轻而坚定："叶律师，我不是要抢他家的东西，这些房子，每一分钱都是我自己出的。我只是想让他走得安心，想让他的遗嘱，算数。"

我的当事人苏晚晴，与她的先夫沈知年于 2016 年登记结婚，两人均是再婚，婚前各自与前婚育有一个儿子。在外人看来，这段中年相遇的婚姻，本应是彼此扶持、安稳度日的归宿。可命运残酷，婚后不到一年，沈知年便被确诊为癌症。此后数年，苏晚晴放下自己的生活，日夜照料、四处求医，几乎撑起了他全部的治疗与尊严。

婚姻存续期间，苏晚晴出于对伴侣的信任与托付，用自己婚前个人财产出资购买了三处房产，却登记在了沈知年名下。从法律形式上看，这几处房产形成了夫妻共同财产。因为苏晚晴对这段婚姻非常看重，她没有私心，只希望两人能安稳相伴，无论健康疾病，都能互相依靠。只是她没有想到，风雨同舟的日子，会那么快走到尽头。

2021 年 8 月，沈知年病情持续加重，自知时日无多，在意识清醒、精神正常的状态下，沈知年亲笔写下一份自书遗嘱。遗嘱内容清晰而明确：苏晚晴出资购买并登记在沈知年名下的三处房产是婚内夫妻共同财产，在沈知年去世后，属于他本人的份额，全部由苏晚晴继承；沈知年婚前个人房屋的拆迁回购房，则由他与前妻所生的儿子沈亦辰继承。同时，遗嘱中特意指定，由相交多年的好友江柏舟担任遗嘱执行人，负责日后遗嘱的执行与遗产的分配。

沈知年郑重签名，注明年、月、日。写完后，他将这份承载着全部心意与安排的遗嘱原件，亲手交给了江柏舟保管。他以为，这样一来，身后之事便再无纷争。

2021 年 10 月，沈知年因病离世。葬礼刚过，苏晚晴便联系江柏舟，希望他依照遗嘱，协助办理遗产分割与过户手续。她也主动联系继子沈亦辰，希望平和沟通，互不亏欠。可让她万万没有想到的是，江柏舟态度冷淡，一再拖延；沈亦辰更是直接拒绝配合，认为遗嘱无效，不肯退让半步。一方手握遗嘱却拒不露面，一方质疑遗嘱拒不配合，苏晚晴一夜之间，从尽心尽力的妻子，变成了"外人"。

她无数次联系江柏舟，但对方电话不接，信息不回，人更是见不到。那位被逝者托付重任、本该中立公正的遗嘱执行人，成了一个彻底消失的遗产管理人。万般无奈之下，2021 年 11 月，苏晚晴向法院提起诉讼，将沈亦辰列为被告，请求法院确认沈知年的自书遗嘱合法有效，依照遗嘱分割遗产。

可诉讼一开始，苏晚晴就陷入了致命的困境。江柏舟始终拒绝配合，拒不提交遗嘱原件。而法庭之上，证据规则极为严苛：主张遗嘱继承，应当提交遗嘱原件。如今原件在第三人手中，对方隐匿不出，苏晚晴几乎要承担"举证不能"的不利后果，一旦法院以此为由驳回，她将一无所有。在陷入困境之际，苏晚晴找到我，寻求破局之策。

我仔细梳理案情，提出新的诉求和事实理由，我们认为，虽原告方未能出示遗嘱原件，但我们有证据证明，本案遗嘱设有遗嘱执行人，且遗嘱原件保存在遗嘱执行人处，我们请求追加遗嘱执行人江柏舟为第三人，要求其参与诉讼、履行职责、以让法庭查明事实，执行遗嘱内容。法院采纳了我方的主张。又经我方申请，法院再次组织开庭。但遗憾的是，江柏舟经法院传唤却拒绝出庭。

庭审中，沈亦辰的律师提出：遗嘱无法核对真实性，应认定无效；沈知年的遗产应按法定继承处理，也即该三套夫妻共有的房产由继子和原告共同参与继承分割。

局势对苏晚晴显然非常不利。一旦法院以"无法提供原件"为由判决苏晚晴败诉，她数年付出、倾尽财力、悉心照料的一切，都将化为泡影。

我在法庭上清晰阐述我方观点：

第一，案涉自书遗嘱合法有效。被继承人沈知年亲笔书写、签名、注明年月日，形式完整、内容明确，是其真实意思表示，不存在欺诈、胁迫、无民事行为能力等无效情形。被告主张遗嘱无效，却未能提供任何相反证据，其抗辩不能成立。

第二，案涉房产的来源和家庭的经济贡献，均系原告苏晚晴投入的巨大付出和形成的财富价值。且沈知年的治疗照护也均由苏晚晴尽心竭力操持，儿子却始终缺位床前。

第三，江柏舟作为遗嘱指定的执行人，继承开始后即成为遗产管理人，依法具有独立诉讼地位，与本案存在直接法律上的利害关系，应当作为第三人参加诉讼，履行遗产管理职责，不得逃避、推诿。遗产管理人负有法定职责，应当妥善保管遗产、执行遗嘱、协助分配，不得因个人懈怠损害继承人利益。江柏舟拒不交出遗嘱、拒不协助办理手续，已经构成严重不作为。

在最艰难的时刻，我没有放弃程序内的每一次努力，也没有放弃调解的可能。我多次与承办法官沟通案情，与对方代理人反复释法明理，与江柏舟联系沟通，充分阐明客观事实：案涉房产出资来源、苏晚晴多年照料的事实、遗嘱的真实背景、遗产管理人的法律责任。我告诉他们：法律尊重逝者遗愿，也保护真正付出、无愧于心的人。拖延与对抗，伤害的不只是当事人，更是逝者的安宁。最终，在法院的主持下，在事实与法律的双重说服下，沈亦辰终于被说服松口。江柏舟也终于将这一纸遗嘱的原件出示到法庭上。

双方达成调解协议：

确认被继承人沈知年自书遗嘱真实有效，各方同意严格按照遗嘱内容分割遗产，沈亦辰配合办理全部房产过户登记手续。苏晚晴同时撤回对第三人江柏舟的起诉。一场几乎要败诉的继承纠纷，最终以最接近逝者本意的方式，尘埃落定。

走出法院那天，苏晚晴红了眼眶，轻轻说了一句："他总算可以安心了。"我知道，她赢得的不只是财产，更是一段被看见、被尊重、没有被辜负的真心。

案后结语

本案是中国《民法典》实施遗产管理人制度以来，极具典型意义的一起继承纠纷。它让我们看到，一份合法有效的遗嘱，仍可能因执行人的懈怠、逃避、不作为，而陷入僵局；也让我们清晰认识到遗产管理人的法律地位、职责边界与民事责任。

自书遗嘱由遗嘱人亲笔书写、签名、注明年月日，形式完备、意思真实，即合法有效。即便一方对遗嘱提出质疑，如无相反证据，亦不能否定其效力。而被指定的遗嘱执行人，在继承开始后即成为遗产管理人，享有独立的诉讼主体地位，负有保管遗产、执行遗嘱、协助分配、维护继承人合法权益的法定义务。

现实中，有人因人情、顾虑、偏袒，选择沉默、隐匿、拖延，以为"不参与、不表态"便可置身事外，却不知这种消极逃避，反而会让逝者不安、让亲人反目、让信任崩塌。

婚姻也好，继承也罢，它的珍贵之处，是经得起利益的诱惑和考验，守住承诺、尊重真心、不负所托。真正的体面，不是沉默消失，而是在责任面前，不缺位、不逃避、不辜负。

The Vanishing Estate Administrator

Introduction

A handwritten will should be the deceased's final peace and arrangement for those left behind. Yet when the designated executor holds the will firmly in his hands, it becomes a locked door that no one can open. On one side stands a remarried wife who gave everything and stayed by her husband's side through his severe illness. On the other stands the son from his first marriage, convinced that "the stepmother is plotting the family fortune". And between them lingers a "vanishing estate administrator" who holds the original will but refuses to show up. Is the will valid? How should the estate be divided? What could have ended peacefully has turned into a long deadlock, all because of the silence and evasion of one key person. When I took on this case, my client was on the verge of losing. My mission was to defend everything rightfully hers, even in the desperate situation where the original will was missing.

I will never forget the exhaustion and helplessness in Su Wanqing's eyes when we first met. She sat on the sofa in my office, her voice soft but determined: "Lawyer Rachel J. Ye, I am not trying to seize his family's property. Every penny of these houses came from my own money. I just want him to rest in peace, and I want his will to count."

My client, Su Wanqing, and her late husband, Shen Zhinian, registered their marriage in 2016. Both were remarried, and each had a son from their previous marriages. To outsiders, this mid-life union seemed like a safe harbor of mutual support and steady living. But fate was cruel. Less than a year into the marriage, Shen Zhinian was diagnosed with cancer. In the years that followed, Su Wanqing put her own life on hold, caring for him day and night, seeking medical help everywhere, and supporting nearly his entire treatment and dignity.

During their marriage, out of trust and devotion to her partner, Su Wanqing used her pre-marital personal assets to buy three properties, which were registered under Shen Zhinian's name. Legally, these properties became marital community property. Because Su Wanqing cherished the marriage deeply, she had no selfish motives; she only wished they could stay together in sickness and in health. Little did she know that their life through thick and thin would end so soon.

In August 2021, Shen Zhinian's condition worsened dramatically. Knowing his time was short, and with full consciousness and sound mind, he personally wrote a holographic will. The content was clear and explicit: the three properties purchased by Su Wanqing but registered under Shen Zhinian's name are marital community property. Upon his death, his share shall be inherited solely by Su Wanqing; the replacement apartment from the demolition of his pre-marital personal house shall be inherited by Shen Yichen, his son from his first marriage. At the same time, the will specifically appointed Jiang Baizhou, his friend of many years, as the executor to oversee the execution of the will and the distribution of the estate.

Shen Zhinian signed it solemnly and dated it. After finishing, he personally handed this original will, carrying all his wishes and arrangements, to Jiang Baizhou for safekeeping. He thought that this would ensure no disputes after his passing.

In October 2021, Shen Zhinian passed away. Just after the funeral, Su Wanqing contacted Jiang Baizhou, hoping he would assist with the estate division and transfer procedures according to the will. She also reached out to her stepson, Shen Yichen, hoping for peaceful communication with no ill feelings. But to her absolute surprise, Jiang Baizhou was cold and kept stalling; Shen Yichen outright refused to cooperate, claiming the will was invalid and refusing to yield an inch. With one side holding the will but refusing to appear, and the other questioning the will and refusing to cooperate, Su Wanqing turned overnight from a devoted wife into an "outsider".

She tried contacting Jiang Baizhou countless times, but her calls went unanswered, her messages ignored, and she could not even see him in person. The executor, entrusted with a heavy responsibility by the deceased and expected to be neutral and fair, had become a completely vanished estate administrator. In desperation, in November 2021, Su Wanqing filed a lawsuit with the court, naming Shen Yichen as defendant, asking the court to confirm the validity of Shen Zhinian's handwritten will and divide the estate accordingly.

But from the start, the lawsuit plunged Su Wanqing into a fatal dilemma. Jiang Baizhou consistently refused to cooperate, refusing to appear in court or submit the original will. And in court, the evidence rules are extremely strict: to claim inheritance by will, the original will must be presented. Now with the original hidden by a third party, Su Wanqing risked being found "unable to bear the burden of proof". If the court dismissed her claim on that basis, she would be left with nothing. It was at this difficult moment that she came to me, seeking a way out.

After carefully reviewing the case, I put forward new claims and factual arguments. We believed that although the plaintiff could not produce the original will, we had evidence proving that an executor was appointed and the original was in his custody. We requested to add the executor Jiang Baizhou as a third party, ordering him to join the litigation, fulfill his duties, to allow the court to ascertain the truth, and enforce the will. The court accepted our position. At our request, the court held another hearing. Regrettably, however, Jiang Baizhou refused to appear despite being summoned by the court.

During the trial, Shen Yichen's lawyer argued: the authenticity of the will could not be verified, so it should be deemed invalid; Shen Zhinian's estate should be distributed according to statutory succession, meaning the three jointly owned properties should be inherited and divided jointly by the stepson and the plaintiff.

The situation was obviously very unfavorable for Su Wanqing. Once the court ruled against her because of the "inability to provide the original", all her years of devotion, financial investment, and meticulous care would be reduced to nothing.

I clearly stated our position in court:

First, the holographic will in question is legally valid. The decedent Shen Zhinian personally wrote, signed, and dated it. The form was complete, the content clear, and it represented his true intention. There were no grounds for invalidity such as fraud, duress, or lack of civil capacity. The defendant claimed the will was invalid but provided no contrary evidence, so his defense cannot stand.

Second, the source of the properties in question and the economic contributions to the family were all due to the immense effort invested and wealth value created by the plaintiff, Su Wanqing. Furthermore, Shen Zhinian's treatment and care were entirely managed by Su Wanqing with all her might, while his son was entirely absent from his bedside.

Third, Jiang Baizhou, as the designated executor, became the estate administrator upon the commencement of inheritance. He has an independent litigation status and a direct legal interest in the case, and must participate as a third party, perform his estate administration duties, and not evade or shirk responsibility. An estate administrator is legally obligated to properly keep the estate, execute the will, and assist in distribution, and must not harm the heirs' interests through personal negligence. Jiang Baizhou's refusal to hand over the will and assist with the procedures constitutes a severe omission of duty.

In the most difficult moments, I did not give up any procedural effort, nor did I abandon the possibility of mediation. I repeatedly communicated the case details with the presiding judge, explained the law to the opposing counsel, and contacted Jiang Baizhou, fully presenting the objective facts: the source of funding for the properties, Su Wanqing's years of care, the true background of the will, and the legal responsibilities of the estate administrator. I told them: The law respects the wishes of the deceased and protects those who have truly given with a clear conscience. Delay and confrontation hurt not only the parties involved but also the peace of the deceased. Finally, under the court's mediation, and persuaded by both facts and the law, Shen Yichen finally relented. Jiang Baizhou also finally presented the original will to the court.

The parties reached a mediation agreement:

The holographic will of the decedent Shen Zhinian was confirmed as authentic and valid, and all parties agreed to strictly divide the estate according to the will, with Shen Yichen cooperating in processing all property transfer registrations. Su Wanqing simultaneously withdrew her lawsuit against the third party, Jiang Baizhou. An inheritance dispute that almost ended in defeat was finally settled in the manner closest to the deceased's true intention.

As we walked out of the court that day, Su Wanqing's eyes turned red and she whispered softly: "He can finally rest in peace now." I knew she had won more than property — she had won a genuine heart that was seen, respected, and not betrayed.

Post-Case Conclusion

This case is a highly representative inheritance dispute since the Civil Code introduced the estate administrator system. It shows us that even a legally valid will can become deadlocked due to the executor's negligence, evasion, or inaction; it also clearly reveals the legal status, scope of duties, and civil liability of an estate administrator.

A holographic will is legally valid if it is entirely handwritten, signed, and dated by the testator, with complete form and true intent. Even if one party challenges it, the validity cannot be denied without contrary evidence. The designated executor, upon the opening of the succession, becomes the estate administrator, enjoying independent litigation standing, and is legally obligated to safeguard the estate, execute the will, assist in distribution, and protect the lawful rights of heirs.

In reality, some people choose silence, concealment, and delay due to personal feelings, hesitation, or bias, thinking they can stay out of trouble by "not participating, not commenting". Yet they do not realize that such passive evasion will instead disturb the deceased, turn relatives against each other, and destroy trust.

Whether in marriage or inheritance, its true value lies in withstanding the temptation and test of interests, keeping promises, respecting sincerity, and living up to trust. True dignity is not vanishing in silence, but showing up, not evading, and not betraying when duty calls.

英伦遥望：十年空守，一纸传票唤醒良知，跨境调解终获解脱

引言

十年，可以让一个青涩孩童长成挺拔少年，也可以让一段婚姻，在无尽等待与孤独中，消磨成一纸空文。我的当事人方卉，在上海浦东的家中，守了整整十年。她的丈夫远在英国伦敦经商，早已形同陌路、另筑爱巢，当她决心离婚时，对方却彻底失联。我以《民事诉讼法》管辖规则为基石，在上海浦东法院全程代理，从公告送达唤醒失联被告，到法庭调解促成和解，最终用一份调解书，为她十年的孤独坚守，画上了体面且圆满的句号。

方卉的书房里，摆着一张一家三口的老照片，照片上的她温婉浅笑，眼神里满是对未来的憧憬。她 45 岁，是浦东一所重点中学的语文老师，气质沉静、性格坚韧，做事认真、待人温和，是学生眼中的好老师，也是亲友口中的贤妻良母。

2005 年，她与大她两岁的王瀚文自由恋爱结婚，王瀚文彼时意气风发，心怀闯荡世界的梦想，对方卉体贴入微、承诺满满。婚后第二年，儿子王一凡出生，小家庭温馨安稳，充满烟火气。2013 年，王瀚文以“拓展海外贸易、给家人更好生活”为由，只身前往英国伦敦，从此踏上了一条远离家庭的路。

起初，分离的思念还能维系感情。王瀚文每周都会打视频电话，给方卉分享伦敦的生活，给儿子寄玩具、奶粉与衣物，节日里也会准时送上祝福。可渐渐地，视频越来越少，通话越来越短，信息常常已读不回，寄回家的生活费也开始断断续续、一拖再拖。

方卉起初默默体谅，以为他只是生意繁忙、压力巨大，她独自扛起家庭全部重担：每天上班教书育人，下班接孩子、做饭、辅导功课，周末还要照顾双方年迈的父母，家里大小事全靠她一人支撑，从无怨言。

直到 2016 年的一天，方卉在王瀚文许久未更新的社交平台上，无意间看到一张照片：他与一名金发碧眼的外国女子亲密依偎，怀里抱着一个刚出生的混血婴儿，配文满是温柔。那一刻，方卉坚守多年的信念轰然崩塌，全世界仿佛瞬间安静下来，只剩下心脏碎裂的声音。

她颤抖着手拨通王瀚文的电话，得到的只有长久的沉默与随后的冰冷挂断。从那以后，王瀚文彻底切断联系：更换手机号、拉黑微信、注销社交账号，彻底消失在英国的人海里。他不再支付儿子抚养费，不再过问父母身体，对这个远在上海的家，彻底弃之不顾。

十年光阴，方卉从年轻少妇熬成鬓角微白的中年女性，儿子从懵懂孩童长成挺拔大学生，公婆从健朗身躯变得步履蹒跚，而王瀚文，始终是那个遥不可及、不负责任的名字。

2023 年夏天，儿子考上大学离家求学，临走时抱着方卉认真说："妈，你为这个家撑了十年，现在我长大了，你别再等了，为自己活一次吧。"儿子的话，彻底点醒了方卉。她看着镜中疲惫的自己，终于下定决心，结束这段早已名存实亡的婚姻。可现实难题接踵而至：丈夫定居英国十年、下落不明、拒不配合，她该向哪个法院起诉？对方不到庭，婚还能不能离？她辗转咨询多位律师，均因"跨境送达、对方失联"难以推进，最终在朋友推荐下，找到了我。

"叶律师，他在英国十年，找不到人、不接电话，我真的还能在国内离婚吗？"方卉的眼神里，满是期待与不安。我握住她的手，告诉她，不要担忧，中国法院会保护你的合法权利。

接受委托后，我们认为，根据我国《民事诉讼法》第二十三条及司法解释明确规定：对不在中华人民共和国领域内居住的人提起的有关身份关系的诉讼，由原告住所地人民法院管辖；中国公民一方在国外、一方在国内，国内一方住所地法院有权管辖。方卉常住上海浦东，因此上海浦东法院对本案具有管辖权。

我指导方卉收集、固定关键证据：王瀚文的英国永久居留证明、出入境记录，从而证实他连续十年未回国、长期定居国外；双方多年无沟通、无经济往来的记录，证实夫妻感情早已破裂；王瀚文境外同居生子的相关证据，证实他具有重大过错；方卉独自抚养儿子、照顾老人的证人证言与近十年的开支明细（包括学费、生活费、医疗费等），清晰核算出王瀚文拖欠的抚养费和私立学校教育费共计 82 万元；同时补充了儿子王一凡的书面证言，陈述十年来父亲缺位的成长经历。

随即，我们以"夫妻感情彻底破裂、要求离婚并支付拖欠抚养费"为诉讼请求，向上海市浦东人民法院申请立案，同步提交全套证据材料，案件被法院顺利受理。

审理中，因王瀚文下落不明、无法直接送达起诉状，我依法向法院申请涉外公告送达，严格按照法定程序，在《人民法院报》及法院公告栏同步公告起诉状、开庭传票等法律文书。公告发布后的第二个月，我突然接到了浦东法院承办法官的电话，告知王瀚文已知晓其被起诉离婚，通过其国内亲友联系到法院，并委托了上海的一名律师作为诉讼代理人，正式提交了答辩状。

这个意外的消息让方卉既高兴又忐忑，而我深知，这是案件从"缺席判决"转向"实质解决"的关键契机。王瀚文在答辩状中虽承认长期分居的事实，却以"境外生意亏损、经济困难"为由，辩称并非故意不支付抚养费，同时表示"愿意协商离婚，但希望减免抚养费"。

为了最大程度维护方卉的合法权益，也为了给这段十年的婚姻留一份体面，我主动联系承办法官，申请启动法庭调解程序。法官欣然同意，考虑到王瀚文远在英国，最终确定采用"线上 + 线下"结合的方式进行调解：王瀚文通过视频连线参与，其代理律师到庭，我陪同方卉现场参加。

调解当天，法庭氛围庄重而平和。视频画面里的王瀚文，比十年前苍老了许多，眼神里带着明显的愧疚。我首先代表方卉，清晰陈述了核心诉求：“第一，双方感情已彻底破裂，无任何和好可能，我方坚决要求离婚；第二，被告十年来未履行抚养义务，拖欠的 82 万元抚养费和私立学校教育费是其应当支付的法律责任，这是对孩子十年成长的弥补，也是法律的底线。”随后，我当庭逐一展示证据：方卉独自支付的学费票据、儿子的医疗记录、老人的护理费用清单，还有王一凡那封字字恳切的信——信里写着“我不怪爸爸，但我希望他能为自己的责任画上句号”。

看着这些证据，读着儿子的文字，视频那头的王瀚文沉默了许久。他的代理律师试图继续以“经济困难”为由协商减免，却被王瀚文抬手制止。“别说了。”王瀚文的声音沙哑，看向视频里的方卉，郑重地说了一句，“对不起，方卉，这十年，是我对不起你和孩子。”那一刻，一直强忍情绪的方卉，眼泪夺眶而出，浑身颤抖不已。

王瀚文随后明确表态：“我同意离婚，没有任何异议。拖欠的 82 万元抚养费，我分文不少，下个月就一次性打到孩子的账户上。”他还主动提出，“孩子以后读研究生的费用，我也会承担一半，这是我作为父亲的责任。”

我立刻抓住这一契机，与法官一同拟定调解协议条款，明确约定：

一、准予方卉与王瀚文离婚；

二、王瀚文于调解书生效后三十日内，一次性支付拖欠的抚养费 82 万元；

三、双方就子女后续教育费用的承担方式达成补充约定。

最终，双方在调解协议上签字确认，法官当场出具了民事调解书。这份调解书，兼具判决书的强制执行力与调解书的自愿性，彻底解决了所有争议。

拿到调解书的那天，方卉这次没有再哭，只是轻轻舒了一口气。她给儿子发了一条信息：“一切都结束了，爸爸也承担了他该承担的。”很快，儿子回复：“妈，我们都解脱了。”

案后结语

方卉的故事，打破了“跨境失联离婚必缺席判决”的固有认知。公告送达并非终点，它更像一声跨越重洋的警钟，唤醒了被告沉睡的良知。

作为家事律师，我的价值不仅在于精准适用法律、搭建完整证据链，更在于把握案件的每一个转机，用专业的调解策略，为当事人争取更圆满的结果。相较于冰冷的缺席判决，调解不仅快速解除了婚姻关系，更让被告主动承担了抚养责任，既维护了方卉的合法权益，也为孩子的成长画上了相对完整的句号。

婚姻的破裂或许无法挽回，但责任的承担永远不晚。法律的意义，不仅在于定纷止争，更在于唤醒人性的良知，让每一段走到尽头的婚姻，都能少一份纠葛，多一份体面。

Across the Oceans: A Decade of Waiting, a Summons to Conscience, and Freedom Through Cross-Border Mediation

Introduction

Ten years can turn a young child into a tall youth. It can also wear a marriage down to nothing but empty words, amid endless waiting and loneliness. My client, Fang Hui, waited faithfully at her home in Pudong, Shanghai, for an entire decade. Her husband, away doing business in London, had long become a stranger and built another family. When she finally decided to divorce, he completely disappeared. Grounded in the jurisdiction rules of the Civil Procedure Law, I represented her throughout the case in the Shanghai Pudong People's Court. From public service that reached the absent defendant, to court mediation that brought reconciliation, I finally helped her put a dignified and complete end to ten years of lonely waiting with a mediation judgment.

In Fang Hui's study, there has always been an old photo of the family of three. In it, she smiles gently, her eyes full of hope for the future. Now 45, she is a Chinese teacher at a key middle school in Pudong – calm, strong, earnest, and kind. She is a beloved teacher to her students and a devoted wife and mother to her family and friends.

In 2005, she married Wang Hanwen, whom she had dated freely. Wang was two years older, ambitious and passionate about seeing the world, thoughtful and full of promises to Fang Hui. Their son Wang Yifan was born the year after marriage, and the small family was warm and peaceful. In 2013, claiming he wanted to "expand overseas trade and give the family a better life," Wang Hanwen left alone for London, setting off on a path far from home.

At first, longing sustained their bond. Wang called by video every week, sharing his life in London, sending toys, milk powder and clothes for their son, and greeting them faithfully on festivals. But gradually, videos grew fewer, calls shorter, messages often read but unanswered, and living expenses sent home became irregular and delayed.

Fang Hui tried to understand at first, thinking he was simply busy and under great pressure. She shouldered the entire family burden alone: teaching during the day, picking up her son, cooking and tutoring after work, caring for elderly parents on weekends. She never complained.

Then one day in 2016, Fang Hui accidentally saw a photo on Wang Hanwen's long-dormant social media: he was cuddling closely with a blonde foreign woman, holding a newborn mixed-race baby, with tender captions. In that moment, the faith she had held for years collapsed. The world went quiet, except for the sound of her heart breaking.

Trembling, she called Wang Hanwen — only long silence, then a cold hang-up. After that, Wang cut off all contact completely: changing his phone number, blocking WeChat, deleting his social accounts, vanishing into the crowd in Britain. He stopped paying child support, stopped asking about his parents' health, and abandoned the family in Shanghai entirely.

Ten years passed. Fang Hui grew from a young woman into a middle-aged lady with faint gray at her temples. Her son grew from a little boy into a tall university student. Her parents-in-law grew frail and slow. But Wang Hanwen remained only a distant, irresponsible name.

In the summer of 2023, their son was admitted to university and left home. Before leaving, he hugged Fang Hui and said earnestly: "Mom, you've held this family up for ten years. Now I'm grown up. Stop waiting. Live for yourself for once."

His words woke her completely. Staring at her tired reflection in the mirror, she finally made up her mind: end this marriage in name only. But real difficulties followed: Her husband had settled abroad for ten years, his whereabouts unknown, uncooperative. Which court could she sue in? Could she get a divorce without him appearing?

She consulted several lawyers, but all found the case difficult due to "cross-border service and the defendant's disappearance." On a friend's recommendation, she came to me.

"Lawyer Ye, he's been in the UK for ten years. I can't find him, he won't answer calls. Can I really divorce him in China?" Fang Hui's eyes were filled with hope and anxiety.

I held her hand and told her: Do not worry. Chinese courts will protect your lawful rights.

After taking the case, we confirmed that under Article 23 of the Civil Procedure Law and relevant judicial interpretations: A lawsuit concerning personal relationship brought against a person not residing within the territory of the People's Republic of China shall be under the jurisdiction of the people's court of the plaintiff's domicile. Where one Chinese citizen is abroad and the other is in China, the court in the domestic party's place of residence definitely has jurisdiction. Fang Hui had long resided in Pudong, Shanghai. Therefore, the

Shanghai Pudong People's Court had jurisdiction.

I guided Fang Hui to collect and secure a full set of key evidence:

1. Wang Hanwen's UK permanent residence documents and entry-exit records, proving he had not returned to China for ten consecutive years and was long settled abroad;
2. Records showing no communication or financial exchanges for years, proving the marriage had completely broken down;
3. Evidence of Wang's cohabitation and having a child abroad, proving his serious fault;
4. Witness testimony and detailed expense records over nearly ten years (tuition, living costs, medical fees, etc.), showing Fang Hui raised the son and cared for the elderly alone;
5. A clear calculation that Wang Hanwen owed 820,000 yuan in back child support and private school education fees;
6. A written statement from their son Wang Yifan, describing growing up without a father for ten years.

We then filed a lawsuit with the Pudong People's Court of Shanghai, claiming:

1. The marriage had irretrievably broken down;
2. Divorce should be granted;
3. The defendant should pay the arrears of child support.

The case was duly accepted.

During the proceedings, as Wang Hanwen's whereabouts were unknown and direct service was impossible, I lawfully applied for public service — publishing the complaint, court summons and other legal documents in the People's Court Daily and on the court's notice board in accordance with formal procedures.

In the second month after publication, I suddenly received a call from the presiding judge: Wang Hanwen had learned he was being sued for divorce, contacted the court through relatives in China, and had appointed a lawyer in Shanghai as his legal representative, formally submitting a defense.

This unexpected news delighted and worried Fang Hui. I knew it was a critical turning point — from a possible default judgment to a substantive resolution.

In his defense, Wang admitted long-term separation but claimed he had not intentionally refused to pay support, citing "overseas business losses and financial difficulties." He expressed willingness to negotiate a divorce but asked for a reduction in support.

To protect Fang Hui's rights to the fullest and preserve dignity for this ten-year marriage, I proactively contacted the judge and applied to launch court mediation.

The judge agreed. Given Wang's distance in the UK, mediation was held online plus offline: Wang joined by video link, his lawyer appeared in person, and I accompanied Fang Hui on-site.

On the day of mediation, the courtroom was solemn and peaceful. On the screen, Wang looked much older than ten years ago, his eyes clearly guilty.

I first stated Fang Hui's core demands clearly:

1. The marriage has completely broken down with no possibility of reconciliation. We firmly request a divorce.

2. The defendant has failed to fulfill his parental duties for ten years. The 820,000 yuan in arrears for child support and private education is his legal obligation — compensation for ten years of the child's growth, and the bottom line of the law.

I then presented evidence one by one: tuition receipts paid solely by Fang Hui, her son's medical records, elderly care bills, and Wang Yifan's sincere letter, which read: "I don't blame Dad, but I hope he can fulfill his responsibilities and bring this to a close."

After watching and listening, Wang Hanwen fell silent for a long time. His lawyer tried to argue again for a reduction based on "financial hardship," but Wang raised his hand to stop him.

"Stop," Wang said hoarsely. He looked into the camera at Fang Hui and said solemnly: "I'm sorry, Fang Hui. These ten years, I let you and our son down."

At that moment, Fang Hui, who had held back her emotions, burst into tears and trembled all over.

Wang Hanwen then made his position clear: "I agree to the divorce, no objection. The 820,000 yuan in arrears I will pay in full, every cent, into the child's account in one lump sum next month."

He voluntarily added: "I will also cover half of the son's future postgraduate tuition fees. It is my responsibility as a father."

I immediately seized the moment and, together with the judge, drafted the mediation agreement:

1. The divorce between Fang Hui and Wang Hanwen is granted;
2. Wang Hanwen shall pay the arrears of 820,000 yuan in child support in one lump sum within 30 days after the mediation document takes effect;
3. The parties reach a supplementary agreement on future education expenses for the child.

Both parties signed the agreement. The judge issued a civil mediation judgment on the spot — enforceable, voluntary, and resolving all disputes completely.

On the day she received the mediation judgment, Fang Hui did not cry. She only let out a soft, relieved breath.

She sent her son a message: "It's all over. Dad has taken the responsibility he should have."

Her son quickly replied: "Mom, we are both free."

Post-Case Conclusion

Fang Hui's story broke the stereotype that "cross-border divorce with a missing spouse must end in default judgment."

Public service was not the end — it was a warning across oceans, awakening the defendant's dormant conscience.

As a family law attorney, my value lies not only in accurately applying the law and building a complete evidence chain, but also in seizing every turning point and using professional mediation strategies to achieve a more complete outcome for my client.

Compared with a cold default judgment, mediation not only quickly dissolved the marriage but also made the defendant voluntarily take up parental duties. It protected Fang Hui's rights and brought a relatively complete closure to the child's growth.

A broken marriage may be beyond repair, but it is never too late to take responsibility.

The purpose of the law is not only to resolve disputes, but also to awaken human conscience — so that every marriage that reaches its end can have less entanglement and more dignity.

孕途风波里，法理与温情共护新生

引言

婚姻里的裂痕，有时会隐藏在未曾言说的过往，又会被突如其来的变故而放大。这起离婚纠纷，缘起一场寻常相亲缔结的姻缘，却因女方婚前隐瞒的精神病史、孕期激素诱发的旧疾，陷入生育与离婚的双重困局。男方忧心孩子的健康与家庭安稳，女方渴望守护腹中骨肉，立场相悖间，矛盾一触即发。作为女方代理律师，我摒弃对立博弈的办案思路，既共情男方的现实顾虑，更坚守女性生育自由的法律底线，用法理和温情化解了这场家庭风波，也让破碎的婚姻之外，新生的亲情得以圆满。这起案件，尽显家事法律的温度，也道尽平凡人在婚姻变故里的挣扎与和解。

陈麟与覃遥遥的相遇，是市井里最常见的缘分。经亲友介绍相识，两人年岁相当，家境般配，相处中性情相投、默契渐生。交往半年后，他俩便从热恋走向谈婚论嫁，订婚、结婚的流程顺理成章，在外人看来，这是一段安稳可期的烟火姻缘。

无人知晓的是，覃遥遥心底藏着一段过往。高中时期，她曾罹患精神疾病，曾因病发休学半年，后经系统治疗与规律服药，病情已痊愈。大学求学与步入职场的数年间，她生活顺遂、工作如常，与常人无异，从未出现病情反复的迹象。也正因这份对过往病痛的释然，面对倾心的陈麟，她始终未提及这段病史，只愿以当下完好的状态，奔赴这段婚姻，未曾想，这份沉默和疏忽，埋下了婚姻里的隐患。

婚后一年，覃遥遥怀上身孕，小生命的降临，本是这个小家庭最珍贵的期许，可孕期体内激素的剧烈波动，成了诱发旧疾的导火索。渐渐地，覃遥遥的状态出现异样，情绪变得焦躁易怒，行为也愈发古怪反常，这份异常，最先被陈麟的母亲察觉。她满心焦灼地问询儿子，陈麟却茫然无措，对妻子的病史一无所知，只当是孕期常见的情绪波动，并未深究。

直至一次覃遥遥病情急性发作，情绪彻底失控，行为举止明显癫狂，陈麟一家惊惶不已，连夜将她送往医院救治，覃家父母也匆匆赶来。在医生全面问诊、梳理既往病史时，覃母才如实道出女儿早年的患病经历，这个真相如平地惊雷，让陈麟与家人震惊之余，更陷入了难以释怀的懊恼和愠怒。

事已至此，陈家唯一的期盼，便是让覃遥遥尽快接受治疗，稳住病情。可覃遥遥满心牵挂腹中胎儿，固执地认定药物会伤及宝宝健康，任凭丈夫、公婆苦劝，即便亲生父母出面劝导，她依旧坚决抗拒诊疗，情绪愈发狂躁，病情也随之持续加重。看着女儿深陷病痛与执念之中，覃家父母心疼又无措，与陈家商议后，只能忍痛将她送往专业精神病医院，接受约束性治疗与药物干预，病情才渐渐得到控制。

围绕腹中胎儿的去留，双方的矛盾彻底激化，陷入无法调和的僵局。主治医生给出客观专业的医学意见：当前产检结果显示，胎儿各项发育指标暂无异常，状态平稳，但结合孕妇自身病史、孕期已接受药物治疗的实际情况，无法完全排除孩子出生后的健康隐患，从医学角度考量，建议终止妊娠。

陈麟及家人听闻此言，担忧愈发深重，执意要求覃遥遥引产，他们惧怕孩子出生后伴随健康问题，更担心这个家庭从此被病痛拖累。可覃遥遥轻抚隆起的腹部，感受着胎儿细微的胎动，满心皆是不舍，这份与生俱来的母性执念，让她无论如何都不愿放弃孩子，谁也无法动摇她的决心。

孕期逐月推进，覃遥遥的病情虽有缓解却未痊愈，双方的争议始终没有突破口，这段婚姻也彻底耗尽了温情，走到了尽头。陈麟最终通过他的律师向覃遥遥提出离婚请求，同时要求覃遥遥终止妊娠。孤立无援的覃遥遥，带着满心倔强与无助，找到我寻求帮助，期盼能守住生下孩子的权利。

听完覃遥遥的故事，我知道由于覃遥遥尚在妊娠期，陈麟是无权向法院起诉离婚，但对于胎儿何去何从的现实问题，仍是双方必须面对解决的。我接受了覃遥遥的委托，和男方陈麟及其代理人建立联系，展开沟通和协调。在双方的调解中，我向对方表达道，陈麟一家顾虑胎儿健康、担忧家庭未来的心情，我们深表理解，为人亲者，这份顾虑本就是情理之中的牵挂。旋即，我的意见核心聚焦于法理与事实的客观呈现：其一，生育权是法律赋予女性的独立人身权利，是女性与生俱来的核心权益，不因婚姻关系存续、不因自身过往病史而被剥夺，男方作为胎儿生父，亦无权替代女方决定胎儿的去留，孩子的留存与否，决定权全然归于覃遥遥本人；其二，覃遥遥婚前未告知病史，确有不妥之处，有违婚姻里的坦诚原则，但她的病情早已痊愈，多年无发作迹象，孕期病发实属无法预知的意外，并非刻意欺瞒，且在明确风险后，她始终积极配合孕期产检与病情监测，拼尽全力守护胎儿安全；其三，覃遥遥坦然同意解除婚姻关系，也明确承诺，孩子出生后，她愿独自承担全部抚养责任，同时不会阻拦男方行使父亲的探视与抚养权利，绝不因婚姻破裂，阻隔孩子与父亲的亲情联结。

这场纠纷调解现场，没有剑拔弩张的对峙，没有极端偏颇的指责，唯有法理的清晰阐释，与情理的平和表达。而命运的温柔巧合，恰在此时降临。双方达成离婚协议的次日，覃遥遥在医院顺利产下一名女婴，婴儿哭声清亮，各项身体指标均属正常，是个健康的宝宝。

怀抱软糯的女儿，覃遥遥泪落不止，过往的委屈、挣扎与坚守，在这一刻都有了归宿。此后，她放下心中芥蒂，积极配合后续康复治疗，心态日渐平和，病情恢复的远超预期。她全身心投入到陪伴女儿成长的日常里，日子慢慢归于安稳。

案件落幕之后，我持续关注着这对母女的境况，也收获了暖心的后续。陈麟得知女儿健康降生，心中的隔阂渐渐消散，主动前往探望，慢慢履行父亲的责任，父女间的亲情越来越浓厚。多年后，覃遥遥的病情完全康复，她从容地陪伴女儿成长。在一场儿童画展上，覃遥遥看着女儿的画作亮相展台，眉眼间满是为人母亲的骄傲与从容，过往的风波早已烟消云散，只留下岁月静好的温情。

案后结语

这起案件，没有跌宕起伏的戏剧冲突，没有非黑即白的是非对错，只是万千家庭遭遇婚姻变故的真实写照，也让我对家事法律服务的意义，有了更为深刻的认知。

婚姻的长久，离不开彼此坦诚。覃遥遥婚前隐瞒病史的行为，终究是婚姻里的一处缺憾，也直接引发了后续的一系列风波，这也为每一对即将步入婚姻的人敲响警钟：关乎健康、关乎未来的重要过往，无需刻意隐匿，坦诚相待，才是婚姻稳固的基石，才能从源头避免不必要的矛盾与伤害。

从法律维度来看，女性生育自由是不可撼动的法定权利，家事法律的意义，在于守护每一位当事人的合法权益，更在于平衡法理与情理。办理家事案件，要能体谅当事人的处境与苦衷，化解对立情绪，尽可能减少婚姻破裂对家人、对孩子的伤害。即便婚姻关系走到尽头，也能让孩子拥有完整的亲情，让当事人放下过往，重新开启生活。

这起案件中，新生的婴儿不仅是一段婚姻的句点，更是一段亲情的开端，法理守护了权益，温情治愈了伤痛，这也是家事法律最动人的价值所在，亦是《难结难分》全书想要传递的初心。

Safeguarding New Life with Law and Warmth Amid Pregnancy Disputes

Introduction

Cracks in a marriage sometimes lie hidden in unspoken pasts, only to be amplified by sudden upheavals. This divorce dispute originated from an ordinary marriage arranged through a blind date, yet it fell into a dual dilemma of childbirth and divorce due to the wife's undisclosed history of mental illness before marriage and a relapse triggered by pregnancy hormones. The husband was deeply concerned about the child's health and the family's stability, while the wife was determined to protect the unborn baby. With conflicting positions, the conflict was on the verge of erupting. As the wife's attorney, I abandoned the confrontational approach to case handling. I empathized with the husband's practical worries while firmly upholding the legal bottom line of women's reproductive freedom. Through legal principles and human warmth, I resolved this family turmoil and allowed new familial bonds to flourish despite the broken marriage. This case fully demonstrates the compassion inherent in family law and recounts the struggles and reconciliations of ordinary people amid marital upheavals.

The meeting between Chen Lin and Qin Yaoyao was the most common kind of fate in daily life. Introduced by relatives and friends, they were of similar age, matched family backgrounds, and grew to be congenial and taciturn as they spent time together. After six months of dating, they moved from passionate love to marriage talks, with their engagement and wedding following naturally. To outsiders, it was a stable and promising ordinary marriage.

Unknown to everyone, Qin Yaoyao harbored a secret past. During high school, she suffered from a mental illness and had to suspend her studies for six months due to an outbreak. After systematic treatment and regular medication, she fully recovered. Throughout her university years and early career, she lived a smooth life, worked normally, showed no signs of relapse, and was no different from others. Eager to leave her past illness behind, she never mentioned this medical history to her beloved Chen Lin. She only wished to embrace this marriage as her healthy present self, never imagining that this silence and oversight would plant a hidden danger in their marriage.

One year after marriage, Qin Yaoyao became pregnant. The arrival of a new life was supposed to be the family's most precious blessing, but the drastic hormonal fluctuations during pregnancy triggered her old illness. Gradually, Qin Yaoyao began to act abnormally—she became irritable and her behavior grew increasingly erratic. Her unusual state was first noticed by Chen Lin's mother. She anxiously questioned her son, but Chen Lin was at a loss. Knowing nothing about his wife's medical history, he dismissed it as common mood swings during pregnancy and did not look into it further.

It was not until an acute outbreak of Qin Yaoyao's illness, when she completely lost emotional control and behaved in a visibly manic manner, that Chen Lin and his family were thrown into panic. They rushed her to the hospital for treatment overnight, and Qin Yaoyao's parents also hurried over. During the doctor's comprehensive consultation and review of past medical history, Qin's mother truthfully revealed her daughter's early illness. This truth struck like a thunderbolt, leaving Chen Lin and his family not only shocked but also consumed by lingering regret and anger.

At this point, the Chen family's only wish was for Qin Yaoyao to receive treatment as soon as possible to stabilize her condition. However, Qin Yaoyao was preoccupied with the fetus in her womb and stubbornly insisted that medication would harm the baby. Despite repeated pleas from her husband, parents-in-law, and even her own parents, she firmly refused treatment. Her emotions grew more manic, and her condition worsened accordingly. Watching their daughter trapped between illness and obsession, Qin Yaoyao's parents felt heartache and helplessness. After discussing with the Chen family, they reluctantly sent her to a specialized psychiatric hospital for compulsory treatment and medication intervention, and her condition gradually came under control.

The conflict between the two sides over the fate of the unborn fetus completely escalated into an irreconcilable deadlock. The attending physician provided an objective and professional medical opinion: current prenatal examinations showed that the fetus's development indicators were normal and stable. However, considering the mother's medical history and the medication she had received during pregnancy, potential health risks for the child after birth could not be completely ruled out. From a medical perspective, termination of the pregnancy was recommended.

Upon hearing this, Chen Lin and his family grew increasingly worried and insisted that Qin Yaoyao have an abortion. They feared the child might be born with health problems and that the family would be burdened by illness for years to come. Yet Qin Yaoyao gently stroked her swollen belly, feeling the faint movements of the fetus, and could not bear to let go. This innate maternal instinct made her refuse to abandon the child under any circumstances, and nothing could shake her resolve.

As the pregnancy progressed month by month, Qin Yaoyao's condition improved but did not fully recover. The dispute between the two sides remained deadlocked, and all warmth in the marriage had been exhausted, bringing it to an end. Chen Lin eventually proposed a divorce request to Qin Yaoyao through his lawyer and simultaneously demanded that she terminate the pregnancy. Left isolated and helpless, yet stubbornly determined, Qin Yaoyao came to me for help, hoping to preserve her right to give birth to the child.

After hearing Qin Yaoyao's story, I knew that because she was still pregnant, Chen Lin had no legal right to file for divorce in court. However, the practical issue of the unborn child's fate was something both parties still had to face and resolve. After taking on her case, I established contact with Chen Lin and his representative to initiate communication and coordination. During our mediation, I expressed to the other side our deep understanding of the Chen family's concerns for the fetus's health and their worries about the family's future; as loved ones, such anxieties were only natural and reasonable. I then focused my core opinions on the objective presentation of legal principles and facts: First, reproductive rights are independent personal rights granted to women by law, inherent core rights of women, which cannot be deprived due to the existence of a marital relationship or a past medical history. As the biological father, the husband had no right to make decisions on behalf of the mother regarding the fate of the fetus. The sole decision-maker on whether to keep the child was Qin Yaoyao herself. Second, it was indeed inappropriate for Qin Yaoyao not to disclose her medical history before marriage, violating the principle of honesty in marriage. However, her condition had long been cured with no signs of recurrence for many years. The relapse during pregnancy was an unpredictable accident, not intentional deception. Moreover, after being informed of the risks, she had actively cooperated with prenatal examinations and medical monitoring throughout her pregnancy, doing everything possible to protect the fetus. Third, Qin Yaoyao willingly agreed to dissolve the marriage and clearly promised that after the child was born, she would bear all childcare responsibilities alone. At the same time, she would not prevent the father from exercising his rights of visitation and parenting, nor would she sever the father-child bond simply because the marriage had broken down.

This mediation session was free of tense confrontation and extreme one-sided accusations. Instead, it consisted of clear interpretations of the law and reasonable expressions of empathy. And in a gentle twist of fate, the day after the two parties reached a divorce agreement, Qin Yaoyao successfully gave birth to a baby girl in the hospital. The infant cried loudly, and all physical indicators were normal — a healthy child.

Holding her soft daughter in her arms, Qin Yaoyao burst into tears. All the past grievances, struggles, and perseverance finally found meaning at this moment. Afterwards, she let go of her resentment and actively pursued follow-up rehabilitation. Her state of mind gradually calmed, and her recovery exceeded all expectations. She devoted herself wholeheartedly to raising her daughter, and life slowly returned to peace.

After the case concluded, I continued to follow the mother and daughter, and was heartened by what followed. When Chen Lin learned that his daughter was born healthy, his estrangement gradually faded. He took the initiative to visit, gradually fulfilled his paternal duties, and the father-daughter bond grew stronger over time. Years later, Qin Yaoyao made a full recovery and calmly accompanied her daughter through childhood. At a children's art exhibition, as she watched her daughter's painting on display, her face was filled with the pride and composure of a mother. The storms of the past had long dissipated, leaving only the quiet warmth of peaceful days.

Post-Case Conclusion

This case has no dramatic twists and turns, nor is it a simple matter of absolute right or wrong. It is merely a true reflection of marital crises suffered by thousands of families, and has given me a deeper understanding of the significance of family law services.

A lasting marriage cannot exist without mutual honesty. Qin Yaoyao's act of concealing her medical history before marriage ultimately became a flaw in the marriage and directly triggered a series of subsequent disturbances. This also serves as a warning to every couple about to get married: important past matters concerning health and the future should not be deliberately hidden. Honesty is the cornerstone of a stable marriage and the only way to avoid unnecessary conflicts and harm from the very beginning.

From a legal perspective, women's reproductive freedom is an unshakable statutory right. The purpose of family law is not only to protect the legitimate rights and interests of every party, but also to balance legal principles with human compassion. Handling family cases requires understanding the parties' circumstances and difficulties, easing antagonism, and minimizing the harm caused by marital breakdown to family members and children. Even when a marriage comes to an end, children should still be able to enjoy complete parental affection, and parties should be able to let go of the past and start a new life.

In this case, the newborn baby marks not only the end of a marriage but also the beginning of a new parental bond. Legal principles safeguard rights, while warmth heals wounds. This is the most touching value of family law, and also the original intention that the book Hard to Tie, Harder to Untie aims to convey.

Photograph by Joseph Xu

Chapter 5 | Greed
第五章 | 贪婪

引文

"人的心只容得下一定程度的绝望，就像海绵吸够了水，即使大海流过，也不能再增添一滴。"

——【法】雨果《巴黎圣母院》

婚姻本应以情感为基石，以信任为脉络，可当贪婪的欲望侵入其中，所有温暖与真诚都会被利益一点点消解。在我经办的各类疑难婚姻家事案件里，贪婪以无数种真实的面目显现：为侵占资产而刻意隐匿、转移夫妻共同财产；为争夺遗产不惜撕破血脉亲情；为争夺抚养权将孩子当作博弈筹码；为掌控家族财富而互相算计、攻讦构陷。

曾经相濡以沫的伴侣，却因财产纷争对簿公堂；曾经血脉相连的至亲，却因资产分配反目成仇。欲望的沟壑永远难以填平，执念的枷锁只会让人越困越紧。太多人在一场场争夺里赢得了纸面的胜利，却输掉了一生的体面、安宁与良知。人们追求所谓的"圆满"，却在追逐中失去了比财富更珍贵的东西。

作为长期行走在法理与情理之间的婚姻律师，我始终坚信：法律的使命是守护公平与底线，而非纵容无度的索取。财富只是生活的依托，绝非幸福的全部；得失只是一时的境遇，绝非人生的终极答案。懂得节制，方得长久；心怀知足，方能心安。这是历经世事之后，最朴素也最珍贵的真理。

Epigraph

"The human heart can hold only a certain measure of despair, just as a sponge, once saturated, can absorb no more water even when the ocean flows over it."

— Victor Hugo, The Hunchback of Notre-Dame

Marriage should be built on affection and woven with trust. Yet when greedy desire invades, all warmth and sincerity are gradually eroded by self-interest. In the complex family and marital cases I have handled, greed reveals itself in countless forms: deliberate concealment and transfer of joint marital assets to seize property; willingness to sever blood ties for inheritance; using children as bargaining chips in custody battles; scheming, attacking, and framing one another to control family wealth.

Partners who once shared weal and woe end up in court over property disputes; blood relatives turn against each other over asset distribution. The chasm of desire can never be filled, and the chains of obsession only bind tighter. Too many win paper victories in their struggles, yet lose their dignity, peace, and conscience for a lifetime. In pursuit of so-called "perfection," they lose what is far more precious than wealth.

As a family lawyer walking between law and human compassion, I have always believed: the mission of law is to safeguard fairness and basic decency, not to indulge excessive demands. Wealth supports life, but is never the whole of happiness; gain and loss are temporary, never the ultimate meaning of life. Restraint brings endurance; contentment brings peace. This is the simplest yet most precious truth after experiencing the ways of the world.

法庭微光：以未成年人之名，修复一段濒临破碎的婚姻

引言

执业二十载，我经手的离婚案件千差万别，有的剑拔弩张，有的利益胶着，有的覆水难收。但经常让我铭记于心的，并不是胜负输赢，而是法律在刚性之外，尚能以温情托举家庭，以理性守护童年，以良知唤醒迷途。这起案件并无繁复的财产纠葛，亦无激烈的人际对抗，却以最朴素的婚姻困境、最隐忍的女性痛苦、最无辜的未成年人创伤，诠释了家事司法最珍贵的意义——不止裁判离合，更守护人心；不止厘清权责，更救赎关系。

婚姻的崩塌，往往不是一瞬间的轰然决裂，而是藏在日复一日的疏离与沉默之中。

2022 年盛夏，赵女士坐在我的咨询室里，周身笼罩着一种近乎窒息的沉静。她手中攥着法院送达的起诉状，纸张边缘已被指尖反复摩挲得微微发皱。相伴十四载的丈夫刘先生，以夫妻感情破裂为由，正式向法院提起离婚诉讼，并请求将婚生子刘子轩的抚养权判归原告刘先生。

赵女士与刘先生于 2008 年自由恋爱成婚，从青涩同行走到中年相守，婚姻平稳走过十余年。婚后，赵女士以全部心力经营家庭，照料起居、抚育幼子、维系亲情，将生活打理得安稳有序，是传统意义上温柔隐忍的妻子与母亲。若不是隐秘的裂痕悄然蔓延，这个家庭本应在平淡中安稳前行。

变化始于 2020 年。

最先感知异常的，是女性近乎本能的敏感与直觉。赵女士发现丈夫的作息出现不正常，回家时间也不规律，手机也从不离身，言语间疏离淡漠，曾经的默契与温情悄然消散。那些细微却刺目的异常，在赵女士心中埋下不安的种子，她试图忽略，试图自解，却终究无法无视心底日渐清晰的预感。

在反复的挣扎与迟疑后，她不得不面对现实——通过行踪轨迹与生活细节的观察，那些她最不愿触碰的真相，终于显露和确信：刘先生出轨了，和一名赵女士并不认识的女性。

真相摊开的那一刻，赵女士十四年的托付、信任与坚守，在一瞬间被彻底撼动。她经历了沉默的痛哭、深夜的辗转、自我怀疑与尊严受损的双重煎熬，却始终未曾将伤口暴露于人前。为了维护家庭的完整，为了让幼子在稳定的环境中成长，她选择将所有痛楚吞咽，以隐忍换取暂时的平静，以退让等待丈夫的回心转意。

而她并不知道，丈夫的变化，并非一时糊涂，而是一场始于网络的境外迷局。自 2021 年起，刘先生在社交平台结识了一位华裔菲律宾籍女商人。对方谈吐干练，以跨境投资、海外创业为话题，一步步拉近关系，凭借精心编织的商

业蓝图，让久居安稳生活的刘先生逐渐心生向往。两人交流日益密切，情感越界，最终发展为婚外恋情。

在对方不断游说下，刘先生被所谓"海外商机"深深蛊惑，对方更频频怂恿他抛下国内一切，远赴海外共同创业、开启全新生活。被甜言蜜语与虚幻前景冲昏头脑的刘先生，渐渐变得偏执而狂热，对家庭愈发冷漠，对妻儿愈发疏离，开始频繁夜不归宿，一心扑向这场危险的境外迷梦。

曾经温暖的居所，逐渐沦为压抑、沉默、充满隔阂的空间。夫妻间的冷战与疏离，最直接地投射在孩子身上。儿子刘子轩变得沉默敏感、胆怯内敛，在父母的冷战之间无所适从，过早承受了不属于他年纪的心理负重。

赵女士在煎熬中试图沟通、试图挽回、试图修补濒临破裂的关系，可所有努力都石沉大海。直到 2022 年，离婚诉状送达，她所有的隐忍与期待，彻底落空。多年付出被轻贱，满心真诚被辜负，安稳生活被击碎，她在绝望与不甘之中，来到我面前，寻求法律的帮助。

接受委托后，我并未急于进入对抗式诉讼程序。在完整梳理案情、核实婚姻基础、评估情感状态后，又与赵女士耐心了解沟通后。我得出清晰判断：双方婚姻基础牢固，感情并未彻底破裂，矛盾源于刘先生单方的行为出轨与认知迷失，而非根本性不可调和；而一旦婚姻解除，遭受最持久、最深刻伤害的，必然是未成年人刘子轩。而我获得的一个最重要的信息是，刘先生非常疼爱儿子，也非常在意对儿子的培养和教育。

随即，我让赵女士将孩子带来见我。我和刘子轩进行了非常愉快轻松的沟通，我发现孩子很聪明，很懂事，只是有些胆小，畏惧，但他非常爱他的妈妈，也爱他的爸爸，他不愿意爸爸妈妈分开，更不愿意让他选择单独跟随任何一方生活。我意识到，我已经找到了解开这个婚姻困局的关键一步。

我随即与承办法官深入沟通，提出一个重要的程序建议，请求法官征询孩子关于抚养权的意愿，同时也以亲情唤醒情感，以童真触动人心。我始终坚信，在家事审判之中，最有力量的并非法条与证据，而是血脉相连的亲子之情，是一个孩子最纯粹、最无辜、也最不容伤害的眼神。解决家事矛盾的核心，并非是"解除婚姻"，律师更不应仅仅帮助当事人远离婚姻的泥沼，而在于利益衡平、情感修复、未成年人利益最大化。对这起案件而言，最优解并非判决离婚，而是唤醒良知、化解矛盾、促成和好、守护家庭。法官对我方的意见表示了认同。

庭审当日，气氛凝重。刘先生态度冷淡，坚持离婚诉求，不愿意和好，仿佛婚姻早已成为需要剥离的负担。就在庭审趋于僵持之际，法官宣布休庭。并要求当事人赵女士将孩子从学校接来，准许孩子进入调解室与法官进行交流。

此时，赵女士的哥哥老赵早已等候在庭外，他迅速到学校将刚放学的刘子轩接到法庭。当身形瘦小的刘子轩被匆匆带来，安静的怯生生的站在法庭的门口时，他眼神不安地望向自己的父亲刘先生，他没有哭闹，没有言语，只是以孩童最本真的目光，注视着那个曾经庇护他、如今却决意离开的亲人。

短短一瞬，足以击穿所有坚硬的伪装。前一刻仍坚持诉求的刘先生，在与孩子目光相接的刹那，神情骤然松动，心底最后一道防线彻底崩塌。而几乎同时，他此前已隐隐察觉的真相，终于让他彻底清醒过来，那位菲律宾华裔女商人的海外投资，从头到尾都是一场精心设计的骗局，所谓创业、商机、未来，全是诱骗他离家、掏空他信任的圈套。

悔恨瞬间将他淹没。他看着无辜的儿子，惶惑的站在法庭上，愧疚、自责、心疼与顿悟涌至心底，他情绪失控，冲上去抱住儿子，崩溃痛哭。"儿子，爸爸不离婚了。我们回家。"这一刻，赵女士泪如泉涌，法官，和我，也都难掩感慨，潸然泪下。那悲恸的场景，在我执笔写到此处时，仍记忆犹新，感慨万千。

那天，刘先生当庭承认自身过错，对婚姻中的失责、背叛与冷漠深刻悔过，并向妻子赵女士诚恳致歉。他坦言，自己因一时糊涂迷失在境外迷梦之中，险些葬送整个家庭，如今彻底醒悟，只愿回归妻儿身边，用余生弥补过错。

最终，在法院主持下，双方达成和好调解。刘先生当庭撤回离婚起诉，承诺断绝一切不当交往，踏实回归家庭，全力履行丈夫与父亲的责任。赵女士在目睹丈夫彻底清醒、真心悔改之后，选择以包容与理性放下过往伤痕，给婚姻一次修复的机会，给孩子一个完整安稳的成长空间。

一场濒临破碎的婚姻，在法律的引导与亲情的感召下，重归完整。

案后结语

在大量离婚案件中，成年人往往聚焦于情绪宣泄、利益分割与是非对错，却极易忽略：婚姻的破裂，最沉默、最长久、最难以修复的受害者，是未成年人。父母关系的破裂、家庭结构的崩塌、成长环境的动荡，都可能在孩子心底留下贯穿一生的阴影印记。

因此，家事律师的价值，不能局限于庭审对抗、财产分割或抚养权争夺。真正的专业，是穿透情绪表象，判断婚姻是否具有修复可能；真正的责任，是以未成年人利益最大化为核心，引导案件走向最有利于成长的结局；真正的智慧，是在法律框架内，兼顾情理，唤醒良知，促成和解。

这起案件的意义，不在于“没有离婚”，而在于关系被看见、创伤被抚慰、过错被悔改、家庭被守护。它让我们看见：婚姻可以有裂痕，但裂痕未必意味着终结；人性可以有迷失，但迷途永远留有折返的光亮；法律可以有尺度，但尺度之上，始终有人性的温度。

对我而言，这便是家事律师最核心的使命：以法律为准则，以情理为温度，以未成年人利益最大化为终极目标。在该断的婚姻里守护公平与底线，在可修复的关系中促成谅解与重生，让每一份裁判与调解，都真正护佑家庭、抚慰人心、点亮归途。

A Glimmer of Light in Court: In the Name of a Minor, Mending a Marriage on the Brink

Introduction

Over two decades of practice, I have handled countless divorce cases—some fraught with tension, some entangled in interests, some beyond repair. Yet what has stayed with me most deeply is not victory or defeat, but the fact that beyond its rigidity, the law can also uphold families with compassion, protect childhood with reason, and awaken the lost with conscience. This case involved no complicated property disputes nor fierce personal conflicts. Yet through an ordinary marital crisis, a woman's quiet suffering, and the innocent trauma of a minor, it reveals the most precious meaning of family justice: it does not merely judge separation or union, but guards human hearts; it does not only clarify rights and duties, but redeems relationships.

The collapse of a marriage is rarely a sudden rupture. More often, it hides in day-to-day estrangement and silence.

In the high summer of 2022, Ms. Zhao sat in my consultation room, enveloped in an almost suffocating calm. She clutched a court summons, its edges worn thin from being repeatedly squeezed in her fingers. Her husband of 14 years, Mr. Liu, had formally filed for divorce on the grounds of irreconcilable broken relationship, requesting custody of their son Liu Zixuan.

Ms. Zhao and Mr. Liu married in 2008 after dating freely. From youthful companions to middle-aged life partners, their marriage had lasted steadily for more than a decade. After marriage, Ms. Zhao devoted herself entirely to the family—caring for daily life, raising their son, nurturing family bonds—and kept their home orderly and peaceful. She was, in the traditional sense, a gentle and forbearing wife and mother. But for a quiet crack that gradually spread, this family might have continued peacefully.

Change began in 2020.

Ms. Zhao first sensed something wrong through a woman's almost instinctive sensitivity. Her husband's schedule grew erratic; he often returned late and unreachable; his phone was never out of his hand; his tone turned distant and cold. The once warm understanding quietly faded. Those small but glaring signs planted unease in her heart. She tried to ignore them, to rationalize them, yet could not deny the growing premonition.

After repeated struggle and hesitation, she finally faced the truth. Comparing his whereabouts and daily habits, the reality she least wanted to accept was confirmed: Mr. Liu was having an affair with a woman unknown to her.

In that moment, 14 years of devotion, trust, and commitment were utterly shaken. She cried silently, tossed through sleepless nights, and suffered the double agony of self-doubt and wounded dignity—yet never exposed her pain to others. To keep the family intact and let her son grow in stability, she chose to swallow all her pain, endure for temporary peace, and compromise in hope that her husband would return.

Little did she know, his change was not a momentary lapse, but a foreign trap born online. Starting in 2021, Mr. Liu met a Chinese-Filipino businesswoman on social media. Articulate and capable, she drew close by talking about cross-border investment and overseas entrepreneurship. With an elaborately woven business blueprint, she stirred longing in Mr. Liu, who had long lived a stable life. Their communication deepened, emotions crossed boundaries, and they eventually developed an extramarital affair.

Under constant persuasion, Mr. Liu fell deeply for the so-called "overseas business opportunities." She repeatedly urged him to abandon everything at home and start a new life abroad with her. Blinded by sweet words and illusory promises, Mr. Liu grew obsessed and fanatical. He became increasingly indifferent to his family, distant from his wife and child, often stayed out all night, and chased this dangerous overseas fantasy wholeheartedly.

The once-warm home gradually turned into a place of suppression, silence, and division. The cold war and emotional distance between the couple directly affected their son. Liu Zixuan became quiet, sensitive, timid, and withdrawn. Caught between his parents' estrangement, he bore a psychological weight far beyond his age.

Ms. Zhao struggled to communicate, reconcile, and repair the broken bond, yet all her efforts were in vain. When the divorce petition arrived in 2022, all her endurance and hope shattered. Years of dedication dismissed, sincerity betrayed, peaceful life destroyed—she came to me in despair and unwillingness, seeking legal help.

After accepting the mandate, I did not rush into adversarial proceedings. After fully reviewing the case, examining their marital foundation, assessing their emotional state, and speaking at length with Ms. Zhao, I reached a clear judgment: the marriage had a solid foundation and was not completely broken. The conflict stemmed from Mr. Liu's own misconduct and confusion, not fundamental irreconcilable differences. And if the marriage ended, the most enduring and profound harm would fall on their minor son Liu Zixuan. One crucial detail stood out: Mr. Liu deeply loved his son and cared greatly about his upbringing and education.

I then asked Ms. Zhao to bring the boy to meet me. I spoke with Liu Zixuan in a relaxed and pleasant way. I found him intelligent and sensible, yet timid and fearful. He loved both his mother and father dearly and did not want his parents to separate, let alone be forced to choose only one parent to live with. I realized I had found the key to unlocking this marital impasse.

I immediately communicated thoroughly with the presiding judge and proposed an important procedural suggestion: to solicit the child's opinion on custody, while awakening affection through family bonds and touching the heart with childlike innocence. I have always believed that in family trials, the greatest power lies not in laws or evidence, but in the blood tie between parent and child—the pure, innocent, and vulnerable gaze of a child. The core of resolving family disputes is not simply "ending the marriage." A lawyer should not merely help a client escape a troubled marriage, but pursue balanced interests, emotional healing, and the best interests of the minor. In this case, the optimal outcome was not a divorce judgment, but awakening conscience, resolving conflicts, promoting reconciliation, and protecting the family. The judge agreed with our position.

On the day of the hearing, the atmosphere was solemn. Mr. Liu remained firm in his divorce request, speaking calmly and with restrained emotion, as if the marriage had long been a burden to be cast off. As the hearing reached a stalemate, the judge called a recess and asked Ms. Zhao to bring their son from school, permitting the child to enter the mediation room to speak with the judge.

Ms. Zhao's elder brother, waiting outside, quickly fetched Liu Zixuan from school and brought him to the court. When the small, thin boy arrived quietly and timidly at the courtroom door, he looked uneasily toward his father. He did not cry or speak; he only gazed with pure childish eyes at the man who had once protected him but now intended to leave.

In that brief moment, all tough pretense collapsed. Mr. Liu, who had insisted on divorce moments before, instantly softened upon meeting his son's eyes. His last line of defense crumbled completely. At almost the same time, the truth he had vaguely suspected finally dawned on him: the overseas investment scheme promoted by the Chinese-Filipino woman was an elaborate fraud from start to finish. The so-called entrepreneurship, business opportunities, and future were all traps to lure him away from home and betray his trust.

Remorse overwhelmed him. Looking at his innocent son standing confused in court, guilt, self-blame, heartache, and realization flooded him. He lost control, rushed forward, hugged his son, and broke down crying. "Son, Daddy's not getting divorced. We're going home." At that moment, Ms. Zhao burst into tears. The judge and I were also moved to tears. Even now, as I write this, that heartbreaking scene remains vivid in my memory, filling me with deep emotion.

That day, Mr. Liu admitted his fault in open court, sincerely repented his neglect, betrayal, and coldness toward the marriage, and apologized earnestly to his wife. He confessed that he had been lost in a foreign fantasy and nearly ruined his entire family. Now fully awake, he only wished to return to his wife and child and make amends for the rest of his life.

Ultimately, under the auspices of the court, the couple reached a reconciliation. Mr. Liu withdrew his divorce petition on the spot, promised to cut off all inappropriate relations, return wholeheartedly to his family, and fully fulfill his duties as husband and father. After witnessing her husband's genuine awakening and repentance, Ms. Zhao chose tolerance and reason to let go of past wounds, giving their marriage a chance to heal and their son a complete and stable upbringing.

A marriage on the verge of collapse was made whole again, guided by law and inspired by family love.

Post-Case Conclusion

In many divorce cases, adults often focus on emotional outbursts, dividing property, and proving right or wrong, yet easily overlook one fact: when a marriage breaks, the most silent, long-lasting, and irreparable victim is the minor. Broken parental relations, collapsed family structure, and unstable upbringing can leave lifelong scars on a child's heart.

Therefore, the value of a family lawyer extends far beyond courtroom confrontation, property division, or custody battles. True professionalism lies in seeing through emotional appearances and judging whether a marriage can be repaired. True responsibility lies in centering on the best interests of the minor and steering the case toward the outcome most beneficial to the child's growth. True wisdom lies in balancing reason and empathy within the law, awakening conscience, and fostering reconciliation.

The meaning of this case is not simply that "no divorce happened." It is that the relationship was acknowledged, trauma soothed, wrongdoing repented, and the family protected. It shows us: Marriage can have cracks, yet cracks do not always mean the end. Human nature can stray, yet there is always light to guide the lost back. The law has boundaries, yet above those boundaries lies the warmth of humanity.

For me, this is the core mission of a family lawyer: to uphold the law as principle, to embody compassion as warmth, and to prioritize the best interests of minors as the ultimate goal. In marriages that must end, we safeguard fairness and bottom lines. In relationships that can be mended, we promote forgiveness and renewal. May every judgment and mediation truly protect families, comfort hearts, and light the way home.

跨国婚姻父女分离，“首诉不离”下的贪婪之欲

引言

跨国婚姻本应是文化交融的美好联结，可当文化差异、情感隔阂叠加人性的贪婪，便会沦为一场漫长的煎熬与拉扯。本案的当事人，埃及籍原告卡里姆与云南籍被告邱杉美，因宗教与文化的分歧，陷入长达十年的分居僵局，婚姻早已名存实亡。作为卡里姆的代理律师，我全程参与这场诉讼，亲眼见证原告十年如一日的付出，却遭遇被告突破底线的贪婪索取，一审法院因被告当庭拒不同意离婚，作出首次判决不准予离婚的裁判。这场看似普通的跨国离婚案，不仅撕开了婚姻破裂的残酷真相，更暴露了人性深处的自私与贪婪，也让我们重新审视我国“首诉不离”司法规则的利弊，以及中西离婚审判体系的核心差异。

接手这个案件时，原告卡里姆先生眼中的疲惫与委屈，让我至今印象深刻。他是埃及籍商人，2005 年远赴中国义乌经商，凭借诚信经营在当地站稳脚跟。2006 年，他在义乌结识了在此务工的邱杉美，两人相恋后，因卡里姆信奉伊斯兰教，于同年在清真寺依宗教仪式举办婚礼，又在 2008 年 5 月间赴云南办理结婚登记，正式确立合法夫妻关系，2016 年 3 月，两人的婚生女邱伊莎降生，这个中埃混血的小生命，曾是卡里姆对这段婚姻最后的期许。

婚初，两人感情尚可，一同在义乌生活，可随着相处日久，中埃两国文化背景、宗教信仰、价值观念的巨大差异彻底显现，性格不合的矛盾也日益尖锐，夫妻感情迅速消耗，早已走到破裂边缘。两人曾数次协商离婚，恰逢邱杉美突然怀孕，卡里姆念及腹中胎儿，出于父亲的责任，选择放下矛盾，陪同邱杉美前往杭州医院产检、保胎，满心期待女儿的出生，能让这段婚姻重归于好。

可这份善意，终究是错付了。女儿邱伊莎出生仅两三个月，邱杉美便以父母需要照料、能帮忙带孩子为由，不顾卡里姆的极力反对，执意带着女儿返回云南老家，从此，两人开始了长达十年以上的分居生活，这段婚姻彻底沦为空壳。这十年间，邱杉美仅偶尔带女儿来义乌短暂居住，卡里姆无数次低声请求她带着女儿回义乌共同生活，给孩子一个完整的家，可每一次都被邱杉美无情拒绝，硬生生将卡里姆与女儿分隔两地，让他承受十年父女分离的煎熬，作为父亲，不能陪伴女儿成长，成了卡里姆心中最深的痛。

十年分居，两人早已没有任何夫妻生活，仅有的交集，全是卡里姆对女儿的牵挂与付出。作为父亲，卡里姆从未推卸过抚养责任，十年间持续通过转账、现金等方式，向邱杉美支付女儿的抚养费，累计金额高达 120 多万元，平均每年支付 12 万余元。女儿学龄前，每年都会来义乌与卡里姆同住月余，父女相处融洽，感情深厚，可近几年，邱杉美彻底变本加厉，不仅以各种借口阻拦父女相见，还不断以女儿的名义，以各种理由借口向卡里姆索要高额钱款，甚至教唆

年幼的女儿通过语音、视频主动向父亲要钱，持续不断地索要，仿佛一个无底洞，永远也填不满。

更让卡里姆忧心的是，他倾尽所有支付的大额款项，并未被邱杉美用于女儿的生活与教育。邱伊莎在云南老家衣着朴素，生活条件普通，丝毫看不出父亲支付了高额抚养费，这些钱显然被邱杉美挪作他用，甚至用来供养自己的父母、弟弟一家三口，成了邱杉美全家的生活来源，卡里姆的善意与付出，彻底被邱杉美的贪婪吞噬。

除此之外，邱伊莎是中埃混血，外貌特征更像父亲卡里姆，肤色较深，在云南老家的小县城生活学习时，因外貌异于同龄人，长期遭受同学排挤、歧视，幼小的心灵早已受到严重伤害，身心健康岌岌可危。而卡里姆居住的义乌，是国际化大都市，外籍人士众多，环境包容多元，能给女儿提供平等友善的成长环境，他收入稳定，有足够的能力为女儿提供优质的生活与教育资源，可这一切，都被邱杉美的自私与固执阻断。

眼见婚姻毫无挽回余地，父女分离的痛苦日益加剧，卡里姆无奈之下，委托我向法院提起离婚诉讼，诉讼请求清晰明确：一是判令准予双方离婚；二是判令婚生女邱伊莎由自己抚养，邱杉美每月支付 2000 元抚养费至女儿独立生活。

可庭审中，邱杉美的答辩意见，却完全暴露了她的贪婪与无理，提出的各项诉求毫无法律与事实依据，简直是漫天要价：她先是声称双方感情尚可，坚决不同意离婚，试图继续捆绑这段名存实亡的婚姻，以此继续索取钱财；随后又表示，若法院判决离婚，便要求女儿抚养权归自己，让卡里姆每月支付 1 万元抚养费，同时索要 80 万元家务劳动补偿金，还要求分割卡里姆经营的贸易公司，让卡里姆一次性支付 60 万元财产分割款等等，诉求合计金额高达 250 余万元。

作为卡里姆的代理律师，我在庭审中逐一驳斥邱杉美的无理诉求，清晰阐明其诉求明显违背常理，也毫无证据支撑，并全力还原卡里姆十年的付出与遭遇的不公：

首先，关于抚养费，邱杉美主张的每月 1 万元，漫天要价，毫无依据。邱杉美居住地为云南某乡镇，当地城镇居民人均月收入不足 4000 元，消费支出水平远低于 1 万元，1 万元的抚养费标准，远超当地生活水平与孩子的实际成长需求。卡里姆十年累计支付的 120 多万元，早已远超女儿实际所需，即便按每月 2000 元的宽裕标准计算，十年抚养费也仅 20 余万元，剩余近百万款项，均被邱杉美占有使用，如今她还索要高额抚养费，纯粹是将女儿当成敛财工具，贪婪至极。

其次，关于 80 万元家务劳动补偿金，更是于法无据、于实不符。邱杉美声称是卡里姆要求她遵循宗教教义辞职在家，可事实并非如此，她是因工作不力被辞退，并非卡里姆要求，且双方分居长达十年，早已各自生活，邱杉美根本没有为卡里姆付出任何家务劳动，家中环境脏乱不堪，她也从未尽到照顾家庭、照料丈夫的责任，所谓家务补偿，不过是她贪婪索取的借口。

最后，关于分割贸易公司 60 万元的诉求，同样不成立。卡里姆经营的贸易公司，并无实质资产，反而因近年国际环境的影响和中东战争影响，背负至少 40 万美元的债务，双方根本无夫妻共同财产可分割，邱杉美拿不出任何证据证明公司有可分割资产，却执意索要巨额款项，纯属无理。

反观卡里姆，十年间独自承受父女分离的煎熬，从未间断对女儿的抚养付出，倾尽财力供养邱杉美全家，可换来的不是理解与感恩，而是邱杉美无休止的索取、阻拦父女相见，甚至教唆女儿索要钱财，这段婚姻带给卡里姆的，只有无尽的痛苦、委屈与不公。尽管如此，在法庭上，我们仍充分表达卡里姆先生渴望争取女儿抚养权的强烈意愿。虽然我们清楚，孩子长期在母亲身边生活，形成了客观事实，法院一般会判决孩子抚养权归属母亲。但卡里姆先生深爱着女儿，且洁身自好，完全没有任何生活瑕疵，被告本人也承认丈夫卡里姆先生的人品非常好。卡里姆先生的诚心诚意也让法庭和各方动容。

庭审结束后，一审法院基于“首诉不离”的司法审判实践，因被告坚决不同意离婚，而作出了“不准予离婚”的判决。根据中国法律的规定，卡里姆先生有权在半年之后再次起诉离婚，方能获得最终的离婚判决。

案后结语

这起跨国婚姻纠纷，是婚姻与人性的双重照妖镜，它不仅展现了跨国婚姻中文化差异带来的困境，更将人性的贪婪、自私与婚姻中的不公，展现得淋漓尽致。在原有对婚姻、司法规则的思考基础上，结合本案细节，更能深度剖析人性贪婪在婚姻破裂中的恶劣影响，也让我们对“首诉不离”规则、中西离婚审判差异有更清晰的认知。

从婚姻本质来看，婚姻的基石是情感、坦诚与责任，可本案中，邱杉美抛弃了这些底线，利用父女亲情、十年分居，一味地索取，让原本可以和平解决的离婚纠纷，变成一场充满贪婪与算计的拉锯。卡里姆的善意、责任与十年付出，换来的却是无休止的压榨与父女分离的痛苦，这段婚姻早已失去存在的意义，却因被告的贪婪与固执，被迫延续，尽显婚姻的无奈与悲凉。

人性的贪婪，是婚姻破裂后最伤人的利刃。本案中邱杉美的行为，是人性贪婪的典型体现：她明知双方感情早已破裂，却拒不离婚，以此要挟索取高额补偿；无视卡里姆十年的经济付出，将对方的善意当成理所当然，甚至挪用女儿的抚养费供养自家亲人；不顾女儿的身心健康，为了钱财阻拦父女相聚，将年幼的女儿当成索要钱财的筹码。贪婪让她失去了基本的良知与底线，不仅伤害了真心付出的卡里姆，更让无辜的女儿成为牺牲品，长期处于歧视与亲情缺失的环境中。既毁掉了过往的情分，也让自己陷入道德的困境，最终既得不到想要的利益，也错失了体面放手的机会。

而卡里姆遭遇的不公，更让人唏嘘。他作为外籍人士，在中国打拼，始终坚守父亲的责任，十年付出不计回报，却因对方的贪婪，被迫承受父女分离的煎熬，连陪伴女儿成长的权利都被剥夺，法律虽能维护权益，却难以立刻抚平这份情感与人性带来的伤害，这也让我们看到，婚姻家事纠纷中，人心的复杂，远比法律的约束更难应对。

关于我国司法实践中“首诉不离”的规则，优势在于，坚守维护婚姻家庭稳定的核心，给予双方冷静修复的机会，避免冲动离婚，尤其保护未成年人的成长环境，契合我国传统婚姻观念，也节约司法资源。但弊端也尤为突出：对于本案这种分居十年、感情完全破裂、一方纯粹以不同意离婚为筹码漫天要价的案件，“首诉不离”反而延长了无过错方的痛苦，纵容了过错方的贪婪，违背了婚姻自由的核心原则，让无过错方继续陷入不公的婚姻困境，也不利于未成年人的健康成长。法官虽秉持司法温情，可在人性贪婪面前，这份温情难以驳斥无理诉求，凸显了规则在特殊案件中的局限性。

对比西方普通法系国家的离婚审判规则，二者差异显著。我国以“感情确已破裂”为离婚核心标准，“首诉不离”是惯例，更重家庭稳定与情理考量，法官自由裁量权较大，注重调解化解矛盾，即便感情破裂，也会给予修复机会；而西方普通法系国家多采用无过错离婚原则，只要一方主张婚姻无法维系，法院即可判决离婚，极少出现“首诉不离”，更注重当事人的离婚自由与个人权利，财产、抚养权严格依法裁判，不会因一方不同意离婚而强行维系，对贪婪诉求的约束更直接，更注重形式正义与程序正义。

但对于六个月后第二次起诉离婚的案件，我国法院则基本判决准予离婚。因此离婚仍然是终局的结果，它不会因一方的执意不离而被阻止，也不会让一方的贪财诉求而得逞。西方普通法系的离婚诉讼虽无首诉不离的规则，但它审理期限漫长，往往因一方在诉讼中基于程序上的反复交涉而陷入僵局，离婚诉讼审理期超过一两年也很常态。因此制度本身各有利弊，重要的是对于个案的处理，需要更加人性化的审判精神。

对于卡里姆而言，一审判决虽未如愿，但他为女儿争取幸福的初心从未改变，也希望这场漫长的拉锯，能早日迎来公正的结果，让无辜的孩子摆脱困境，让贪婪者承担应有的代价。因为，婚姻需要责任与坦诚，一旦贪婪占据上风，再美好的缘分也会沦为煎熬。

Separation of Father and Daughter in a Cross-Border Marriage: Greed Under the "No Divorce in First Action" Rule

Introduction

A cross-border marriage should be a beautiful bond of cultural integration. Yet when cultural differences, emotional estrangement, and human greed combine, it can degenerate into a long period of torment and entanglement. The parties in this case—Karim, an Egyptian national as plaintiff, and Qiu Shanmei, a Chinese national from Yunnan Province as defendant—have been trapped in a decade-long deadlock of separation due to religious and cultural divisions, rendering their marriage merely nominal. As Karim's attorney, I participated in the entire litigation and witnessed the plaintiff's decade of unwavering devotion, only to be met with the defendant's unscrupulous and greedy demands. At first instance, the court ruled against divorce because the defendant explicitly refused to consent in court. This seemingly ordinary cross-border divorce case not only exposes the cruel reality of a broken marriage, but also reveals the deep-seated selfishness and greed of human nature. It also prompts us to re-examine the advantages and disadvantages of the judicial practice of "no divorce in first action" in China, as well as the core differences between Chinese and Western divorce adjudication systems.

When I took on this case, the exhaustion and grievance in Mr. Karim's eyes left a deep impression on me. An Egyptian businessman, he traveled to Yiwu, China in 2005 to run a business and established a solid foothold through honest management. In 2006, he met Qiu Shanmei, who was working in Yiwu. After they fell in love, and in light of Karim's Islamic faith, they held a religious wedding ceremony at a mosque in the same year. In 2008, they traveled to Yunnan to register their marriage to formalize their legal spousal relationship. In March 2016, the couple welcomed their daughter, Qiu Yisha. This little Sino-Egyptian girl was once Karim's last hope for the marriage.

At the beginning of the marriage, the couple enjoyed a decent relationship and lived together in Yiwu. However, as time passed, profound differences in cultural background, religious belief, and values between China and Egypt fully emerged, and conflicts over incompatible personalities intensified. Marital affection quickly faded, bringing the relationship to the brink of breakdown. The couple negotiated divorce on several occasions, until Qiu Shanmei suddenly became pregnant. Out of paternal responsibility and consideration for the unborn child, Karim chose to set aside their disputes. He accompanied her to hospitals in Hangzhou for prenatal checks and to protect the fetus, earnestly hoping that the birth of their daughter could reconcile the marriage.

Yet this kindness was ultimately misplaced. Only two to three months after Qiu Yisha was born, Qiu Shanmei insisted on returning to her hometown in Yunnan with the baby, claiming that her parents needed care and could help raise the child—despite Karim's strong opposition. Since then, the couple had been separated for more than ten years, and their marriage became an empty shell. During these ten years, Qiu Shanmei only occasionally brought their daughter to Yiwu for short stays. Karim repeatedly pleaded with her to return to Yiwu with their child to provide a complete family, but each request was ruthlessly rejected. She forcibly kept Karim apart from his daughter, subjecting him to a decade of agony of father-daughter separation. Being unable to accompany his daughter as she grew up became Karim's deepest pain.

After ten years of separation, the couple no longer had any marital relations. Their only interaction revolved around Karim's concern for and support of their daughter. As a father, Karim never shirked his parental responsibilities. Over the decade, he continuously provided child support to Qiu Shanmei via bank transfers and cash payments, totaling more than 1.2 million yuan, averaging over 120,000 yuan per year. Before her daughter reached school age, she would stay with Karim in Yiwu for about a month each year, and the father and daughter enjoyed a warm and close relationship. In recent years, however, Qiu Shanmei has become increasingly excessive. She not only obstructed father-daughter meetings under various pretexts, but also repeatedly demanded large sums of money from Karim in the name of their daughter. She even instigated the young girl to ask her father for money through voice messages and video calls. This endless stream of demands has become a bottomless pit that can never be filled.

What troubles Karim even more is that the large sums he has paid with all his means have not been used for his daughter's daily life or education by Qiu Shanmei. Qiu Yisha lives a plain life with simple clothes in her hometown in Yunnan, showing no sign that her father has been providing high child support. The money has clearly been misappropriated by Qiu Shanmei for other purposes, even to support her parents and her brother's family of three, becoming the entire family's source of income. Karim's kindness and devotion have been completely devoured by Qiu Shanmei's greed.

In addition, Qiu Yisha is of mixed Chinese-Egyptian heritage and bears a strong resemblance to her father Karim, with relatively darker skin. While studying and living in a small county town in Yunnan, she has long been excluded and discriminated against by classmates due to her different appearance. Her young mind has suffered severe harm, and her physical and mental health is in grave danger. By contrast, Yiwu, where Karim resides, is an international metropolis with a large expatriate community and an inclusive, diverse environment that can offer her daughter an equal and friendly upbringing. Karim has a stable income and is fully capable of providing high-quality living and educational resources for his daughter. Yet all this has been blocked by Qiu Shanmei's selfishness and stubbornness.

Seeing no hope of saving the marriage and suffering increasing agony from being separated from his daughter, Karim had no choice but to entrust me to file a divorce lawsuit with the court. His claims were clear and specific:

To grant a divorce between the two parties;

To award custody of their daughter Qiu Yisha to Karim, with Qiu Shanmei paying 2,000 yuan per month in child support until the daughter reaches financial independence;

However, during the trial, Qiu Shanmei's pleadings fully exposed her greed and unreasonableness. Her demands were legally and factually baseless, amounting to exorbitant overcharging. She first claimed that the relationship between the couple remained normal and firmly refused to agree to a divorce, attempting to prolong this empty marriage to continue extorting money. She then stated that if the court granted a divorce, she would demand sole custody of their daughter, require Karim to pay 10,000 yuan per month in child support, claim 800,000 yuan as compensation for housework, demand the division of Karim's trading company, and request a one-time property division payment of 600,000 yuan from Karim. The total amount of her claims exceeded 2.5 million yuan.

As Karim's attorney, I refuted Qiu Shanmei's unreasonable demands one by one in court, clearly demonstrating that they were contrary to common sense and unsupported by evidence. I also fully presented Karim's decade of devotion and the injustice he had suffered.

First, regarding child support, Qiu Shanmei's claim of 10,000 yuan per month was excessive unfounded. Qiu Shanmei lives in a township in Yunnan, where the per capita monthly income of urban residents is less than 4,000 yuan, and the local consumption level is far below 10,000 yuan. Such a child support standard far exceeds the local living standard and the actual needs of the child. The more than 1.2 million yuan Karim had paid over ten years already far exceeded his daughter's actual needs. Even at a generous standard of 2,000 yuan per month, ten years of support would only amount to around 200,000 yuan. The remaining nearly one million yuan was possessed and used by Qiu Shanmei. Her current demand for high child support is nothing more than using her daughter as a tool for profit, revealing extreme greed.

Second, her claim for 800,000 yuan in housework compensation lacks both legal basis and factual support. Qiu Shanmei alleged that Karim required her to resign and stay at home in accordance with Islamic teachings. However, the truth is that she was dismissed due to poor work performance, not at Karim's request. Furthermore, the couple had been separated for ten years and lived independently. Qiu Shanmei had not performed any housework for Karim at all. The home was in a messy and unhygienic condition, and she never fulfilled her duties to care for the family or her husband. The so-called housework compensation was merely an excuse for her greedy demands.

Lastly, her claim for a 600,000-yuan division of the trading company is equally untenable. The trading company owned and operated by Karim has no substantial assets. On the contrary, due to the impact of the international environment and conflicts in the Middle East in recent years, the company is burdened with debts of at least 400,000 US dollars. There are simply no community assets of the couple subject to division. Qiu Shanmei has failed to produce any evidence proving the existence of divisible assets in the company, yet insists on claiming a huge sum of money, which is entirely unreasonable.

For his part, Karim endured a decade of agony of being separated from his daughter. He never ceased providing financial support for his daughter and exhausted his financial means to support Qiu Shanmei's entire family. Yet in return, he received neither understanding nor gratitude, only endless demands from Qiu Shanmei, obstruction of contact between father and daughter, and even instigation of the daughter to ask him for money. This marriage brought Karim nothing but endless pain, grievance and injustice. Even so, in court we fully expressed Mr. Karim's strong wish to obtain custody of his daughter. While we are aware that the child has long lived with the mother as an established fact, and courts generally grant custody to the mother, Mr. Karim deeply loves his daughter and conducts himself with exemplary personal conduct, with no flaws whatsoever. Even the defendant herself acknowledged that her husband Karim is a man of excellent character. Mr. Karim's sincerity moved the court and all parties present.

Following the trial, the court of first instance, based on the judicial practice of "no divorce in first instance" and given the defendant's firm refusal to agree to a divorce, rendered a judgment denying the divorce petition. Pursuant to Chinese law, Mr. Karim has the right to file a second divorce lawsuit six months later, at which point a final divorce judgment may be issued.

Post-Case Conclusion

This transnational marriage dispute serves as a double mirror held up to marriage and human nature. It not only reveals the dilemmas caused by cultural differences in cross-border marriages, but also lays bare the greed, selfishness in human nature and injustices within marriage in the most vivid manner. Building on existing reflections on marriage and judicial rules, and combined with the details of this case, we can conduct an in-depth analysis of the pernicious impact of human greed on marital breakdown, and gain a clearer understanding of the "no divorce in first action" practice and the differences between Chinese and Western divorce adjudication systems.

From the perspective of the essence of marriage, the cornerstones of marriage are affection, honesty and responsibility. Yet in this case, Qiu Shanmei completely abandoned these bottom lines, treating marriage as a tool for amassing wealth. She took advantage of the father-daughter bond and a decade of separation to make unscrupulous demands, turning a divorce dispute that could have been resolved peacefully into a protracted tug-of-war full of greed and calculation. Karim's kindness, sense of responsibility and ten years of devotion were repaid with endless exploitation and the agony of separation from his daughter. This marriage had long lost its meaning, yet it was forced to continue due to the defendant's greed and stubbornness, fully demonstrating the helplessness and cruelty of a failed marriage.

Human greed is the cruellest weapon after a marriage breaks down. Qiu Shanmei's conduct in this case is a typical manifestation of such greed: knowing full well that the relationship had irretrievably broken down, she refused to divorce in order to extort high compensation; ignoring Karim's decade of financial support, she took his kindness for granted, even misappropriating child support funds to support her own relatives; disregarding her daughter's physical and mental health, she blocked father-daughter contact for financial gain, using her young daughter as a bargaining chip for money. Greed deprived her of basic conscience and moral bottom lines. She not only hurt Karim, who had given his all sincerely, but also sacrificed the innocent daughter, who was left in an environment of discrimination and lack of family affection. She destroyed what was left of their past affection, landed herself in moral dilemma, and ultimately gained neither the benefits she craved nor the chance to part with dignity.

The injustice suffered by Karim is deeply lamentable. As a foreigner building a career in China, he faithfully fulfilled his paternal duties, giving selflessly for ten years without asking for anything in return. Yet due to the other party's greed, he was forced to endure the pain of being separated from his daughter, even deprived of the right to accompany her as she grew up. Although the law can uphold his rights and interests, it cannot immediately heal the emotional and human harm inflicted. This also shows that in family and marriage disputes, the evil in human nature is far harder to confront than legal restrictions.

Regarding the judicial rule of "no divorce in first action" in China's practice, its advantage lies in upholding the core principle of maintaining marital and family stability. It gives both parties an opportunity to calm down and repair the relationship, avoiding impulsive divorces, and particularly protecting the upbringing environment for minors. This aligns with traditional Chinese views on marriage and conserves judicial resources. However, its drawbacks are equally prominent: in cases like this one, where the parties have been separated for ten years, the relationship has completely broken down, and one party purely uses their refusal to divorce as a bargaining chip for exorbitant demands, "no divorce in first action" instead prolongs the suffering of the innocent party. It indulges the greedy party, violates the core principle of marital freedom, traps the innocent party in an unfair marital predicament, and is detrimental to the healthy development of the minor. Although the judge upheld judicial compassion, in the face of human greed, this compassion became a protective umbrella for unreasonable demands, highlighting the rule's limitations in exceptional cases.

Comparing this with the divorce adjudication rules in Western common law countries, the differences are significant. China uses the "irretrievable breakdown of affection" as the core standard for divorce, with "no divorce in first action" as the convention. It places greater emphasis on family stability and emotional considerations, grants judges wider discretion, and focuses on mediation to resolve conflicts; even when affection has broken down, an opportunity for repair is provided. In contrast, Western common law countries mostly adopt the principle of no-fault divorce. As long as one party claims the marriage is unsustainable, the court can grant a divorce, and the "no divorce in first action" scenario rarely occurs. They place more emphasis on the parties' freedom of divorce and individual rights. Property and custody are strictly adjudicated according to the law, and a marriage will not be forcibly maintained simply because one party refuses to divorce. Their constraint on greedy demands is more direct, placing greater emphasis on formal and procedural justice.

However, in China, courts almost invariably grant a divorce in the second lawsuit filed six months after the first judgment. Divorce therefore remains the inevitable final outcome. It will not be prevented by one party's stubborn refusal, nor will one party's greedy financial demands prevail. Although Western common law systems do not apply the "no divorce in first action" rule, their divorce proceedings are often extremely lengthy. Cases frequently become deadlocked due to repeated procedural arguments raised by one party, and it is common for divorce litigation to drag on for more than one or two years. Each system thus has its own advantages and disadvantages. What matters most is that the adjudication of individual cases should be conducted with a more human-centered judicial spirit.

For Karim, although the first-instance judgment did not meet his expectations, his original wish to strive for a happy life for his daughter has never wavered. It is hoped that this long tug-of-war will soon reach a just conclusion, freeing the innocent child from her predicament and holding the greedy party accountable for their actions.

After all, marriage requires responsibility and sincerity. Once greed prevails, even the most beautiful relationship will turn into nothing but torment.

狮城余波：新加坡离婚后，我为当事人追回宁波学区房

引言

离婚，或许能斩断情感的牵绊，却未必能厘清财产的纠葛。我的当事人林知夏，与丈夫在新加坡协议离婚，以为从此一别两宽，却不料，一套位于浙江宁波的学区房，成了两人分手后的新战场。当境外离婚协议遇上境内不动产，我以"主要财产所在地管辖"规则为依据，在宁波法院全程代理，为林知夏成功分割了这套承载女儿未来的核心资产。

林知夏第一次坐在我办公室时，手中紧握新加坡的离婚判决书与宁波学区房的房产证，眼神焦急又委屈。她 39 岁，浙江宁波人，是一名资深儿童教育专家，温柔细心、做事有条理，对女儿的教育与成长格外重视。

2010 年，她赴新加坡国立大学攻读教育学硕士，在校园里遇见了同是留学生的山东汉子张磊。张磊比她大两岁，学金融专业，性格沉稳、做事稳妥，在新加坡留学期间对林知夏照顾得无微不至：上课帮忙占座、生病悉心照料、节日精心准备惊喜，这份踏实可靠，让远离家乡的林知夏倍感安心。

两人在新加坡相恋、毕业、结婚，随后一同留在当地定居工作，日子平稳安稳。2015 年，女儿张念宁出生，成为整个家庭的中心。作为教育行业从业者，林知夏从女儿出生起便规划未来教育，两人反复商量后决定：在林知夏的老家——浙江宁波，购买一套重点小学学区房，为女儿将来回国读书做好万全准备。

这套位于海曙区的学区房，总价近千万，由两人婚后共同存款出资购买，登记在双方名下，是他们唯一的不动产，也是为女儿教育预留的核心资产。买房那天，两人还笑着约定：等女儿上小学，就回国生活，一家人安稳相伴。

可这份约定，终究没能抵过生活的磨损。林知夏注重生活品质与教育投入，愿意花重金给女儿报早教班、买绘本、做启蒙培养；张磊则受原生家庭影响，极度节俭务实，甚至到了吝啬的地步，常常因林知夏给女儿买玩具、报兴趣班大发脾气，指责她"乱花钱、没必要"。

生活细节上的冲突更是无处不在：林知夏爱干净、家里收拾得一尘不染，张磊却随意乱扔衣物、从不做家务；林知夏喜欢周末带女儿去公园、图书馆，张磊却宁愿宅在家里玩手机，对母女俩不闻不问。三观不合、消费观悬殊、缺乏陪伴与沟通，让这段婚姻慢慢走向尽头。

2023 年，林知夏与张磊在新加坡家庭法院和平协议离婚，两人对新加坡境内的存款、车辆、家具等财产逐一分割清楚，签字确认。因当时心思慌乱、又专注于女儿抚养权，两人一时疏忽，完全遗漏了国内宁波的学区房，离婚协议里未提及任何关于这套房产的分割约定。

离婚后，林知夏带着女儿回到宁波生活，准备办理入学手续时，却震惊发现：张磊早已偷偷回国，更换了学区房门锁，擅自将房屋出租给陌生人，每月租金全部据为己有，甚至打算长期占有这套房产。林知夏多次联系张磊，要求协商分割这套夫妻共同财产，可张磊态度蛮横、强词夺理：“我们在新加坡已经办完离婚、分完财产，宁波的房子就算没写，也默认归我，你别再来纠缠。”

张磊的霸道与无理，让林知夏又气又急。这套学区房是两人共同出资购买，是女儿未来上学的唯一保障，更是她作为母亲最大的心愿。走投无路之下，林知夏带着全部材料，找到了我。

“叶律师，我们在新加坡离的婚，人也都在新加坡，国内法院还能管这套房子吗？”我看着她焦急无助的模样，非常肯定地告诉她：“当然能。你的房子在宁波，宁波法院有管辖权，我们可以在宁波属地法院起诉依法分割。”根据我国《民事诉讼法司法解释》第十七条明确规定：已经离婚的中国公民，双方均定居国外，仅就国内财产分割提起诉讼的，由主要财产所在地人民法院管辖。本案中，林知夏与张磊均定居新加坡，唯一争议财产就是宁波海曙区的学区房，因此，海曙区人民法院是本案唯一合法管辖法院。

接受委托后，我全程细致代理。

第一步，指导林知夏将新加坡法院出具的离婚判决书，完成中国驻新加坡使馆公证、认证、中文翻译，确保境外法律文书在国内具备合法效力；

第二步，全面收集学区房证据：购房合同、银行转账流水、产权登记证书、双方出资证明，清晰证实该房产为婚后共同出资、属于夫妻共同财产，且未在新加坡离婚时进行分割；

第三步，以“离婚后财产纠纷”为案由，向宁波市海曙区人民法院正式立案，同步申请财产保全，防止张磊私自出售、转移房产；

第四步，庭审中，我针对张磊“已默示分割、归其所有”的无理抗辩，当庭有力反驳：新加坡离婚协议未列明涉案房产，不存在任何“默示分割”的事实与法律依据，该房产仍属双方共同共有，林知夏作为共有人，有权依法平均分割；同时强调，房产为女儿教育购买，林知夏直接抚养女儿，由其持有房屋更有利于子女成长。

法院经审理，完全采纳我方全部代理意见，最终依法判决：涉案学区房归林知夏所有，林知夏在判决生效后向张磊支付房屋折价款 50%。拿到判决书的那一刻，林知夏紧紧握着我的手，眼眶泛红：“叶律师，谢谢你，女儿上学的事终于有着落了。”

案后结语

林知夏与张磊的案例，凸显了跨境离婚最常见的隐患：财产分割不全面、境内外资产未统筹处理。很多当事人在境外离婚时，因疏忽或认知不足，遗漏境内不动产，最终引发不必要的纠纷。

作为家事律师，我的价值，在于精准把握跨境财产纠纷的管辖规则，用专业能力为当事人锁定最佳诉讼路径，守住核心财产利益。我所做的，不过是用法律厘清财产边界，用证据维护公平正义，让每一位当事人，都能在离婚后得到应有的财产保障，让孩子的未来，不因父母离异而受影响。

跨境离婚不是财产分割的终点，中国法院，永远是中国公民财产权益最坚实的守护者。无论婚姻始于何处、财产位于何方，法律都会为你守住应得的公平与希望。

Aftermath in the Lion City: Recovering Ningbo School-District Property for My Client After a Singapore Divorce

Introduction

Divorce may cut the emotional bond, but it does not always clear up complicated property disputes. My client Lin Zhixia reached an amicable divorce with her husband in Singapore, thinking they would go their separate ways peacefully. Unexpectedly, a school-district apartment in Ningbo, Zhejiang, became a new battlefield after their breakup. When an overseas divorce agreement clashed with domestic real estate, I based my case on the rule of jurisdiction at the location of the main property and represented Ms. Lin throughout the proceedings in the Ningbo court. I successfully helped her divide this key asset that held her daughter's future.

When Lin Zhixia first sat in my office, she tightly clutched her Singapore divorce judgment and the ownership certificate of the Ningbo school-district apartment, her eyes anxious and wronged. Aged 39 and a native of Ningbo, Zhejiang, she is a senior expert in early childhood education — gentle, attentive, organized, and deeply focused on her daughter's education and growth.

In 2010, she went to the National University of Singapore to pursue her master's degree in education. There she met Zhang Lei, a fellow student from Shandong. Two years older than her, Zhang studied finance, calm and reliable. During their studies in Singapore, he took excellent care of her: saving seats in class, nursing her when she was ill, and preparing thoughtful surprises on festivals. His steadiness gave Lin Zhixia great comfort far from home.

They fell in love, graduated, and married in Singapore, then settled and worked there together, living a stable life. In 2015, their daughter Zhang Nianning was born and became the center of the family. As an education professional, Lin Zhixia planned her daughter's future from birth. After repeated discussions, the couple decided to buy a key primary school district apartment in Lin Zhixia's hometown — Ningbo, Zhejiang — to fully prepare for their daughter's future education in China.

This school-district apartment in Haishu District cost nearly 10 million yuan. It was purchased with their joint savings after marriage and registered under both names. It was their only real estate and the core asset reserved for their daughter's education. On the day they bought the apartment, they even joked that they would return to China to live together when their daughter started primary school.

Yet this promise could not stand up to the wear of daily life. Lin Zhixia valued quality of life and educational investment, willing to spend generously on early education classes, picture books, and enlightenment training for her daughter. Influenced by his family of origin, Zhang Lei was extremely thrifty and practical, even miserly. He often lost his temper over Lin Zhixia buying toys or enrolling their daughter in interest classes, accusing her of "wasting money unnecessarily."

Conflicts over daily details were everywhere: Lin Zhixia kept a spotless home, while Zhang Lei littered clothes and never did housework. Lin Zhixia loved taking their daughter to parks and libraries on weekends, while Zhang Lei preferred staying home playing on his phone, ignoring mother and daughter. Incompatible values, huge differences in consumption attitudes, and a lack of companionship and communication slowly drove the marriage to its end.

In 2023, Lin Zhixia and Zhang Lei amicably divorced at the Singapore Family Court. They clearly divided all property in Singapore, including savings, vehicles, and furniture, and signed the agreement. Distraught and focused on child custody, they carelessly completely overlooked the school-district apartment in Ningbo. No division of this property was mentioned in the divorce agreement.

After the divorce, Lin Zhixia returned to Ningbo with her daughter to prepare for school enrollment. To her shock, she found that Zhang Lei had secretly returned to China, changed the locks of the apartment, rented it out to strangers without permission, kept all the rent for himself, and even intended to occupy the property permanently. Lin Zhixia contacted Zhang Lei many times, asking to negotiate the division of this joint property. But Zhang Lei was arrogant and unreasonable: "We already completed the divorce and divided property in Singapore. Even if the Ningbo apartment wasn't written down, it belongs to me by default. Don't bother me again."

Zhang Lei's dominance and unreasonableness left Lin Zhixia angry and anxious. The apartment was bought with joint funds, the only guarantee for her daughter's future schooling, and her greatest wish as a mother. With no way out, Lin Zhixia came to me with all the documents.

"Lawyer Ye, we got divorced in Singapore and both live there. Can a Chinese court still rule on this apartment?" Seeing her anxious and helpless look, I told her with complete certainty: "Absolutely. Your apartment is in Ningbo, so the Ningbo courts have jurisdiction. We can file a lawsuit in the local Ningbo court for legal division." According to Article 17 of the Judicial Interpretation of the Civil Procedure Law of the People's Republic of China: Where a Chinese citizen who has been divorced, with both parties residing abroad, institutes an action solely for the division of domestic property, the case shall be under the jurisdiction of the people's court where the main property is located. In this case, Lin Zhixia and Zhang Lei both resided in Singapore, and the only property in dispute was the school-district apartment in Haishu District, Ningbo. Therefore, the People's Court of Haishu District was the only legally competent court for this case.

After accepting the mandate, I provided detailed representation throughout the process.

First, I guided Lin Zhixia to complete notarization, authentication at the Chinese Embassy in Singapore, and Chinese translation of the divorce judgment issued by the Singaporean court, ensuring the overseas legal document was legally valid in China.

Second, I comprehensively collected evidence regarding the school-district apartment: purchase contracts, bank transfer records, property ownership certificates, and proof of contributions from both parties, clearly establishing that the property was jointly purchased after marriage, constituted community property of the couple, and had not been divided in the Singapore divorce proceedings.

Third, under the cause of action "post-divorce property dispute", I formally filed the case with the People's Court of Haishu District, Ningbo, and simultaneously applied for property preservation to prevent Zhang Lei from selling or transferring the apartment without permission.

Fourth, during the trial, I strongly refuted Zhang Lei's unreasonable defense claiming "implied division and sole ownership". I argued in court that the Singapore divorce agreement did not list the property in question, so there was no factual or legal basis for any "implied division". The apartment remained jointly owned by both parties, and Lin Zhixia, as a co-owner, was entitled to an equal division by law. I also emphasized that the apartment was bought for their daughter's education, and that awarding it to Lin Zhixia, who had direct custody, would be more beneficial to the child's growth.

After hearing the case, the court fully accepted all our arguments and rendered a judgment in accordance with the law: the school-district apartment shall belong to Lin Zhixia, who shall pay Zhang Lei 50% of the property's value as compensation within the effective term of the judgment. When she received the judgment, Lin Zhixia held my hand tightly, her eyes red with emotion: "Lawyer Ye, thank you so much. My daughter's schooling is finally settled."

Post-Case Conclusion

The case of Lin Zhixia and Zhang Lei highlights the most common hidden danger in cross-border divorces: incomplete property division and uncoordinated handling of domestic and overseas assets. Many parties, due to carelessness or insufficient understanding, omit domestic real estate when divorcing abroad, eventually triggering unnecessary disputes.

As a family lawyer, my value lies in accurately applying jurisdiction rules for cross-border property disputes, using professional expertise to secure the optimal litigation strategy for clients and protect their core property interests. What I do is simply clarify property boundaries through law, uphold fairness and justice through evidence, ensure every client receives proper financial protection after divorce, and prevent children's futures from being harmed by their parents' separation.

Cross-border divorce is not the end of property division. Chinese courts will always be the most solid guardian of property rights for Chinese citizens. No matter where a marriage begins or where property is located, the law will safeguard the fairness and hope you rightfully deserve.

一纸离婚约定，十四年的侵占，与一场迟来的归还

引 言

一份在民政局备案生效的离婚协议，本该是结束婚姻、安顿未来的契约，可在现实面前，有时却脆弱得不堪一击。我的当事人骆女士，拿着白纸黑字的财产约定，却被前夫霸占房屋长达十四年，她与儿子在恐惧与漂泊中度日，明明是房屋的合法权利人，却连一扇属于自己的家门都打不开。我与金律师接手此案后，没有纠结于难以实现的产权争议，而是另辟蹊径，以使用权为突破口，用最扎实的法律逻辑，帮这对受尽委屈的母子，夺回了本该属于他们的家。

骆女士第一次走进我办公室时，是 2022 年的初秋。她穿着洗得发白的外套，头发简单挽起，说话声音轻得像一阵风，眼神里藏着常年压抑的怯懦与不安。站在她身边的小伙子高高瘦瘦，眼神却带着与年龄不符的沉默与倔强，那是她的儿子小宇。骆女士当年离婚时，小宇只有 8 岁，如今已经 22 岁。正是这个长大了的小伙子，推着母亲走进了律所，说出了那句藏了十几年的话：“妈，我们不能再怕了。”

骆女士与前夫钱某的婚姻，始于平凡，毁于嗜赌。婚后第三年，钱某染上赌博恶习，从此一发不可收拾。家里的积蓄被他一次次输光，柴米油盐的开支都成了难题，争吵成了家常便饭。钱某输钱后便性情大变，摔砸物品、恶语相向，骆女士稍有反驳，便是言语威胁，长期的精神暴力，让骆女士渐渐变得胆小懦弱，在这段关系里失去了所有底气。

2008 年，感情彻底耗尽，两人决定协议离婚。在民政局签署的《离婚协议书》写得清清楚楚：双方婚内唯一的房屋归骆女士所有，银行存款归钱某所有，年仅 8 岁的儿子小宇由骆女士直接抚养，钱某每月支付固定抚养费，直至孩子成年。那套房子，是骆女士和儿子最后的保障，是她以为能给孩子撑起的一片安稳天地。

她万万没有想到，这场离婚，不是苦难的结束，而是长达十四年侵占的开端。

离婚后，钱某非但没有按照约定搬离房屋，反而仗着自己强势蛮横，擅自将房子出租给陌生租客，每月租金稳稳揣进自己腰包，一分钱都没有留给骆女士母子。骆女士鼓起勇气找到钱某，要求清退租户、交还房屋，换来的却是劈头盖脸的辱骂与驱赶。钱某指着她的鼻子威胁，说她一个女人掀不起风浪，敢再来纠缠就让她们母子无处安身。

长期的畏惧让骆女士不敢再反抗，她带着 8 岁的小宇，开始了颠沛流离的生活。先是挤在亲戚家的阳台，狭小拥挤，看人脸色；后来租住在老旧的民房里，漏风漏雨，搬家成了常态。年幼的小宇不懂大人的恩怨，只知道自己明明

有房子，却不能回家，每次看到别的小朋友安稳放学回家，他都会低着头小声问："妈妈，我们什么时候才能回自己的家？"

骆女士只能默默流泪，无言以对。

更让人心寒的是，钱某霸占房屋收取租金牟利的同时，对儿子的抚养费分文未付。十四年里，他从未看过孩子一次，从未买过一件衣服、一份文具，从未过问过儿子的学习与生活。小宇在离异家庭的敏感与缺失中长大，父亲的缺席、暴力、自私，像一根刺扎在他心里。他从小沉默寡言，不敢与人交流，在学校里总是低着头，看到别人的父亲温柔陪伴，都会默默躲开。青春期的他，一度叛逆孤僻，骆女士虽心疼万分，却因为自身的软弱，没有勇气给孩子一个公道。

钱某则愈发肆无忌惮，换了一拨又一拨租客，收了一年又一年租金，住着本该属于方女士的房子，花着本该属于母子俩的收益，活得理直气壮。骆女士母子的委屈与漂泊，在他眼里，仿佛从来都不存在。

直到 2022 年，小宇长大成人，有了保护母亲的能力，他坚定地拉着母亲的手说："妈，房子是你的，我们有协议，我们找律师，把家要回来。"在儿子的鼓励下，骆女士终于鼓起全部勇气，找到了我和金律师。

听完方女士的讲述，我们没有急于表态，而是沉下心仔细梳理全部材料。很快，我们发现了案件的核心障碍：这套房屋在 2008 年离婚时，并未办理正式的不动产权登记手续，产权存在明显瑕疵。如果直接起诉要求确认房屋所有权，极有可能因权利瑕疵被法院驳回，骆女士的合法权利反而无法得到保护。

一边是法律上的程序障碍，一边是母子俩被侵害十四年的紧迫现实。我和金律师反复研判案情，最终放弃了常规的所有权确认思路，确定了最务实、最可行的诉讼策略：不纠结产权归属，仅主张房屋使用权。依据双方备案生效的《离婚协议书》，骆女士享有合法占有、使用房屋的权利，钱某长期霸占、出租牟利，已构成明确侵权，我们请求法院判令钱某立即腾空房屋，交还骆女士使用。

庭审当天，钱某依旧蛮横嚣张。他在法庭上百般抵赖，接连提出多条抗辩理由：声称房屋无产权证、购房合同无效、离婚协议约定无效，甚至颠倒黑白，说自己才是房屋的实际权利人。他言辞激烈，态度嚣张，试图用混乱的逻辑掩盖自己侵占的事实。

我方则始终保持冷静，没有多余的情绪渲染，只是以事实为依据，以证据为核心，逐条驳斥他的抗辩。我们提交了民政局备案的离婚协议书、钱某收取租金的转账记录、租客的书面证言、骆女士多年在外租房的凭证、钱某从未支付抚养费的证据，每一份材料都扎实有力，每一段论述都逻辑严密。

真正让法庭看清钱某本性的，是庭审后的现场勘察。法官组织双方前往房屋核实情况，钱某竟当场情绪失控，当着法官与法警的面，公然抬手企图殴打骆女士。法官当场严厉制止，对钱某予以严厉训诫，并依法作出制裁。这一刻，这场所谓的"产权纠纷"，彻底暴露了本质——这不是权利争议，而是一场持续十四年、恃强凌弱的恶意侵占。

庭审结束后不久，法院作出一审判决：被告钱某于判决生效之日起十日内，将案涉房屋腾空，并交付原告方女士使用。拿到判决书的那一刻，骆女士捂着脸，压抑了十四年的泪水终于决堤。小宇紧紧抱住母亲，这个从小缺失父爱、在漂泊中长大的男孩，终于挺直了脊梁。

几天后，在法院的执行下，钱某彻底搬离，租户清退完毕。当骆女士打开那扇尘封了十四年的家门，阳光照进屋子的瞬间，她轻声对儿子说："小宇，我们回家了。"

案后结语

这起案件没有激烈的戏剧冲突，却道尽了弱势女性在离异后的现实困境。一纸离婚协议，写得再清楚明白，也挡不住恶意侵占；法律赋予的权利，再正当合法，也需要勇敢与专业的支撑才能落地。

骆女士的十四年，是恐惧的十四年，是漂泊的十四年，也是儿子在缺失与伤害中长大的十四年。钱某的嗜赌、自私、暴力与蛮横，不仅摧毁了一段婚姻，更给孩子的童年留下了难以磨灭的阴影。

作为律师，我们能做的，不在意是否有豪言壮语，而是在当事人走投无路时，找到最可行的法律路径。当所有权确认存在障碍时，我们不硬冲、不蛮干，而是转向更务实的使用权主张，用最平实的逻辑、最扎实的证据，帮当事人守住最核心的利益。

法律或许无法抚平已经造成的伤害，但它可以纠正不公，可以让侵占者付出代价，可以让漂泊者重归家园。对于每一位在婚姻中受委屈、被侵害的女性而言，勇敢拿起法律武器，永远不算晚。而我们能做的，就是做她们最坚实的依靠，让正义不迟到，让归家有归途。

A Divorce Agreement
14 Years of Illegal Occupation, and a Long-Overdue Return

Introduction

A divorce agreement duly filed and effective at the Civil Affairs Bureau should have been a contract to end a marriage and settle the future. Yet in reality, it can sometimes be shockingly fragile. My client Ms. Luo held an agreement with clear property terms in black and white, yet her ex-husband had occupied her house for 14 full years. She and her son lived in fear and displacement. Though the legal owner of the home, she could not even open the door that belonged to her. After Attorney Jin and I took over the case, we did not get stuck in a difficult ownership dispute. Instead, we broke new ground—using the right of use as a breakthrough point. With solid legal logic, we helped this wronged mother and son reclaim the home that was rightfully theirs.

Ms. Luo first walked into my office in the early autumn of 2022. She wore a washed-out coat, her hair simply tied back, her voice soft as a breeze, her eyes hiding years of suppressed timidity and unease. Beside her stood a tall, thin young man, with a silence and stubbornness beyond his years—her son, Xiao Yu. When Ms. Luo divorced, Xiao Yu was only 8 years old. Now he was 22. It was this grown young man who pushed his mother into the law firm and spoke the words hidden for more than a decade: "Mom, we can't be afraid anymore."

The marriage between Ms. Luo and her ex-husband Qian started ordinarily and collapsed due to his gambling addiction. Three years after marriage, Qian developed a destructive gambling habit. One by one, the family savings were gambled away; even daily expenses became a struggle, and quarrels became routine. After losing money, Qian turned violent: smashing things, hurling insults, and threatening Ms. Luo if she dared to argue. Long-term mental abuse gradually made her timid and weak, stripping her of all confidence in the relationship.

In 2008, with love completely exhausted, they agreed to divorce. The Divorce Agreement signed at the Civil Affairs Bureau stated clearly: the only marital house belonged to Ms. Luo; bank savings belonged to Qian; their 8-year-old son Xiao Yu was to be raised directly by Ms. Luo, with Qian paying fixed monthly child support until the child reached adulthood. That house was Ms. Luo and her son's final security—the stable shelter she believed she could provide for her child.

She never imagined that this divorce was not the end of suffering, but the beginning of 14 years of illegal occupation.

After the divorce, not only did Qian refuse to move out as agreed, but relying on his aggressive and domineering personality, he secretly rented the house to strangers, pocketing all the rent every month—not a single cent went to Ms. Luo and her son. Ms. Luo mustered the courage to confront Qian, demanding he evict the tenants and return the house. Instead, she was met with furious insults and expulsion. Qian threatened her, saying a woman like her could make no waves, and if she dared to pester him again, he would leave them homeless.

Trapped by long-term fear, Ms. Luo did not dare to resist. With 8-year-old Xiao Yu, she began a displaced life. First, they were crammed on a relative's balcony, cramped and humbled; later, they rented old, leaky houses, where moving constantly became the norm. Young Xiao Yu did not understand adult conflicts. He only knew he had a home but could not return. Every time he saw other children go home safely after school, he would lower his head and whisper: "Mom, when can we go back to our own home?"

Ms. Luo could only weep silently, with no answer.

Even more chilling: while illegally occupying the house and profiting from rent, Qian paid not a penny in child support. In 14 years, he never visited the child, never bought a piece of clothing or stationery, never asked about his studies or life. Xiao Yu grew up amid the sensitivity and absence of a broken family. His father's abandonment, violence, and selfishness pierced his heart like a thorn. He grew up quiet, afraid to communicate, always keeping his head down at school, quietly turning away when seeing other fathers gently accompanying their children. During adolescence, he became rebellious and withdrawn. Ms. Luo was heartbroken, yet weakened by her own fear, she had no courage to seek justice for her son.

Qian grew increasingly unscrupulous: changing tenants one after another, collecting rent year after year, living in the house that belonged to Ms. Luo, spending the income that should have belonged to the mother and son—all with utter righteousness. To him, their grievances and displacement simply did not exist.

Not until 2022, when Xiao Yu reached adulthood and gained the strength to protect his mother, did he firmly take her hand and say: "Mom, the house is yours. We have the agreement. We'll find a lawyer and take back our home." Encouraged by her son, Ms. Luo finally mustered all her courage and found me and Attorney Jin.

After listening to Ms. Luo's account, we did not rush to take a position, but calmed down and carefully sorted through all the materials. We soon identified the core obstacle in the case: the property had not undergone formal real estate title registration at the time of the divorce in 2008, leaving its ownership clearly defective. Filing a direct lawsuit to confirm ownership of the house would most likely be dismissed by the court due to defective title, which would only leave Ms. Luo's legitimate rights unprotected.

On one side stood procedural legal barriers; on the other, the urgent reality of a mother and son having suffered infringement for fourteen years. Attorney Jin and I repeatedly analyzed the case and ultimately abandoned the conventional approach of ownership confirmation, settling on the most pragmatic and feasible litigation strategy: setting aside disputes over title and claiming only the right to use the property. Pursuant to the duly filed and effective Divorce Agreement between the parties, Ms. Luo was legally entitled to possess and occupy the house. Mr. Qian's long-term occupation and rental of the property for profit constituted clear tortious acts. We petitioned the court to order Mr. Qian to immediately vacate the house and return it to Ms. Luo for her use.

On the day of the trial, Mr. Qian remained arrogant and unruly. He repeatedly denied the allegations in court and put forward a series of defenses: claiming the house had no property ownership certificate, that the purchase contract was invalid, that the provisions of the divorce agreement were void, and even distorting the facts by asserting that he was the actual right holder of the property. He spoke fiercely and behaved arrogantly, attempting to cover up his misappropriation with confused reasoning.

Our side remained calm throughout, without unnecessary emotional rhetoric. Grounded in facts and focused on evidence, we refuted his defenses one by one. We submitted the divorce agreement filed with the civil affairs bureau, bank transfer records of Mr. Qian collecting rent, written testimony from tenants, proof of Ms. Luo renting accommodation elsewhere for years, and evidence that Mr. Qian had never paid child support. Every piece of material was solid and compelling, and every argument tightly reasoned.

What truly revealed Mr. Qian's true nature to the court was the on-site inspection after the trial. When the judge arranged for both parties to verify the conditions of the property, Mr. Qian lost control on the spot. In front of the judge and bailiffs, he raised his hand and attempted to assault Ms. Luo. The judge immediately stopped him harshly, reprimanded him severely, and imposed legal sanctions. At that moment, the so-called "title dispute" laid bare its true nature: it was not a dispute over rights, but a malicious misappropriation lasting fourteen years, an act of bullying the weak.

Shortly after the trial concluded, the court issued its first-instance judgment: the defendant, Mr. Qian, shall vacate the subject property and deliver it to the plaintiff, Ms. Luo, for her use within ten days from the date the judgment takes effect. When she received the judgment, Ms. Luo covered her face, and the tears she had suppressed for fourteen years finally burst forth. Xiaoyu held his mother tightly. Having grown up without a father's love and in a state of displacement, the boy finally stood tall and straight.

A few days later, under court enforcement, Mr. Qian moved out completely and all tenants were evicted. As Ms. Luo opened the door to the home that had been locked up for fourteen years, and sunlight streamed into the house, she whispered to her son: "Xiaoyu, we're home."

Post-Case Conclusion

This case lacks dramatic conflict, yet it lays bare the real hardships faced by disadvantaged women after divorce. Even the clearest written divorce agreement cannot stop malicious misappropriation; rights conferred by law, no matter legitimate, can only be realized with courage and professional legal support.

Fourteen years of Ms. Luo's life were filled with fear, displacement, and a childhood scarred by absence and harm for her son. Mr. Qian's gambling addiction, selfishness, violence, and arrogance not only destroyed a marriage but also left an indelible mark on the boy's childhood.

As lawyers, our work is not about grand rhetoric. It is about finding the most viable legal path when our clients are driven to despair. When ownership confirmation is blocked, we do not recklessly push forward but shift to a more practical claim of usage rights. With plain logic and solid evidence, we help our clients safeguard their core interests.

The law may not heal the wounds already inflicted, but it can correct injustice, make occupiers pay the price, and help the displaced return home. For every woman wronged and violated in marriage, it is never too late to bravely wield the weapon of the law. And what we can do is be their strongest support, ensuring justice is not delayed and that a way home is always within reach.

致命的婚姻——哀悼一位沉入海底的美丽新娘

引言

“深海中那点光，昏暗的诱惑；她以为抓得住，名为爱的泡沫。人心扑朔晦涩，幽蓝如墨。怎么猜透看透故事的结果。为何绚烂叫人扑空，为何爱我者予我牢笼。”

这首歌名为《笼》，是2023年上映的电影《消失的她》的主题歌。影片中白富美的女主角被他的丈夫杀害在海底的观鲨笼内。这个故事让我想起我曾经办理的一起剧情非常相似的案件。同样是一位美丽的对爱充满憧憬和信念的真纯善良的女孩，同样被她所爱的丈夫谋杀在海底。海面的波澜下藏着致命的阴谋，璀璨的海底星空成了生命的墓碑。这场以爱为名的婚约，从缔结之初就是赌徒精心编织的猎网，温柔是精心伪装的演技，深情是掩盖罪恶的面纱。当时，我接受被害人乐芸的母亲许爱媛女士的委托，代理这起性质恶劣的刑事附带民事诉讼案件。在公诉机关追究被告人故意杀人罪刑事责任的同时，我将为枉死的女儿、尚未出世的胎儿，争取公平和正义。从一位母亲基于生活细节的本能疑虑，到真相层层揭开的刺骨寒意，这段难结难分的致命婚约，撕开了人性贪婪的狰狞面目，也见证了母爱执念下的正义追讨。

盛夏的海风裹挟着咸湿的气息，却吹不散电话那头传来的绝望与颤抖。我接到了许爱媛老师的来电，这位相识多年的退休语文教师，一生温婉平和，此刻的声音却破碎得如同被海浪拍打的贝壳。

“叶律师，芸芸失踪了……和章克吉出海一天了，搜救队都没找到人。”

彼时，警方已接到章克吉的报案，据他的讲述，他和妻子乐芸刚新婚一周，正在新婚蜜月期。这天他俩开着刚买不久的私人游艇出海游玩。傍晚时分，乐芸在甲板拍摄海面落日时不慎失足坠海，海域洋流湍急，经过一整天的全力搜救，依旧没有任何踪迹，生还概率已趋近于零。

许爱媛赶到海边时，看到的是一个声泪俱下、对着海面一遍遍呼喊妻子名字的男人——她的女婿章克吉。他的悲伤看起来如此真切，可母亲的直觉像一根尖锐的刺，扎进了许爱媛的心底。她太了解自己的女儿乐芸了，那是一个被温柔包裹、却命运多舛的女孩，她的美好，是刻在骨子里的纯粹与善良。她平时那么热爱生命、谨小慎微，怎么可能在出海中将自己置于危险的境地。

乐芸的人生，是一幅带着遗憾却依旧温柔的画卷。父母早年离异，她跟随父亲长大，父亲是当地一位知名企业家，富庶阔绰，离婚后他未再娶，将所有的爱与温柔都倾注在这个独生女身上。乐芸生得清丽温婉，眉眼间带着江南女子的柔和，气质干净得不染尘埃。25 岁那年，父亲突发车祸意外离世，留下偌大的家业与上亿遗产。孤独像潮水般将她淹没，她渴望温暖，渴望被爱，这份对情感的极致渴求，成了她人生中最致命的软肋。

章克吉的出现，恰逢其时。这个出身平凡的男人，拥有出众的外形，更拥有一套精湛的“温柔话术”。他精准捕捉到乐芸的孤独与渴望，用无微不至的体贴、海边的日落、温柔的陪伴，一点点攻陷了乐芸的心防。他记得她的喜好，倾听她的悲伤，将所有的爱意包装得完美无缺，让乐芸坚信，自己终于找到了那个可以托付一生的人。

许爱媛最初便心生隐忧。她见过太多趋炎附势的人，深知女儿的单纯与善良，极易被虚假的温柔欺骗。可看着女儿眼中闪烁的幸福光芒，她终究不忍强行拆散。她也偶尔前往女儿家中小住，那些藏在温情表象下的细碎破绽，被她一一记在心里，成为日后揭开真相的关键线索。

章克吉看似对乐芸百依百顺，却总在深夜躲在阳台低声通话，语气里满是焦躁与催促，挂掉电话后，便会以各种理由向乐芸索要钱财，创业周转、朋友应急、偿还小额债务，理由永远冠冕堂皇。他从不允许乐芸翻看自己的手机，手机屏幕始终设置着复杂的密码，偶尔醉酒时，会无意识地说出“赌债”“催债”“还钱”等字眼，酒醒后又矢口否认，编造谎言搪塞。

乐芸曾悄悄向母亲倾诉，说章克吉对她的财产格外上心，屡次旁敲侧击询问遗产的打理方式，甚至提议将资产转到两人共同名下。那时的乐芸，还在为丈夫找借口，说他只是一时遇到了困难，许爱媛反复叮嘱女儿多加防备，可深陷爱河的乐芸，根本不愿相信自己深爱的人会心怀歹意。

出事前一周，乐芸哭着拨通了母亲的电话，声音哽咽得几乎无法成声：“妈，我发现他一直在赌博，欠了一大笔钱，我帮他还了一次又一次，可他根本改不了……我怀孕了，我本想用孩子拉他回头，守住我们的家，可我现在好害怕，我觉得他要毁了我和孩子。”

这个未出世的小生命，是乐芸对婚姻最后的期许与救赎。她计划在这次结婚周年出海之旅中，将怀孕的消息告诉章克吉，她天真地以为，孩子的到来能让这个男人浪子回头，能让破碎的家庭重归完整。她不知道，这份对未来的美好憧憬，最终成了催命符，将她和孩子一同推向了冰冷的深海。

章克吉报案后的种种表现，让许爱媛的疑虑彻底化为坚冰。他对着镜头声泪俱下，扮演着痛失爱妻的痴情丈夫，言辞却漏洞百出：他说乐芸失足落水，却始终记不清具体的海域位置；他声称自己奋力施救，却浑身干爽，没有任何挣扎的痕迹；面对警方的询问，他反复强调是意外，却刻意回避两人婚后的矛盾与争吵。

“叶律师，我的芸芸胆小又谨慎，甲板有牢固的护栏，她绝不会靠近危险边缘，更不可能无故失足。”许爱媛坐在我的办公室里，眼底布满狰狞的红血丝，手里紧紧攥着乐芸的照片，指尖因为用力而泛白，“她那么善良，还有肚子里的孩子，怎么可能就这么没了？章克吉一定有问题，我求你，帮我查明真相，为我的女儿，为那个还没来到这个世界的孩子，讨回公道！”

我当即接受了委托，一方面向警方了解梳理案件线索，固定关键证据；另一方面，提前筹备刑事附带民事诉讼的全部材料，为后续的追责与赔偿做好准备。一场揭开深海谎言的追凶之路，就此拉开序幕。

随着警方的深入侦查，章克吉精心编织的谎言被层层撕碎。他根本不是什么上进青年，而是一个嗜赌成性、背负巨额赌债的亡命之徒。接近乐芸，从一开始就是一场处心积虑的骗局，他的目标只有一个——夺取乐芸的上亿遗产，填补自己的赌债窟窿。

与乐芸恋爱期间，他的赌瘾非但没有收敛，反而愈发疯狂。催债人的步步紧逼，让他陷入了绝境，最终，他将罪恶的双手伸向了深爱自己的妻子。那场看似浪漫的新婚出海之旅，是他精心策划的谋杀局。

他驾驶着私人游艇，带着乐芸驶向深海无人区。乐芸满心欢喜地沉浸在落日的美好里，她都还没来记得告诉丈夫，她已经有了他们爱的结晶，但章克吉却在乐芸最放松、最信任他的时刻，狠下心肠，将她推入了冰冷刺骨的海水之中。

他亲眼看着乐芸在海中挣扎、呼救，看着那个鲜活的生命在海浪中逐渐沉寂，他不知道他那个未出世的孩子随母亲一同沉入海底，他杀了妻子，也亲手扼杀了他亲生的孩子。没有丝毫犹豫，他调转船头，伪造了意外落水的假象，妄图用这场完美的意外，继承乐芸的全部遗产，彻底摆脱赌债的纠缠，开启新的人生。

终于，乐芸的尸体被警方打捞上来。法医的鉴定报告，成了压垮所有伪装的最后一根稻草。鉴定结果显示，乐芸遇害时，刚刚怀孕一个多月，这个还未来得及看一眼世界、未来得及感受一丝母爱的小生命，与母亲一起，永远沉睡在了冰冷的深海里。

得知真相的那一刻，许爱媛瘫软在地，撕心裂肺的哭声在空旷的房间里回荡。她失去了唯一的女儿，也失去了那个未曾谋面的外孙，一生的牵挂，在一夜之间化为乌有。章克吉的残忍，不仅剥夺了一个年轻女孩的生命，更扼杀了一个家庭最后的希望，其泯灭的人性，令人发指。

案件进入司法程序后，公诉机关以故意杀人罪对章克吉提起公诉。许爱媛委托我，作为刑事附带民事诉讼的代理人，向法院提起诉讼，要求章克吉赔偿死亡赔偿金、丧葬费、精神损害抚慰金等全部民事损失，用法律的惩戒，告慰女儿与外孙的在天之灵。

庭审现场，是一场对人性的终极审判。章克吉依旧试图狡辩、推诿责任，可铁证如山，游艇航行轨迹、银行流水、赌债凭证、法医鉴定报告、被告人的认罪供述，尤其是犯罪现场的情景模拟演示，和游艇的厂家提供的安全性能证据，更显示这个新购的游艇具备高度的安全性能，人不可能在甲板上失足落水，只有在外力的施加下才会摔出护栏掉入海中。所有证据环环相扣，彻底戳破了他所有的谎言。当我将乐芸的孕检报告、她生前写给孩子的寄语、对未来的憧憬一一呈现在法庭上时，章克吉仿佛雷劈一样怔住了，瞬间嚎啕大哭。全场陷入了无尽的静默，这个未出世孩子的悲剧，让这场杀戮更添了几分撕心裂肺的悲凉。法庭进行到最后陈述环节，章克吉终于对犯罪行为供认不讳。

最终，法院依法作出判决：被告人章克吉犯故意杀人罪，判处死刑，剥夺政治权利终身；同时判令章克吉赔偿附带民事诉讼原告人许爱媛全部经济损失及精神损害抚慰金。

听到判决结果的那一刻，许爱媛缓缓站起身，对着法庭深深鞠躬，泪水无声地滑落。这场跨越深海的正义追讨，终于落下了帷幕。凶手为自己的罪恶付出了生命的代价，可那个温柔善良的女儿，那个懵懂无辜的孩子，却再也回不来了。

案后结语

深海的谎言被戳破，罪恶得到了法律的严惩，可这场以爱为名的猎杀，留下的伤痛永远无法愈合。章克吉以赌徒的病态执念为刃，将虚假的爱情化作最锋利的凶器，亲手摧毁了深爱自己的妻子与未出世的孩子，贪婪最终将他拖入了万劫不复的深渊。

乐芸的悲剧，源于她对爱的极致渴求与对人性的全然信任。她用真心对待感情，用包容填补孤独，却错信了披着深情外衣的恶魔，将自己的一生乃至未出世孩子的生命，都葬送在了一场精心策划的骗局里。而许爱媛，以母亲的执念为光，在迷雾中坚守真相，用法律为武器，为女儿和外孙追索正义，这份沉重而伟大的母爱，是黑暗中唯一的光亮。

生活中真实的案件，远比电影中的故事更加惊心动魄，揭示人性之恶。每一个善良的人，都要在感情中保持清醒的认知，守住内心的底线，远离贪婪、病态、毫无底线的人，这是对自己最基本的保护。在深深的哀悼这位沉入海底的美丽新娘之时，我只愿这起发生在深海的血色悲剧，能成为所有人的警钟，别让真心错付，别让浪漫的婚约，最终变成吞噬生命的血色牢笼。

A Deadly Union — Mourning the Beautiful Bride Who Sank to the Ocean Depths

Introduction

"A glimmer of light in the deep sea, a dim temptation; She thought she could grasp the foam they call love. The human heart is obscure and murky, dark blue as ink. How can one foresee or see through the end of the story? Why does splendor leave us empty? Why do those who love me cage me?"

This song is titled Cage, the theme song of the 2023 film Lost in the Stars. In the movie, the wealthy and beautiful leading lady is murdered by her husband inside an underwater shark-watching cage. This story reminds me of a strikingly similar case I once handled. A beautiful, pure, and kind girl, full of hope and faith in love, was also murdered at the bottom of the sea by the husband she loved. Beneath the calm waves lay a deadly conspiracy, and the brilliant starry sky under the sea became a tombstone for her life. This marriage, forged in the name of love, was from the very beginning a carefully woven trap set by a gambler. Tenderness was a well-rehearsed act, and affection a veil to conceal his crimes.

At that time, I was entrusted by Ms. Xu Aiyuan, the mother of the victim Le Yun, to represent her in this heinous criminal case with attached civil litigation. While the public prosecution authority pursued the defendant's criminal liability for intentional homicide, I fought for fairness and justice for the wrongfully killed daughter and her unborn child. From a mother's instinctive suspicion rooted in trivial daily details to the bone-chilling cold as layer upon layer of truth was uncovered, this tangled and fatal marriage tore off the hideous mask of human greed and bore witness to the pursuit of justice driven by a mother's unyielding love.

The salty summer sea breeze could not blow away the despair and trembling coming through the phone. I received a call from Ms. Xu Aiyuan, a retired Chinese language teacher I had known for years. Gentle and peaceful all her life, her voice at this moment was broken like seashells shattered by the waves.

"Lawyer Ye, Yunyun is missing... She went out to sea with Zhang Keji a day ago, and the search and rescue team has found no trace of her."

By then, the police had already received Zhang Keji's report. According to his account, he and his wife Le Yun had been married for just one week and were on their honeymoon. That day, they went out to sea on a newly purchased private yacht for leisure. In the evening, Le Yun accidentally fell overboard while taking photos of the sunset on the deck. Amid the swift ocean currents, after a full day of intense search and rescue efforts, there was still no sign of her, and her chance of survival was nearly zero.

When Xu Aiyuan rushed to the seaside, she saw a man weeping bitterly, calling out his wife's name repeatedly to the sea—her son-in-law Zhang Keji. His grief seemed utterly genuine, yet a mother's intuition pricked at Xu Aiyuan's heart like a sharp thorn. She knew her daughter Le Yun all too well: a girl wrapped in tenderness yet plagued by misfortune, whose kindness and purity were ingrained in her very being. Le Yun had always cherished life and been cautious; how could she have put herself in such mortal danger at sea?

Le Yun's life was a painting of tenderness tinged with regret. Her parents divorced when she was young, and she was raised by her father, a prominent local entrepreneur. Wealthy and unmarried after the divorce, he lavished all his love and care on his only daughter. Le Yun was delicate and gentle, with the soft grace of a Jiangnan maiden, her purity untainted by the world. When she was 25, her father died suddenly in a car accident, leaving behind a vast family estate and hundreds of millions in inheritance. Loneliness overwhelmed her like a tidal wave; she longed for warmth and to be loved. This desperate yearning for affection became her fatal vulnerability.

Zhang Keji appeared at just the right moment. A man of humble origins, he possessed striking good looks and a masterful command of "gentle rhetoric." He precisely targeted Le Yun's loneliness and longing, winning her over little by little with meticulous care, sunset walks by the sea, and tender companionship. He remembered her preferences, listened to her sorrows, and packaged his so-called love perfectly, making Le Yun convinced that she had finally found someone she could entrust her life to.

Xu Aiyuan had harbored misgivings from the start. She had seen far too many opportunistic people and knew well that her daughter's innocence and kindness made her an easy target for false tenderness. Yet unable to bear destroying the happiness shining in her daughter's eyes, she did not force them apart. She occasionally stayed at her daughter's home, and those small flaws hidden beneath the warm surface were etched in her mind, becoming crucial clues that would later unravel the truth.

Zhang Keji appeared obedient to Le Yun in every way, yet he would often sneak onto the balcony late at night to make low voice calls, his tone filled with anxiety and urgency. After hanging up, he would ask Le Yun for money under all kinds of high-sounding excuses: business startup capital, emergency help for friends, paying off small debts. He never allowed Le Yun to look through his phone, which was always locked with a complicated passcode. Occasionally, when drunk, he would unconsciously utter words like "gambling debts", "debt collectors", and "pay up", only to deny everything once sober and make up lies to cover his tracks.

Le Yun once confided quietly to her mother that Zhang Keji seemed unusually obsessed with her fortune, repeatedly asking about the management of her inheritance and even suggesting transferring the assets into their joint names. At that time, Le Yun still made excuses for her husband, saying he was just going through a hard time. Xu Aiyuan repeatedly warned her daughter to be on guard, but Le Yun, deeply in love, refused to believe the man she loved could harbor evil intentions.

A week before the incident, Le Yun called her mother in tears, her voice choking almost to silence: "Mom, I found out he's been gambling the whole time and owes a huge amount of money. I've paid for him again and again, but he just won't stop... I'm pregnant. I thought the baby could bring him back to his senses and save our marriage, but now I'm so scared. I think he's going to destroy me and our baby."

This unborn child was Le Yun's last hope and redemption for their marriage. She planned to tell Zhang Keji about her pregnancy during their wedding anniversary trip at sea. Naively, she believed the arrival of the baby would reform this man and mend their broken family. Little did she know that this beautiful vision for the future would become a death sentence, pushing both her and the child into the icy deep sea.

Zhang Keji's behavior after reporting Le Yun missing turned Xu Aiyuan's doubts into cold certainty. He wept bitterly in front of the camera, playing the part of a devoted husband grieving for his beloved wife, yet his words were full of contradictions. He claimed Le Yun had fallen overboard accidentally, but could never remember the exact location. He said he had tried desperately to save her, yet his clothes were completely dry with no signs of struggle. When questioned by police, he repeatedly insisted it was an accident, yet deliberately avoided any mention of their marital conflicts and arguments.

"Lawyer Ye, my Yunyun was timid and careful. The deck had sturdy railings. She would never go near the edge, let alone fall for no reason." Sitting in my office, Xu Aiyuan's eyes were bloodshot, her hands tightly clutching a photo of Le Yun, her fingertips white with pressure. "She was so kind, and there was our grandchild in her belly. How could they both be gone? Zhang Keji must be guilty. Please, help me find out the truth and get justice for my daughter, for that baby who never got to see this world!"

I accepted the retainer immediately. On one hand, I coordinated with the police to review case clues and secure key evidence; on the other, I prepared all materials for the criminal lawsuit with civil damages in advance, laying groundwork for subsequent accountability and compensation. Thus began the quest to uncover the lies hidden beneath the deep sea.

As the police investigation deepened, the elaborate web of lies woven by Zhang Keji was torn apart layer by layer. He was no ambitious young man, but a desperate, compulsive gambler drowning in massive gambling debts. His pursuit of Le Yun had been a premeditated fraud from the very start, with only one goal: to seize Le Yun's hundreds of millions in inheritance and fill his gambling debt hole.

During their relationship, his gambling addiction only grew worse, not better. Hounded relentlessly by debt collectors, he was driven to desperation and finally turned his murderous hands on the wife who loved him deeply. That seemingly romantic honeymoon voyage at sea was a carefully planned murder.

He steered the private yacht toward an uninhabited area of the deep ocean. Le Yun, full of joy, was lost in the beauty of the sunset. She never even got the chance to tell her husband she was carrying their child. Yet at the moment when she was most relaxed and trusting, Zhang Keji hardened his heart and pushed her into the bitterly cold seawater.

He watched Le Yun struggling and screaming for help in the sea, as that vibrant life gradually faded away amid the waves. He did not know that his unborn child had sunk to the bottom of the sea with its mother. He killed his wife and also snuffed out his own flesh and blood with his own hands. Without the slightest hesitation, he turned the bow around and faked an accidental drowning, hoping to inherit all of Le Yun's fortune through this "perfect accident," free himself from gambling debts once and for all, and start a new life.

Finally, Le Yun's cold body was recovered by the police. The forensic report became the final straw that broke through all his disguises. The examination confirmed that Le Yun had been just over one month pregnant at the time of her death. This little life, which had not yet seen the world or felt a trace of maternal love, lay forever in the icy deep sea alongside its mother.

When Xu Aiyuan learned the truth, she collapsed to the ground, her heart-wrenching sobs echoing through the empty room. She had lost her only daughter and her unborn grandchild. All her lifelong hopes were wiped out in a single night. Zhang Keji's cruelty had not only taken the life of a young woman but also snuffed out the last hope of a family. His inhumanity was unspeakable.

After the case entered judicial proceedings, the public prosecution authority indicted Zhang Keji on the charge of intentional homicide. Xu Aiyuan entrusted me to act as her agent in the incidental civil action, filing a lawsuit with the court demanding that Zhang Keji compensate for all civil losses, including death compensation, funeral expenses, and solatium for mental suffering. Legal punishment would bring comfort to the spirits of her daughter and grandchild.

The court trial was a final judgment on humanity. Zhang Keji still tried to quibble and shift blame, but the evidence was overwhelming. The yacht's navigation route, bank transaction records, gambling debt documents, forensic reports, the defendant's confession, and especially the crime-scene reenactment, together with safety performance evidence provided by the yacht manufacturer, all proved that the newly purchased yacht was highly secure. A person could not accidentally fall from the deck; only external force could throw someone over the railing into the sea. All the pieces of evidence interlocked, completely exposing his lies.

When I presented Le Yun's pregnancy test report, the messages she had written for her baby, and her hopes for the future one by one in court, Zhang Keji froze as if struck by lightning and burst into loud cries. The entire courtroom fell into heavy silence. The tragedy of the unborn child added an even more heart-shattering sorrow to the killing. In the final statement session, Zhang Keji finally pleaded guilty to his crimes.

In the end, the court handed down its judgment in accordance with the law: the defendant Zhang Keji was found guilty of intentional homicide, sentenced to death and deprived of political rights for life. He was also ordered to compensate Xu Aiyuan, the plaintiff in the incidental civil action, for all economic losses and mental distress damages.

Upon hearing the verdict, Xu Aiyuan rose slowly, bowed deeply to the court, and tears fell silently. This pursuit of justice across the deep sea had finally come to an end. The murderer paid with his life for his crimes, yet her gentle and kind daughter, along with the innocent unborn child, would never return.

Post-Case Conclusion

The lies of the deep sea were exposed, and evil received severe legal punishment. Yet the wounds left by this hunt in the name of love would never heal. Using his pathological gambler's obsession as a blade, Zhang Keji turned false love into the sharpest weapon, personally destroying the wife who loved him deeply and their unborn child. Greed ultimately dragged him into an abyss of eternal damnation.

Le Yun's tragedy stemmed from her desperate longing for love and complete trust in human nature. She treated relationships with sincerity and filled her loneliness with tolerance, yet she mistakenly trusted a devil disguised as a devoted lover, sacrificing her own life and that of her unborn baby in a carefully planned fraud.

As for Xu Aiyuan, guided by a mother's unyielding faith, she clung to the truth through the darkness and fought for justice for her daughter and grandchild with law as her weapon. This heavy yet great maternal love was the only light in the darkness.

Real-life cases are far more thrilling than movie stories, revealing the true evil of human nature. Every kind person must maintain a clear mind in relationships, hold fast to their bottom line, and stay away from greedy, pathological, and unscrupulous people — this is the most basic protection for oneself.

As I mourn this beautiful bride buried in the deep sea, I can only hope that this bloody tragedy beneath the waves will serve as a warning to all: do not give your heart to the wrong person, and never let a romantic marriage turn into a bloodstained cage that devours lives.

Photograph by Joseph Xu

CHAPTER 6 | GLUTTONY

第六章 | 暴食

引文

"过度的欲望，是灵魂最深的耗损；节制，才是生命真正的秩序。"

——【英】雪莱

暴食之罪，不止于口腹之欲的放纵，更是人性中对情感、物质、权力与欢愉进行无节制的攫取与挥霍。在婚姻家庭里，它化身为不知边界的索取、毫无克制的挥霍、肆意放纵的行为、永不满足的需求。有人在亲密关系中一味汲取温暖与供养，却吝于付出分毫；有人在欲望中彻底迷失，将婚姻当作满足自我的工具；有人在物质享受中沉沦，让整个家庭背负无尽的压力与裂痕。

在我亲历的诸多疑难纠纷中，许多悲剧的发生并非源于意外，而是源于长期的失控与失度。情感被肆意透支，信任被反复消耗，责任被刻意漠视，原本稳固的关系从内部慢慢溃烂，最终走向无可挽回的境地。跨国婚姻中的文化冲突与欲望失序、家族财产中的无度攫取、夫妻关系中的索取无度，皆是如此。

法律可以约束行为、弥补损害、定分止争，却无法重建被挥霍殆尽的温情与信任。人生最珍贵的，不是无限占有，而是懂得适可而止；婚姻最长久的，不是肆意放纵，而是克制、敬畏与用心守护。唯有守住欲望的边界，才能守住关系的长久，守住内心的安宁。

Epigraph

"Excessive desire is the deepest depletion of the soul; temperance is the true order of life."

— Percy Bysshe Shelley

The sin of gluttony lies not merely in overindulgence of appetite, but in unrestrained craving and squandering of emotion, material goods, power, and pleasure. In marriage and family, it becomes boundless taking, reckless spending, unrestrained behavior, and insatiable demands. Some drain warmth and support from intimacy without giving anything in return; some lose themselves in desire and treat marriage as a tool for self-gratification; others drown in material luxury, placing endless pressure and rifts on the whole family.

In many difficult disputes I have experienced, many tragedies arise not from accident, but from long-term loss of control and excess. Affection is recklessly overdrawn, trust repeatedly worn away, responsibility deliberately ignored. Once stable relationships rot from within, eventually reaching a point of no return. This is seen in cultural conflicts and disordered desires in transnational marriages, excessive seizure of family assets, and endless taking between spouses.

The law can restrain conduct, compensate harm, and resolve conflicts, yet cannot rebuild warmth and trust once squandered. The most precious thing in life is not endless possession, but knowing when to stop. The most enduring quality in marriage is not indulgence, but restraint, reverence, and careful protection. Only by guarding the boundaries of desire can we preserve lasting relationships and inner peace.

恋爱炼狱——伪装的"高富帅"的重重骗局

引言

爱情里，当温柔体贴是演的、家境优渥是装的、山盟海誓是圈套，那么所有的倾心付出，都将成为骗子敛财得逞的祭品。本案当事人黄嫣然，家境良好、单纯善良，却在一段看似完美的恋爱中，被精心包装的"富二代"男友榨取钱财、反复操控，直至身心俱疲、满目疮痍。作为她的代理律师，我帮她通过刑事附带民事诉讼追回部分损失，更陪她走过那段信任崩塌、自我怀疑的黑暗时光。这起包含多名受害者的婚恋诈骗案，也给所有单纯善良的女孩敲响警钟：甜言蜜语之下，可能藏着深不见底的陷阱。

第一次见到黄嫣然时，她刚从一场持续近两年的"完美恋爱"里惊醒，现实给了她沉重一击的是，她遭遇到了一个彻头彻尾的恋爱骗局。她眼神空洞、神情憔悴，与照片里那个明媚开朗的女孩判若两人。这个出身知识分子家庭、父母均为大学教授的姑娘，从小在安稳环境中长大，海外留学归来后在培训机构任教，人生平顺简单，对爱情充满天真期待。也正是这份未经世事的纯粹，让她一步步落入了骗子布下的罗网。

改变她命运的相遇，始于一个社交平台。1998 年出生的黎涛，顶着双一流高校英语专业的光环，却从未想过踏实谋生。他早早选定了一条邪路：把自己包装成出手阔绰、前途无量的青年才俊，专挑家境尚可、情感单纯的女孩下手，以恋爱为名，行诈骗之实。为了让伪装无懈可击，他长期租赁豪车撑场面，朋友圈精心营造创业奔波、商务应酬的假象，说话做事精准拿捏女性情绪需求，堪称职业级的"情感操控者"。

黄嫣然毫无防备地被这份"完美"吸引。黎涛的体贴、风趣、见多识广，再加上刻意营造的富二代光环，让几乎没有情感经历的她彻底沦陷。确定关系不久，黎涛便露出了贪婪的真面目。他开始以项目周转、创业急需资金、临时应急等各种理由开口借钱，每一次都搭配对未来生活的美好承诺，用"以后我们会更好""这笔钱很快回来"不断画饼。

深陷恋爱脑的黄嫣然毫无招架之力。父母给的生活费、自己工作的收入、珍藏的大牌饰品、甚至透支信用卡，她源源不断地把钱输送给黎涛，近两年时间里，累计被骗金额高达 150 万元。每当她犹豫、迟疑，黎涛便立刻切换手段：冷暴力施压、下跪示弱、痛哭博取同情，软硬兼施，直到她再次妥协。

更让她不安却又被迫接受的，是这段感情始终"见不得光"。黎涛从不肯与她合照发朋友圈，从不公开她的身份，甚至拒绝让她进入自己的生活圈子。他给出的理由听起来无懈可击：父母对事业要求极高，必须创业有成才能公开恋情。黄嫣然虽失落、困惑，却还是选择了相信。

她不知道的是，自己并不是黎涛的唯一。早在 2023 年，黎涛就与家境优渥的刚毕业女生张茜恋爱同居，套路如出一辙；2024 年与张茜短暂分手后，他无缝衔接黄嫣然，同时又转头挽回张茜，两段关系高度重叠。长期的情感压榨与金钱掏空，让黄嫣然痛苦不堪，只能在社交平台隐晦抒发情绪。

正是这条动态，成了戳破骗局的裂口。张茜在刷到内容后瞬间警觉，两人私信联系上，并核对时间线、转账记录、对方谎言细节，真相轰然倒塌：她们都是同一骗局里的受害者。很快，另一名受害者方芳也找上门来。三人比对后震惊地发现，彼此与黎涛的交往时间完全重合。

于是三位女性迅速选择了报案。与此同时，还有多名女性也向警方报案涉嫌被诈骗。而随着警方调查深入，真相更加骇人：黎涛同时交往的女友多达 9 名，堪称"时间管理大师"，而她们的年龄横跨 18 岁至 40 岁，清一色是家境不错、性格单纯、容易情感上头的女性，有人被骗数万，有人像黄嫣然一样损失百万。

骗局败露后，黎涛还想百般抵赖。但调查证据确凿：他无业、无收入、无还款能力，所谓生意、富二代身份全是虚构，豪车、排场、日常挥霍，全部来自诈骗所得。黎涛因涉嫌诈骗罪被检察机关批准逮捕，最终被依法判刑。

黄嫣然带着满身伤痕与满腔愤恨，委托我提起刑事附带民事诉讼，要求追回被骗款项。坐在我面前的她，情绪几度崩溃，两年的真心付出变成一场算计，百万元财产损失，加上被反复操控、精神压榨的创伤，让她对爱情彻底失去信任，甚至陷入强烈的自我否定。我一边协助她整理完整转账记录、聊天记录、消费凭证等证据，依法推进诉讼程序；一边也在漫长的代理过程中，一点点安抚她破碎的内心。庭审与追赃过程艰难，好在最终法院支持了我方诉求，结合黎涛退赔能力，黄嫣然成功追回了部分款项。

对她而言，这笔钱已不是最重要。走出被欺骗、被贬低、被掏空的心理困境，重建对人与世界的信任，才是真正的救赎。

案后结语

婚恋骗局最残忍之处，在于它不仅掠夺财产，更摧毁一个人对爱的信任、对人的善意，甚至摧毁自我价值感。黎涛式的骗子，精准瞄准善良、单纯、恋爱脑的女性，用精心设计的人设、情绪价值与未来承诺，构建一个看似真实可触的幸福幻境，实则步步为营、敛财不止。

黄嫣然的经历，是无数单纯女孩在情感世界里遭遇的缩影。家境良好、教养得体，并不意味着能识别人性之恶；真心待人、全心付出，也未必能换来真心相待。越是甜得反常的温柔，越是滴水不漏的完美，越值得警惕。不公开的关系、频繁以各种理由借钱、前后矛盾的行踪、永远无法兑现的承诺，都是危险信号。

我始终想对黄嫣然说：你失去的是一段骗局，不是爱的权利；你看错了一个人，不是看错了整个人生。被骗不是受害者的错，不必因此否定全部的自己，更不必因此否定整个世界。伤疤会慢慢愈合，警惕会变成铠甲，而真心，终将遇见值得的真心。愿每一个在婚恋中受伤的人，都能走出阴影，重拾勇气，依然相信，这世间仍有干净、真诚、值得奔赴的爱。愿那些受伤的女孩在恋爱的炼狱中获得重生。

Love's Inferno: The Elaborate Scams of a Fake "Rich, Tall and Handsome" Player

Introduction

In love, when tenderness is an act, wealth a pretense, and vows a trap—every sincere offering becomes a sacrifice for the scammer's greed. My client Huang Yanran, from a good family, innocent and kind, was manipulated and financially drained by her carefully packaged "rich heir" boyfriend in what seemed a perfect relationship, leaving her physically and mentally broken. As her attorney, I helped her recover part of her losses through a criminal incidental civil lawsuit and supported her through the dark period of collapsed trust and self-doubt. This romance fraud case, with multiple victims, serves as a warning to all kind-hearted girls: beneath sweet words may lie an unfathomable trap.

When I first met Huang Yanran, she had just woken up from a nearly two-year "perfect relationship." The harsh reality hit her hard: she had been caught in an out-and-out romance scam. Her eyes were empty, her face haggard—barely recognizable from the bright, cheerful girl in old photos. Born into an intellectual family with university professor parents, she grew up in a stable environment, returned from overseas study, and taught at a training institution. Her life had been smooth and simple, and she held innocent expectations for love. It was this unworldly purity that led her step by step into the scammer's snare.

The fateful encounter began on a social media platform. Li Tao, born in 1998, claimed a prestigious English degree from a top-tier university but had no intention of earning an honest living. He chose a crooked path early on: packaging himself as a generous, promising young talent, targeting financially comfortable, emotionally naive girls, and defrauding them under the guise of love. To perfect his disguise, he rented luxury cars for show, carefully curated a social media image of a busy entrepreneur attending business events, and tailored his words and actions to women's emotional needs—a professional "emotional manipulator."

Huang Yanran was defenselessly drawn to this "perfection." Li Tao's thoughtfulness, wit, and worldly charm, combined with his fabricated wealthy persona, completely overwhelmed her, as she had almost no prior romantic experience. Shortly after they began dating, Li Tao revealed his greedy true self. He started asking for money under various pretenses: project cash flow shortages, urgent startup capital, emergency expenses. Each request was paired with rosy promises about their future, using lines like "we'll be better off soon" and "the money will come back quickly" to keep her hooked.

Blinded by love, Huang Yanran could not resist. She gave him living expenses from her parents, her entire salary, valuable luxury accessories, and even maxed out her credit cards. Over nearly two years, she was defrauded of a total of 1.5 million yuan. Whenever she hesitated or doubted, Li Tao immediately switched tactics: cold violence, kneeling to show weakness, tearful pleas for sympathy—alternating harshness and charm until she gave in again.

Even more disturbing, yet forced upon her, was that their relationship was always "kept in the dark." Li Tao refused to post photos with her on social media, never acknowledged her publicly, and even barred her from his social circle. His excuse sounded airtight: his parents demanded career success before any relationship could be made public. Though sad and confused, Huang Yanran chose to believe him.

What she did not know was that she was never Li Tao's only girlfriend. As early as 2023, he had been dating and living with Zhang Qian, a well-off recent graduate, using the same tricks. After a brief breakup with Zhang Qian in 2024, he immediately started seeing Huang Yanran while reconciling with Zhang Qian—two overlapping relationships. Long-term emotional manipulation and financial depletion left Huang Yanran in agony, and she could only express her feelings vaguely on social media.

It was exactly this post that tore open the scam. As soon as Zhang Qian saw it, she became alert. The two connected via private message, compared timelines, transfer records, and details of his lies, and the truth collapsed completely: they were both victims of the same scheme. Soon another victim, Fang Fang, also came forward. After comparing notes, the three women were shocked to discover that their relationships with Li Tao had overlapped entirely.

The three women immediately reported the case to the police. Meanwhile, several other women also filed police reports alleging they had been defrauded. As the police investigation deepened, an even more horrifying truth emerged: Li Tao had been dating as many as nine girlfriends at the same time, a true "time management master." They ranged in age from 18 to 40, all from decent families, simple-natured, and easily emotionally invested. Some were defrauded of tens of thousands, while others, like Huang Yanran, lost over a million.

After the scam was exposed, Li Tao tried every means to deny it. But the evidence was conclusive: he was unemployed, had no income, and no ability to repay. His so-called business career and wealthy heir identity were entirely made up. The luxury cars, lavish lifestyle, and daily spending all came from scam proceeds. Li Tao was arrested by the procuratorate on suspicion of fraud and eventually sentenced in accordance with the law.

Bruised and full of resentment, Huang Yanran entrusted me to file a criminal incidental civil lawsuit to recover the defrauded funds. Sitting before me, she broke down emotionally several times. Two years of sincere devotion had turned into a calculated trap. Along with the loss of a million yuan in property, the repeated manipulation and mental exploitation left her completely distrustful of love and trapped in intense self-doubt. On one hand, I helped her organize complete evidence — transfer records, chat logs, consumption vouchers — and advance the legal proceedings in accordance with the law; on the other, throughout the long representation, I gently comforted her broken heart. The trial and asset recovery process was difficult, but fortunately, the court ultimately upheld our claims. Considering Li Tao's ability to repay, Huang Yanran successfully recovered part of her losses.

For her, the money was no longer the most important thing. Escaping the psychological pain of being deceived, degraded, and drained, and rebuilding trust in people and the world — that was her real salvation.

Post-Case Conclusion

The cruellest part of romance scams is that they do not just steal money — they destroy a person's trust in love, goodwill toward others, and even their sense of self-worth. Scammers like Li Tao target kind, love-starved, emotionally vulnerable women. They build a seemingly tangible happy illusion through carefully crafted personas, emotional support, and promises of the future, all while calculating every step and steadily extracting money.

Huang Yanran's experience reflects the suffering of countless innocent girls in relationships. Coming from a good family and being well-educated does not guarantee immunity to human cruelty. Sincerity and wholehearted devotion do not always earn sincerity in return. The more abnormally sweet the affection, the more flawlessly perfect the performance, the greater the reason for vigilance. Secret relationships, repeated money-asking under various excuses, inconsistent alibis, and forever-unfulfilled promises are all red flags.

I have always wanted to say to Huang Yanran: What you lost was a scam, not the right to love. You misjudged one person, not your whole life. Being deceived is not the victim's fault. You do not have to reject your entire self, nor condemn the whole world because of it. Scars will slowly heal; vigilance will become armor; and a sincere heart will eventually meet one worthy of it. May everyone hurt in love walk out of the shadows, regain courage, and still believe that pure, genuine love worth pursuing exists in this world. May these wounded girls be reborn from the purgatory of romance.

塞纳河畔的亲情谜题：一场中法跨国非婚生子抚养权的拉锯战

引言

一场始于巴黎蒙马特高地的相遇，一段缠绕八年的爱恨，一个无辜降生在异国的孩子，最终演变成一场牵动中法两国司法程序的抚养权拉锯战。非婚生子的身份、跨境监护的争议、电子证据的抗辩、儿童利益最大化的考量，让这起案件从始至终都充满了现实的锋利与人性的拉扯。我接手此案时，孩子已被悄悄带离熟悉的生活环境，父亲焦急如焚，母亲困在名利的滤镜里不肯清醒，而我要做的，是在国界与法条之间，为一个孩子守住最安稳的归途。

我第一次见到林远，是在 2023 年盛夏，我的律所办公室里。窗外车水马龙，他却安静得像一座沉在水底的岛，指尖反复摩挲着一枚小小的、刻着法文名字的银质长命锁。那是他给远在巴黎的儿子林念安求的平安符，也是这段始于浪漫、终于破碎的感情，唯一剩下的温柔物证。

"叶律师，我请求你，帮我把孩子带回正常的生活里。"

他的故事，始于 2015 年春天的巴黎蒙马特。那时林远是深耕实验室的纳米材料学者，白珊珊是闯荡欧洲的代购博主。一次偶然的相识——白珊珊手机断电，林远把他的充电宝借给她。这次举手之劳的相助，让两个本无交集的人，在塞纳河畔纠缠了整整八年。

2017 年秋，他们的儿子念安在巴黎皮提耶医院降生。由于林远和白珊珊并未建立合法婚姻，因此孩子是非婚生子。但非婚生的身份，并未削减林远的半分期待。他全情投入父亲的角色，医院诊断书、考勤表、夜间陪护记录、出院病历、保姆的沟通、家里的监控，桩桩件件都留下了他日夜守在孩子床边的痕迹。而白珊珊，则一头扎进代购的浪潮里，在流量与订单中，渐渐忽视了母亲的身份。

他们曾在巴黎十六区租住月租四千多欧元的公寓，生活开销高昂，念安的蒙台梭利托儿所费用更是不菲。但白珊珊代购的收入，却从未拿出来用于家庭和孩子的消费。林远默默承担一切，请来专业的育儿嫂照料孩子的饮食起居。但这份安稳，终究抵不过欲望的拉扯——白珊珊从代购到直播带货，一心投资大卖场的生意，更无暇照管孩子。林远则渴望稳定的生活现状，一切以孩子为重心。2019 年圣诞，两人之间的裂痕彻底爆发，也为后来的跨国争夺孩子的抚养权，埋下了最深的伏笔。

2023 年 6 月，双方终于达成并签订了《共同监护协议》，约定一起抚育和照顾孩子。但这份协议还未完成认证手续，白珊珊便抓住法律程序的空窗，悄无声息地收拾了念安的衣物，带着孩子从巴黎消失。等林远发现时，孩子的衣柜空了大半，地上只留着被撕破的行李箱防尘罩，而他准备好的儿子六岁生日礼物，甚至还没来得及拆开。

一夜之间，父亲变成了千里之外的追寻者，孩子成了跨境争夺里最无辜的棋子。

我接受委托后，与团队迅速启动应对方案。一边以林远作为原告名义，向中国管辖法院提起子女抚养权之诉，并申请人格权侵害禁令，即要求被告白珊珊不得藏匿子女，保护原告林远对儿子的监护权和探望权，一边收集和固定大量证据，一点点拨开双方共同生活期间对孩子所承担的抚育之责。

我们调取了白珊珊账号近三年的全部数据，进行电子证据存证固定。那些屏幕前光鲜亮丽的“巴黎倩姐”，那些动辄宣称千万业绩的神话，在真实的物流、流水、仓储记录面前不堪一击。更让人心惊的是，多段直播回放里，清晰录下孩子哭喊、物品摔碎的声音，而镜头前的她，依旧面不改色地推销着奢侈品童装，将孩子的无助，淹没在百万流量的喧嚣里。

《未成年人保护法》的条文清晰而坚定：监护人不得利用未成年人从事营利性活动，更不得忽视其身心健康。可在这场流量狂欢里，母亲的职责早已被搁置一旁。2024 年 4 月，庭审正式开启。这是一场罕见的、横跨中法两国的电子证据攻防战。对方律师提出白珊珊能提供优渥的教育条件，出示“名校名额”以争夺孩子抚养权。而我们在法庭上，以完整严密的证据链，充分印证：直播记录和飞行轨迹证实白珊珊长期奔波于市场和停留在直播间，并没有时间和精力陪伴孩子；消费记录与生活照片对比，揭示孩子长期穿着旧衣，与母亲直播里的奢华形成刺眼反差；孩子在法国期间均由父亲林远亲自抚育和照管的全面证据；孩子在法国已经有入园入学稳定有序的生活，却被母亲擅自带离出境，父子被迫分离的证据；以及酒店监控、医疗记录、宠物店消费凭证，甚至孩子无意间说出的只言片语，都指向同一个真相——孩子被母亲带离法国回到中国后并未得到稳定、安全、充满爱的照料；而更为重要的一点是，白珊珊在法国的收入均未用于孩子的抚育，而是供她个人花销和留存。

庭审的转折，出现在八岁的念安开口的那一刻：“我想回到爸爸身边。”

他抱着小小的毛线熊，轻声说出那些藏在心里的不安与恐惧。没有刻意引导，没有成人编排，只是一个孩子最真实的感受。而这，恰恰是《民法典》中“尊重未成年子女真实意愿”最温暖、也最有力的体现。我们并非简单听取选择，而是用完整的证据体系，印证孩子陈述的可信度，坚守儿童利益最大化这一终极原则。

法庭最终采纳了我们的观点，孩子的抚养权判归由父亲林远抚养。可判决在手，真正的考验才刚刚开始。2024 年 9 月的孩子交接的执行现场，状况频发。白珊珊召集了很多亲友围堵阻挠孩子的交接，一度让局面混乱不堪。幸而在紧张的时刻，法警协助全程护送孩子。最终，念安顺利回到父亲身边，回到了稳定、安心、被认真呵护的生活里。这场横跨欧亚的亲情拉锯战，终于以法律的正义、孩子的安宁，落下帷幕。

案后结语

这是一起具有时代意义的跨国抚养权纠纷，也是家事司法实践中，非婚生子女保护、跨境监护争议、电子证据运用、儿童利益最大化原则的集中体现。

法律明确规定，非婚生子女享有与婚生子女同等的权利，生父对孩子的抚养监护既是义务也是权利，不因未办理结婚登记而遭遇障碍。在跨境监护的争议里，国界不应成为阻隔，程序也不应成为漏洞，成年人的恩怨与选择，更不应由孩子买单。

随着数字时代的到来，直播记录、消费流水、出行轨迹、音视频资料等电子数据，成为家事案件中至关重要的证据。它们客观、静默、不可篡改，能够刺破伪装，还原最真实的生活样貌，也能为司法裁判提供最坚实的依据。

而此案最核心的价值，是儿童利益最大化。抚养权的归属，不能成为父母之间"输赢"的较量，不是财富与条件的简单比拼，而是谁能真正为孩子提供稳定、安全、充满尊重与爱意的成长环境，谁能真正把孩子的身心健康放在第一位。法律守护最弱小、最无辜的生命，让每一个孩子都能在阳光下安稳长大，不被利用，不被忽视，不被裹挟在成人的欲望里。

塞纳河的流水不息，亲情的谜题终有答案。而司法的温度，就在于无论跨越多远的山海，都要为孩子守住一条回家的路。

Family Puzzle on the Banks of the Seine: A Sino-French Transnational Custody Battle Over a Child Born Out of Wedlock

Introduction

A meeting that began on Montmartre in Paris, a love-hate entanglement spanning eight years, an innocent child born in a foreign land — all eventually evolved into a transnational custody battle that involved judicial proceedings in both China and France. The status of a child born out of wedlock, disputes over cross-border guardianship, defenses based on electronic evidence, and the principle of acting in the best interests of the child have made this case, from start to finish, full of harsh realities and human conflicts. When I took on this case, the child had been secretly taken away from his familiar living environment. The father was distraught with anxiety, while the mother remained trapped in the illusion of fame and fortune and refused to face reality. What I had to do was to secure the safest possible future for the child, between national borders and legal provisions.

I first met Lin Yuan in the summer of 2023, in my law firm office. Outside the window, traffic was heavy, but he was as quiet as an island submerged underwater. His fingers repeatedly stroked a small silver longevity lock engraved with a French name. It was a safety charm he had bought for his son Lin Nian'an, who was far away in Paris. It was also the only gentle physical evidence left from a relationship that began in romance but ended in heartbreak.

"Lawyer Rachel J. Ye, I beg you — help me bring my child back to a normal life."

His story began in the spring of 2015, on Montmartre, Paris. Back then, he was a nanomaterials scholar deeply engaged in laboratory research; she was Bai Shanshan, a cross-border shopping blogger building her career in Europe. A chance encounter — Bai Shanshan's phone had died, and Lin Yuan lent her his power bank. This small act of kindness entangled two people who otherwise would have never met, on the banks of the Seine, for a full eight years.

In the autumn of 2017, their son Nian'an was born at Pitié-Salpêtrière Hospital in Paris. Since Lin Yuan and Bai Shanshan were not legally married, the child was born out of wedlock. Yet this status did not diminish Lin Yuan's expectations in the slightest. He wholeheartedly embraced the role of a father. Hospital diagnoses, attendance records, night-shift care logs, discharge medical records, communication with nannies, home surveillance footage — every detail bore witness to his days and nights by his son's bedside. Bai Shanshan, however, plunged headlong into the wave of cross-border e-commerce. Amid online traffic and orders, she gradually neglected her identity as a mother.

They once rented an apartment in the 16th arrondissement of Paris for over €4,000 a month. Living expenses were exorbitant, and the tuition for Nian'an's Montessori daycare was equally costly. Yet Bai Shanshan never contributed any income from her resale business to family or child-related expenses. Lin Yuan bore all costs in silence and hired a professional nanny to take care of the boy's daily life. But this stability could not resist the pull of desire. Bai Shanshan moved from cross-border resale to livestream sales, pouring all her energy into investing in a large marketplace business, leaving her with even less time to care for her son. Lin Yuan, by contrast, longed for a steady life centered on their child. On Christmas 2019, the rift between them erupted completely, planting the deepest seed for the cross-border custody battle that followed.

In June 2023, the two parties finally reached and signed a Joint Custody Agreement, promising to raise and care for the child together. But before the agreement could be authenticated, Bai Shanshan seized the gap in legal procedures, quietly packed Nian'an's clothes, and disappeared from Paris with the boy. When Lin Yuan discovered what had happened, most of the child's wardrobe was empty; only a torn suitcase dust cover lay on the floor, and the birthday gift he had prepared for his son's sixth birthday remained unopened.

Overnight, the father became a seeker thousands of miles away, and the child the most innocent pawn in a cross-border struggle.

After accepting the mandate, my team and I quickly launched a response plan. On one hand, we filed a lawsuit for child custody with the competent Chinese court on Lin Yuan's behalf as plaintiff, and applied for an injunction against personality rights infringement, ordering the defendant Bai Shanshan to cease concealing the child and protecting Lin Yuan's rights to custody and visitation. On the other hand, we collected and preserved extensive evidence to clarify the childcare responsibilities each party had assumed during their cohabitation.

We retrieved all data from Bai Shanshan's social media and sales accounts over the previous three years and secured them as electronic evidence. The glamorous "Sister Qian from Paris" seen on screen, the myth of tens of millions in sales revenue, collapsed in the face of authentic logistics, transaction records, and warehouse documents. Even more disturbing was that multiple livestream replays clearly captured the sound of the child crying and objects breaking, while she remained composed on camera, promoting luxury children's clothing and drowning the child's helplessness in the noise of millions of views.

The provisions of the Law on the Protection of Minors are clear and firm: guardians shall not use minors for profit-making activities, nor shall they neglect their physical and mental health. Yet in this frenzy of online traffic, maternal duty had long been cast aside. In April 2024, the trial officially began. It was a rare battle of electronic evidence spanning China and France. Counsel for the opposing side argued that Bai Shanshan could provide superior educational conditions and presented offers from prestigious schools to strengthen her custody claim. In court, we presented a complete and rigorous chain of evidence proving: livestream records and travel itineraries confirmed that Bai Shanshan was constantly traveling markets and hosting broadcasts, with no time or energy to accompany her child; a comparison of consumption records and daily photos revealed the child was often dressed in old clothes, in stark contrast to the luxury depicted in her livestreams; comprehensive evidence showed that during the child's time in France, he was personally raised and cared for by his father Lin Yuan; evidence that the child had established a stable routine in French daycare and school, only to be taken abroad by his mother without consent, forcing separation from his father; and hotel surveillance footage, medical records, pet store receipts, and even casual remarks by the child all pointed to the same truth — after being brought back to China from France, the child had not received stable, safe, and loving care; and more importantly, none of Bai Shanshan's income in France had been used for the child's upbringing — it was spent on personal expenses or saved for herself.

The turning point of the trial came when eight-year-old Nian'an spoke up: "I want to go back to Daddy."

Holding a small woolen bear, he softly spoke of the anxiety and fear hidden in his heart. There was no deliberate guidance, no adult coaching — only a child's most genuine feelings. This was precisely the warmest and most powerful expression of the principle in the Civil Code of respecting the true will of minor children. We did not merely accept his choice; we used a full evidentiary system to confirm the credibility of his statement, upholding the ultimate principle of the best interests of the child.

The court ultimately accepted our arguments and awarded custody of the child to his father, Lin Yuan. Yet holding the judgment, the real challenge had only just begun. In September 2024, the enforcement scene of the child's handover was fraught with incidents. Bai Shanshan gathered many relatives and friends to surround and obstruct the handover of the child, causing the situation to become chaotic for a time. Fortunately, at the critical moment, judicial police escorted the child throughout. In the end, Nian'an safely returned to his father and to a stable, peaceful, and carefully cared-for life. This cross-continental family tug-of-war finally came to a close with legal justice and the child's peace of mind.

Post-Case Conclusion

This is a cross-border custody dispute of great contemporary significance, and a concentrated reflection in family justice practice of the protection of non-marital children, cross-border custody disputes, the use of electronic evidence, and the principle of the best interests of the child.

The law clearly states that non-marital children enjoy the same rights as marital children. The biological father's obligation and right to support and custody are not impaired by the absence of a marriage registration. In cross-border custody disputes, national borders should not be barriers, procedures should not become loopholes, and children should not pay the price for adult grievances and choices.

With the arrival of the digital age, electronic data such as livestream records, consumption statements, travel tracks, and audio and video materials have become crucial evidence in family cases. Objective, silent, and tamper-proof, they can pierce through pretense, restore the most authentic appearance of daily life, and provide the firmest foundation for judicial decisions.

The core value of this case remains the best interests of the child. Custody should not be a contest of "winning or losing" between parents, nor a simple comparison of wealth and conditions. It depends on who can truly provide a stable, safe, respectful, and loving environment for the child, and who places the child's physical and mental health above all else. The law protects the weakest and most innocent lives, so that every child can grow up safely in the sun, free from exploitation, neglect, and being caught up in adult desires.

The Seine flows endlessly, and the puzzle of family affection eventually finds its answer. The warmth of justice lies in this: no matter how far the mountains and seas, a path home shall always be secured for the child.

一纸遗嘱锁终身：当继承权困住婚姻自由权

引言

一份遗嘱，三套房产，半生财富，却藏着一句冰冷的约束："继承遗产，便不得改嫁"。一方是倾尽温柔、陪他走完最后岁月的年轻妻子，一方是恪守遗愿、寸步不让的前妻之子与老父。财富可以分割，自由能否标价？爱与陪伴可以衡量，婚姻自主权又怎能被一纸遗嘱捆绑？这起看似简单的继承纠纷，撕开的是人性的占有欲，更是法理与情理、契约与公序良俗的激烈碰撞。作为代理律师，我全程亲历这场纷争，也亲眼见证法律如何为自由与尊严撑腰，如何打破用遗产捆绑人生的荒唐约定。

我第一次见到邓琳琳，是在一个阴雨绵绵的午后。

她不过三十岁出头，怀里抱着年幼的儿子，眼神里有委屈，有茫然，更有不甘。坐在我对面，她轻声开口，每一个字都带着无力："叶律师，我照顾他到最后一刻，没有半点亏欠。可他走了，留给我的不是安稳，是一道枷锁——要房子，就不能再嫁；要再嫁，就一无所有。这样的要求，真的合法吗？"

她口中的"他"，是她已故的丈夫高智余。高智余白手起家，打拼半生，是众人眼中事业有成的老板。他前一段婚姻平淡收场，与前妻协议离婚，两人育有一子高嘉宣。年过半百之际，他在工作中结识了还在读大学、年仅二十多岁的邓琳琳。年龄差距悬殊，却挡不住相互吸引，两人迅速相恋、结婚，不久后又生下小儿子高嘉骐。

谁也没有想到，安稳日子只过了五年，命运便猝然转向。高智余查出肝癌，病情一路恶化。在病榻之上，他自知时日无多，亲笔写下一份自书遗嘱，对自己名下三套房产、存款、股票及理财逐一安排：

1、第一套房产，由与前妻所生之子高嘉宣继承；

2、第二套房产，由与现任妻子邓琳琳所生之子高嘉骐继承；

3、第三套房产及全部存款、股票、理财，由现任妻子邓琳琳继承——但附带条件：邓琳琳必须承诺终身不再改嫁，否则丧失全部继承权。

遗嘱末尾，高智余郑重签名，注明年、月、日。在他看来，这是对身后事的周全安排，是对年轻妻子的"约束"，也是对这段婚姻最后的占有。可他不曾想到，这份带着强烈控制欲的遗嘱，会在他离世后，将邓琳琳推入一场漫长的诉讼。

遗嘱中，第三套房产及所有存款、理财，均由邓琳琳继承，但附带的这个近乎残酷的条件——邓琳琳必须承诺终身不改嫁，否则丧失全部继承权，却让邓琳琳陷入焦虑和迷茫。她才三十岁不到，带着年幼的孩子，未来还有漫长的人生要走。可遗嘱却强行将她的人生定格在“改嫁”和“遗产”二选一之上：想要有更好的物质条件活下去、养好孩子，就要放弃重新爱与被爱的权利；若想追求自由与幸福，就要失去她应有的遗产继承，变得一无所有。

这种无形的精神重压，远比生活的艰难更折磨人。她不敢向亲友倾诉，不敢流露委屈，只能在深夜里独自流泪，在尊严与生存之间反复挣扎。遗嘱里的财产是她和孩子活下去的希望，可附加的条件，却是对她人格与自由最彻底的剥夺。

高智余病逝不久，遗产之争迅速爆发。邓琳琳带着年幼的儿子，要求依照法定继承分割财产。可高智余与前妻所生的儿子高嘉宣、以及高智余的老父亲，坚持要求邓琳琳遵守遗嘱，承诺不改嫁方可继承财产，否则一分一厘都不能拿。他们将遗嘱视作逝者遗愿，不容违背；可在邓琳琳心中，这份遗愿早已越过了法律与人性的底线。

一方要自由，一方要履约。邓琳琳不愿用一生的自由去换取财产，更不愿让孩子跟着自己颠沛流离。在长久的考虑后，她最终选择通过法律途径，维护自己最基本的权利与尊严。她委托我提起继承之诉，将全部法定继承人诉至法院，请求认定遗嘱中对她的人生自由限制性条款无效，要求继承遗产。

案件起诉至法院后，核心争议焦点很明确：遗嘱中“不得改嫁方可继承”的内容，是否合法有效？

作为邓琳琳的代理人，我当庭明确指出：

这份遗嘱，形式上虽符合自书遗嘱的要求，但内容严重违背法律与公序良俗。

婚姻自由，是我国法律赋予每个公民的基本权利，任何人不得加以干涉、限制、剥夺。高智余以遗产为筹码，强制要求邓琳琳终身不改嫁，本质上是用财产捆绑人身自由，用遗嘱干涉婚姻自主权，明显违反《民法典》规定，这部分内容应当认定无效。法院经审理后，采纳了我们的观点。判决书写道：民事主体从事民事活动，不得违反法律，不得违背公序良俗。遗嘱中对邓琳琳附加“不得改嫁”的条件，限制其婚姻自主权，违背社会公共秩序与善良风俗，该部分内容无效。无效部分所涉遗产，依法按照法定继承处理。

同时，法院根据我方的举证，查明一个不争的事实：高智余患病直至离世，全程由邓琳琳陪伴照料、日夜守护、不离不弃。相较其他继承人，她尽到了更多扶助、照顾义务。依据法律规定，与被继承人共同生活、尽了主要扶养义务的继承人，分配遗产时可以多分。最终，法院依法判决：遗嘱中有效部分，仍按遗嘱执行；“不得改嫁”的无效条款所涉遗产，由各法定继承人继承，其中邓琳琳分得 40%。

一纸判决，既守住了法律的底线，也给了真心付出的人一份公道。走出法院那天，邓琳琳红了眼眶，却终于挺直了脊背。她赢的，不只是财产，更是一个女人最基本的尊严与自由。

案后结语

这是一起具有典型意义的继承案件，它清晰地告诉我们：遗嘱可以安排财富，却不能捆绑自由；可以处分财产，却不能违背公序良俗。一份合法有效的遗嘱，必须同时满足四个条件：立遗嘱人具备完全民事行为能力、意思表示真实、形式符合法律规定、内容不违反法律、不违背公序良俗。以继承财产为条件，限制他人婚姻自由、人身自由，即便出自真实意愿，也会因触碰法律红线而无效。

更重要的是：遗嘱部分无效，不代表整份遗嘱无效。无效的内容依法剔除，按照法定继承处理；合法有效的部分，依然得到法律尊重。这既维护了被继承人处分个人财产的权利，也守住了社会最基本的公平与正义。

现实中，不少人希望通过遗嘱对继承人附加种种条件：学业、婚姻、生育、品行……但强行限制人身自由的约定，往往事与愿违。真正稳妥、合法、能够落地的财富传承，并非靠强制与约束，而是靠科学的规划，甚至可以借助遗嘱信托等制度，在不违背法律与公序良俗的前提下，让财富真正守护所爱之人，而非成为束缚一生的枷锁。

爱到最后，最好的模样不是占有与控制，而是尊重与成全。

法律如此，人心亦然。

A Will Bound for Life: When Inheritance Traps the Freedom of Marriage

Introduction

A single will, three properties, a lifetime of wealth — yet hidden within it a cruel condition: "He who inherits the estate shall not remarry." On one side stood a young wife who had tenderly cared for him until his last breath; on the other, his son from a previous marriage and elderly father, who insisted on upholding the will without compromise. Wealth can be divided, but can freedom be priced? Love and companionship have weight, but how can the right to marry freely be chained by a piece of paper? This seemingly simple inheritance dispute exposes the possessiveness of human nature, and a fierce clash between law and morality, contract and public order and good morals. As her attorney, I witnessed the entire conflict and saw how the law upheld freedom and dignity, breaking the absurd agreement that used inheritance to chain a life.

I first met Deng Linlin on a rainy afternoon. In her early thirties, she held her young son in her arms, her eyes filled with grievance, confusion, and unwillingness. Sitting across from me, she spoke softly, every word weak and helpless: "Lawyer Rachel J. Ye, I cared for him until his last moment. I owed him nothing. But after he passed away, what he left me was not peace, but a shackle: keep the houses, and never remarry; remarry, and lose everything. Is such a demand really legal?"

The man she spoke of was her late husband, Gao Zhiyu. A self-made businessman, he was regarded as successful by everyone. His first marriage ended peacefully by mutual divorce, and he had a son named Gao Jiaxuan from that union. In his fifties, he met Deng Linlin, a woman in her twenties still attending university, through work. Despite the large age gap, they fell in love, married quickly, and soon had a younger son, Gao Jiaqi.

No one expected that their stable life would last only five years before fate took a sudden turn. Gao Zhiyu was diagnosed with liver cancer, and his condition deteriorated rapidly. Confined to bed, knowing his days were numbered, he personally wrote a holographic will, arranging his three properties, savings, stocks, and wealth management products one by one:

1. One property to be inherited by Gao Jiaxuan, his son from his first marriage;

2. One property to be inherited by Gao Jiaqi, his son with his current wife Deng Linlin;

3. The third property, all savings, stocks, and wealth management products to be inherited by his current wife Deng Linlin — on the condition that she must promise never to remarry for life, otherwise she shall forfeit all inheritance rights.

At the end of the will, Gao Zhiyu signed solemnly and dated it. In his eyes, this was a thorough arrangement for his affairs, a "restraint" on his young wife, and a final act of possession over their marriage. What he never foresaw was that this controlling will would push Deng Linlin into a long lawsuit after his death.

In the will, the third property and all financial assets were left to Deng Linlin, yet the cruel condition attached — lifelong celibacy in exchange for inheritance — plunged Deng Linlin into anxiety and confusion. She was not yet thirty, raising a young child, with a long life ahead. Yet the will forcibly froze her life into a choice between "remarriage" and "inheritance": to live securely and raise her child, she must give up the right to love and be loved again; to pursue freedom and happiness, she must lose her rightful inheritance and be left with nothing. This invisible mental pressure tortured her more than hardship itself. She dared not confide in relatives, nor show her grievance, only weeping alone at night, struggling between dignity and survival. The inheritance was her and her child's hope for survival, yet the attached condition stripped her of dignity and freedom entirely.

Shortly after Gao Zhiyu's death, the inheritance dispute erupted. Deng Linlin, with her young son, requested division of the estate according to statutory inheritance. However, Gao Jiaxuan and Gao Zhiyu's elderly father insisted that she obey the will and promise not to remarry to inherit — otherwise she would receive nothing. They viewed the will as the deceased's last wish, unbreakable; yet to Deng Linlin, it had already crossed the bottom line of law and humanity.

One side demanded freedom; the other demanded compliance. Deng Linlin refused to trade her lifelong freedom for property, nor let her child suffer instability. After long consideration, she chose to defend her basic rights and dignity through legal channels. She entrusted me to file an inheritance lawsuit against all legal heirs, asking the court to declare the restrictive clause on her personal freedom invalid and to claim her inheritance.

Once the case was filed, the core dispute was clear: Was the condition "no remarriage to inherit" in the will legal and valid? As Deng Linlin's attorney, I argued clearly in court: Although the will met the formal requirements of a holographic will, its content seriously violated the law and public order and good morals. Freedom of marriage is a fundamental right granted to every citizen under Chinese law, which no one may interfere with, restrict, or deprive. Using inheritance as leverage to force lifelong celibacy essentially chains personal freedom to property and interferes with marital autonomy through a will, clearly violating the Civil Code. This part of the content must be deemed invalid.

After hearing the case, the court accepted our position. The judgment stated: Civil persons engaging in civil activities must not violate the law nor public order and good morals. The condition attached to Deng Linlin — prohibiting remarriage — restricts her marital autonomy and violates public order and good morals; this part is invalid. The estate involved in the invalid clause shall be distributed according to statutory succession.

Meanwhile, based on our evidence, the court confirmed an undeniable fact: From the onset of illness until his death, Deng Linlin accompanied, nursed, and stayed with Gao Zhiyu day and night without desertion. Compared with other heirs, she fulfilled far more obligations of support and care. Under the law, an heir who lived with the decedent and performed main support obligations may receive a larger share. Ultimately, the court ruled according to the law: the valid parts of the will remained enforceable; the estate covered by the invalid "no remarriage" clause was distributed among legal heirs, with Deng Linlin awarded 40%.

One judgment upheld the bottom line of the law and delivered justice to one who had given sincerely. Leaving the courthouse that day, Deng Linlin's eyes were red, but she finally stood tall. She had won not only property, but also the basic dignity and freedom of a woman.

Post-Case Conclusion

This is a landmark inheritance case. It clearly teaches us: A will may arrange wealth, but cannot chain freedom; it may dispose of property, but cannot violate public order and good morals. A legally valid will must satisfy four conditions: the testator has full civil capacity, the intent is genuine, the form complies with the law, and the content does not violate laws or public morals. Restricting another's marital or personal freedom in exchange for inheritance — even if truly intended — is invalid for crossing legal red lines.

Importantly, partial invalidity of a will does not invalidate the entire document. Invalid provisions are removed and handled by statutory succession, while lawful parts remain respected. This both protects the testator's right to dispose of property and upholds basic fairness and justice.

In reality, many seek to attach conditions to inheritance: education, marriage, childbearing, conduct... yet restrictions on personal freedom often backfire. Truly stable, lawful, and workable wealth succession relies not on coercion, but on scientific planning — such as testamentary trusts — to protect loved ones within legal boundaries, rather than binding them for life.

At the end of love, the finest form is not possession or control, but respect and fulfillment. So it is with the law, and so it is with the human heart.

隐瞒配偶“被网络诈骗”，离婚因“挥霍”而少分财产

引言

婚姻里的财产，是夫妻二人并肩打拼的底气，更是彼此信任的载体。可当一方违背忠诚，瞒着配偶陷入婚外情感陷阱，又被诱惑卷入所谓“高回报投资”时，那么婚姻就将走向家财散尽、感情破碎的可悲结局。这类因网络交友、婚外情感引发的投资诈骗，是近年来频发的新型家庭财产“杀手”，它不仅夺走真金白银，更彻底摧毁婚姻根基。我代理的这起离婚案中，受害丈夫彭先生，面对妻子擅自挥霍夫妻共同财产、遭遇网络诈骗后留下的烂摊子，凭借法律武器，最终在离婚财产分割中为自己争取到了公平结果，也让过错方为自己的鲁莽与背叛付出了代价。

彭先生和周女士的婚姻，原本是旁人眼中安稳踏实的小家庭。彭先生踏实肯干，深耕新零售行业多年，起早贪黑跑业务、谈合作，一点点积攒起家庭财富，出于对妻子的信任，他始终把家里的存款、账户都交由周女士打理，自己一心扑在事业上，想着多赚点钱，让全家人的生活过得更好。

起初两人感情尚可，可随着彭先生生意越来越忙，两人在创业规划、生活琐事上的分歧渐渐多了起来，沟通越来越少，感情也慢慢淡了，家里时常弥漫着沉默的氛围，再也没有了往日的温馨。彭先生虽觉得遗憾，却从未想过放弃家庭，只想着慢慢磨合，总能回到从前的样子。

变故悄无声息地发生在周女士沉迷网络之后。闲来无事的周女士，在社交软件上结识了一名陌生男子，对方言辞温柔体贴，对她百般关怀，恰好填补了她内心的空虚。一来二去，两人越聊越亲密，很快发展成了婚外不正当关系，周女士对这名男子言听计从，彻底迷失在了虚假的温柔里。

这名男子看似温情，实则居心叵测，没多久便开始向周女士吹嘘自己有“内部投资渠道”，声称做的是低风险、高回报的理财项目，投进去的钱短时间就能翻倍，还不断发一些虚假的盈利截图，哄骗周女士投钱。被情感冲昏头脑的周女士，丝毫没有察觉这是精心设计的骗局，反而对男子的话深信不疑。

她心里清楚，家里的 200 万存款是夫妻共同财产，擅自投钱丈夫肯定不会同意，可在情人的诱惑和一夜暴富的贪念驱使下，她选择了刻意隐瞒。她背着彭先生，悄悄从自己管理的家庭账户里转出一笔笔钱，少则几万，多则几十万，陆陆续续投入了对方推荐的所谓“投资平台”。

一次偶然的机会，彭先生发现账户资金异常，几番追问下，周女士才支支吾吾说出了自己网络投资的事，但她并不承认与该男子有不正当关系。彭先生又气又急，立刻察觉到这是典型的网络投资诈骗，他苦口婆心劝阻妻子，反复告诉她这是骗局，让她赶紧停止投钱，立刻报警处理，想办法追回损失。

可此时的周女士早已被洗脑，非但听不进丈夫的劝告，反而觉得彭先生是在

阻拦她赚钱，对彭先生的劝阻置之不理，甚至拒绝沟通，把自己封闭起来，执意继续与该男子联系交往，往平台投资款达到 200 万元，幻想着能赚回大钱。直到没过多久，所谓的投资平台突然无法登录，之前的" 投资导师"也彻底失联，200 万存款血本无归，周女士才如梦初醒，慌忙去公安机关报案，可此时钱款早已被转移，追回的希望微乎其微。

骗局败露，存款尽失，周女士陷入了巨大的自责与崩溃中，整日以泪洗面，几度寻死觅活，可再多的悔恨也换不回损失的钱财，更挽不回被彻底伤透的夫妻感情。彭先生看着眼前的一切，心彻底凉了：自己辛辛苦苦打拼多年的积蓄，被妻子因为一段婚外情、一场荒唐的骗局挥霍一空，妻子不仅违背了夫妻间的忠实义务，更是擅自处置夫妻共同财产，全然不顾家庭利益。多年的信任瞬间崩塌，这段婚姻再也没有维系的可能，绝望又愤怒的彭先生，找到了我，委托我代理他的离婚诉讼。

接手案件后，我仔细梳理了案件的全部细节，固定了关键证据：周女士与婚外男子的聊天记录、转账凭证、投资平台的操作记录、公安机关的报案回执，以及彭先生多次劝阻周女士的聊天记录、通话录音等。这类案件的核心争议点，在于周女士" 被网络诈骗"的行为，是否属于离婚财产分割中应当少分财产的" 挥霍夫妻共同财产"情形。很多人误以为，被诈骗的一方本身也是受害者，无需承担财产损失的责任，可在婚姻关系中，擅自处分大额共同财产、因重大过错导致财产损失，法律也不会纵容。

我结合案件事实与法律规定，明确了案件的代理核心，重点围绕三个关键事实展开论证：

首先，核实诈骗事实的真实性。我整理了周女士的全部资金流水、与诈骗人员的往来记录，以及公安机关出具的立案回执，证实 200 万存款确实因网络投资诈骗损失殆尽，不存在周女士故意转移、隐藏财产的情形，但这一损失，完全是她自身重大过错导致。

其次，论证财产处置行为的不合理性。这笔 200 万属于大额夫妻共同财产，周女士在夫妻感情本就不和的情况下，基于婚外不正当关系，隐瞒配偶擅自投钱，在配偶明确劝阻后仍执意为之，且投资项目无任何正规资质、风险极高，她未尽到丝毫审慎注意义务，更没有履行夫妻间的告知、协商义务，属于严重不当处置夫妻共同财产。

最后，界定该行为属于法律意义上的" 挥霍"。根据《民法典》相关规定，挥霍夫妻共同财产，并非单指奢侈消费，更包括非为家庭共同生活、未经配偶同意、因自身重大过错导致共同财产重大损失的行为。周女士的行为，完全符合" 非必要、拒协商、损害性"的挥霍核心，且款项已经无法追回，造成难以弥补的损失后果。既违背夫妻忠实义务，又严重侵害彭先生的财产权益，理应在离婚分割共同财产时承担少分的比例。

庭审中，周女士的代理人辩称，周女士也是网络诈骗的受害者，不应因此少分财产。我当庭提交全部证据，逐一阐述论证观点，明确指出：周女士的受害，源于自身违背婚姻忠诚、贪图不当利益、擅自处分夫妻共同财产的重大过错，其行为与家庭财产损失存在直接因果关系，不能以“被诈骗”为由，免除自身应承担的责任，法律保护受害者，但绝不保护因自身过错损害配偶合法权益的一方。

法院经过审理，采纳了我的代理意见，认定周女士在婚姻关系存续期间，违背夫妻忠实义务，未经配偶同意，擅自处分大额夫妻共同财产，经劝阻后仍未停止，最终导致财产全部损失，属于重大过错、挥霍夫妻共同财产的行为，严重损害了彭先生的合法权益。最终判决准予双方离婚，在夫妻共同财产即一套婚内房产的分割中，彭先生分得 65%，周女士分得 35%。

拿到判决书那天，彭先生长长舒了一口气，他说，这笔财产分割，不是为了争多少利益，而是为了讨一个公道，为自己多年的付出和被辜负的信任，要一个说法。

案后结语

这起案件，是当下网络诈骗破坏家庭、摧毁婚姻的典型缩影，也给无数家庭敲响了警钟。

网络交友诈骗、虚假投资诈骗，已经不再是单纯的财产犯罪，它更像一颗埋在婚姻里的炸弹，利用人性的贪婪与情感的空虚，不仅让受害者一夜之间倾家荡产，更彻底撕裂夫妻间的信任，毁掉原本安稳的家庭。近年来，此类新型犯罪频发，多少人因为一时糊涂、心存贪念，瞒着配偶陷入骗局，最终落得家财散尽、妻离子散的下场，其社会危害不言而喻，它夺走的不仅是财产，更是家庭的安稳与婚姻的底线。

婚姻的根基，是信任与忠诚，夫妻共同财产，是双方共同打拼的成果，任何一方都无权擅自处分。《民法典》之所以规定挥霍夫妻共同财产一方离婚时应少分财产，核心就是保护婚姻中的无过错方，维护婚姻关系的公平与正义。本案中，周女士本是婚姻里的一方，却因违背忠诚、漠视配偶权益，最终既承受了财产损失的苦果，又在离婚时少分财产，亲手毁掉了自己的家庭。

这起案件也提醒每一对夫妻：身处网络时代，诱惑无处不在，唯有守住婚姻的忠诚底线，拒绝一夜暴富的贪念，遇事相互沟通、彼此信任，才能避开各类骗局的陷阱；唯有珍惜夫妻共同打拼的成果，尊重彼此的财产权益，才能守住家庭的安稳与幸福。而婚姻里最珍贵的，是彼此的信任与相守，守住这份信任，才是守住家庭的根本。

Concealing that the Spouse Was "Online Scam", and the Divorce Divided Less Property Due to "Squander"

Introduction

Marital property is not only the foundation built by a couple through joint hard work, but also the embodiment of mutual trust. However, when one party breaches their duty of loyalty, conceals an extramarital affair from their spouse, and is lured into so-called "high-return investments", the marriage will head toward the tragic end of financial ruin and emotional breakdown. Investment fraud triggered by online dating and extramarital affairs has emerged as a prevalent new-type "killer" of family property in recent years. It not only takes away tangible wealth but also completely destroys the foundation of marriage. In this divorce case I represented, the aggrieved husband Mr. Peng, facing the mess left by his wife's unauthorized waste of community property and her falling victim to online fraud, used legal weapons to secure a fair outcome in the division of marital property, and made the culpable party pay for her recklessness and betrayal.

The marriage of Mr. Peng and Ms. Zhou was once a stable and down-to-earth small family in the eyes of others. Diligent and hardworking, Mr. Peng had been deeply engaged in the new retail industry for years. He worked from dawn to dusk running business and negotiating cooperation, accumulating family wealth bit by bit. Out of trust in his wife, he had always left the management of family savings and accounts to Ms. Zhou, while devoting himself wholeheartedly to his career, hoping to earn more money and provide a better life for the whole family.

At first, the couple had a decent relationship. But as Mr. Peng's business grew busier, disagreements between them over career plans and daily trivialities gradually emerged. Communication grew scarce, their affection faded, and the home was often filled with silence, losing the warmth it once had. Although Mr. Peng felt regretful, he never thought of giving up the family, hoping that they could reconcile and return to how things were.

The misfortune befell quietly after Ms. Zhou became obsessed with the internet. With plenty of spare time, Ms. Zhou met a strange man on a social media app. The man spoke tenderly and considerately, showering her with care, which just filled the emptiness in her heart. As they chatted more and more intimately, they soon developed an improper extramarital relationship. Ms.

Zhou obeyed the man in everything, completely lost in the false affection.

The man seemed warm-hearted but was actually harboring ulterior motives. Before long, he began bragging to Ms. Zhou about having "internal investment channels", claiming to run low-risk, high-return financial projects where invested money could double in a short time. He kept sending fake profit screenshots to coax Ms. Zhou into investing. Blinded by emotions, Ms. Zhou did not realize it was an elaborate scam at all; instead, she believed every word the man said.

She knew full well that the 2 million yuan in family savings was community property, and her husband would never approve of unauthorized investment. Yet driven by her lover's temptation and greed for getting rich overnight, she chose to deliberately conceal the truth. Behind Mr. Peng's back, she quietly transferred sums of money from the family accounts she managed—ranging from tens of thousands to hundreds of thousands yuan—and successively invested them in the so-called "investment platform" recommended by the man.

By chance, Mr. Peng noticed abnormal fund flows in the accounts. After repeated questioning, Ms. Zhou hesitantly admitted her online investment, but denied having an improper relationship with the man. Furious and anxious, Mr. Peng immediately recognized it as a typical online investment scam. He earnestly dissuaded his wife, repeatedly telling her it was a fraud, urging her to stop investing at once, report to the police immediately, and try to recover the losses.

However, Ms. Zhou had already been brainwashed. Not only did she refuse to listen to her husband's advice, but she also thought Mr. Peng was preventing her from making money. She ignored his dissuasion, even refused to communicate, isolated herself, and insisted on continuing to associate with the man. She eventually invested a total of 2 million yuan in the platform, dreaming of huge profits. It was not until shortly afterward that the so-called investment platform suddenly became inaccessible and the former "investment mentor" completely disappeared, leaving the 2 million yuan savings totally lost, that Ms. Zhou finally came to her senses. She hurried to report the case to the public security authority, but by then the money had long been transferred, with little hope of recovery.

When the scam was exposed and all savings were lost, Ms. Zhou fell into deep remorse and collapse. She cried all day long and even attempted suicide several times. Yet no amount of regret could bring back the lost money, let alone repair the thoroughly broken marital relationship. Looking at what had happened, Mr. Peng was completely disheartened: the savings he had worked so hard to accumulate over the years had been squandered by his wife due to an extramarital affair and an absurd scam. His wife not only breached the duty of fidelity between spouses but also disposed of the community property without authorization, with total disregard for the interests of the family. Years of trust collapsed in an instant, and there was no longer any possibility of saving the marriage. In despair and anger, Mr. Peng came to me and entrusted me to represent him in his divorce lawsuit.

After taking over the case, I carefully sorted out all the details of the case and preserved key evidence: chat records between Ms. Zhou and the extramarital man, transfer vouchers, operation records of the investment platform, receipt of police report, as well as chat records and call recordings of Mr. Peng repeatedly dissuading Ms. Zhou. The core controversial issue in such cases is whether Ms. Zhou's act of "being a victim of online fraud" constitutes "wasteful dissipation of community property" that warrants a smaller share of property in divorce property division. Many people mistakenly believe that the defrauded party is also a victim and thus shall not be liable for property losses. However, in a marital relationship, the law will not tolerate unauthorized disposal of large amounts of community property or property losses caused by gross fault.

Based on the facts of the case and legal provisions, I clarified the core of the representation and focused my arguments on three key facts:

First, verifying the authenticity of the fraud. I compiled all of Ms. Zhou's capital flow records, correspondence with fraudsters, and the case-filing receipt issued by the public security authority, confirming that the 2 million yuan in savings was indeed completely lost due to online investment fraud, and there was no intentional transfer or concealment of property by Ms. Zhou. Nevertheless, this loss was entirely caused by her own gross fault.

Second, demonstrating the unreasonableness of the property disposal. The 2 million yuan constituted a large sum of community property. At a time when the marital relationship was already strained, Ms. Zhou, motivated by an improper extramarital relationship, concealed the investment from her spouse and made the payment without authorization. She persisted even after her spouse explicitly dissuaded her. Moreover, the investment project lacked any formal qualification and carried extremely high risks. She failed to fulfill the slightest duty of care, let alone the duty of notification and consultation between spouses, constituting a serious improper disposal of community property.

Third, defining the act as "wasteful dissipation" in the legal sense. According to the relevant provisions of the Civil Code, wasteful dissipation of community property does not merely refer to luxury consumption, but also includes acts that cause substantial losses to community property for non-family living purposes, without the spouse's consent, and due to one's own gross fault. Ms. Zhou's conduct fully conformed to the core elements of dissipation: unnecessary, non-consultative, and damaging. The funds were irrecoverable, resulting in irreparable losses. Having breached both the spousal duty of fidelity and seriously infringed upon Mr. Peng's property rights and interests, she deserved a reduced share in the division of community property upon divorce.

During the trial, Ms. Zhou's representative argued that Ms. Zhou was also a victim of online fraud and should not receive a smaller share of property for that reason. I presented all evidence in court and elaborated my arguments one by one, clearly pointing out: Ms. Zhou's victimhood stemmed from her gross fault of breaching marital fidelity, coveting improper gains, and disposing of community property without authorization. There was a direct causal link between her conduct and the loss of family property. She could not be exempted from liability on the ground of "being defrauded." The law protects victims, but in no way protects a party who infringes upon the legitimate rights and interests of their spouse due to their own fault.

After trial, the court adopted my agency opinions. It held that during the existence of the marital relationship, Ms. Zhou breached the duty of fidelity between spouses, disposed of a large sum of community property without her spouse's consent, refused to desist despite dissuasion, and ultimately caused the total loss of the property, constituting gross fault and wasteful dissipation of community property, which seriously harmed Mr. Peng's legitimate rights and interests. The court finally granted a divorce to both parties. In the division of community property,namely a marital home, Mr. Peng was awarded 65% and Ms. Zhou 35%.

On the day he received the judgment, Mr. Peng let out a long sigh of relief. He said that the property division was not about pursuing more benefits, but about seeking justice—a fair outcome for his years of dedication and the trust that had been betrayed.

Post-Case Conclusion

This case epitomizes how online fraud destroys families and marriages in the present day, serving as a stark warning to countless households.

Online dating scams and fake investment fraud are no longer mere property crimes. They are like bombs planted in marriages, preying on human greed and emotional emptiness. Such scams not only reduce victims to ruin overnight but also shatter the trust between spouses and destroy once-stable families. In recent years, these new types of crimes have occurred frequently. Many people, blinded by momentary foolishness and greed, hide the truth from their spouses and fall victim to scams, ending up penniless and separated from their families. The social harm is self-evident: what is taken away is not just property, but also family stability and the bottom line of marriage.

Marriage is founded on trust and loyalty, and the community property of husband and wife is the fruit of their joint efforts. Neither party has the right to dispose of it without permission. The reason why the Civil Code stipulates that a party who squanders the community property shall receive a smaller share of property upon divorce is to protect the innocent party in the marriage and uphold fairness and justice in marital relations. In this case, Ms. Zhou, as one party in the marriage, violated the duty of loyalty, failed to resist temptation, and disregarded her spouse's rights and interests. As a result, she not only suffered the bitter consequences of property loss but also received a smaller share of property in divorce, personally ruining her own family.

This case also reminds every couple: in the internet age, temptations are everywhere. Only by upholding the bottom line of marital loyalty, rejecting the greed for getting rich quick, communicating with each other and trusting one another when facing problems can we avoid the traps of various scams. Only by cherishing the fruits of joint hard work and respecting each other's property rights can we safeguard the stability and happiness of the family. The most precious thing in marriage is mutual trust and companionship. To guard this trust is to safeguard the very foundation of the family.

Photograph by Joseph Xu

CHAPTER 7 | LUST

第七章 | 色欲

引文

"爱情不是一时的情欲，不是彼此的占有，而是两个人灵魂相依、共担风雨的漫长旅程。"

——【俄】列夫·托尔斯泰

色欲是人性最原始的冲动，也是最易摧毁婚姻根基的暗流。它常常以激情为外衣，以欢愉为诱饵，在短暂的绚烂之后，留下忠诚的崩塌、信任的碎裂与家庭长久的创伤。在我经办的大量婚姻案件中，因情欲失控引发的纷争比比皆是：婚外情感的纠缠拉扯、背叛之后的关系撕裂、非婚生子女的身份争议、大额婚外赠与的法律追索、身份与情感的双重欺骗。

激情褪去，只剩一地残局需要法律来收拾；冲动过后，只剩无辜者承受漫长而深刻的伤害。婚姻的本质，不应只是片刻的感官欢愉，而是长久的陪伴、坚守与责任；亲密关系的真谛，更不是冲动的沉溺，而是灵魂的契合、尊重与守护。无论是普通婚姻，还是跨越国界的涉外结合，忠诚与底线，永远是关系存续的基石。

法律可以清晰界定对错、公平分割利益、依法确认归属，却无法复原一颗被彻底背叛的心，无法拼凑一段破碎无余的信任。真正的爱，始于心动，终于心安；始于激情，终于长久的忠诚与担当。这是我在无数案件背后，最深切的体悟。

Epigraph

"Love is not temporary passion, nor possession of each other, but a long journey where two souls stand by each other and share all storms."

— Leo Tolstoy, Russia

Lust is the most primitive impulse of human nature, and an undercurrent that most easily destroys the foundation of marriage. It often disguises itself as passion, lures with pleasure, and leaves behind collapsed loyalty, shattered trust and lasting family trauma after its brief brilliance. In numerous marriage cases I have handled, disputes triggered by uncontrolled lust are everywhere: tangled extramarital affairs, fractured relationships after betrayal, disputes over the identity of illegitimate children, legal claims for large-scale extramarital gifts, and double deception of identity and affection.

When passion fades, only a messy aftermath is left for the law to settle; when impulse subsides, only the innocent endure long and profound harm. The essence of marriage should not be mere momentary sensual pleasure, but long-term companionship, commitment and responsibility. The true meaning of an intimate relationship is not indulgence in impulse, but spiritual compatibility, respect and protection. Whether in an ordinary marriage or a cross-border union, loyalty and moral boundaries are always the cornerstones of a lasting relationship.

The law can clearly define right and wrong, divide interests fairly and confirm legal entitlements, yet it cannot mend a heart utterly betrayed, nor piece together trust that has been completely broken. True love begins with attraction and settles in peace of mind; it starts with passion and endures in lasting loyalty and duty. This is my deepest realization behind countless cases.

分手后的"阴影期"，终有"人身安全保护令"的守护

引言

爱情的终点，本该是体面告别，或是相忘于江湖。但总有一些偏执的灵魂，把分手当成不甘的执念，用无休止的纠缠、骚扰，把昔日温情彻底碾碎，变成困住他人的枷锁。婚恋关系结束后的恶意滋扰，已超出正常情感纠纷的范畴，是对他人安宁与人格尊严的公然侵犯。
本案当事人万紫珊，在分手之后便长期陷入被前男友骚扰的恐惧之中。第一道人身安全保护令曾为她短暂驱散阴霾，可禁令到期后，骚扰卷土重来，甚至变本加厉。作为她的代理律师，我全程协助她启动司法救济，以更严密的法律屏障阻断纠缠、震慑越界，最终帮她彻底走出阴影，重归平静生活。

我第一次对万紫珊留下深刻印象，是在一个阴雨连绵的午后。她走进办公室时神情紧绷，周身笼罩着一种长期处于不安中的紧绷感，语速轻而急促，条理却异常清晰。摆在我面前的，是厚厚一叠整理好的短信截图、通话记录、投诉凭证，以及一份已经过期的人身安全保护令裁定文书。作为长期处理婚恋纠纷与人身保护案件的律师，看了她的资料和听完她的讲述后，我知道她正处在"分手后持续性骚扰"的困境中，且已濒临心理承受的极限。

在随后的案情梳理中，一段令人窒息的纠缠经过逐渐完整呈现。万紫珊与韩安牧本是恋爱关系，因性格与价值观难以磨合，双方于2022年9月正式分手。本应是各自安好的结局，却在韩安牧的偏执执念下，演变成一场漫长的侵扰。自分手之日起，他便持续对万紫珊实施骚扰：不分昼夜发送侮辱、恐吓信息，深夜反复拨打电话滋扰，甚至专程前往万紫珊任职的医院进行恶意投诉、散布不实言论，试图干扰其正常工作与职业声誉。

长期被辱骂、被威胁的处境，早已让万紫珊身心俱疲。她于2024年向法院申请人身安全保护令，禁令生效期间，对方一度有所收敛，万紫珊也终于获得片刻喘息。

可这份安宁并未持续太久。首份人身安全保护令有效期届满后，韩安牧迅速故态复萌，并且手段更加激进。他通过非法途径获取万紫珊的新住址后，多次在小区门口、单元楼下尾随、蹲守。有一次万紫珊下班回家，刚走出电梯口，韩安牧突然从楼道拐角出现，径直朝她逼近并出言威胁。万紫珊受到剧烈惊吓，当场出现心慌、发抖、站立不稳等症状，事后连续多日不敢独自乘坐电梯、不敢在天黑后归家，精神高度惊恐，正常生活几近崩溃。

为固定这一关键事实，我协助万紫珊向小区物业申请调取了事发时段的公共监控录像。录像清晰记录下韩安牧长时间逗留守候、突然现身逼近女方、双方发生近距离对峙的全过程，画面连贯、时间明确，形成了极具说服力的客观证

据，完整印证了其跟踪、威胁、现实滋扰的侵权事实。

接受委托后，我立即将前后两段骚扰事实、短信恐吓记录、医院恶意投诉材料、小区监控录像等证据整合闭环，重点印证韩安牧屡教不改、持续升级的主观恶意。同时严格依据《妇女权益保障法》第二十九条之规定，向法院明确主张：终止恋爱关系后的纠缠、骚扰已被法律明确禁止，万紫珊面临现实、紧迫的人身危险，再次申请人身安全保护令具有充分且扎实的法律依据。

庭审中，我向法庭完整呈现证据链条，着重指出：韩安牧在司法禁令到期后立即重启骚扰，并升级为上门尾随、近距离威胁，已对万紫珊造成明显精神恐惧与现实危险，若不施以更全面、更严格的行为限制，受害人的人身安全与正常生活将难以得到根本保障。

法院经审理后认定，被申请人韩安牧在首份人身安全保护令有效期届满后，再次实施上门骚扰、跟踪、威胁等行为，已构成法律规定的终止恋爱关系后纠缠、骚扰妇女的情形，申请人万紫珊面临明确、现实、紧迫的人身安全危险，其再次申请人身安全保护令符合法定条件，依法应予支持。

据此，法院作出第二份更为全面、严苛的人身安全保护令裁定：

一、禁止被申请人韩安牧对申请人万紫珊实施殴打、威胁、恐吓等一切形式的暴力及暴力倾向行为；

二、禁止被申请人韩安牧以任何方式骚扰、跟踪、尾随、窥视、接触申请人万紫珊及其近亲属；

三、禁止被申请人韩安牧以电话、短信、微信、电子邮件、社交媒体留言及其他任何通讯方式，对申请人万紫珊及其近亲属实施侮辱、诽谤、威胁、恐吓等行为；

四、禁止被申请人韩安牧进入申请人万紫珊的实际居住地、工作单位及其他经常出入场所，禁止在上述场所周边一定范围内逗留、守候、聚集，不得实施任何可能影响申请人正常生活、工作、学习秩序的行为；

五、如被申请人韩安牧违反上述禁令，人民法院将依法视情节轻重予以罚款、拘留；构成犯罪的，依法追究刑事责任。

裁定生效后，强大的司法震慑效果立显。韩安牧自知证据确凿、禁令刚性极强，未再实施任何骚扰、尾随、威胁或通讯滋扰行为。后续跟进中，万紫珊的精神状态逐步平复，能够正常上下班、正常出入居住小区，持续近两年的阴影彻底散去。即便在该份保护令有效期届满之后，韩安牧亦未再有任何越界之举，万紫珊终于真正回到了安宁、不被打扰的生活。

案后结语

恋爱有聚散，人心有亲疏，可再浓烈的执念，也不能成为侵犯他人自由与安宁的理由。分手不是纠缠的借口，告别更不是骚扰的许可，任何以“放不下”为名的持续尾随、恐吓、滋扰，都已越过情感边界，踏入法律禁区。

中国法院裁定的人身安全保护令已突破传统家庭暴力的适用场景，成为守护婚恋关系结束后受害人人身权益的重要利器。尤其是《妇女权益保障法》明确将分手后纠缠、骚扰、泄露隐私等行为纳入保护范围，为陷入恐惧的当事人提供了可及时启动、可刚性执行的司法屏障。本案中，第二道保护令的价值，不仅在于制止正在发生的侵害，更在于对反复侵权、主观恶意明显的行为人作出更强的司法否定，以全方位、多层次、可追责的禁令设计，实现从“临时制止”到“源头阻断”的升级。

监控录像、通讯记录、投诉凭证等客观证据，在这类案件中往往具有一锤定音的作用。它让抽象的恐惧变成具象的事实，让模糊的骚扰变成可认定的违法，也让司法保护更加精准有力。婚恋之间的难结难分，应是情感上的余韵，而非行为上的挟持。真正的体面，是放手；真正的尊重，是不打扰。对受害人而言，懂得留存证据、果断寻求救济，就是对自己最可靠的保护；对施扰者而言，保护令不是“到期即解禁”的通行证，任何无视他人安宁、挑战司法权威的行为，终将面临相应的法律后果。

The Post-Breakup "Shadow": Finally Guarded by a Personal Safety Protection Order

Introduction

The end of love should be a dignified farewell, or letting go and moving on. Yet some obsessive souls take breakup as resentment, crushing all past warmth with endless harassment, turning it into a cage for others. Malicious disturbance after a relationship ends goes beyond normal emotional disputes; it is a blatant violation of one's peace and personal dignity.

My client Wan Zishan lived in long-term fear of harassment by her ex-boyfriend after their breakup. An initial personal safety protection order briefly lifted the shadow, but the harassment returned and intensified once the order expired. As her attorney, I assisted her throughout the judicial relief process, blocking the stalking and deterring further violations with a tighter legal barrier, finally helping her step out of the shadow and return to a peaceful life.

My first strong impression of Wan Zishan was on a rainy afternoon. She entered the office tense, wrapped in the constant anxiety of someone living in fear. Her voice was soft but hurried, yet her logic unusually clear. Lying before me was a thick stack of organized screenshots of threatening messages, call records, complaint vouchers, and an expired personal safety protection order ruling. As a lawyer specializing in relationship disputes and personal protection cases, after reviewing her materials and listening to her story, I knew she was trapped in persistent post-breakup harassment and was at the limit of her mental endurance.

As we sorted out the case, a suffocating story of stalking unfolded in full. Wan Zishan and Han Anmu had been in a romantic relationship. Due to irreconcilable differences in personality and values, they officially broke up in September 2022. What should have been a peaceful separation turned into prolonged harassment under Han Anmu's obsession. From the day of the breakup, he harassed Wan Zishan nonstop: sending insulting and threatening messages day and night, repeatedly calling late at night, and even traveling to the hospital where she worked to file malicious complaints and spread false rumors, attempting to disrupt her normal work and damage her professional reputation.

Long-term verbal abuse and threats left Wan Zishan physically and mentally exhausted. In 2024, she applied to the court for a personal safety protection order. During its validity, the respondent restrained his behavior to some extent, granting her a short respite.

But this peace did not last. As soon as the first protection order expired, Han Anmu quickly resumed his old ways, with even more aggressive tactics. After illegally obtaining Wan Zishan's new address, he repeatedly stalked and lurked outside her residential compound and building entrance. On one occasion, as Wan Zishan returned home from work and stepped out of the elevator, Han Anmu suddenly appeared from the stairwell corner, approached her directly, and threatened her verbally. Wan Zishan suffered severe shock, experiencing palpitations, shakiness, and unsteady standing on the spot. For days afterward, she dared not take the elevator alone or go home after dark, living in intense fear with her normal life on the verge of collapse.

To preserve this crucial fact, I assisted Wan Zishan in applying to the property management for public surveillance footage from the incident period. The video clearly recorded Han Anmu lingering and waiting for a long time, suddenly appearing and approaching the victim, and their close confrontation. The continuous footage with precise timestamps formed highly persuasive objective evidence, fully confirming his infringement through stalking, threatening, and in-person harassment.

After accepting the mandate, I immediately formed a complete evidence package combining both phases of harassment, threatening text records, malicious hospital complaints, residential surveillance footage, and other materials, highlighting Han Anmu's repeated malice and escalating behavior. Meanwhile, in strict accordance with Article 29 of the Law on the Protection of Women's Rights and Interests, I clearly argued to the court: Stalking and harassment after the termination of a romantic relationship are explicitly prohibited by law. Wan Zishan faced real and imminent personal danger, and her reapplication for a personal safety protection order was supported by sufficient and solid legal grounds.

During the trial, I presented the full chain of evidence to the court and emphasized that: Han Anmu immediately resumed harassment right after the judicial restraining order expired, escalating to stalking and close-range threats, which had caused obvious psychological fear and real danger to Wan Zishan. Without more comprehensive and strict behavioral restrictions, the victim's personal safety and normal life could not be fundamentally guaranteed.

After hearing the case, the court held that the respondent Han Anmu had again engaged in home harassment, stalking, threats, and other acts after the expiration of the first personal safety protection order, which constituted the statutory scenario of harassing a woman after the termination of a romantic relationship. The applicant Wan Zishan faced a clear, real, and imminent threat to her personal safety, and her reapplication for a personal safety protection order met the legal requirements and should be upheld in accordance with the law.

Accordingly, the court issued a second, more comprehensive and stringent personal safety protection order, ruling that:

1. The respondent Han Anmu is prohibited from committing any form of violent or violent-tendency acts against the applicant Wan Zishan, including beating, threatening, and intimidating.
2. The respondent Han Anmu is prohibited from harassing, stalking, tailing, spying on, or contacting the applicant Wan Zishan and her close relatives in any manner.
3. The respondent Han Anmu is prohibited from insulting, defaming, threatening, or intimidating the applicant Wan Zishan and her close relatives via phone calls, text messages, WeChat, email, social media messages, or any other means of communication.
4. The respondent Han Anmu is prohibited from entering the actual residence, workplace, and other frequently visited places of the applicant Wan Zishan; prohibited from lingering, waiting, or gathering within a certain perimeter around the above locations; and prohibited from committing any acts that may disrupt the applicant's normal life, work, or study.
5. If the respondent Han Anmu violates the above prohibitions, the People's Court shall, in accordance with the law, impose fines or detention according to the seriousness of the circumstances; if the act constitutes a crime, criminal liability shall be pursued in accordance with the law.

After the ruling took effect, strong judicial deterrence was immediately achieved. Realizing that the evidence was conclusive and the order was strictly enforceable, Han Anmu no longer engaged in any harassment, stalking, threats, or communication interference. In follow-up checks, Wan Zishan's mental state gradually stabilized. She was able to commute to and from work normally and move freely in her residential community. The shadow that had loomed over her for nearly two years finally lifted completely. Even after the expiration of this second protection order, Han Anmu did not cross any boundaries again, and Wan Zishan finally returned to a truly peaceful and undisturbed life.

Post-Case Conclusion

Romance has its beginnings and endings; human feelings grow closer or drift apart. But even the strongest obsession cannot justify violating another person's freedom and peace. Breaking up is not an excuse for harassment, and letting go is not permission for intrusion. Any persistent stalking, intimidation, or disturbance in the name of "not being able to let go" crosses the line of emotion and enters the forbidden zone of law.

Personal safety protection orders issued by Chinese courts have expanded beyond traditional domestic violence scenarios and become a crucial tool for protecting victims' personal rights after the end of romantic relationships. In particular, the Law on the Protection of Women's Rights and Interests explicitly includes post-breakup stalking, harassment, privacy disclosure, and other acts within its scope of protection, providing a timely and enforceable judicial barrier for terrified parties. In this case, the value of the second protection order lies not only in stopping ongoing violations but also in delivering a stronger judicial rejection of a repeatedly infringing party with obvious malicious intent. Through a comprehensive, multi-layered, and accountable prohibition order, the protection was upgraded from "temporary cessation" to "fundamental prevention at the source."

Objective evidence such as surveillance footage, communication records and complaint vouchers often plays a decisive role in such cases. It turns abstract fear into concrete facts, ambiguous harassment into identifiable illegal acts, and makes judicial protection more precise and effective. The entanglement and inseparability in love and marriage should be an emotional aftertaste, not behavioral coercion. True dignity lies in letting go; true respect lies in non-interference. For victims, preserving evidence properly and seeking relief resolutely is the most reliable form of self-protection. For harassers, a protection order is not a pass that expires and lifts all restrictions. Any act that disregards others' peace and challenges judicial authority will eventually bear corresponding legal consequences.

新婚疑云，揭开亲子谜团的惊天秘密

引言

一场表面完美的婚姻，却藏着隐秘的暗流和波澜，也从一开始就埋下了悲剧的伏笔。这起案件的离奇与曲折，远超寻常家事纠纷，我的当事人乔培旻，本以为遇见了真心的人生伴侣，开启安稳的婚姻生活，却在新婚仅十天便陷入亲子疑云，"孩子究竟是不是自己亲生的"，一场亲子鉴定揭开的真相，震碎了两个家庭，也让身处其中的每个人，都背负起无法回避的人生代价。真实的生活从无剧本，那些猝不及防的变故，那些难以言说的苦衷，最终都化作家事案件里，最让人唏嘘的过往，也让我们看清，婚姻里的坦诚，从来都是容不得半点敷衍的底线。

乔培旻是一名才华出众的建筑设计师，从业多年，凭借扎实的专业能力在行业内站稳脚跟，身边从不乏倾慕者，可他心性清高、眼光挑剔，年过三十，依旧没有遇到中意的结婚对象，婚事成了全家人的心头事。

2022 年 9 月，乔培旻的妹妹牵线搭桥，介绍他认识了女青年木芬芳。木芬芳是一名中学教师，举止大方得体，周身带着知性温婉的气质，难能可贵的是，她对美术颇有见解与造诣，恰好与从事设计工作的乔培旻志趣相投，两人一见如故，总有聊不完的话题，感情升温得极快，相识不到一个月，便敲定了终身大事。

双方家长对这门亲事都十分满意，觉得两人年龄相当、职业般配，又到了适婚年纪，便纷纷催促尽快完婚。2022 年国庆节，乔培旻与木芬芳按照当地风俗举办订婚仪式，乔家拿出 30 万元现金作为聘礼，礼数周全，场面和睦。同年 11 月底，两人正式举办婚礼，同步在民政局办理结婚登记，婚后搬进乔培旻刚装修好的新房，开启了二人世界。

起初的新婚生活，看似平静顺遂，可乔培旻渐渐发现，木芬芳经常深夜归家，问及缘由，她总以学校加班、批改作业为由搪塞，乔培旻忙于设计工作，起初并未多想，直到 12 月中旬的一件事，彻底勾起了他的疑心。

乔培旻时常在家伏案制图，某天上午，木芬芳出门匆忙，将手机落在了家里。乔培旻正专注工作，手机突然响起，是陌生号码来电，他刚准备接听，对方便挂断了，紧接着发来一条短信："在上课吗？你的身体怎样了？"

这条语气亲昵的短信，让乔培旻心头泛起异样，他下意识翻看木芬芳的手机通讯记录，发现这个陌生号码与她往来频繁，通话记录众多，短信却寥寥无几，其中一条木芬芳的回复格外刺眼："我担心我有了。"短短五个字，让乔培旻心里瞬间蒙上阴影，隐隐觉得事情并不简单。

当晚木芬芳回家后，乔培旻拿出手机，平静地让她解释短信与通话的缘由，木芬芳神色略显慌乱，只称对方是普通好友，生活琐事会相互倾诉，并无出格关系。紧接着，她抛出了一个让乔培旻心绪复杂的消息：自己已怀孕一个多月，医院检查结果已经证实。

乔培旻当场愣在原地，仔细推算时间后，怒火与疑虑瞬间涌上心头。他与木芬芳 9 月相识，10 月订婚，11 月底才正式登记结婚、开启夫妻生活，满打满算，新婚不过十天，从医学常理来看，绝无可能如此短时间内查出怀孕，他当即断定，腹中孩子绝非自己的骨肉，可木芬芳拒不解释，也不正面回应质疑，只是默默搬去客卧居住，两人的关系瞬间降至冰点。

此后，两人多次因孩子的血缘问题爆发争吵，木芬芳始终一口咬定孩子是乔培旻的，不肯吐露半句实情。乔培旻顾及家族颜面，不敢将此事对外声张，也不忍心让满怀期待的父母担忧，只能把痛苦与煎熬藏在心底，看着父母盼着抱孙子的欣喜模样，他内心备受折磨。

僵持的状态一直持续，两人冷战不断，木芬芳的孕期慢慢推进，肚子渐渐隆起，怀孕半年后，她索性搬回娘家居住，两人正式分居，这段本就仓促的婚姻，彻底名存实亡。

2024 年 5 月，两人再次因孩子的问题发生激烈争执，乔培旻忍无可忍，要求木芬芳终止妊娠，木芬芳却斥责他无理取闹。积攒已久的情绪彻底爆发，乔培旻最终将双方父母都请到家中，坦言自己的质疑，明确表示腹中胎儿绝非乔家血脉。双方父母听闻此事，皆震惊不已，木芬芳却依旧没有做出任何辩解，只坚持乔培旻是无端猜忌，这场家庭会面最终不欢而散，孩子的去留与血缘争议，依旧没有任何结果。

2024 年 6 月，木芬芳在医院产下一名女婴，出院回家坐月子期间，两人又围绕孩子血缘、抚养问题产生激烈矛盾。乔培旻正式提出离婚，并要求对孩子做亲子鉴定，确认自己非生父，拒绝承担抚养义务，木芬芳却坚决反对亲子鉴定，要求乔培旻先支付经济补偿，才同意离婚。社区居委会出面调解，可双方分歧过大，始终无法达成一致，调解最终以失败告终。

2024 年 7 月，木芬芳坐完月子，带着孩子搬回娘家，临走时将家中的家电、床品、厨具等生活用品悉数搬走，从此再未回过新房，这场婚姻的纠葛，彻底陷入僵局。

满心绝望与困惑的乔培旻，最终找到我，坚定地要求通过法律途径解决问题，一是离婚，二是做亲子鉴定，撇清与孩子的亲子关系，拒绝抚养非亲生子女。

接手案件后，我先结合现行法律梳理了诉讼思路：根据《民法典》婚姻家庭编相关规定，女方在分娩后一年内，男方原则上不得提出离婚诉讼，乔培旻此时无法直接起诉离婚；但依据最高人民法院关于适用《中华人民共和国民法典》婚姻家庭编的解释（一）相关条款，夫妻一方起诉请求确认亲子关系不存在，并提供必要证据证明，另一方无相反证据又拒绝做亲子鉴定的，人民法院可推定请求方主张成立。据此，我们可先提起亲子关系否认之诉，厘清血缘问题，再择机处理离婚事宜，乔培旻当即认可了这个方案。

随后我们正式提起诉讼，请求法院确认乔培旻与女婴不存在亲子关系。诉讼的核心，是提交足以支撑质疑的必要证据：我们整理了木芬芳的可疑短信记录、结婚登记时间、孕期检查时间等证据，形成完整的证据链，证明新婚仅十天查出怀孕，明显违背医学常理；同时提交两人婚前的聊天记录，记录中明确显示，乔培旻对待婚姻十分慎重，双方约定婚后入住新房再开启夫妻生活，这一细节足以印证乔培旻的质疑符合生活逻辑，并非无端猜忌。

庭审初期，木芬芳并未亲自到庭，仅委托律师出庭应诉，律师仅出具出生医学证明，以证明父亲一栏登记为乔培旻为由，坚决拒绝亲子鉴定。乔培旻当庭提出异议，出生医学证明是依据结婚证、准生证办理，仅为形式登记，并非亲子关系的实质依据，且木芬芳生产时，两人已分居许久，自己并未在医院陪护，对该证明的出具流程持有异议。

因木芬芳缺席，关键事实无法核实，法庭宣布休庭，并向其释明法律后果：若无法对抗辩意见作出合理解释、提交相反证据，又拒绝亲子鉴定，法院将依法推定乔培旻的主张成立，其需承担相应法律后果。

第二次开庭，木芬芳终于亲自到庭，让人意想不到的是，她沉默许久后，终于松口同意亲子鉴定，却当庭提出一个震惊全场的要求：追加乔培旻的弟弟乔培浩为鉴定对象。

这句话如同平地惊雷，在场所有人都愣住了，乔培旻更是如遭晴天霹雳，完全不敢相信自己的耳朵。随后，木芬芳缓缓道出了隐藏已久的真相：孩子确是乔家血脉，但并非乔培旻的，而是弟弟乔培浩的。

原来，木芬芳早在两年前就与乔培浩相识，两人早已确立恋爱关系，可乔培浩有吸毒史，品行不稳，两人一直分分合合，始终藕断丝连。木芬芳结识乔培旻后，下定决心与乔培浩彻底了断，乔培浩也表示愿意放手，两人最后一次见面后，乔培浩便远赴国外。木芬芳本想斩断过往，安心与乔培旻过日子，没想到婚后很快发现怀孕，她清楚孩子是乔培浩的，却想刻意隐瞒，试图让乔培旻相信孩子是他的，可时间线的破绽，终究没能瞒过乔培旻的眼睛，她既愧疚又无措，不知该如何坦白，只能一直隐瞒到孩子出生。

真相大白的那一刻，乔培旻彻底懵了，他设想过无数种可能，却唯独没料到，这场婚姻的骗局，竟与自己的亲弟弟息息相关，这份伤害，早已超出了案件本身，扎进了亲情与尊严的深处。双方家人得知真相后，皆陷入崩溃与难堪，有人愤怒，有人愧疚，有人无奈，而这场闹剧里，受伤最深的，始终是从头到尾被蒙在鼓里的乔培旻。

最终，乔培旻选择撤回诉讼，没有再追究更多，只是默默收拾好心情，离开了这座装满伤心与难堪的城市，放下了这段荒唐又痛苦的婚姻。

多年后，我辗转得知众人的近况：乔培旻远赴外地工作，重新组建了家庭，有了属于自己的孩子，日子渐渐回归安稳；乔培浩依旧留在国外，生活过得并不顺遂；木芬芳独自带着孩子，与父母一同生活，始终没有再婚。而那个懵懂长大的孩子，至今仍不知道，自己的生父究竟是谁。

案后结语

这起离奇的亲子关系纠纷案，是家事案件中极具代表性的一例，既牵扯出婚姻里的隐瞒与背叛，又夹杂着亲情的纠葛与破碎，也让我们对亲子关系的法律认定，有了更清晰的认知。

近年来，涉及亲子鉴定的家事纠纷日益增多，司法实践中常出现一方坚持鉴定、另一方拒不配合的情况。现行《民法典》婚姻家庭编司法解释，明确了亲子关系推定规则：夫妻一方起诉否认亲子关系，且提交必要证据支撑主张，另一方无相反证据又拒绝亲子鉴定的，法院可推定亲子关系不存在。法律作出这样的规定，核心是兼顾血缘真实性与亲子关系的安定性，将亲子关系否认权限定在夫妻双方范围内，既尊重真实的血缘联结，也避免随意打破既有的亲子关系，守护未成年人的合法权益。

从情理层面来看，这起案件的悲剧，始于仓促的婚姻，终于刻意的隐瞒。乔培旻与木芬芳相识过短，未充分了解彼此便步入婚姻，本就埋下了隐患；而木芬芳隐瞒过往情感纠葛与孩子的真实血缘，更是触碰了婚姻的底线，不仅毁了自己的婚姻，伤害了无辜的乔培旻，也让两个家庭陷入长久的难堪，更让孩子从出生起，就背负着本不该属于他的身世谜团。

婚姻不应是一时冲动的选择，而需要坦诚与担当的长久承诺。隐瞒与欺骗，最终都会酿成无法挽回的后果。法律的存在，既是为了厘清是非、维护公平，更是为了让每一个在婚姻中受伤害的人，都能有途径走出困局，重新开启属于自己的人生。那些走过的弯路、受过的伤害，终究会成为过往，而守住坦诚与底线，才是规避婚姻悲剧的根本。

Newlywed Doubts: Uncovering the Shocking Truth Behind Parentage

Introduction

A marriage that seemed perfect on the surface hid undercurrents and turmoil, planting the seeds of tragedy from the very beginning. This bizarre and twisted case goes far beyond ordinary family disputes. My client, Qiao Peimin, thought he had found his true life partner and embarked on a stable married life, only to be caught in a paternity controversy just ten days after the wedding. The question of "whether the child is his own" lingered. The truth revealed by a paternity test shattered two families, leaving everyone involved to bear unavoidable lifelong consequences. Real life has no script. Those unexpected twists and unspeakable difficulties eventually became the most lamentable stories in family law cases. They also made us realize that honesty in marriage is a bottom line that tolerates no perfunctoriness.

Qiao Peimin is a talented architect. After years of practice, he has established himself in the industry with solid professional expertise. He has never lacked admirers, yet he is principled and discerning. Well into his thirties, he still had not found a suitable marriage partner, making his wedding a constant concern for his entire family.

In September 2022, Qiao Peimin's sister introduced him to a young woman named Mu Fenfang. Mu Fenfang was a middle school teacher with graceful manners and an elegant, gentle temperament. What was particularly rare was that she had a deep understanding and attainments in fine art, which matched Qiao Peimin's interest as a designer. The two hit it off immediately, with endless topics to share. Their relationship developed rapidly, and they decided to get married within a month of meeting.

Both parents were highly satisfied with the match, believing the couple were well-matched in age and careers and of suitable marrying age, so they urged them to wed as soon as possible. On China's National Day 2022, Qiao Peimin and Mu Fenfang held an engagement ceremony according to local customs. The Qiao family provided 300,000 yuan in cash as betrothal gifts with thoughtful etiquette and a harmonious atmosphere. At the end of November the same year, the couple held a formal wedding and registered their marriage at the Civil Affairs Bureau. After the wedding, they moved into Qiao Peimin's newly decorated home and began their life together.

At first, their newlywed life appeared calm and smooth. But Qiao Peimin gradually noticed that Mu Fenfang often came home late at night. Whenever he asked why, she always made excuses about working overtime at school or grading homework. Busy with his design projects, Qiao Peimin did not think much of it at first—until an incident in mid-December completely aroused his suspicion.

Qiao Peimin often worked on drawings at home. One morning, Mu Fenfang left in a hurry and forgot her phone. While Qiao Peimin was focused on his work, the phone suddenly rang. It was an unknown caller. Just as he was about to answer, the caller hung up, followed by a text message: "Are you in class? How are you feeling?" This intimate message made Qiao Peimin feel uneasy. Instinctively, he checked Mu Fenfang's call logs and found frequent contact with this unknown number, with many calls but very few text messages. One reply from Mu Fenfang was particularly striking: "I'm worried I'm pregnant." These five words immediately cast a shadow over Qiao Peimin's heart, and he sensed something was deeply wrong.

That night, when Mu Fenfang returned home, Qiao Peimin showed her the phone and calmly asked her to explain the messages and calls. Mu Fenfang looked slightly flustered, claiming only that the person was an ordinary friend with whom she shared daily trivialities, and that there was nothing improper between them. Then she dropped a piece of news that left Qiao Peimin in turmoil: she was more than a month pregnant, confirmed by a hospital examination. Qiao Peimin froze on the spot. After carefully calculating the timeline, anger and doubt welled up in him at once. He met Mu Fenfang in September, got engaged in October, and they only formally registered their marriage and began their life as a couple at the end of November. Counting from their wedding day, it had barely been ten days. Medically speaking, it was impossible to confirm a pregnancy in such a short time. He immediately concluded that the unborn child could not be his own. Yet Mu Fenfang refused to explain or respond directly to his doubts, instead moving into the guest bedroom in silence. Their relationship plummeted to freezing point.

After that, the two quarreled repeatedly over the child's parentage. Mu Fenfang insisted the child was Qiao Peimin's and would not reveal the truth. Mindful of his family's reputation, Qiao Peimin dared not make the matter public, nor could he bear to worry his parents who had been looking forward to a grandchild. He could only bury his pain and torment deep in his heart.

Watching his parents' joy at the expectation of a grandson, he suffered immensely inside.

The stalemate dragged on, with constant cold wars between them. As Mu Fenfang's pregnancy progressed, her belly gradually grew. Halfway through her pregnancy, she simply moved back to her parents' home, and the couple formally separated. This already hasty marriage was completely dead in name only.

In May 2024, they had another fierce argument over the child. Having run out of patience, Qiao Peimin demanded that Mu Fenfang terminate the pregnancy, only to be scolded by her for being unreasonable. His long-suppressed feelings finally erupted. Qiao Peimin invited both sets of parents to his home, laid out his suspicions, and stated clearly that the unborn baby was not of the Qiao family blood. Both parents were shocked by the news, but Mu Fenfang still offered no explanation, insisting only that Qiao Peimin was being paranoid. The family meeting ended on bad terms, with no resolution to the dispute over the child's parentage or future.

In June 2024, Mu Fenfang gave birth to a baby girl at the hospital. During her postnatal recovery at home, the two clashed fiercely again over the child's biological father and custody. Qiao Peimin formally filed for divorce and demanded a paternity test to prove he was not the biological father, refusing to bear any child support. Mu Fenfang firmly opposed the paternity test, insisting on financial compensation from Qiao Peimin before agreeing to a divorce. The community committee stepped in to mediate, but the two sides remained deeply divided and failed to reach an agreement, resulting in a failed mediation.

In July 2024, after her postnatal period ended, Mu Fenfang moved back to her parents' home with the baby. Before leaving, she took all household appliances, bedding, kitchenware and other daily necessities. She never returned to the marital home, and the marital dispute descended into total deadlock.

Overwhelmed by despair and confusion, Qiao Peimin finally came to me, determined to resolve the matter through legal channels: first, to obtain a divorce; second, to conduct a paternity test to disclaim any parental relationship with the child and refuse to raise a child that was not his own.

After taking on the case, I first mapped out the litigation strategy in accordance with current laws. Pursuant to the relevant provisions of the Marriage and Family Part of the Civil Code of the People's Republic of China, a husband is generally prohibited from filing for divorce within one year after the wife gives birth, meaning Qiao Peimin could not directly sue for divorce at that time. However, under the relevant clauses of the Judicial Interpretation (I) of the Supreme People's Court on the Application of the Marriage and Family Part of the Civil Code of the People's Republic of China, if one spouse sues to confirm the non-existence of a parent-child relationship and provides necessary evidence to support the claim, while the other party has no contradictory evidence yet refuses a paternity test, the people's court may presume the plaintiff's claim is valid. Accordingly, we could first file a lawsuit to disaffirm the parent-child relationship to clarify the bloodline issue, and then handle the divorce at an appropriate time. Qiao Peimin immediately approved this plan.

We then formally filed a lawsuit requesting the court to confirm that there was no parent-child relationship between Qiao Peimin and the baby girl. The core of the litigation was to submit sufficient necessary evidence to support the suspicion: we compiled evidence including Mu Fenfang's suspicious text messages, the marriage registration date, and prenatal examination dates to form a complete chain of evidence, proving that a pregnancy detected merely ten days after the wedding clearly violated common medical sense. We also submitted their pre-marriage chat records, which clearly showed that Qiao Peimin took marriage very seriously, and the couple had agreed to start conjugal life only after moving into their new house after marriage. This detail sufficiently confirmed that Qiao Peimin's suspicion was logically grounded in real life, not unfounded speculation.

At the initial trial, Mu Fenfang did not appear in person, but only authorized a lawyer to represent her. The lawyer only produced a medical birth certificate, insisting on refusing the paternity test on the grounds that Qiao Peimin was registered as the father on the document. Qiao Peimin raised an objection in court, stating that the medical birth certificate was issued based on the marriage certificate and birth permit, serving only as a formal registration rather than substantive proof of parent-child relationship. Furthermore, the couple had been separated for a long time when Mu Fenfang gave birth; he had not accompanied her at the hospital, and he questioned the process by which the certificate was issued. As Mu Fenfang was absent and key facts could not be verified, the court adjourned the trial and explained the legal consequences to her: if she failed to give a reasonable explanation to the defense, submit contradictory evidence, and still refused the paternity test, the court would presume Qiao Peimin's claim valid in accordance with the law, and she would bear corresponding legal liabilities.

At the second hearing, Mu Fenfang finally appeared in person. Unexpectedly, after a long silence, she finally agreed to the paternity test, but made a shocking demand in court: to add Qiao Peimin's younger brother, Qiao Peihao, as a subject for the test.

The remark struck like a thunderbolt, stunning everyone present. Qiao Peimin was especially devastated, unable to believe his ears. Then Mu Fenfang slowly revealed the long-hidden truth: the child was indeed of the Qiao family's blood, but not Qiao Peimin's — it was his younger brother Qiao Peihao's.

It turned out that Mu Fenfang had met Qiao Peihao two years earlier, and they had already been in a romantic relationship. However, Qiao Peihao had a history of drug use and unstable conduct; the two had been on-again, off-again and never fully cut ties. After meeting Qiao Peimin, Mu Fenfang made up her mind to end things with Qiao Peihao for good. Qiao Peihao also agreed to let her go, and after their final meeting, he went abroad. Mu Fenfang intended to leave her past behind and live a stable life with Qiao Peimin, only to discover she was pregnant soon after marriage. Knowing the child was Qiao Peihao's, she deliberately concealed the truth, trying to make Qiao Peimin believe the child was his. Yet the flaws in the timeline ultimately failed to escape Qiao Peimin's notice. Overwhelmed with guilt and helplessness, she did not know how to confess and kept the secret until the child was born.

When the truth finally came out, Qiao Peimin was utterly stunned. He had imagined countless possibilities, yet never once did he foresee that the deception in this marriage was so closely tied to his own younger brother. The pain ran far deeper than the case itself; it pierced into the very core of his family bonds and dignity.

When both families learned the truth, they were thrown into shock and embarrassment—some filled with rage, some with guilt, others with helplessness. In this whole farce, the one who suffered the most was none other than Qiao Peimin, who had been kept completely in the dark from beginning to end. In the end, Qiao Peimin chose to withdraw the lawsuit and seek no further accountability. He simply gathered his emotions quietly and left the city filled with sorrow and humiliation, letting go of this absurd and painful marriage.

Years later, I learned through various channels about how everyone was getting on: Qiao Peimin moved to work in another place, started a new family, had a child of his own, and gradually settled into a stable life; Qiao Peihao remained abroad, but his life was far from smooth; Mu Fenfang raised her child alone, living with her parents and never remarrying. As for the child who grew up innocently, to this day she still has no idea who her biological father is.

Post-Case Conclusion

This bizarre paternity dispute is a highly representative case in family law. It not only exposes the deception and betrayal in marriage, but also involves tangled and broken family bonds, giving us a clearer understanding of the legal determination of parent-child relationships.

In recent years, family disputes involving paternity testing have been on the rise. In judicial practice, it is common for one party to insist on a paternity test while the other refuses to cooperate. The current judicial interpretations of the Marriage and Family Part of the Civil Code have clarified the presumption rules of parent-child relationship: where one spouse sues to deny the existence of a parent-child relationship and provides necessary evidence to support the claim, and the other spouse refuses to take a paternity test without presenting contradictory evidence, the people's court may presume that the parent-child relationship does not exist. The core of this legal provision is to balance the authenticity of blood ties and the stability of parent-child relationships, restricting the right to deny parent-child relationship to the spouses. It not only respects the real blood bond but also prevents the arbitrary disruption of existing parent-child relationships, safeguarding the legitimate rights and interests of minors.

From an emotional and moral perspective, the tragedy of this case began with a hasty marriage and ended with deliberate concealment. Qiao Peimin and Mu Fenfang knew each other for too short a time and entered marriage without fully understanding each other, which already planted the seeds of trouble. Moreover, Mu Fenfang concealed her past emotional entanglements and the child's true biological origin, crossing the bottom line of marriage. This not only ruined her own marriage and hurt the innocent Qiao Peimin, but also plunged the two families into long-term embarrassment. Worse still, the child has been burdened with a life mystery that should never have belonged to her since birth.

Marriage should not be a choice made on impulse, but a long-term commitment based on honesty and responsibility. Concealment and deception will eventually lead to irreversible consequences. The law exists not only to distinguish right from wrong and uphold justice, but also to provide a way for those harmed in marriage to break free from their predicament and restart their lives. The detours taken and the hurts suffered will eventually become the past. Upholding honesty and moral bottom lines is the fundamental way to avoid marital tragedies.

性瘾执念下的婚姻废墟，绝望主妇的涅槃重生

引言

婚姻本应是彼此忠诚、相互扶持的港湾，可当一方被畸形的病态心理裹挟，将婚外滥情当作生活的必需品，这座港湾便会瞬间沦为吞噬一切的废墟。本案中的海潮，曾因家庭压力仓促闪婚，以为新生命能唤醒丈夫的良知，却不料遭遇丈夫姜继辉根深蒂固的病态滥情与家庭暴力。从孕期的背叛、哺乳期的持续出轨，到荒唐的"婚外交友自由协议"，甚至拳脚相向的家庭暴力，海潮在隐忍与绝望中挣扎，最终在二审法院的公正判决中挣脱枷锁，完成了从绝望主妇到独立女性的涅槃重生。这起案件撕开了病态婚恋观下的婚姻真相，也让我们看清，忠诚与尊重，才是婚姻不可动摇的基石。

三十多岁的海潮，有着体面的工作和稳定的收入，是旁人眼中的"优质剩女"。可在母亲的催逼下，在家人施加的无形压力下，她对爱情失去了期待，也对婚姻变得草率。在一次相亲中，她结识了家境优渥的姜继辉，这个被包装成精英子弟的男人，用短暂的热情打动了她。不到两个月的时间，两人便闪婚组建了家庭，海潮以为，这是她人生幸福的开端，却没想到，这只是一场精心编织的噩梦的开始。

婚后不久，海潮怀孕，七个多月的身孕让她对未来充满了憧憬，她坚信，孩子的到来会让这个家庭变得完整，也会让丈夫收心。然而，一次偶然的机会，她翻看姜继辉的手机，触目惊心的微信记录让她浑身冰冷——丈夫频繁与多名女子相约开房，甚至留宿在对方家中。这个发现如同惊雷，炸碎了她所有的幻想。她颤抖着质问姜继辉，面对铁证，男人无从辩驳，只能低头承认，还信誓旦旦地承诺会彻底悔改。

海潮选择了相信，她抱着最后一丝希望，等待着丈夫的改变。随着双胞胎女婴的顺利降生，看着丈夫初为人父时脸上的喜悦与兴奋，海潮的心又软了下来，她以为，血脉的联结能唤醒这个男人的责任，两个小宝贝的新生命将会一扫这个家庭的阴霾，彻底改变丈夫的劣根。可她错了，月子里的她，再次翻看丈夫的手机，发现他依旧与多名女子保持着暧昧不清的关系。她试图与姜继辉沟通，换来的却是厚颜无耻的辩解："我的生活里，必须要有很多女人。"

这句冷漠的话语，彻底击碎了海潮的幻想。她本应愤怒地反抗，可内心的顾虑让她选择了隐忍。她寄希望于用自己的真诚与包容，挽回这段摇摇欲坠的婚姻，却不知姜继辉的病态早已深入骨髓——他对婚外女性的迷恋，并非简单的情感出轨，而是一种无法自控的性瘾执念，婚外滥情于他而言，是生活的必需品，是刻在骨子里的病态需求，而非一时的冲动。

姜继辉不仅没有丝毫收敛，反而变本加厉。他甚至起草了一份荒唐的《婚

内协议》，白纸黑字写明“夫妻双方各自有权利寻找婚外伴侣，对方不得干涉”。这份协议是对婚姻忠诚原则的公然践踏，是对海潮人格的极致侮辱。海潮忍无可忍，与他爆发了激烈的争吵，两人的关系降到了冰点。姜继辉见状，索性提出离婚，声称要还她“自由”。海潮不甘心，她无法接受自己苦心经营的婚姻就此破碎，无法目睹两个新生儿一降生就陷入了破碎的原生家庭。更让她绝望的是，她的这份委屈和痛苦，连娘家人都无法理解。

农村出身的母亲，习惯了一辈子逆来顺受。当她得知所有真相后，虽然很心疼女儿，但她的观念里，女儿离婚是并不光彩的事情。而且想到两个幼小的外孙女，离婚后都要女儿独自一人来抚养，她又非常担心海潮母女三人未来的生活。于是她劝女儿海潮“为了孩子，为了家庭，忍一忍就过去了”。母亲的不理解，让海潮陷入了孤立无援的境地，她像迷失在浓雾中的人，找不到任何方向。长期的精神折磨让她终日神情恍惚、彻夜难眠，最终，她不得不从原本稳定的公司辞职。失去工作的她，生活陷入了困境，找新工作屡屡碰壁，曾经经济独立的她，如今连基本的生活都成了问题。

走投无路之下，海潮向姜继辉索要孩子的抚养费和家庭生活费，这是一个母亲最基本的诉求。可姜继辉的回应，比寒冬更刺骨：“你不是有工作吗？连自己都养不活，我娶你还有什么用？”他将婚姻的责任抛之脑后，将海潮的付出视作理所当然，甚至用言语进行无情的贬低。这一刻，海潮对这段婚姻彻底绝望了，可她不敢离婚，她不知道自己离开这个家后，能去哪里，能给孩子一个怎样的未来。

姜继辉早已厌倦了海潮的隐忍与争吵，一次次催逼她离婚。在海潮的坚决拒绝下，这个病态的男人彻底暴露了狰狞的面目。一次争吵中，他对海潮大打出手，拳打脚踢落在了这个脆弱的母亲身上。身体的疼痛与精神的羞辱，让海潮的身心遭受了前所未有的创伤。

走投无路的海潮，在好友的鼓励下，终于鼓起勇气向法院提起离婚诉讼。法庭上，她泣不成声地控诉了姜继辉的婚外滥情行为，揭露了他婚前伪装、婚后肆意践踏婚姻忠诚的卑劣行径，以及实施家庭暴力的严重过错，要求姜继辉承担精神损害赔偿责任，并要求两个女儿由她抚养，由姜继辉支付抚养费。

一审法院判决双方离婚，却以“被告殴打原告未造成严重后果”为由，驳回了海潮的精神损害赔偿诉求。且判决两个女儿分别由海潮和姜继辉一人抚养一个。这个结果，让海潮再次陷入了绝望。但她没有放弃，毅然提起了上诉。

二审的法庭上，我作为海潮的代理律师，清晰地还原了案件的全貌。首先，我们提交了姜继辉曾起草的那份荒唐无耻的《婚内协议》，其中明确记载了姜继辉承认在外乱搞男女关系、与多名女子发生婚外性关系行为。姜继辉当庭否认这一事实，辩称他并没有起草过婚内协议。我们立即申请对这份协议进行笔迹鉴定，姜继辉当场变了脸色。经法庭询问，他最终承认了该协议是他本人起草，内容也是他当时的真实意思。其次，我们提交了家里的监控记录，清晰呈现了海潮被姜继辉当着孩子和保姆的面施暴的场景，这不仅让海潮遍体鳞伤，更给年幼的孩子留下了心理阴影，这种对孕期、哺乳期的妻子实施精神摧残与身体暴力的双重伤害，已然构成严重的家庭暴力。第三，基于姜继辉在婚内的严重过错，人格败坏和不负责任，根本不适合抚养两个女儿。且两个年幼的双胞胎女儿不适合分开抚养，从尊重未成年人利益最大化的原则，应将两个女儿都判归由母亲海潮抚养。

二审法院最终采纳了我们的全部观点。法院认定，姜继辉存在明确的婚外性关系的过错行为，同时其家庭暴力行为给海潮造成了严重的身心伤害，判决姜继辉赔偿海潮精神损失费 5 万元。并判决两个孩子的抚养权都给海潮，由姜继辉支付两个女儿每月抚养费 5000 元直至孩子成年为止。

拿到二审判决书和赔偿款的那一刻，海潮泪流满面。这段短暂却充满血泪的婚史，终于画上了句号。曾经的她，以为隐忍和包容能感化一个病态的人，却换来变本加厉的伤害与拳脚相加。是那场家暴，让她彻底幡然醒悟，挣脱了婚姻的枷锁。如今，她终于可以放下过去，重拾被压抑的自我，开始属于自己的新生活，完成了属于自己的涅槃重生。

案后结语

这起婚姻悲剧，是病态婚恋观、畸形心理与家庭暴力交织的产物，它不仅摧毁了一个家庭，更让一个无辜的女性在婚姻的废墟中挣扎求生。作为代理律师，我全程见证了海潮从满怀期待到绝望隐忍，再到涅槃重生的全过程，也深刻认识到，婚姻的存续，不仅需要感情的基础，更需要双方对忠诚、尊重、责任的坚守，而当一方被根深蒂固的病态心理裹挟，任何忍让都只会让伤害变本加厉。

从人性与心理的角度剖析，姜继辉的行为，绝非简单的婚内出轨，而是一种典型的性瘾执念与病态占有欲的体现。他将婚外滥情当作生活的必需品，无视婚姻的基本准则，无视妻子的情感与尊严，甚至将妻子的隐忍视作软弱。这种病态的心理，源于其自身价值观的扭曲与人格的缺陷，他不仅背叛了婚姻，更践踏了人性的基本良知。而海潮的悲剧，在于她对婚姻抱有不切实际的幻想，用包容与隐忍对抗一个毫无底线的病态之人，最终沦为婚姻的牺牲品。母亲的不理解、社会的偏见，进一步加剧了她的困境，让她在绝望中独自承受所有的伤害。

姜继辉的家暴行为，是对法律与人性的双重践踏。在孕期、哺乳期遭受丈夫的精神摧残与身体暴力，这种伤害是不可逆的。而他当着孩子的面施暴，更是突破了道德与法律的双重底线，给孩子的成长埋下了隐患。二审法院对家暴的认定与精神损害赔偿的判决，是对海潮尊严的捍卫，也是对家庭暴力的有力回击，更是对《反家庭暴力法》的生动践行。

从婚姻与法律的层面反思，本案深刻印证了我国《民法典》中婚姻家庭编的核心要义：夫妻应当互相忠实、互相尊重、互相关爱。草率的闪婚、缺乏感情基础的婚姻，本身就埋下了隐患；而当一方肆意践踏婚姻的忠诚底线、实施家庭暴力时，法律绝不会坐视不管。长期以来，家庭暴力被视作“家务事”的观念，让无数女性陷入沉默，而 2016 年《反家庭暴力法》的实施，打破了这一桎梏，让“家务事”有了国法可依，为受害者提供了坚实的法律保护。本案中，二审法院的判决，正是这一法律精神的体现，用法律的武器，捍卫了受害者的合法权益。

海潮的涅槃重生，是悲剧中的一抹微光。她的经历告诉我们，婚姻不是一场独角戏，更不是一个人的自我牺牲。在婚姻中，永远不要为了所谓的“隐忍”放弃自己的尊严与底线。当一段婚姻只剩下伤害与折磨，当对方被病态心理裹挟、毫无悔改之意时，及时止损、勇敢维权，才是对自己、对孩子最好的保护。尊严与自我，永远值得被守护、被重生。

The Ruins of Marriage Under Sex Addiction: The Nirvana and Rebirth of a Desperate Housewife

Introduction

Marriage should be a harbor of mutual loyalty and support. Yet when one partner is consumed by a distorted, pathological state of mind, treating extramarital promiscuity as a necessity of life, this harbor instantly turns into ruins that devour everything. In this case, Hai Chao rushed into a flash marriage under family pressure, hoping a new life would awaken her husband's conscience. Instead, she endured her husband Jiang Jihui's deeply rooted pathological promiscuity and domestic violence. From betrayal during pregnancy, repeated infidelity while she was breastfeeding, to the absurd "extramarital dating freedom agreement," and even physical domestic abuse, Hai Chao struggled between endurance and despair. Finally, with a fair judgment from the second-instance court, she broke free from her chains and completed her nirvana from a desperate housewife to an independent woman. This case exposes the truth of marriage under a pathological view of love and marriage, and makes it clear that loyalty and respect are the unshakable foundations of marriage.

Hai Chao, in her thirties, had a decent job and stable income, and was seen by others as an "elite leftover woman." But pressured by her mother's urging and invisible family expectations, she lost hope in love and became reckless about marriage. At a blind date, she met Jiang Jihui, who came from a wealthy background. Presented as an elite young man, he won her over with temporary passion. Within two months, they had a flash marriage and started a family. Hai Chao thought this was the beginning of happiness in her life, never imagining it was only the start of an elaborately woven nightmare.

Shortly after marriage, Hai Chao became pregnant. Seven months into her pregnancy, she was full of hope for the future, firmly believing the arrival of a child would complete the family and bring her husband to his senses. But by chance, she looked through Jiang Jihui's phone and was chilled to the bone by shocking WeChat records: her husband was repeatedly meeting multiple women for hotel hookups and even staying overnight at their homes. The discovery struck like thunder, shattering all her illusions. Trembling, she confronted Jiang Jihui. Faced with irrefutable evidence, the man could not deny it, lowered his head to admit his affairs, and promised earnestly that he would completely repent.

Hai Chao chose to believe him, clinging to one last hope that he would change. When twin baby girls were born safely, she softened again at the joy and excitement on her husband's face as a new father. She thought blood ties would awaken the man's sense of responsibility, and the lives of the two little babies would clear the darkness in the family and completely reform her husband's bad nature. But she was wrong. While she was still in confinement, she checked his phone again and found he was still maintaining ambiguous relationships with multiple women. She tried to communicate with Jiang Jihui, only to be met with his brazen justification: "I have to have many women in my life."

Those cold words completely shattered Hai Chao's illusions. She should have angrily resisted, yet inner worries made her choose to endure. She hoped to save the crumbling marriage with sincerity and tolerance, unaware that Jiang Jihui's pathology was deeply ingrained. His obsession with extramarital women was not simple emotional cheating, but an uncontrollable obsession of sex addiction. For him, extramarital promiscuity was a necessity of life, a pathological need rooted in his bones, not a momentary impulse.

Jiang Jihui not only showed no restraint but intensified his behavior. He even drafted an absurd Marital Agreement, stating in black and white that "both husband and wife have the right to seek extramarital partners, and the other party shall not interfere." This agreement openly trampled on the principle of marital loyalty and was an extreme insult to Hai Chao's dignity. Hai Chao could bear it no longer, and a fierce quarrel erupted. Their relationship plummeted to freezing point. Seeing this, Jiang Jihui simply filed for divorce, claiming he would grant her "freedom." Hai Chao refused to give up. She could not accept that the marriage she had worked so hard to build was falling apart, nor could she bear seeing her two newborn babies trapped in a broken family from birth. To make matters worse, even her own family could not understand her grievance and pain.

Her mother, from a rural background, had endured hardships all her life. After learning the truth, she felt deep sympathy for her daughter, yet in her mind, divorce would bring shame to the family. Thinking of the two infant granddaughters, who would have to be raised alone by her daughter after divorce, she worried constantly about the future of Hai Chao and the twins. So she urged Hai Chao to "endure for the children, for the family — it will pass." Her mother's lack of understanding left Hai Chao isolated and helpless, like someone lost in thick fog with no direction. Long-term mental torment left her dazed all day and sleepless all night. Eventually, she had to resign from her stable job. Unemployed, she fell into financial hardship and struggled repeatedly to find new work. Once financially independent, she now could barely make ends meet.

With nowhere else to turn, Hai Chao asked Jiang Jihui for child support and living expenses — the most basic demand of a mother. But Jiang Jihui's response cut sharper than the bitter cold: "Don't you have a job? If you can't even support yourself, what use was it marrying you?" He cast aside all marital duty, took Hai Chao's devotion for granted, and even degraded her with cruel words. In that moment, Hai Chao lost all hope in the marriage. Yet she dared not divorce; she had no idea where she would go if she left, or what kind of future she could give her children.

Jiang Jihui had long grown tired of Hai Chao's endurance and quarrels, and pressed her to divorce again and again. When Hai Chao refused firmly, the pathological man revealed his true vicious nature. During one argument, he violently attacked her, beating and kicking the fragile mother. Physical pain and mental humiliation inflicted unprecedented trauma on her body and mind.

With her back against the wall, and encouraged by her friends, Hai Chao finally summoned the courage to file for divorce. In court, she tearfully accused Jiang Jihui of rampant extramarital affairs, exposed his pre-marital pretense, his post-marital betrayal of marital loyalty, and his serious domestic violence. She demanded mental distress compensation from him, sought sole custody of their two daughters, and asked Jiang Jihui to pay child support.

The first-instance court granted the divorce but dismissed Hai Chao's claim for mental damages, ruling that "the defendant's beating did not cause serious harm." It also ordered that each parent raise one daughter. This result plunged Hai Chao into despair once more. But she did not give up — she resolutely filed an appeal.

At the second-instance trial, acting as Hai Chao's attorney, I presented a full and clear account of the case. First, we submitted the absurd and shameless Marital Agreement drafted by Jiang Jihui, which clearly documented his acknowledgment of promiscuity and extramarital relations with multiple women. When Jiang Jihui denied drafting it in court, we immediately applied for handwriting verification, at which point his face paled. Under further questioning, he finally admitted writing the agreement and that its content reflected his true intentions at the time. Second, we presented home surveillance footage clearly showing Jiang Jihui assaulting Hai Chao in front of the children and the nanny. This left her physically injured and traumatized the young children. The combined mental cruelty and physical violence against his wife during pregnancy and breastfeeding constituted serious domestic violence. Third, given Jiang Jihui's severe marital faults, moral corruption, and irresponsibility, he was clearly unfit to raise the girls. Furthermore, the infant twins should not be separated. In line with the principle of maximizing the interests of minors, both daughters should be placed in the custody of their mother, Hai Chao.

The second-instance court ultimately accepted all our arguments. It confirmed Jiang Jihui's fault in engaging in extramarital relations and that his domestic violence caused severe physical and mental harm to Hai Chao. The court ordered Jiang Jihui to pay Hai Chao 50,000 yuan in mental distress compensation. It also granted full custody of both children to Hai Chao, with Jiang Jihui to pay 5,000 yuan per month in child support for each daughter until they reach adulthood.

When Hai Chao received the second-instance judgment and the compensation, she broke down in tears. Her short, blood-and-tear marriage had finally come to an end. She had once believed endurance and tolerance could reform a pathological man, only to receive escalating harm and violence. That act of abuse finally woke her up and broke her marital chains. Now, she could finally let go of the past, reclaim her suppressed self, start a new life of her own, and complete her own nirvana and rebirth.

Post-Case Conclusion

This marital tragedy was born of a distorted view of love and marriage, deformed psychology, and domestic violence. It not only destroyed a family but also forced an innocent woman to struggle for survival amid the ruins of her marriage. As her attorney, I witnessed Hai Chao's entire journey—from hopeful expectation to desperate endurance, and finally to nirvana and rebirth. It also made me deeply aware that a marriage lasts not only on emotional foundation but also on mutual commitment to loyalty, respect, and responsibility. When one partner is trapped in deep-rooted pathological psychology, any tolerance only escalates the harm.

From a human and psychological perspective, Jiang Jihui's behavior was far from simple infidelity. It was a classic manifestation of sex addiction, obsessive compulsion, and pathological possessiveness. He treated extramarital promiscuity as a necessity of life, ignored basic marital norms, disregarded his wife's feelings and dignity, and even took her endurance as weakness. Such pathology stemmed from his distorted values and flawed personality. He not only betrayed his marriage but also trampled on basic human conscience.

Hai Chao's tragedy lay in her unrealistic fantasies about marriage. She tried to confront an unscrupulous, pathological man with tolerance and patience, ultimately becoming a victim of her own marriage. Her mother's misunderstanding and social prejudice worsened her plight, leaving her to bear all harm alone in despair.

Jiang Jihui's domestic violence violated both law and humanity. The mental torture and physical abuse inflicted on his wife during pregnancy and breastfeeding caused irreversible harm. Beating her in front of their children crossed both moral and legal boundaries, planting hidden dangers in the children's growth. The second-instance court's recognition of domestic violence and award of mental damages defended Hai Chao's dignity, struck a powerful blow against domestic violence, and vividly upheld the Anti-Domestic Violence Law.

From a marital and legal perspective, this case profoundly reflects the core spirit of the Marriage and Family Part of China's Civil Code: husband and wife shall be faithful, respectful, and caring toward each other. Hasty flash marriages and unions without emotional foundation already contain hidden risks. When one party wantonly violates the bottom line of marital loyalty and commits domestic violence, the law will never stand idly by. For a long time, the view that domestic violence was a "family matter" silenced countless women. The implementation of the Anti-Domestic Violence Law in 2016 broke this shackle, subjecting "family affairs" to national law and providing solid legal protection for victims. The judgment in this case embodied this legal spirit, using the power of law to safeguard the victim's legitimate rights and interests.

Hai Chao's nirvana and rebirth is a faint glimmer of light amid tragedy. Her experience teaches us that marriage is not a one-man show, nor is it self-sacrifice for one person. In marriage, never abandon your dignity and bottom line for the sake of so-called "endurance." When a marriage brings nothing but harm and torture, and when the other party remains unrepentant trapped in pathological behavior, cutting losses in time and bravely defending your rights is the best protection for yourself and your children. Dignity and self-worth always deserve to be protected and reborn.

一场婚外虐恋引发的亲子鉴定之诉

引言

婚外情无疑是隐藏在婚姻里的暗礁，更是牵扯无辜生命的漩涡。这起案件里，来自双方当事人截然相反的陈述，将一段隐秘的婚外纠葛摊开在眼前，一边是孤身携女、辗转维权的母亲，为孩子讨要身份与抚养费；一边是矢口否认、直指对方蓄意讹诈的男方及其家人，称孩子与己无关。真相扑朔迷离，稚弱的孩子成了情感博弈里最无辜的牺牲品。作为代理律师，我唯有循着证据与法理，拨开谎言与隐瞒交织的迷雾，为非婚生子女守住法定的权利，也看清这场婚外虐恋里，没有赢家的结局，以及破碎家庭里永远无法抹平的伤痛。

2021 年深秋，我见到了戚宛如，她抱着刚满一岁的女儿，面容憔悴，衣衫朴素，眼神里满是疲惫与倔强，从沿海小城辗转到律所，身上几乎没了余钱，却紧紧护着怀里的孩子，见到我时，声音哽咽：“叶律师，求你帮帮我的孩子，给她一个名分，让她能好好活下去。”

戚宛如的遭遇，藏着一段满是欺骗与纠葛的过往。2020 年初，28 岁的她在小城的服装品牌店做销售顾问，家中境况窘迫，父亲早年病逝，母亲患有脑部神经萎缩，常年生活无法自理，底下还有弟弟妹妹在读大学，全家的重担都压在她一个人身上，为给母亲治病，家里早已负债累累。

也就是这时，她认识了顾屿。顾屿比她小一岁，是店里的大客户，时常来定制高端服饰，出手阔绰，开着豪车，言谈间尽显家境优渥，后来戚宛如才知道，他父母是当地知名私营企业主，家境殷实。两人因往来频繁渐渐熟悉，顾屿很快开始主动约她，声称自己单身未婚，对家境困难的戚宛如十分体贴，得知她母亲的病情后，还主动帮忙联系上海的脑科专家，跑前跑后安排就医事宜，这份温柔与相助，让孤立无援的戚宛如渐渐动了心，两人顺理成章确立恋爱关系，不久后，顾屿带她住进市中心的一套公寓，称是家人为他购置的婚房，两人开始同居生活。

顾屿一直承诺会娶她，戚宛如满心期待，可每当她提出想见顾屿家人，顾屿都以母亲看重门当户对，需要慢慢做工作为由推脱，戚宛如虽有疑虑，却还是选择相信。2020 年 6 月，戚宛如发现自己怀孕，欣喜万分，顾屿表面也表现得十分开心，让她安心养胎，说会尽快和家人商量婚事。可随着孕期渐长，顾屿的态度愈发闪躲，在戚宛如的反复催促下，他终于道出真相：他早已结婚，他自己的女儿刚满两岁。原来他和宛如的这段感情，从一开始就是欺骗。

这个消息如同晴天霹雳，戚宛如这才明白，自己自始至终都是局外人，是别人婚姻里的第三者。顾屿却劝说她，自己与妻子是奉父母之命结婚，毫无感情，正在筹备离婚，只是碍于家族生意无法立刻办妥，他劝戚宛如先生下孩子，又给出一个荒唐的提议：让戚宛如回老家找个熟人假结婚，先给孩子一个名义上的身份，等顾屿与他妻子离婚后，再做打算。

万般无奈又不舍腹中胎儿，戚宛如想起老家的同学苏哲，苏哲一直对她心存好感，单身未婚，是个挺不错的可托付的对象。戚宛如遂回到老家，找到了苏哲。两人相见后，苏哲仍对戚宛如一往情深。戚宛如并没有向苏哲隐瞒，而是将自己的遭遇和盘托出，并表示如果他愿意娶她，她从此就能跟苏哲安心的过日子，养育孩子。苏哲考虑后同意了，两人按照老家风俗举办婚礼，随后办理了结婚登记。2020 年 12 月，戚宛如顺利生下一名女婴，可从她怀孕后期到生产、坐月子，顾屿彻底失联，不仅没来看过一次，电话也极少接听。婚后苏哲的收入并不宽裕，但他对戚宛如母女却很好。然而戚宛如对苏哲心有愧疚，决定要找顾屿追讨孩子的抚养费。

但当戚宛如回到曾经同居的公寓，发现门锁已换，保安告知她顾屿早已搬走，她一遍遍拨打顾屿电话，好不容易接通，顾屿却直言两人关系到此为止，对孩子绝口不提。戚宛如要求他对孩子负责，顾屿才称会让母亲出面协商抚养费，可当戚宛如见到顾屿母亲，对方却态度强硬，拒不承认这个孩子，双方不欢而散。

戚宛如不甘心，抱着孩子四处奔走，从律所到司法鉴定中心，只为给孩子讨一个公道，走投无路之下，找到了我。听完她的陈述，我心中存有诸多疑虑，这段感情的始末，似乎另有隐情，而想要解开谜团，必须听听另一方的说法。

在戚宛如的恳请下，我主动联系了顾屿的母亲，这位举止端庄的女士，来到律所后，说出了一个完全不同的版本。

她坦言，自己对儿子管教严苛，顾屿的学业、工作、婚姻全由她安排，也正因如此，顾屿内心有些叛逆，与戚宛如的交往，他一开始便刻意隐瞒家人与妻子。但顾屿绝非欺骗，戚宛如从一开始就知道顾屿有家室，并非无辜受害，她比顾屿成熟，看中顾家的家境，一心想上位取代顾屿妻子。两人同居的公寓，并非顾屿的房产，只是朋友空置的房子，两人同居不过两个月，便因戚宛如逼婚分手，分手时戚宛如称自己怀孕，顾屿虽有怀疑，还是给了她二十万元，让她终止妊娠，戚宛如当场答应，也承诺从此不再纠缠。

可没多久，戚宛如便与苏哲结婚生子，婚后因苏哲家境贫寒，戚宛如又多次找顾屿借钱，顾屿先后借给她十五万元，直到戚宛如突然声称孩子是顾屿的，要求巨额抚养费，顾屿才彻底不再理会。顾家并非不讲情理，可戚宛如拿着钱后另嫁他人，孩子户口也落在苏哲名下，如今又找上门来，分明是蓄意讹诈，顾家绝不会认，也拒绝配合亲子鉴定。

双方各执一词，真相变得模糊，而案件的核心，始终是孩子的血缘归属。当下孩子的户籍登记生父为苏哲，想要确认顾屿与孩子的亲子关系，第一步便是排除苏哲的生父身份。好在苏哲始终配合，愿意做亲子鉴定，鉴定结果很快出具，苏哲与孩子并无血缘关系，这一结果，也印证了戚宛如的部分说辞。

我将鉴定结果告知顾屿母亲，希望她能顾及血脉亲情，劝说顾屿配合亲子鉴定，对方虽有动容，却依旧态度强硬，称即便孩子是顾家血脉，也不愿孩子留在戚宛如身边，想要直接抱走抚养。戚宛如得知后，坚决不同意放弃抚养权，协商彻底破裂，只能通过法律途径解决。

2021 年 11 月，我代理戚宛如向法院提起诉讼，请求确认顾屿与孩子的亲子关系，并要求其承担抚养费。庭审前，法院向顾屿释明法律后果，结合戚宛如提交的同居证据、转账记录、苏哲的亲子鉴定报告等证据，顾屿最终同意配合亲子鉴定。2022 年 1 月，鉴定报告出具，顾屿与孩子的亲权概率高达 99.99%，孩子确系顾屿的非婚生女儿。

真相大白，顾屿及其家人再无辩驳的理由，在法院的调解下，双方达成协议：孩子抚养权归戚宛如，顾屿每年支付抚养费十万元，直至孩子成年。

本以为案件就此落幕，可调解书签收次日，顾屿的妻子温冉来到了律所。她清秀斯文，眼神里满是疲惫与绝望，见到我便直言，这段婚姻早已让她痛苦不堪，她早就知道顾屿的婚外情，一直为了女儿隐忍，如今真相彻底揭开，她再也无法维系这段破碎的婚姻，决心离婚。

我试图劝说她，为了年幼的女儿慎重考虑，可温冉去意已决，她坦言，这场婚外情，早已耗尽了她所有的感情与信任，婚姻早已名存实亡，她只想带着女儿离开，重新开始。不久后，我得知，顾屿与温冉正式协议离婚，女儿由温冉抚养，顾屿孤身一人远赴国外，再也没有回来。

而戚宛如，依旧和苏哲生活在一起，苏哲默默帮她照顾孩子，承担起家庭的重担，只是这段始于欺骗、纠葛多年的往事，成了所有人心里无法抹去的伤疤，那个无辜的孩子，也终究要在不完整的亲情里，慢慢长大。

案后结语

这是一起典型的非婚生子女亲子关系确认纠纷，也是婚外情引发家庭悲剧的真实写照，案件的处理，既关乎法理的公正，更关乎无辜孩童的合法权益。

根据《中华人民共和国民法典》婚姻家庭编及相关司法解释规定，对亲子关系有异议且有正当理由的，父或者母可以向人民法院提起诉讼，请求确认或者否认亲子关系。若一方起诉请求确认亲子关系，并提供必要证据予以证明，另一方没有相反证据又拒绝做亲子鉴定的，人民法院可以推定确认亲子关系一方的主张成立。非婚生子女享有与婚生子女同等的权利，任何组织或者个人不得加以危害和歧视，不直接抚养非婚生子女的生父或者生母，应当负担未成年子女的抚养费，直至子女成年，这是法律对未成年人权益的硬性保障，也是对过错方责任的明确追究。

本案中，戚宛如与顾屿的婚外情，本身就是违背婚姻忠诚、违背公序良俗的行为，两人的隐瞒与欺骗，不仅毁掉了顾屿原本的家庭，更让无辜的孩子从出生起，就背负着身世的争议，承受着本不该承受的偏见与困境。顾屿的欺骗、戚宛如的妥协，最终酿成了多方皆输的结局：温冉失去了婚姻，顾屿远走他乡，戚宛如独自带着孩子背负生活压力，最无辜的孩子，生来便缺失了完整的亲情。

这起案件也给所有人敲响警钟：婚外情不是浪漫的邂逅，而是摧毁家庭、伤害他人的利刃，一时的放纵与自私，最终会让自己、家人、甚至无辜的孩子付出沉重代价。而法律的意义，在于守护弱者的权益，为非婚生子女撑起保护伞，却无法弥补情感的裂痕、修复破碎的家庭。

婚姻的忠诚、情感的责任，历来都是不容触碰的底线，唯有守住本心、敬畏婚姻，才能避免这样的悲剧，才能让每一个孩子，都能在健康、完整的家庭里成长，这也是家事法律之外，最该铭记的人生道理。

Extramarital Love Woes Leading to a Paternity Suit

Introduction

An extramarital affair is undoubtedly a hidden reef lurking within marriage, and even more a whirlpool that drags innocent lives into its vortex. In this case, starkly conflicting accounts from both parties laid bare a secret extramarital entanglement. On one side stood a mother, alone with her baby daughter, struggling to defend her rights and claim legal identity and child support for her child. On the other side were the man and his family, who flatly denied paternity and accused the mother of deliberate blackmail, claiming the child was unrelated to them. The truth was confusing and obscure, and the vulnerable child became the most innocent victim in this emotional struggle. As her attorney, I could only follow the evidence and legal principles to cut through the fog woven from lies and concealment, safeguard the statutory rights of the child born out of wedlock, and also bear witness to the fact that in this tormented extramarital affair, there were no winners — only irreparable pain in a broken family.

In the late autumn of 2021, I met Qi Wanru. Holding her one-year-old daughter, she looked haggard, plainly dressed, and her eyes were filled with exhaustion and stubbornness. She had traveled from a small coastal city to my law firm with almost no money left, yet she held the baby tightly in her arms. When she saw me, her voice choked with sobs: "Attorney Ye, please help my child. Give her a legal identity so she can live a decent life."

Qi Wanru's ordeal concealed a past full of deception and entanglement. In early 2020, the 28-year-old worked as a sales consultant at a clothing boutique in the small city. Her family was in dire straits: her father had passed away from an illness in his early years, her mother suffered from cerebral atrophy and was permanently unable to care for herself, and she had younger siblings attending university. The entire family burden rested solely on her shoulders. To pay for her mother's medical treatment, the family had already fallen heavily into debt.

It was around this time that she met Gu Yu. Gu Yu was a year younger than her and a major client at the shop. He often came to order high-end clothing, spent money freely, drove a luxury car, and his words and manners revealed his wealthy background. Qi Wanru later found out that his parents were well-known local private business owners with a prosperous family. The two gradually grew close through frequent interactions. Gu Yu soon began asking her out actively, claiming to be single and unmarried. He was extremely considerate toward Qi Wanru, who came from a poor family. After learning about her mother's illness, he even took the initiative to contact a brain specialist in Shanghai and went out of his way to arrange medical treatment. This tenderness and help gradually won over the helpless Qi Wanru, and the two logically entered a romantic relationship. Not long after, Gu Yu brought her to live in an apartment in the city center, saying it was a wedding apartment his family had bought for him, and they began living together.

Gu Yu kept promising to marry her, and Qi Wanru was full of expectation. But whenever she asked to meet his family, Gu Yu would put her off, saying his mother valued social status and he needed time to persuade her. Despite her doubts, Qi Wanru chose to trust him. In June 2020, Qi Wanru discovered she was pregnant and was overjoyed. On the surface, Gu Yu also appeared delighted, telling her to rest easy and that he would discuss the marriage with his family as soon as possible. But as her pregnancy progressed, Gu Yu's attitude grew increasingly evasive. Under repeated urging from Qi Wanru, he finally revealed the truth: he had already been married, and his own daughter had just turned two. The relationship between him and Wanru, it turned out, had been a lie from the very beginning.

The news hit her like a bolt from the blue. Qi Wanru finally realized she had been an outsider all along — the other woman in someone else's marriage. Yet Gu Yu tried to persuade her that his marriage to his wife was arranged by their parents and lacked any affection, and that he was preparing for a divorce but could not go through with it immediately due to family business interests. He urged Qi Wanru to abort the child first, then made a ridiculous suggestion: that she return to her hometown, fake a marriage with an acquaintance, give the child a nominal identity first, and wait until Gu Yu divorced his wife before making further plans.

Feeling utterly helpless yet unwilling to give up the unborn child, Qi Wanru thought of Su Zhe, a former classmate from her hometown. Su Zhe had long been fond of her; he was single and seemed a reliable person to rely on. Qi Wanru therefore returned to her hometown and met with Su Zhe. When they reunited, Su Zhe still held deep affection for her. Instead of hiding the truth, Qi Wanru told him everything about her situation. She said that if he was willing to marry her, she would live a peaceful life with him and raise the child together. After thinking it over, Su Zhe agreed. They held a wedding according to local customs and then registered their marriage. In December 2020, Qi Wanru gave birth to a baby girl. However, from the late stage of her pregnancy through delivery and her postpartum recovery, Gu Yu completely disappeared. He never visited once and rarely answered her calls. After marriage, Su Zhe's income was modest, but he treated Qi Wanru and the baby with great kindness. Yet Qi Wanru felt guilty towards Su Zhe and decided to claim child support from Gu Yu.

When Qi Wanru returned to the apartment where they had once lived together, she found the locks changed. The security guard told her that Gu Yu had already moved out. She called Gu Yu repeatedly, and when she finally got through, he bluntly said their relationship was over and refused to mention the child at all. When Qi Wanru demanded that he take responsibility for the baby, Gu Yu said he would ask his mother to negotiate child support. But when Qi Wanru met Gu Yu's mother, she took a tough stance and refused to acknowledge the child. The two parted on bad terms.

Refusing to give up, Qi Wanru wandered from place to place with her baby, going from law firms to forensic appraisal centers, all to seek justice for her child. In desperation, she came to me. After hearing her story, I had many doubts. There seemed to be more to this relationship than met the eye, and to uncover the truth, I had to hear the other side.

At Qi Wanru's request, I took the initiative to contact Gu Yu's mother. This dignified lady arrived at the firm and told a completely different story.

She admitted that she had strict control over her son. Gu Yu's studies, career, and marriage were all arranged by her, which made him somewhat rebellious. He deliberately hid his relationship with Qi Wanru from his family and wife from the very beginning. But Gu Yu was not a liar, she claimed. Qi Wanru knew from the start that Gu Yu was married and was not an innocent victim. She was more mature than Gu Yu, coveted the wealth of the Gu family, and was determined to replace his wife. The apartment they shared was not owned by Gu Yu, but a vacant property belonging to a friend. They only lived together for two months before breaking up because Qi Wanru pressured him to marry her. When they separated, Qi Wanru said she was pregnant. Although suspicious, Gu Yu gave her 200,000 yuan to have an abortion. Qi Wanru agreed on the spot and promised never to bother him again.

Soon after, however, Qi Wanru married Su Zhe and gave birth to a child. After the marriage, because Su Zhe's family was poor, she repeatedly asked Gu Yu for money, and he lent her a total of 150,000 yuan. It was not until Qi Wanru suddenly claimed the child was Gu Yu's and demanded a large sum in child support that Gu Yu cut off all contact. The Gu family was not unreasonable, but after taking the money and marrying someone else, with the child's household registered under Su Zhe, Qi Wanru's return was clearly deliberate extortion. The Gu family would never recognize the child and refused to cooperate with a paternity test.

With both parties sticking to their own versions, the truth became unclear. Yet the core of the case was always the child's biological parentage. At that time, the child's household registration listed Su Zhe as her biological father. To confirm the parent-child relationship between Gu Yu and the child, the first step was to rule out Su Zhe as the birth father. Fortunately, Su Zhe cooperated fully and willingly took a paternity test. The result came out quickly: there was no biological relationship between Su Zhe and the child. This finding partly supported Qi Wanru's account.

I informed Gu Yu's mother of the test result, hoping she would consider the blood tie and persuade Gu Yu to cooperate with a paternity test. Although she was moved, she remained firm, stating that even if the child was of the Gu family blood, they did not want the child to stay with Qi Wanru and intended to take the child away to raise her themselves. When Qi Wanru learned of this, she firmly refused to give up custody. Negotiations completely broke down, leaving no choice but to resolve the dispute through legal proceedings.

In November 2021, I represented Qi Wanru in filing a lawsuit with the court, requesting confirmation of the biological relationship between Gu Yu and the child, and demanding that he bear child support expenses. Prior to the trial, the court clarified the legal consequences to Gu Yu. Combined with the evidence submitted by Qi Wanru—including records of cohabitation, money transfers, and the paternity test report involving Su Zhe—Gu Yu finally agreed to undergo a paternity test. In January 2022, the appraisal report was issued, showing a probability of parentage of 99.99% between Gu Yu and the child, confirming that the girl was indeed Gu Yu's daughter born out of wedlock.

With the truth revealed, Gu Yu and his family had no grounds for further rebuttal. Under the mediation of the court, the two parties reached an agreement: custody of the child was granted to Qi Wanru, and Gu Yu would pay

100,000 yuan in child support each year until the child reached adulthood.

I thought the case would end there. However, on the day after the mediation agreement was signed and received, Gu Yu's wife Wen Ran came to the law firm. She was delicate and gentle, with exhaustion and despair filling her eyes. Upon seeing me, she stated directly that this marriage had long been unbearable for her. She had known about Gu Yu's extramarital affair for a long time and endured it for the sake of their daughter. Now that the truth was fully exposed, she could no longer maintain this broken marriage and was determined to divorce.

I tried to persuade her to think carefully for her young daughter, but Wen Ran's mind was made up. She admitted frankly that the affair had exhausted all her affection and trust, and the marriage existed only in name. She only wanted to leave with her daughter and start over. Shortly afterward, I learned that Gu Yu and Wen Ran had formally divorced by agreement. Their daughter was raised by Wen Ran, while Gu Yu left alone for abroad and never returned.

As for Qi Wanru, she continued to live with Su Zhe. Su Zhe quietly helped her take care of the child and bore the burden of the family. Yet this past, which began with deception and dragged on for years, became an indelible scar in everyone's heart. And the innocent child would eventually grow up amid incomplete family bonds.

Post-Case Conclusion

This case is a typical dispute over the confirmation of paternity regarding a child born out of wedlock, and a true reflection of family tragedies caused by extramarital affairs. The adjudication of this case concerns not only the justice of the law but also the legitimate rights and interests of the innocent child.

Pursuant to the provisions on marriage and family in the Civil Code of the People's Republic of China and relevant judicial interpretations, a father or mother who objects to a paternity relationship with just cause may file a lawsuit with a people's court to request the confirmation or denial of such paternity. Where one party sues to confirm a paternity relationship and provides necessary evidence to prove it, while the other party refuses to undergo a paternity test without presenting contrary evidence, the people's court may presume that the claim of the party seeking confirmation is valid. Children born out of wedlock shall enjoy the same rights as legitimate children; no organization or individual may endanger or discriminate against them. The biological father or mother who does not directly raise such a child shall bear the child support until the child reaches adulthood. This is a mandatory legal protection for the rights and interests of minors, as well as a clear accountability for the party at fault.

In this case, the extramarital affair between Qi Wanru and Gu Yu was inherently a breach of marital loyalty and public order and good morals. Their concealment and deception not only destroyed Gu Yu's original family but also subjected the innocent child to disputes over his identity from birth, bearing prejudice and hardships that he should never have endured. Gu Yu's deception and Qi Wanru's compromise ultimately led to a lose-lose outcome for all parties: Wen Ran lost her marriage, Gu Yu left his hometown, Qi Wanru raised the child alone under financial strain, and the most innocent child was deprived of complete family affection from birth.

This case also serves as a warning to everyone: an extramarital affair is never a romantic encounter, but a sharp blade that destroys families and hurts others. Momentary indulgence and selfishness will eventually exact a heavy price on oneself, family members, and even innocent children. While the law exists to protect the rights of the vulnerable and shield children born out of wedlock, it cannot mend emotional rifts or repair broken families.

Marital loyalty and emotional responsibility are inviolable bottom lines. Only by upholding one's conscience and respecting marriage can such tragedies be avoided, allowing every child to grow up in a healthy and complete family. This is a life truth worth bearing in mind beyond the scope of family law.

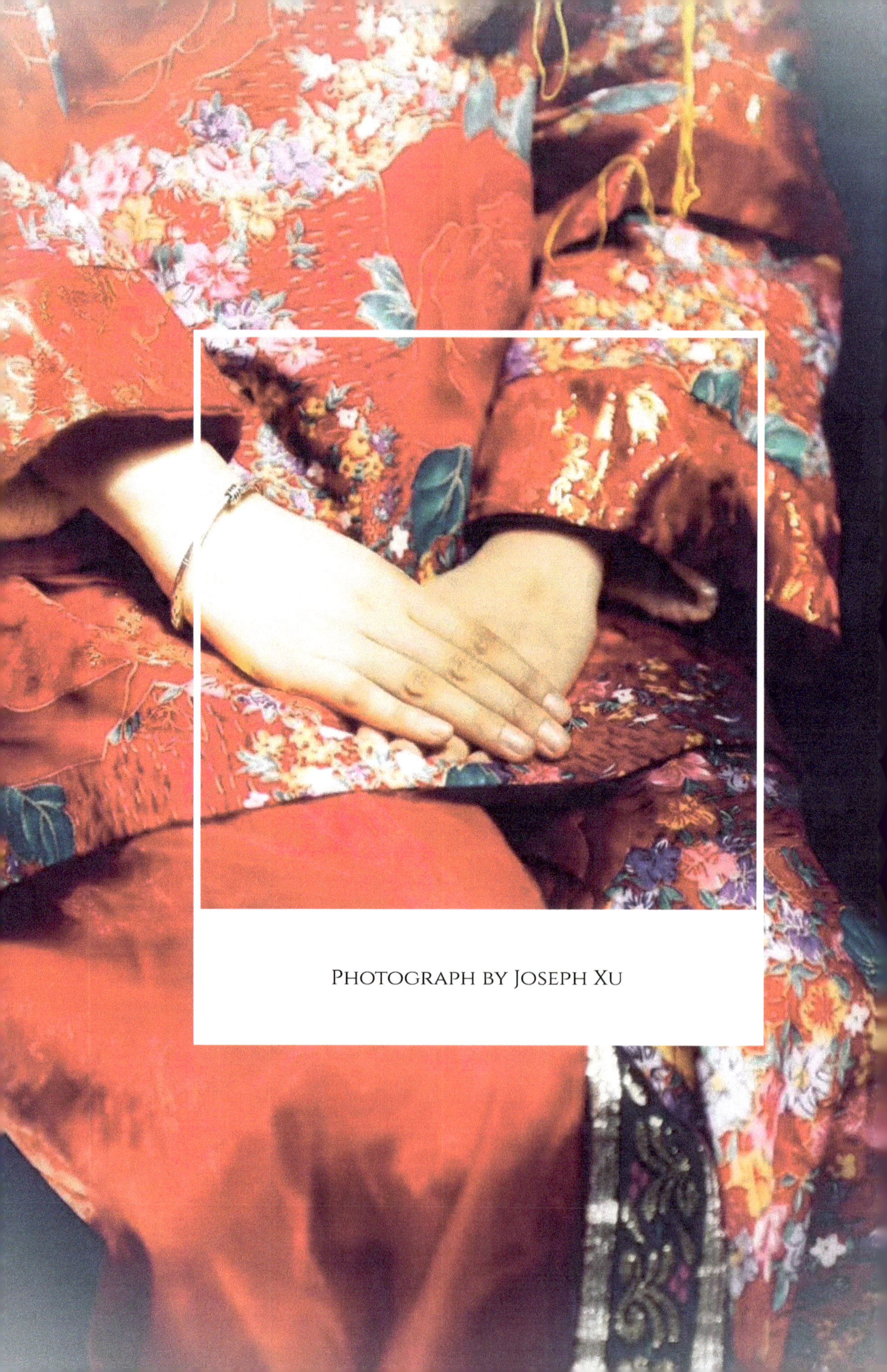

Photograph by Joseph Xu

THE END

全书完

扫码关注

www.ingramcontent.com/pod-product-compliance
Lightning Source LLC
LaVergne TN
LVHW070849210926
848482LV00016B/898
9798902590262